Advancing Women's Careers

# Advancing Women's Careers: Research and Practice

Edited by

## Ronald J. Burke
School of Business
York University

and

## Debra L. Nelson
College of Business Administration
Oklahoma State University

Copyright © Blackwell Publishers Ltd 2002

Editorial matter and arrangement copyright © Ronald J. Burke and Debra L. Nelson 2002

The moral right of Ronald J. Burke and Debra L. Nelson to be identified as authors of the editorial material has been asserted in accordance with the Copyright, Designs and Patents Act 1988.

First published 2002

2 4 6 8 10 9 7 5 3 1

Blackwell Publishers Ltd
108 Cowley Road
Oxford OX4 1JF
UK

Blackwell Publishers Inc.
350 Main Street
Malden, Massachusetts 02148
USA

*British Library Cataloguing in Publication Data*

A CIP catalogue record for this book is available from the
British Library.

*Library of Congress Cataloging-in-Publication Data*

Advancing women's careers : research and practice / edited by Ronald J. Burke and Debra L. Nelson.
    p.   cm.
  Includes bibliographical references and index.
  ISBN 0–631–22389–4 (alk. paper)–ISBN 0–631–22390–8 (pb.)
  1. Vocational guidance for women.   2. Career development.   3. Women–
Promotions.   I. Burke, Ronald J.   II. Nelson, Debra L.

HF5382.6 .A38 2002
331.4 — dc21

                                                        2001037473

Typeset in 10 on 12 pt Photina
by Best-set Typesetter Ltd., Hong Kong
Printed in Great Britain by MPG Books, Bodmin, Cornwall

This book is printed on acid-free paper.

# CONTENTS

# FIGURES

# TABLES

# CONTRIBUTORS

Nancy Adler, Faculty of Management, McGill University, 1001 Sherbrooke Street West, Montreal, H3A 1G5, Canada

Lotte Bailyn, Sloan School of Management E52–585, Massachusetts Institute of Technology, 50 Memorial Drive, Cambridge, Massachusetts, 02142-1347, USA

Gayle M. Baugh, Department of Management, College of Business, University of West Florida, 11000 University Parkway, Pensacola Florida, 32514-5752, USA

Myrtle P. Bell, College of Business Administration, University of Texas at Arlington, UTA Box 19467, Arlington Texas, 76109-0467, USA

Laura W. Brody, Bestfoods, International Plaza, 700 Sylvan Avenue, Englewood Cliffs, New Jersey, 07632-9976, USA

Ronald J. Burke, School of Business, York University, 4700 Keele Street, Toronto, Ontario M3J 1P3, Canada

Marilyn J. Davidson, Manchester School of Management, UMIST, PO Box 88, Manchester M60 1QD, England

Lori Engler, Faculty of Management, McGill University, 1001 Sherbrooke Street West, Montreal, Quebec, H3A 1G5, Canada

Valerie Hammond, Chief Executive, Roffey Park Management Institute, Forest Road, Horsham, West Sussex, RH12 4TD, England

Vicki Holton, Ashridge Centre for Business and Society, Ashridge Management College, Ashridge, Berkhamsted, Hertfordshire, HP4 1N5, England

Katie Isbister, Workplace Equality, Bank of Montreal, 55 Bloor Street West, 6th Floor, Toronto, Ontario, M4W 3N5, Canada

Nuzhat Jafri, Workplace Equality, Bank of Montreal, 55 Bloor Street West, 6th Floor, Toronto, Ontario, M4W 3N5, Canada

Mary Dean Lee, Faculty of Management, McGill University, 1001 Sherbrooke Street West, Montreal, Quebec, H3A 1G5, Canada

Suzan Lewis, Department of Psychology and Speech Pathology, Manchester Metropolitan University, Elizabeth Gaskell Campus, Heathersage Road, Manchester, M13 0JA, England

Mary C. Mattis, Catalyst, 120 Wall Street, 5th Floor, New York, NY 10005, USA

Mary E. McLaughlin, College of Business Administration, University of Texas at Arlington, UTA PO Box 19467, Arlington, Texas, 76109-0467, USA

Dorothy Perrin Moore, Department of Business Administration, The Citadel, 171 Moultrie Street, Charleston, South Carolina, 29409-0215, USA

Debra L. Nelson, Department of Management, College of Business Administration, Oklahoma State University, Stillwater, Oklahoma, 74078, USA

Joyce S. Osland, Dr Robert B. Pamplin Jr, School of Business Administration, University of Portland, 5000 N, Williamette Blvd., Portland, Oregon, 97203-5798, USA

Terri Scandura, Department of Management, 414 Jenkins Building, School of Business Administration, University of Miami, Coral Gables, Florida, 33124-9145, USA

Val Singh, School of Management, Cranfield University, Cranfield, Bedford, MK43 0AL, England

Bret L. Simmons, School of Management, University of Alaska Fairbanks, PO Box 756080, Fairbanks, Alaska, 99775-6080, USA

Nora Spinks, President, Work Life Harmony Enterprises, 207 Shaughnessy, Toronto, Ontario, Canada, M2J 1J9

Phyllis Tharenou, Department of Management, Monash University, PO Box 197, Caulfield East, Victoria, 3145, Australia

Norma Tombari, Corporate Human Resources, Royal Bank of Canada, Royal Bank Plaza, 200 Bay Street, 11th Floor, North Tower, Toronto, Ontario, M5J 2J5, Canada

Susan Vinnicombe, School of Management, Cranfield University, Cranfield, Bedford, MK43 0AL, England

Leanne Wright, Faculty of Management, McGill University, 1001 Sherbrooke Street West, Montreal, Quebec, H3A 1G5, Canada

# ACKNOWLEDGMENTS

I would like to acknowledge two individuals who got me interested in research and writing while I was in graduate school in organizational psychology at the University of Michigan: the late Norman R. F. Maier and L. Richard Hoffman. Norm had the brilliant capacity to make complex things simple. I admired his maverick quality even though it cost him professionally. In addition, he was one of the first academics to take psychology into organizations. Dick exemplified the methodical process of research and writing through data collection and analysis, highlighting the importance of putting pencil to paper. This one's for them. I am also grateful to our international contributors. In addition, I thank my friend and colleague Debra Nelson; working with her has always been a fruitful and rewarding collaboration. Finally, I am indebted to the editorial and production staff at Blackwell for their guidance and diligence and their general enthusiasm for our projects.

Ronald J. Burke
Toronto, Ontario


I am very grateful to my colleagues in the Management Department at Oklahoma State University for their support and encouragement. Ron Burke has played a pivotal role in assembling this collection; I appreciate his friendship and our collaboration. Our contributors have done an outstanding job of producing cutting-edge chapters, and I thank them for sharing their work with us.

Debra L. Nelson
Stillwater, Oklahoma

# I

# OVERVIEW

# 1

# ADVANCING WOMEN IN MANAGEMENT: PROGRESS AND PROSPECTS

*Ronald J. Burke and Debra L. Nelson*

During the past two decades there has been a dramatic increase in the number of women who are pursuing managerial and professional careers (Fagenson, 1993). Many of these women have prepared themselves for careers by undertaking university education and they now comprise almost half of the graduates of professional schools such as accounting, business and law (Catalyst, 1999a, 2000). Research evidence suggests that these graduates enter the workforce at levels comparable to their male colleagues and with similar credentials and expectations, but it seems that women's and men's corporate experience and career paths begin to diverge soon after that point (Davidson and Burke, 2000).

It is evident that although managerial and professional women are at least as well educated and trained as their male counterparts and are being hired by organizations in approximately equal numbers, they are not entering the ranks of senior management at comparable rates. The supply of qualified women for these management jobs has increased steadily as more women accumulate experience and education. Women are more likely to occupy managerial jobs in fields in which more women are employed in non-management jobs. Women in executive and managerial jobs are more likely to be found in services, insurance, and real estate industries. They are less likely to be found in manufacturing, construction, transportation, and public utilities (Catalyst, 1999a, 2000).

Women are gaining the necessary experience and paying their dues but they still encounter a "glass ceiling" (Powell, 1999a). The relative failure of these women to

Preparation of this chapter was supported in part by the School of Business, York University and the College of Business Administration, Oklahoma State University.

move into the ranks of senior management, in both private- and public-sector organizations in all developed countries, has been well documented (Adler and Izraeli, 1988; Davidson and Cooper, 1993).

Why should organizations be interested in developing and utilizing the talents of women? Schwartz (1992) summarizes reasons why supporting the career aspirations of talented and successful managerial women makes good business sense. These include: obtaining the best people for leadership positions; giving the chief executive officer (CEO) experience in working with capable women; providing female role models for younger high-potential women; ensuring that companies' opportunities for women will be noticed by both women graduates in recruiting and women customers; and guaranteeing that all ranks of management will be filled with strong executives. The recruitment, hiring, and development of managerial women is increasingly seen as a bottom-line issue related to corporate success.

Research on women in management has reflected these changes in organizations. The first women in management researchers asked: "Why are there so few women in management?", and their work had an impact on the practice of management. Early writers (for example Riger and Galligan, 1980; Hennig and Jardim, 1977) considered both person-centered (personality traits, skills, education) and situation-centered factors (different rewards and training opportunities, men's attitudes, token status). It was concluded that person-centered variables were less important than situation-centered variables in explaining the small numbers of women in management.

The appearance of *Breaking the Glass Ceiling* (Morrison, White, and Van Velsor, 1987) gave renewed energy to women in management research. This book, with its attendant publicity, captured the attention of women managers and professionals, researchers interested in women in management issues, and organizations interested in furthering the careers of managerial and professional women. Later reviews (Burke and McKeen, 1992; Davidson and Cooper, 1992; Morrison and Von Glinow, 1990) showed that women had made considerable progress in some areas (entering the workforce, occupying managerial and professional jobs) but limited progress in other areas (senior management jobs, top wage earners, clout positions, corporate directorships).

This interest, coupled with increased research attention, highlighted the importance to business leaders and educators of understanding the impact of large numbers of managerial and professional women entering the workplace. These demographic changes are some of the most significant organizational changes taking place in the industrialized world. During the 1980s and 1990s the numbers of women in management (broadly defined) increased substantially, yet the numbers of women holding top management positions held fairly constant at about 5 percent. This leads to a second, and more contemporary, question: "Why are there so few women in top management?"

## ■ Good news: progress and success stories ■

The advancement picture for women, in some respects, contains reasons for optimism. Of the corporate officers in *Fortune* 500 companies, 12 percent are women. Of these women, 149 hold the high-ranking positions of CEO, president, COO, and EVP (Catalyst, 1999a). Three quarters of the *Fortune* 500 have at least one woman corporate officer. Recent Canadian data is consistent with the progress in the US. Thus 43 percent of all managers and administrators are female, up from 29 percent in 1982; but women are relatively rare at the top (Catalyst, 2000).

Notable examples of females who lead major corporations are Marion Sandler of Golden West Financial Corporation, Andrea Jung of Avon, and Carly Fiorina of Hewlett-Packard. A recent addition to this small group is Anne Mulcahy, president and chief operating officer of Xerox Corporation. Interestingly, Fiorina of Hewlett-Packard has argued that there are no glass ceilings for women; Mulcahy wrote an angry response detailing the low number of women leaders in technology companies.

Women's presence on corporate boards is also increasing (Catalyst, 1999b, 1999c). Since 1993, the number of *Fortune* 500 boards with women directors has increased 21 percent. The greatest gains in women directors has come in companies that already hold three or more women directors. Given more women in top leadership positions and more women serving on corporate boards, women's influence at the top of organizations is increasing. While this news looks encouraging, it must be acknowledged that still among *Fortune* 1500, a larger group, 95 to 97 percent of vice-presidents and above are men.

The proportion of women in management jobs overall has increased substantially in recent years. In the US, over 7.1 million women were employed in full-time executive, managerial, or administrative positions. This represents a gain of 29 percent over 1993. These statistics represent progress: more women at the top of organizations (but still few and far between), more women on corporate boards, and more women in management jobs overall. It is important to examine the reasons for this progress. Why has the proportion of women in management overall increased in recent years? Powell (1999) offers a number of reasons for the gains women have enjoyed. Women have increased their human capital through increasing their education. Falling birth rates mean that there are fewer candidates for managerial jobs. There are simply more women who want to work and fewer men who are available. Societal norms regarding women's roles have facilitated women's move into management. Equal opportunity and affirmative action, along with organizational programs that support women's advancement, have played a role. And, women at more senior levels influence the numbers of women at more junior levels of management. These societal forces have undoubtedly played a role in women's progress.

It is also important to ask women why they believe they succeed. Catalyst surveyed 325 CEOs and 461 women at levels of vice-president and above to determine how women attribute their success (Catalyst, 1996). Consistently exceeding performance expectations (77 percent), developing a style with which male managers were comfortable (61 percent), and seeking out difficult or high-visibility assignments (50 percent) were the factors women believed were most important to their progress. Many women managers believed that women must over-perform to demonstrate their abilities in a male-dominated environment. In addition to exemplary performance, women had to make men feel comfortable with them. Others (Morrison, White, and Van Velsor, 1997; Ragins, Townsend and Mattis, 1998) have reported very similar findings in other samples of women.

## ■ The bad news: substantial barriers remain ■

Women are making great inroads in some executive ranks; in others, their progress has been slow. Organizations seem to be doing a good job at recruiting and hiring capable women, but they appear to have difficulty in developing and retaining managerial women and advancing them into ranks of senior management: estimates of women in "clout" jobs in senior management remain at 5 percent. Clout titles are those that convey policy-making power, and include chairman, CEO, COO, and executive vice-president. Most of the women in senior management are in staff functions without direct line responsibility. This indicates the existence of not only the glass ceiling but also glass walls. Men hold 93.2 percent of the top line officer jobs (those with profit and loss responsibility). A notable exception is Southwest Airlines, where 56 percent of the line officers in the company are women.

Women's earnings are still not at parity with men's. Women continue to earn approximately 76 percent as much as their male counterparts (US Department of Labor, 1998). The lack of comparable earnings is magnified by the fact that benefits are tied to salary, extending women's disadvantages to such benefits as health care and retirement.

Three major hypotheses have been offered to explain why these barriers have kept most women from senior levels of organizations (Fagenson, 1990). The first builds on ways in which women are different from men and concludes that these deficiencies in women are responsible for their lack of career progress. This hypothesis suggests that women's characteristics, such as attitudes, behaviours, traits, and socialization, handicap them in particular ways. It also suggests that women may lack the education and job training necessary to qualify for managerial and professional jobs. However, research support for this explanation is limited (Morrison and von Glinow, 1990). Almost all the evidence shows little or no difference in the traits, abilities, education and motivations of managerial and professional women and men (Powell, 1990).

A second hypothesis builds on notions of bias and discrimination by the majority toward the minority. It suggests that managerial and professional women are held back as a result of bias toward, and stereotypes of, women. The dynamics of this situation are well explained by Kanter (1977) in *Men and Women of the Corporation*. Such bias or discrimination is either sanctioned by the labor market or rewarded by organizations despite the level of job performance of women. In addition, there is widespread agreement that the good manager is seen as male or masculine (Schein, 1973, 1975). Thus there is some research support for this hypothesis.

The third hypothesis emphasizes structural and systematic discrimination as revealed in organizational policies and practices which affect the treatment of women and which limit their advancement (Morrison, 1992). These policies and practices include women's lack of opportunity and power in organizations, the existing sex ratio of groups in organizations, tokenism, lack of mentors and sponsors, and denial of access to challenging assignments. This hypothesis has also received empirical support. In attempting to identify specific reasons for women's lack of advancement, it is important to remember that managerial and professional women live and work in a larger society that is patriarchal, a society in which men have historically had greater access to power, privilege and wealth than women. The mechanisms by which this has occurred and is perpetuated are the subject of feminist theory and research. A useful analogy for conceptualizing the intricacy of the structure enforcing this status quo is presented by Frye, quoted by Code (1988). She envisions a bird cage in which if one examines each individual wire one cannot understand why the cage is so confining. It is only by stepping back to contemplate the entire structure, the interconnected and mutually enforcing system of barriers, that one can see why the bird is trapped.

Catalyst (1998) has identified the following as the most powerful barriers to female career advancement:

- negative assumptions in executive ranks about women, their abilities, and their commitment to careers
- perceptions that women don't fit with the corporate culture
- lack of career planning and the range of job experiences commensurate with the future needs of the organization
- lack of core opportunities for female employees who have management potential
- assumption that women will not relocate for career advancement
- failure to make managers accountable for advancing women
- management reluctance to giving women line (that is, revenue-generating) experience
- absence of, or too limited, succession planning
- "negative mentoring" and self-selection where women move into staff areas instead of line positions
- lack of mentoring and exclusion from informal career networks, where men have typically learned the unwritten rules of success
- appraisal and compensation systems that are not uniform for men and women
- corporate systems designed prior to women's large-scale infusion into the workplace, such as benefits systems and productivity measures that don't take into account new policies such as flexible work arrangements
- other forms of "cultural discouragement," like a work environment that values long hours over actual performance or that offers limited support for work–family initiatives and limited commitment to diversity programs in general
- discrimination and sexual harassment.

The barriers that Catalyst identified are in line with the second and third hypotheses about the barriers to women's advancement; they follow a theme of bias and discrimination, whether individual or structural.

Powell (1999a) addressed more specifically the issue of why the proportion of women in top management has remained relatively small. He noted that there are many interested and qualified male candidates for senior jobs. It is difficult to prevent bias and discrimination at these levels, because objective credentials (for example, more education) are less important at these levels, and male decision makers at the top more are likely to use gender-based models and criteria in selection. Men may be more comfortable with other men, and may view women as less competent. Decision processes at top levels of the organization are often unstructured and unscrutinized. Women at lower organizational levels may not be developed or groomed as often or as well, and may have more trouble getting mentors. In addition, women themselves may select out of top jobs because of family responsibilities, and the desire to make fewer personal sacrifices. Frustrated by the glass ceiling, they may quit, often to start their own businesses.

It is notable that sometimes CEOs and senior female managers do not agree on what constitutes barriers to women's advancement (Ragins, Townsend, and Mattis, 1998). Key barriers noted by male CEOs were: lack of general management or line experience (82 percent), not being in the pipeline long enough (64 percent) male stereotyping and preconceptions (25 percent), an inhospitable corporate culture (18 percent) and exclusion from informal networks (15 percent). The major barriers noted by senior women were: male stereotypes and preconceptions (52 percent), exclusion from informal networks (49 percent), lack of general management or line experience (47 percent), an inhospitable corporate culture (35 percent) and women not in the pipeline long enough (29 percent). Thus, while there was agreement on some barriers there remained disagreement on others. This may contribute to the problems facing managerial women.

A Canadian study (Conference Board of Canada, 1997) showed similar results, in that women cited male stereotyping, preconceptions of women's roles and abilities, and exclusion from informal networks as barriers more often than did male CEOs. Male CEOs noted lack of significant general management or line experience and lack of time in the pipeline more often than did senior women. More senior women than CEOs believed that commitment to family responsibilities and having children hindered women's advancement.

Pollara, a strategic public opinion and market research firm located in Toronto conducted a telephone interview study of 350 executive women in Canada for the Women's Executive Network (Pollara, 2000). In addition, a survey of 1,000 Canadians was undertaken to determine the influence of gender in the workplace. When executive women ($n = 350$) were asked to estimate the period it will take for equality to be achieved in ten key areas, most estimates fell between 2017 and 2034. They believed that women would be equally represented on corporate boards of directors until 2027 and that women will not hold half of all CEO positions in large companies until 2033. They were most pessimistic about gender-based discrimination completely disappearing from the workplace, estimating that this will take until 2034. Interestingly, younger women were more pessimistic than older executive women in each of the ten areas. 42 percent of Canada's executive women believed that gender-based discrimination would never completely disappear in Canadian workplaces. One quarter of these women (26 percent) believed that women would never hold half of all CEO positions in large, private sector companies in Canada. Surprisingly, 47 percent of the executive women could not name a Canadian organization that does the most to reduce the barriers to women's advancement to senior positions.

The sample of executive women believed that the equal representation of men and women in corporate management would have very favorable effects in the way employees were treated, productivity, and the profitability of businesses. Younger women generally saw more benefits from equal representation than did older executive women.

There is also recently emerging evidence that fewer people, both women and men, may be pursuing undergraduate and graduate business education programs in universities. Catalyst, the University of Michigan Business School and the University of Michigan's Center for the Education of Women, undertook a study of women and men MBA graduates of 12 prestigious American business schools. The results showed that women as a group did not recognize the advantages of an MBA degree because they did not believe that they would have the same access to opportunities for income and achievement that the MBA degree has afforded men.

The current environment for women in management reflects progress, but not enough. Glass ceilings, glass walls, prejudices, and discrimination remain. There are many changes that must be made for women to see additional strides in career advancement.

## ■  The challenge of change  ■

Of the three hypotheses presented earlier concerning the factors that limit women's career advancement, two are viable: those that argue that discrimination and prejudices, and organizational policies/practices, hinder women's progress. It follows, then, that change efforts should be directed toward these obstacles. It is also important to understand the forces that affect the overall proportion of women in management. Efforts to increase this proportion should not diminish. Powell (1999a) notes that there are a number of factors that affect the number of women in management, including societal norms regarding women's roles and women's educational attainment. Other factors relate to the demand for labor, the participation rates of women relative to men, and the structure of the economy. There are organizational factors cited by Powell as well: enforcement of equal opportunity/affirmative action, organizational attitudes toward diversity, and organizational work/family initiatives. These factors should be the target of ongoing efforts to ensure women's participation in management positions.

The new challenge in the women in management arena is to foster the advancement of capable women into the ranks of executive leadership. The evidence available to date suggests that this challenge will be formidable. Success here requires addressing the issues posed by Powell (1999b) concerning the forces that will influence the proportion of women in top management positions. One such force is societal norms regarding women's status. A reduction in norms of male superiority and patriarchy will help women. Another influence is the persistence of masculine stereotypes of effective managers (Butterfield and Grinnell, 1999). A change in stereotypes emphasizing traditionally female characteristics will increase perceptions of women's abilities to fill these jobs. Increasing visibility of successful high-profile women executives will counter the prevailing masculine stereotypes.

The use of gender schemas by senior male decision makers also affects the proportion of women in top level jobs. More female candidates for these jobs will create a more gender-neutral decision making situation. This assumes that there will be an increasing number of women in lower-level managerial jobs to vie for these positions. In addition, a more structured and accountable decision-making process is called for.

Another force affecting women's progression to top leadership positions is the uncertainty associated with having women in top management positions. As more women enter top management, this uncertainty is likely to diminish, leading to an increase in the proportion of women in top management. Organizational attitudes toward diversity must also be reckoned with. Organizations valuing diversity, with specific initiatives to attract and retain female executives, will increase the proportion of women in top management. Opening up more development experiences to women will also provide a broader talent pool.

Some efforts involve attracting women to top positions. If women show less interest in balance (or men show more) this will increase the number of women in top management. Greater availability of meaningful family support will make it easier for women with family responsibilities to hold managerial jobs, thus increasing the proportion of women interested in holding top management jobs. Women may be inclined to quit the corporate world when faced with limited career opportunities. Reducing the number of women in management who quit when frustrated will increase the proportion of women in top management.

Increasing the proportion of women in top leadership positions inevitably involves changes in the way those currently in top management positions view the necessity of supporting women's advancement and involving themselves in systemic (total culture) change. Fortunately, there are signs of increasing movement in this direction. A number of publications have appeared highlighting the importance of such efforts providing detailed descriptions of how leading-edge organizations are responding to this need and the identification of common themes associated with more successful change efforts. And there are some bright spots. Avon, for example, has a global mission of being the "company for women." CEO Andrea Jung leads a team with 47 percent female officers and 89 percent female managers. In a more traditionally male-dominated industry, Charles Schwab has a strong initiative to develop its female employees so it can promote from within. Networking and mentoring programs are key parts of the initiative, and 37 percent of the brokerage's managers are female (Cleaver, 2000).

Meyerson and Fletcher (2000) offer what they term "a modest manifesto for shattering the glass ceiling." Instead of a revolution, Meyerson and Fletcher advocate a series of small wins, incremental changes aimed at long-entrenched biases in the organizational system. Their research, undertaken in 11 organizations over the past eight years, showed that the small-wins approach was successful in tackling some of the barriers holding women back without creating high levels of resistance or backlash. The small-wins strategy starts with a gender-related problem, moves to a diagnosis of possible causes, attempts to identify cultural patterns in the organization that serve as the root cause, and concludes with the design of the small wins.

Catalyst (1998) has distilled best practices for advancing women in business based on their work with companies trying to eliminate gender barriers to executive levels and undertaking initiatives supporting the advancement of capable women and their retention. This volume, emphasizing as it does an inclusive, problem-solving, comprehensive approach, identifies characteristics of successful change initiatives as well as detailed illustrations of model company efforts. Characteristics of successful change initiatives are:

- motivation and rationale linked to business strategy and profitability
- support from the highest levels of the organization
- built-in communication plan clearly stating how the best practices are linked to business issues
- built-in accountability mechanism so that the initiative doesn't become a management fad that employees can ignore.

Aspects of a systemic women's initiative are:

- leadership development programs
- identification and development of high-potential women
- cross-functional training
- supports that ensure women gain line experience
- succession planning
- mentoring programs
- women's networks
- worklife balance and flexibility initiatives
- accountability
- measuring of results
- training
- evaluating and modifying the initiative.

Senior women who have made it to top management attribute their success, in part, to company strategies. The factors they report as most beneficial include identification and development of high-potential employees, high visibility assignments, and cross-functional job rotations. CEOs in the Catalyst study who were asked to identify strategies for advancing women to top positions also cited high visibility assignments as important. The CEOs added succession plans that incorporate gender diversity, formal mentoring programs, and programs that hold managers accountable for women's career advancement.

Increasing the proportion of women in management, and the proportion of women in top leadership positions, will not be accomplished by implementing a few women's programs. Instead, it requires systemic and cultural changes in organizations. In particular, it requires support and commitment from top management. A clear case must be communicated from the top of the organization that new policies and practices are good for women; and, that what is good for women benefits the business as a whole.

The last ten years has demonstrated increased attention to women in management research (Davidson and Burke, 1994; Fagenson, 1993; Nelson and Burke, 2000; Sekaran and Leong, 1992). We have a good understanding of the barriers women face as they pursue careers in medium-size and large organizations (Morrison, 1992; Catalyst, 1998). An increasing number of organizations have realized that the full utilization and development of the talents of all employees has become a business imperative (Schwartz, 1992). Supporting the career aspirations of women is not just the right thing to do: it is the smart thing to do if organizations are to remain productive and competitive in an increasingly demanding marketplace (Totta and Burke, 1995).

It is important to integrate research and practice in this area. Research findings are now being used to develop strategies for organizational change. A range of initiatives are increasingly being undertaken by organizations to create a level playing field on which women and men are similarly advantaged.

Unfortunately, there are relatively few case studies of such corporate initiatives and few evaluations of corporate policies and programs supportive of women's career aspirations (Kinsley, 1993). Much more research and descriptive work is needed here. We need to learn from the experiences of these model organizations so that future corporate initiatives can benefit from the learnings (and mistakes) of others (Mattis, 1994).

Finally, there is the range of available options and how they might proceed. Organizational leaders are more likely to be influenced by the activities and attitudes of their peers than by researchers in universities.

The intent is to encourage more organizations to take action to bring about cultural change. In addition, there is a role for consultants and researchers to initiate, chronicle, and evaluate these efforts. Research and practice should combine in efforts to foster women's development in organizations.

At least three countries (Canada, the US and the UK) have begun to monitor the progress of women in management in various sectors in a meaningful way, to highlight companies that are doing well (and not so well) and to identify both model programs and best practices.

## ■ Rhetoric versus reality ■

In a recent discussion about the value of corporate initiatives for advancing women in management, a colleague, Leonie Still, raised the issue of rhetoric versus reality. That is, might this particular collection contain contributions outlining what could be done to support women's career aspirations coupled with a few success stories, or would it convey a reality of slow (or no) progress and even backsliding? On the latter point, some industrialized countries have taken steps to eliminate employment equity/affirmative action initiatives. These equity initiatives, however imperfect, have had a positive effect on the numbers of women hired and advanced in organizations. The reality that we encounter in some Canadian and US organizations is somewhere between these two extremes. We have observed organizations that are different now as a result of initiatives to support women's career aspirations. Is the playing field level and are there no instances of male advantage in these firms? Absolutely not. But progress is slowly being made. Hopefully this collection of articles from three countries will contribute to further movement.

## Conclusions

One of the great social paradoxes of the past two decades involves the massive influx of women into managerial and professional ranks and the continuation of inequality in both employment and family responsibilities. Women now represent over 40 percent of the workforce and will be an even more significant component in the future, but organizations have been slow to capitalize on the potential of their women employees. In particular, competent, promising female professionals and managers represent a human resource that is frequently left underdeveloped. It is important that organizational leaders recognize the valuable resource that women represent in management and administrative positions and use them effectively (Bass and Avolio, 1994). Managers at all levels need to develop the attitudes and expertise to make full use of their female managers and professionals.

Research can provide a recognition of the major issues involved and the knowledge of how to deal with them that will add to the knowledge and practical experience of managers, more of whom are becoming increasingly aware of their responsibilities in increasing the women friendliness of their organizations. As for researchers, research on women in corporate management should lead to increasing the satisfaction and well-being of both women and men in management.

A pressing need in this regard is to document efforts by organizations to develop the talent of women managers and professionals. This will serve to identify what works and does not work, and why. In addition, the successful efforts of some organizations will provide a blueprint for others in their own efforts. Efforts by organizations in this area will be more credible to senior corporate leaders. It is also important to have successful CEOs committed to full partnership for women at senior ranks, so that they can influence others at those levels.

Understanding the experiences of this large and growing segment of the workforce, in whom education, effort, and hopes have been invested, is critical for economic survival. Organizations cannot afford to under-utilize or lose this talent. Educators need to understand the barriers encountered by women, both in the organizations employing them and in their own educational institutions, and managerial and professional women need to understand why they are experiencing particular work situations.

We hope this collection will serve to interest more organizational researchers to consider women-in-management issues; to develop projects in areas that are just now emerging; and to envision projects that will have value to the individuals whose work and life experiences we are trying to better understand women and men in managerial and professional jobs, and organizations that are currently struggling with developing a level playing field. These demographic changes and the questions they raise have the potential for creating new ways of thinking about work, careers, and organizational purposes and policies as well as family and leisure. Organizations must grasp the significance of these issues, adjust to them, and focus on the positive opportunities these forces offer. The economic success of business hinges on their efforts.

## REFERENCES

Adler, N. J. and Izraeli, D. N. (1988): *Women in management worldwide*. Armonk, NY: M. E. Sharpe.

Bass, B. M. and Avolio, B. J. (1994): Shatter the glass ceiling: Women may make better managers. *Human Resource Management*, 33, 549–60.

Burke, R. J. and McKeen, C. A. (1992): Women in Management. In C. L. Cooper and I. T. Robertson (eds) *International Review of Industrial and Organizational Psychology*, New York: Wiley, 245–84.

Butterfield, D. A. and Grinnell, J. P. (1999): Re-viewing gender, leadership, and managerial behavior: Do three decades of research tell us anything? In G. N. Powell (ed.), *Handbook of gender and work*. Thousand Oaks, CA: Sage Publications, 223–38.

Catalyst (1996): *Women in corporate leadership: progress and prospects*. New York: Catalyst.

Catalyst (1998): *Advancing women in business: the Catalyst guide*. San Francisco, CA: Jossey-Bass.

Catalyst (1999a): *The 1999 Catalyst census of women corporate officers and top earners*. New York: Catalyst.

Catalyst (1999b): *The 1998 Catalyst census of women board directors of Canada*. New York: Catalyst.

Catalyst (1999c): *The 1999 Catalyst census of women directors of the Fortune 1000*. New York: Catalyst.

Catalyst (2000): *The 1999 Catalyst census of women corporate officers of Canada*. New York: Catalyst.

Cleaver, J. (2000): Top 25 companies for executive women. *Working Woman*, 25, 48–60.

Conference Board of Canada (1997): *Closing the gap: Women's advancement in corporate and professional Canada*. Ottawa: Conference Board of Canada.

Davidson, M. J. and Burke, R. J. (2000): *Women in management: Current research issues. Vol. II*, Thousand Oaks, CA: Sage Publications.

Davidson, M. J. and Cooper, C. L. (1992). *Shattering the glass ceiling: The women manager.* London: Paul Chapman.

Davidson, M. J. and Cooper, C. L. (1993). *European women in business and management.* London: Paul Chapman.

Fagenson, E. A. (1990): At the heart of women in management research: Theoretical and methodological approaches and their biases. *Journal of Business Ethics,* 9, 267–74.

Fagenson, E. A. (1993): *Women in Management.* Newbury Park, CA: Sage Publications.

Frye, S. (1988): cited in L. Code. Feminist Theory. In S. Burt, L. Code, and L. Dorney, (eds), *Changing Patterns: Women in Canada,* Toronto: McClelland and Stewart, 18–50.

Hennig, M. and Jardim, A. (1977): *The managerial woman.* New York: Anchor/Doubleday.

Kanter, R. M. (1977): *Men and women of the corporation.* New York: Basic Books.

Kinsley, M. J. (1993): A pragmatic approach to workplace equality. *Business and the Contemporary World,* 5, 171–84.

Mattis, M. C. (1994): Organizational initiatives in the USA for advancing management women. In M. J. Davidson and R. J. Burke (eds), *Women in management: Current research issues.* London: Paul Chapman, 261–76.

Meyerson, D. E. and Fletcher, J. K. (2000): A modest manifesto for shattering the glass ceiling. *Harvard Business Review,* January–February, 127–36.

Morrison, A. M. (1992): *The new leaders.* San Francisco, CA: Jossey-Bass.

Morrison, A. M. and Von Glinow, M. A. (1990): Women and Minorities in Management. *American Psychologist,* 45, 200–08.

Morrison, A. M., White, R. P., and Van Velsor, E. (1987): *Breaking the glass ceiling.* Reading, MA: Addison-Wesley.

*Moving Forward (2000): The experiences and attitudes of executive women in Canda.* Toronto: Pollara, July 2000.

Nelson, D. L. and Burke, R. J. (2000): Women Executives: Health, Stress and Success. *Academy of Management Executive,* 14, 107–21.

Pollara (2000): *Moving Forward 2000: The experiences and attitudes of executive women in Canada.* Toronto: Pollara.

Powell, G. N. (1990): One more time: Do male and female managers differ? *Academy of Management Executive,* 4, 68–75.

Powell, G. N. (1999a): Reflections on the glass ceiling: Recent trends and future prospects. In G. N. Powell (ed.), *Handbook of gender and work.* Thousand Oaks, CA: Sage Publications, 325–45.

Powell, G. N. (1999b): *Handbook of gender and work.* Thousand Oaks, CA: Sage Publications.

Ragins, B. R., Townsend, B., and Mattis, M. (1998): Gender gap in the executive suite: CEOs and female executives report on breaking the glass ceiling. *Academy of Management Executive,* 12, 28–42.

Riger, P. and Galligan, S. (1980): Women in management: An exploration of competing paradigms. *American Psychologist,* 35, 902–10.

Schein, V. A. (1973): The relationship between sex role stereotypes and requisite management characteristics, *Journal of Applied Psychology,* 57, 95–100.

Schein, V. A. (1975): The relationship between sex role stereotypes and requisite management characteristics among female managers. *Journal of Applied Psychology,* 60, 340–44.

Schwartz, F. N. (1992): *Breaking with tradition: Women and work, the new facts of life.* New York: Warner.

Sekaran, V. and Leong, F. (1992): *Woman power.* Newbury Park, CA: Sage Publications.

Totta, J. and Burke, R. J. (1995): Integrating diversity and equality into the fabric of the organization. *Women in Management Review,* 10, 46–53.

US Department of Labor (1998): Usual weekly earnings summary. *Labor Force Statistics from the Current Population Survey.* Washington, DC: US Government.

# 2

# DEVELOPING WOMEN AS GLOBAL LEADERS: LESSONS AND SENSE MAKING FROM AN ORGANIZATIONAL CHANGE EFFORT

*Joyce S. Osland, Nancy J. Adler, and Laura W. Brody*

> The best reason for believing that more women will be in charge before long is that in a ferociously competitive global economy, no company can afford to waste valuable brainpower simply because it's wearing a skirt.
> **A. Fisher, Fortune Magazine (1992)**

According to many managers and researchers, global competitiveness in the twenty-first century will depend on the quality of leadership guiding today's and tomorrow's organizations (Zahra, 1998). In a *Fortune 500* survey, however, 85 percent of the US-based firms said they do not have an adequate number of global leaders, and 67 percent thought their existing leaders needed additional skills and knowledge in the area of global leadership Gregerson, Morrison, and Black (1998). To ensure a sufficient supply of global leaders with the needed competencies, firms must pay greater attention to the process of developing global leaders and expand their pool of potential leaders. The best global leadership programs are inclusive – they include multiple nationalities in the development of global leadership criteria (which differs from domestic leadership criteria in any given country) and they draw from a candidate pool that includes all nationalities, both women and men, and representatives of majority as well as minority subcultures Osland and Taylor (2001). This chapter describes one company's efforts to increase its overall global competitiveness by enhancing the global leadership competencies of its high-potential and senior women.

## ■ Women and global leadership ■

Despite predictions that globalization will increase the number of women at senior levels, there has not been a significant change in the proportion of women in the executive suite.[1] At present, only two women are CEOs of US-based *Fortune 500* firms (Catalyst, 2000). Although women hold half of all managerial and professional positions at lower levels in these firms (Catalyst, 2000), they hold only 6.1 percent of the highest corporate titles and represent only 4.1 percent of the top earners. In Europe, women hold less than two percent of all senior management positions (Dwyer, Johnston, and Miller, 1996).

As global competition continues to intensify, the opportunity cost of relying on the historic men-only pattern of senior leadership escalates. There is evidence, however, that some countries and companies are gradually shifting away from the traditional pattern. For example, of the 47 women who have served in their country's highest political leadership position – either as president or prime minister – over 60 percent have come into office in just the last decade; all but seven are the first women ever selected for such a position in their country (Adler, Brody, and Osland, under review).[2] Similarly, the statistics are slowly improving for women in some of the world's leading companies. Three of General Motors' six vehicle divisions, for example, are now headed by women, which prompted the president for North American operations to note: "If you looked at GM in the past, it was run by 12 white guys from Cleveland. In today's world, 12 white guys from Cleveland are not going to make a successful, globally diverse company."[3] Harvard professor Rosabeth Moss Kanter confirms this view, emphasizing that in a global economy, "Meritocracy – letting talent rise to the top regardless of where it is found and whether it is male or female – has become essential to business success."[4] In 1996 a small number of global companies, led by IBM, began major initiatives to promote their most talented women from among all nationalities into previously all-male executive positions. This chapter outlines the key steps in such an initiative, an innovative change effort at Bestfoods.

### Global competitiveness and leadership: the situation faced by Bestfoods

At the time of its purchase by Unilever in 2000, Bestfoods was one of the most internationally oriented food companies, with over ninety years of operating experience in Europe, seventy years in Latin America, and more than sixty-eight years in Asia. The company earned 60 percent of its revenues from non-US sources, operated in more than sixty countries, and marketed products in 110 countries. It was among the largest US-branded food companies, with annual sales in 1999 of $8.4 billion.[5]

Bestfoods's leadership was as global as the company's operations. Almost half of the 20 corporate officers came from outside the United States and represented eight nationalities. Its 14-member board of directors consisted of five nationalities. Two of the CEOs sitting on Bestfoods's board were women. Of the company's 44,000 employees, two-thirds worked outside the United States.

Bestfoods had a highly decentralized structure which gave general managers and local management the autonomy to adapt and modify changes suggested by corporate headquarters. One of the company's strengths was its global strategic vision, which it combined with a local focus in its decision making. Bestfoods's CEO, Dick Shoemate, had a clear sense of the difficult balance between giving the local divisions geographic power to make their own decisions and integrating these units into a coherent whole. Combining a global strategic vision with local focus and decision making, as he noted, is "our strength, but it's also a challenge when we try to make changes."

Bestfoods used a strategic performance measurement system called the balanced scorecard to implement their vision in four areas (customer satisfaction, people development, business practices, and innovation and learning), all of which combined to produce financial performance. Instead of one uniform global measurement system, each division, affiliate, department, and functional group within the company created its own balanced scorecard that identified the key activities, or "strategic drivers," that would move its particular business closer to the company's goals. Nevertheless, the CEO could announce specific goals to add to the Corporate Balanced Scorecard at WorldTeam Meetings held about every three years with the firm's most senior executives.

Dick Shoemate, chairman, president and chief executive officer of Bestfoods, joined the company in 1962 and worked his way to the top. Shoemate, in his late fifties, wanted one of his legacies at Bestfoods to be increased diversity in the company's leadership ranks.

## Diversity at Bestfoods

Shoemate was aided in his effort to increase diversity by Laura Brody, Director of Diversity and Development.[6] Brody and her two staff members gathered data showing that in the US division, Bestfoods had 10 to 15 percent more minorities than the industry norm, but 5 to 10 percent fewer women. With some exceptions, women at Bestfoods tended to hit the "glass ceiling" at the middle-management level. Moreover, retention analyses revealed that at every management level, women and minorities had more turnover than men, and especially white men. As a result of these findings, Brody's objective within the United States was to have better retention and development of both women and minorities. When Brody and her staff did a global analysis of female employees, they discovered that only 15 percent of the employees who had been designated as "high potential" were women. Brody knew that attitudes toward promoting women varied widely throughout the company, from extremely supportive to indifferent – or even chauvinistic in a few cases. For the most part, she felt that managers were well intentioned but uncertain about what improvements regarding career advancement for women could be made and how to make them.

While the number of senior women, corporate officers, and board members at Bestfoods was respectable when compared to many companies, neither Brody nor Shoemate thought it was adequate to support the future they envisioned for Bestfoods. To succeed in a highly competitive global environment, Bestfoods needed to attract and retain the best talent available globally and to have local employees from each country reflect the consumer base. With women making more than 80 percent of purchasing decisions for Bestfoods's products, the company would suffer if it failed to understand women's perspectives and needs. Shoemate saw promoting women into senior management positions as a matter of strategic competitive advantage. On numerous occasions, he expressed his commitment to developing the most highly talented women and men from around the world:

> We believe that one of Bestfoods' unique competitive strengths is a management team that delivers outstanding performance in the local marketplace and also works together to build the "Best International Food Company in the World." . . . We actively seek to identify and to develop high performing Bestfoods' managers throughout the company, including men and women from all countries and ethnic backgrounds.

Shoemate knew, however, that words were not enough to change the organization. He personally appointed all three of the female corporate officers during his tenure as CEO. Nevertheless, he wanted to see more rapid progress on the goal of including more women in senior management and leadership.

## Managing change at Bestfoods

No CEO can simply mandate change in a highly decentralized multinational that values local independence. Focusing on diversity further complicates change efforts because it is often viewed as a "US issue." Within some cultures, equity among women and men is not a well-publicized concern, and diversity is locally defined to refer to other group-ings within the population. Therefore, the leadership of companies headquartered in the US often tread lightly in this area until a consensus can be developed.

Organizational culture was another consideration. Both within the food industry and within Bestfoods, employees tend to work their way up. Executives brought in from the outside often do not adjust to the informal norms and values of the company. This practice has the advantage to the company of providing continuity and a strong organizational culture but the downside of introducing less new blood and fewer innovations. Brody described Bestfoods's culture as traditional, conservative, polite, "gentlemanly," and non-confrontational. While the politeness contributed to the pleas-ant relations Bestfoods was noted for, it also made face-to-face confrontations rare: criti-cism and dissent tended to go underground. The emphasis on tradition made change slow and risky. Some executives were leery of being blamed if changes did not work out. As a result, many managers preferred the "drip method" of change – small changes over time that eventually add up to real progress.

Although individual managers approached change somewhat cautiously, Bestfoods developed a very effective group method for taking advantage of opportunities and resolving issues that affected all divisions. Global action-learning task forces convened and analyzed global problems and then make recommendations to senior management.

As a result of all these organizational dynamics, Brody's strategy was to focus on getting the decision makers "on board" and then making incremental changes. Her style was to plant the seeds of change by providing ideas, information, and options to the executive team so that they would begin thinking about diversity more broadly and from new perspectives.

## Laying the groundwork for change

Bestfoods already had a US-focused diversity advisory council (DAC) when Brody first assumed her position. It was composed of 14 members – senior executives in the US business, corporate staff, and vice-presidents of Human Resources from each unit. The council was chaired by the CEO and facilitated by Brody. Brody adopted a team-building approach with the council and helped them establish a common vision and agree on a definition of diversity. She worked to ensure that Bestfoods defined diversity very broadly, for two reasons: 1) to avoid excluding white males and 2) so other countries would not see diversity only in light of US equal employment opportunities (EEO) legislation and requirements. The council linked diversity to the corporate vision and developed a balanced scorecard for diversity that mirrored the Corporate Balanced Scorecard. Brody noted:

> In corporate life, you only make progress on things you measure, and you only measure things that are important – such as operating income, profitability, ROI, ROA, and market share. These things are all measured and tracked very, very frequently. So in terms of making progress on diversity, the measurable goal was increased career opportunity – promotions, salary levels, and representation at senior management levels – and not the "nice-to-haves," like calendars with every ethnic holiday posted or "feeling included;" it was in fact about *being* included. I preached that you could not have an effective diversity function without, at a minimum, having effective EEO policies and actions in place.

Brody's team building with the DAC paid off. After about two years the council wanted to raise the bar on diversity and chose to go forward in a proactive way. To learn what leading companies were doing to increase their business competitiveness by leveraging workforce inclusion, Brody invited outside practitioners involved in best-practice efforts to make presentations to the council. She also disseminated a variety of benchmarking and best-practice studies and reports to them.

At her suggestion, in 1997 Shoemate sent out an open letter to all employees regarding the company's diversity initiative and another "state of diversity" letter to US employees in 1998. When Shoemate was in the midst of reviewing the 1997 employee survey data, he asked, "Laura, if you could do one thing to improve things for women in the company, what would it be?" Brody answered that she would like to engage a significant number of women in a dialogue on this question. She suggested holding a global forum for high-potential and senior women from around the world representing all Bestfoods's businesses. The forum would be structured just like Bestfoods' other action-learning initiatives – starting with the presentation of a business issue, followed by gathering information and participants making recommendations on how both to proceed immediately and to make long-term progress. The forum would also include activities to increase participants' global leadership competencies. Shoemate suggested she flesh out the idea with her immediate boss, Dick Bergeman, VP Human Resources. Together they prepared a position paper that Bergeman discussed with the Corporate Strategy Council (CSC). The all-male CSC was composed of the six most senior corporate officers, who were responsible for each of the company's five divisions and the corporate staff. The CSC immediately approved the idea to hold a forum. Shoemate requested that the forum take place no later than the end of July, which meant Brody had only 90 days to organize her company's first-ever Women's Global Leadership Forum.

Brody's primary concern was how to ensure that the forum resulted in real organizational change. She worried that participants might leave feeling good, with raised expectations about what the company would do for women, only to become disillusioned if nothing came to pass afterwards. As it turned out, senior management shared Brody's concern about unrealistically raising expectations. Some senior managers also wondered how they could participate and interact with the attendees so that neither the women nor the current group of senior male managers would feel threatened.

## Forum invitations and reactions

To create a comprehensive list of senior and high-potential women, Brody solicited nominations from all division presidents, which she personally reviewed along with the corporate high-potential lists and succession plans. Next, the CEO sent a letter to the six members of the CSC describing the forum and requesting that they rank order their nominees. Brody's goal was to invite 50 participants, of which at least half would come from outside the United States; spaces were allocated according to the relative size of each division and geographical area to ensure balanced representation. The divisions requested additional spaces, so Brody increased the number of participants to 60 and chose 10 of these as facilitators for small-group sessions. Shoemate personally sent a letter of invitation to each participant. Fifty-five women accepted the invitation.

Brody felt that merely asking the division presidents to identify their high-potential women, thereby adding them to the talent pool for the company's future leadership, was a significant intervention in and of itself. "Even if we'd never held the forum at all, it was a good exercise for the senior executives to stop and consider how many highly talented women managers they had and where they were in the company. One president promoted a woman a few months earlier than he had planned as a result of thinking about whom he wanted to nominate!"

Women's reactions to the announcement of the forum were, for the most part, very positive. Many were gratified to be nominated to attend such an innovative meeting. Some senior women, however, worried that their participation in an all-women forum might send a message that their success was due to the fact that they were women rather than to their competence; they had no desire to be at the forefront of women's issues. Some women who were not invited, from secretaries to senior managers, felt excluded from yet another "private club." Some invitees were also concerned about the reactions of their male colleagues and bosses; some worried about a possible male backlash.

There were dismissive and sceptical comments by both men and women who doubted that the forum would result in anything more than a "bitch session." One senior male manager told a subordinate, "Have a good time at the coffee-klatch" as she left for the forum. Some men complained of discrimination because they were not invited. Other men thought the forum was long overdue and emphasized their support. Brody kept Shoemate and Bergeman informed of the resistance she encountered so there would not be any surprises among the senior managers regarding this controversial meeting.

## Planning the forum

As far as Brody was aware, no other company had ever held this type of global meeting for senior and high-potential women with the intent of opening a dialogue on global leadership and organizational change. There were no models to follow, so she began searching for an outside consultant to help design the forum. After some difficulty finding someone with expertise on both women's leadership and global management, she hired Nancy Adler, an international management professor and consultant. To get a feel for the organization, Adler interviewed Shoemate, Bergeman, all corporate officers, including the three female corporate officers, and one of the female board members. Adler and Brody began designing the meeting to fit Bestfoods's needs and meet the forum's goals.

- Increase the global competitiveness of Bestfoods.
- Develop the global leadership skills of Bestfood's most highly talented and senior women.
- Create an internal network among Bestfoods's women leaders to facilitate their global effectiveness.
- Develop both global and local recommendations for enhancing Bestfoods' ability to support the career advancement and success of an increasing number of highly talented and senior women.

Adler suggested hiring another consultant to conduct cross-cultural training for the group facilitators and to present research at the forum itself. Brody hired Joyce Osland, a management professor and long-term expatriate with experience in organization development consulting and designing leadership workshops for female executives in Latin America. Brody wanted consultants with expatriate knowledge for two reasons. First, companies frequently identify women's lack of international experience as a reason why they are not promoted into top jobs. Second, Brody was convinced that senior women would be better positioned to lead the company if they had more "cross-border" and international experience.

Early in the process, Brody warned Bergeman that the cost of the program would be higher than original estimates. His response was, "Spend whatever you need to put on an outstanding program." Bergeman was aware that some people who felt ambivalent about the forum might try to find reasons for it to fail. Therefore, he insisted that everything about the forum be first rate.

## Pre-forum survey

Brody's team carried out a survey–feedback process in hopes that the data would serve as a baseline and cause people to re-examine their thinking about the opportunities and barriers for women's career advancement and contributions to the company's leadership. Beyond generating results, Brody viewed the survey as a means to involve senior women and men in the questions that the company needed to address as well as to build their support for implementing the recommendations that the forum would generate. The confidential survey was modelled after Catalyst's[7] studies and administered to all 20 corporate officers, the next 125 most senior executives, of whom 92 percent were male, and all 60 women nominated to attend the forum. The response rate to the survey was 70 percent.

The survey documented the benefits to the company, as perceived by both women and men, of having more women in leadership positions. The results identified the actual strategies participants used to advance their careers, along with the barriers they faced. The survey solicited recommendations about what both individual women and the company could do to increase the number of women in senior positions. As with similar surveys at other firms,[8] the results indicated some similarities as well as highly significant differences. For example, one of the perceived gaps pertained to the extra barriers women report, gaps which are invisible to men. Another gap concerned the greater importance women give to organizational strategies for helping them advance in their careers, for which men see less need.

Brody reported these results during the forum and also sent a written report to all the survey participants after the forum. She hoped the feedback would serve to trigger discussion at the forum, so more people would become motivated to eliminate the gaps in perceptions and find new ways for women and men to work together.

## The Women's Global Leadership Forum

Given the goals of the forum, most events were designed for the 55 women participants. The decision to hold a primarily women-only event, rather than inviting both men and women, was carefully considered. There are advantages and disadvantages to both approaches. Women-only events theoretically allow women to discuss issues more openly in a group that understands the context of their remarks without needing much interpretation or background. The opportunity to address the unique aspects of their situation often allows women to form relationships that provide ongoing support. On the other hand, including both women and men provides an opportunity to hear different perspectives, build a mutual agenda for change, and may prevent a backlash from those who were not present. To gain both types of advantages, the forum design included primarily women-only sessions combined with a series of sessions for women and men together. In particular, since the long-term success of this effort depended on the continued support of senior executives and their reaction to the forum, the majority of Bestfoods's most senior executives (CEO, CSC, DAC, corporate officers, and a board member) attended the welcome dinner, as well as other sessions (where their presence would not be inhibitive), and the all-important presentation of recommendations at the closing session. The inclusion of the male senior executives allowed them to see the women in action, hear their opinions first hand, and learn for themselves what went on at the forum.

The design of the forum aimed at enhancing the women's preparation for proactive roles in the company's future leadership. There were three types of sessions: 1) individual professional development sessions focusing on global leadership skills; 2) organization development sessions aimed at gathering information and making recommendations on retention, development and career advancement; and 3) sessions designed to help the women form a network.[9]

The forum had some challenging moments as Brody and the consultants facilitated a widely diverse group of 55 women with different goals, opinions, experiences, and communication and behavioral styles, which are discussed in a later section. However, the participants, as well as the senior executives, were very positive about the experience and the outcomes of the forum. The women's pleasure in meeting and working with their very impressive female colleagues from around the world was evident.

## Forum recommendations and executive response

On the last day of the forum the participants presented their recommendations to the CEO, the CSC, and the DAC. Before the presentations began, Shoemate assured the women that they could be totally candid and honest in their feedback. Their specific recommendations focused on three key areas: career development (enhancing career opportunities); diversity (increasing representation of women in senior and high-level positions); and work – life balance (enabling women to perform to their highest capabilities). The women also identified what they themselves could do to enhance their career opportunities.

Immediately following the presentations, Shoemate and the senior executives met to discuss the women's recommended actions and plan their response. Shoemate suggested separating the recommendations into three categories:

1  *Current company initiatives* – recommendations for actions the company was already involved in but which needed to be accelerated and better communicated throughout the company
2  *New corporate-wide recommendations*, which the corporate strategy council would consider at its next meeting
3  *New "local" recommendations*, best addressed within specific countries, regions, or divisions.

When the women rejoined the executives, Shoemate responded to each recommendation, some of which he accepted instantly. He was very open to feedback and did not argue with or become defensive about any points the women raised. He promised to look into existing programs and policies that were not consistently working to the benefit of women's development and retention. Shoemate reiterated his belief that the company's strength lies in its local decision making and explained why he hesitated to mandate all policies from corporate headquarters. He also clarified, however, what he could do as CEO to make change happen and assured the women that he would communicate the outcome of each recommendation to them as soon as possible. Shoemate's obvious sincerity and thoughtfulness made a positive impression on the women, as did the helpful responses of other senior executives.

The immediate positive feedback from those in attendance seemed to indicate that the forum had achieved one of its primary goals: to served as a successful catalyst in the change process. However, the challenge of institutionalizing the proposed changes still remained.

## The aftermath – institutionalization

There was a great deal of curiosity about what occurred at the forum. Many participants were asked by their bosses to present a report the very next day after their return. At Brody's request, Shoemate sent a cease-and-desist order to senior executives, asking them to hold off requesting a formal report until an official communication strategy was in place. Brody prepared a communication packet for each participant, including overheads they could use in their presentations to colleagues. A week later, Shoemate sent a letter to participants and members of the DAC and CSC, thanking them for their input, complimenting them the recommendations, responding in writing to each recommendation, and laying out the company's plan for the next steps to be taken.

Brody and Shoemate also circulated ideas about the forum's recommendations that the CSC would be considering at their September meeting, just two months after the forum. Brody discussed the recommendations with the members individually, so that she could answer any questions and address any reservations they had before the CSC meeting. At their September meeting, the CSC approved all the women's recommendations and even added two of their own. They agreed to take responsibility for oversight of the company's global diversity strategy. In addition, the CSC members, as division presidents, as well as the unit presidents reporting to them, agreed to establish diversity councils in their respective businesses. Rather than simply adding international members to Brody's DAC, they voted to establish local councils and invite the women who had attended the forum to participate. This represented a major change from the previous attitude that "diversity is just a US issue." The forum had successfully demonstrated that diversity and global leadership development is a strategic issue and a global challenge that appears in various forms throughout the world.

A month later, at the October WorldTeam Meeting attended by the company's top 125 managers, Brody announced Shoemate's decision to set a new Balanced Scorecard goal: by the year 2005, 25 percent of high-potential employees will be women – an increase from the company's current 16 percent figure. To Brody's pleasure, some male executives stated that the goal was too low and recommended increasing it.

Changes occurred at an even faster pace following the WorldTeam Meeting. Local division councils were formed all over the world. Several Latin American countries – Argentina, Brazil, Colombia, and Mexico – began benchmarking themselves against other multinationals. They discovered that Bestfoods was in the forefront in establishing diversity policies and measurable objectives, and in advising employees on their performance and career enhancement opportunties. Both Argentina and Mexico held their own women's forums, modeled after the earlier company-wide event. Europe's newly formed diversity council created a regional strategy for retaining women and enhancing their development opportunities, and was considering a training program for senior executives on managing inclusion.

The Women Leaders Network, established at the forum, became very active. Immediately following the forum, the women shared their re-entry strategies and stories via email or telephone. The women continued to use the network for coaching, disseminating information about career opportunities, professional support, and strategy.

Even though the forum was designed to benefit the company by focusing on women, other groups also profited from increased attention to the concerns the women raised. For example, Bestfoods instituted additional management development training for mid-level managers of both genders to ensure that development opportunities occur before employees attain senior management positions. More flexible work options and assignments also benefited a broad group of employees.

## ■ Making sense of the experience: lessons learned ■

Any innovation, particularly in emerging fields like global leadership, warrants reflection on what has been learned. This section focuses on the challenges that we, as the forum designers, faced, our attempts to make sense of the experience, and finally, the lessons we learned. Many of the lessons grew out of the unique challenges of bringing together women from 25 nationalities for a forum of this nature.

### The first major challenge: who's to blame?

Our first challenge grew out of the forum's joint goals of addressing business issues while simultaneously focusing on enhancing individuals' global leadership capabilities. Experts acknowledge that global leadership requires simultaneous organizational and individual transformation.[10] The dual organizational- and individual-level agenda of the forum, however, inadvertently raised the question of who was primarily to blame for the underrepresentation of women leaders within the company. Was it the company – thus implying that the organizational change initiatives should take precedence – or was it some perceived deficiency in the women themselves – thus implying that the leadership development initiatives should take precedence?[11] Given their familiarity with the systemic issues, the first priority of many women was to recommend ways in which the organizational culture could be changed. Among the women holding organizational change as their priority, some consequently viewed the personal development aspects of the agenda as secondary, and, at times, as taking them away from their primary goal of changing the organization. A group of primarily American participants asked the designers to modify the agenda for the third day to give them more time to prepare their recommendations for the final day's presentation.

Perhaps the lesson to be learned regarding first meetings of this sort is that participants – especially those as sophisticated in understanding organizational dynamics as this group – may initially view sessions aimed at individual leadership development as superfluous or even counter-productive. Designers must take care to ensure that organizational change and individual leadership development goals complement, rather than compete with, each other. As companies shift from multi-domestic to global strategies, this balance becomes particularly important, because all managers, whether male or female, and whether from Asia, Africa, Europe, or the Americas, need to upgrade their global leadership skills.

## The second major challenge: going beyond the myth that all women are the same

The second major challenge emerged from what cross-cultural experts term "assumed similarity" (Adler, 1997). There was an implicit expectation among the participants that women attending the forum would have had similar experiences and therefore would share similar perspectives on most important professional issues, simply because they are women. Given that many women's experiences and opinions are not identical to those of men – as the survey results had clearly documented – it is understandable that some women arrived at the forum expecting, consciously or otherwise, that they would finally be among a community of professionals who saw the world as they did. Their diverse backgrounds and career experiences soon became apparent. As the forum progressed, the company and the participants learned – not without a certain degree of frustration – to accept that differences in the women's cultural background, age, tenure, rank, and personal experience meant that the group could not, and should not, come to a consensus on a uniform "women's" perspective or position. The women expressed markedly divergent opinions, for example, on the existence, or lack thereof, of a "glass ceiling." Some of the most senior women, a disproportionate number of whom had begun their professional lives as trail blazers in a very different social climate than that of the late 1990s, now saw their careers as having plateaued, albeit at a very senior level, below a very real glass ceiling. These senior women held attitudes and objectives that differed markedly from those of many younger women whom the company had only recently identified as fast trackers, and for whom the glass ceiling held no personal meaning. Moreover, the most senior women often chose not to describe their most negative experiences to their junior colleagues so as not to discourage them. This choice made it easy for some younger women to blame their senior colleagues for not having progressed further and faster, rather than appreciating the systemic barriers these trail-blazing women had faced. Thus, in this forum (as in all other women-only meetings we have facilitated) it was necessary for the facilitators to remind participants that a uniform "women's point of view" seldom exists, and neither companies nor women should expect one.

As highlighted in the forum, helping people appreciate different realities – not just between women and men, but also among the women themselves – is a crucial step in allowing them to move beyond the need to reach consensus on either "the state of women" or explanations about why women do or do not make it to the top of major companies. A lack of consensus, however, neither indicates that such companies have no systemic issues, nor that there is no need for corporate action. Developing an understanding of the range of experiences and explanations makes it more likely that companies can achieve real change.

## The third major challenge: recognizing that cultural differences do make a difference

The third set of challenges also related to assumed similarity, in this case regarding styles of behavior and communication that were, in fact, influenced by culture. Some participants expected, consciously or unconsciously, that others would work and communicate as they did; instead, cultural differences significantly influenced group dynamics and the learning climate. Erroneously assuming a level of homogeneity among the women that simply did not exist caused problems in both conducting and interpreting the forum.

The key cultural differences were evident in problem-solving approaches, agenda preferences, and communication styles. The interaction of various cultural dimensions, described below, helps to explain the role culture played in the forum.[12]

***Problem solving: inductive versus deductive approaches.*** Following the typical cultural pattern of people from Canada and the United States, many North American women preferred to use a more inductive approach to resolving issues and formulating recommendations. They wanted to start with the specifics of their own and others' personal experience and later arrive at generalizations. Women from many other regions – for example, many Europeans, and especially those from France – preferred to take the opposite, more deductive approach (Samovar, Porter, and Stefani, 1998; Hall and Hall, 1990). They chose to begin with a general understanding and broad concepts and then work down toward the specifics of their own and others' lives. Both approaches ultimately arrive at an integration of general patterns and specifics. The processes for arriving at integration, however, are culturally defined, opposite, and, if not made explicit, often difficult to bridge. Global leaders need to be able to use the strengths of both inductive and deductive approaches, rather than merely negating one in favor of the other.

***Power distance: the influence of status and hierarchy.*** Cultures also vary in their relationship to power and to what cross-cultural management scholars refer to as power distance – the extent to which individual cultures accept that power in society and organizations is distributed unequally (Hofstede, 1980; Hofstede, Geert, and Bond, 1988). Power distance impacts the degree of respect given to authority, position, and hierarchical status. As noted previously, at the end of the second day a group of primarily American women assertively requested a change in the agenda for the following day to allow participants more time to work in their teams on organizational development issues – a change they believed would allow them to make best use of their time. It is not uncommon for American participants in US workshops to "take over" the agenda toward the end, behavior that is viewed as a positive sign by some US organizational development consultants. When the forum organizers announced the schedule changes, some Asian and Latin American women – who come from higher power-distance countries – expressed surprise that participants would attempt to change the agenda. Their reaction is a strong reminder that people from different cultures vary in their needs and reactions, and that it is often difficult to fulfill all needs simultaneously.

***The source of truth: experts versus experience.*** Another cross-cultural difference that global teams frequently experience relates to what anthropologists refer to as the source of truth – how a group seeks the "right" answer, or in the case of the forum, the "right" recommendations. Is truth believed to come primarily from scientific research, legal precedent, the opinion of experts, tradition, personal experience, or trial-and-error experimentation (Phillips and Boyacigiller, 1998)? Participants' varied reactions to changing the forum agenda, described above, may reflect this cultural difference regarding the source of truth. Beyond expressing surprise, some Asian and Latin American women were also disappointed because the new agenda left less time for the originally scheduled presentations by experts. Hearing the opinion of experts held more value for these women than for many of their North American colleagues, which is not surprising given their more deductive and higher power-distance approaches.

Whereas Americans also value expert opinion, they are much more likely to question authority than are most other cultures. Influenced by their more inductive approach and greater acceptance of change, most Americans at the forum welcomed the agenda change, believing it would give them more time to develop excellent recommendations based on their own personal experience. Typical of lower power-distance cultures, these Americans were placing less importance on expert input and hierarchical status. Which approach is correct? Neither – they simply differ. Global leadership involves bridging and integrating diverse approaches, not labeling one culture's approach as superior to that of other cultures.

***Communication styles: direct versus indirect.*** The most obvious communication differences were rooted in culturally based preferences for direct versus indirect communication (Gudykunst and Ting-Toomey, 1988). The formality and reserved nature of many women from outside the United States contrasted dramatically with the behavior of the many highly verbal Americans. These differences were evident in the planning sessions for the final presentations. Indirect communicators were sometimes shocked by the bluntness and greater willingness to confront senior management on the part of direct communicators. By contrast, some of the direct communicators misinterpreted the more formal respect and deference of women from indirect cultures as being too accepting of the status quo. The difference is not so much in the level of respect each culture shows, but rather in the ways in which respect is communicated. As is usually true in such situations, a number of cross-cultural influences were operating simultaneously, and, for the most part, below the level of conscious awareness of most of the people involved. In the work sessions, as in most multicultural teams, the women differed in their culturally-based orientations toward direct versus indirect communication, group versus individual decision making, faster- versus slower-paced problem solving, more versus less formal ways of conveying respect, and in their proclivity to accept, versus attempting to change, situations.

Alerting participants to potential cross-cultural differences increases their ability to manage the impact of culture and benefit from its presence. At a pre-forum session, team leaders received cross-cultural training on differences in both culturally based values dimensions and communication styles. During the forum, when it became apparent that all participants needed similar coaching, we added a brief orientation on communication-style differences and effective approaches to communicating between native and non-native English speakers. In retrospect, we should have included more cross-cultural training for all participants at the beginning of the forum since, for many attendees, it was their first global meeting. Such presentations do not mitigate the cross-cultural differences themselves. When differences are made explicit, however, the inevitable discovery of differing cultural and value-based norms regarding appropriate behavior and communication styles can, if well managed, become a source of potential synergy rather than merely a source of frustration, misleading interpretations, and inappropriate evaluations.

## ■ Global sense making ■

As consultants and facilitators, we struggled at times to understand the different perspectives and reactions we observed at the forum as well as throughout the overall change process. One framework that was particularly helpful in making sense of the experience was Osland and Bird's (2000) cultural sense making model. As shown in figure 2.1, the model, which was originally designed as a tool for understanding the importance of context in decoding cultural paradoxes, consists of five components.

### Framing the situation

The sense-making process begins when individuals attempt to understand a situation or context. They engage in indexing behavior, which involves noticing – or attending to – stimuli that provide cues about the nature or meaning of the situation. In determining what to attend to and what to ignore, individuals "frame the situation." The varied reactions to the forum can be traced in part to differences in how various participants framed the situation. Some women, for example, felt honored when the CEO invited them, as some of the highest-potential and most senior business leaders in the company, to participate in what they saw as an important and exciting change process. Upon receiving the same invitation, other women felt offended that they had been invited to a women-only meeting, fearing that they were being invited only because they were women and that the invitation itself, therefore, de-emphasized, and detracted from their professional accomplishments. Although operating below the level of conscious awareness of most, if not all, participants, the underlying cross-cultural values clash guiding the women's sense making was between what anthropologists and cross-cultural management scholars refer to as ascribed versus achieved status (Trompenaars and Hampden-Turner, 1998). Did the women perceive that the CEO was inviting them primarily because they were women (ascribed status) or primarily because of their performance as top business professionals (achieved status)?

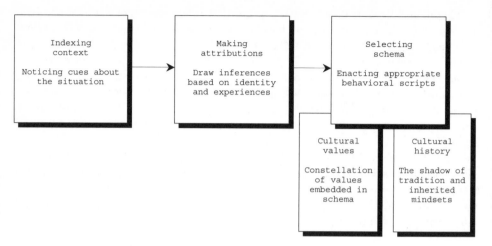

**Figure 2.1**   Cultural sensemaking model

Similarly, when attempting to make sense of (to index) the context (or meaning) of a women-only meeting, many participants focused on a single dimension, similarity. They assumed that they would be with other women who were "just like themselves" and who would therefore share similar perspectives. In subconsciously determining what to attend to, they chose to focus on characteristics that reinforced similarity – the most prominent of which was that the group included all women – while choosing to ignore, or downplay, the participants' dissimilarity – the fact that the women came from a wide range of cultures, countries, and backgrounds. This "assumed similarity" prevented some participants from framing the forum as a gathering of people with disparate views and different cultural styles – in addition to their similarity of all being women. Without the moderating appreciation of the simultaneous impact of similarities and differences, the exaggerated emphasis on the single dimension of similarity at times resulted in inaccurate sense making and consequent misattributions.

## Making attributions

The next step in the model is attribution, a process by which contextual cues are analysed in order to make sense of their meanings. This is done by matching the contextual clues with appropriate schema. The matching process is moderated or influenced by one's social identity (for example, ethnic or religious background, gender, social class, organizational affiliation, and nationality) and one's personal history (for example, experiences and chronology). Throughout the forum and overall change process, being a man or a woman played a heightened role in people's attributions, as did age and cultural background. Most male corporate officers at Bestfoods, for example, were in their late fifties and early sixties, and had stay-at-home wives. They had never watched their wives struggle to climb the corporate ladder or to juggle the competing demands of professional and private life. Nor were their own careers affected by the demands of dual-career marriages. As a result, they had a different appreciation from that of the women participating in the forum of the barriers, challenges, and opportunities faced by most women today.

Age similarly influenced some of the attributions the women made at the forum. The older women, for example, had experienced more hardships in previous decades related to the fact that they were women than had most of the younger women. Many older women had already bumped up against the glass ceiling while their younger colleagues often had no personal experience of discrimination. As a result, these two groups differed in their appreciation of what it would take for the company to deal effectively with the problem of retaining and developing women as global leaders. Equally apparent, and perhaps equally unsurprising, the older and younger women exhibited somewhat different ways of behaving with the senior executives.

## Selecting a script

Schema are cultural scripts, patterns of social interaction that are characteristic of particular cultural groups (Triandis et al., 1984). Cultural scripts are accepted as appropriate ways of behaving, specifying certain patterns of interaction. From personal or vicarious experience, people learn how to select schema that are appropriate for specific situations. By watching and working with senior executives, for example, people develop scripts that guide how they believe they should act when they themselves take on senior-executive roles. People learn the appropriate vocabulary and gestures of senior executives, which then elicit fairly predictable responses. Differing cultural scripts among participants explain many of the cultural clashes experienced during the forum. The women from the United States who requested the agenda change, for example, framed the forum as a situation that primarily offered an opportunity to change the organization. From their perspective, it was therefore appropriate to behave proactively in attempting to modify the agenda to meet their needs. Unlike participants from most other cultures, the American women had observed similar behavior in other meetings. In contrast, the scripts learned by the Asians and Latin Americans involved paying respectful attention to expert presenters and accepting the agenda as it had been originally designed.

## The influence of cultural values

All schemas reflect not only the underlying cultural values of the particular individuals or groups involved, but also the hierarchical importance of those values relative to each other. For example, similar to their Asian and Latin American colleagues, the participants from the United States also valued experts. However, at the forum, other cultural values were more important to them when they requested that the forum convenors change the agenda – for example, low power distance (less importance given to expert input and hierarchical status), inductive problem solving, the positive value of change, and status gained through achievement, which in this case meant preparing an excellent presentation. The dynamic of one value trumping – or taking precedence over – another value in guiding action reveals the ways in which the constellation of values related to a particular schema is hierarchical. It also helps us understand why cultural decoding by members of other cultures is often extremely difficult.

## The influence of cultural history

When decoding schema, we often find vestiges of cultural history and tradition. Mindsets inherited from previous generations – or what is often referred to in organizations as administrative heritage – explain how history is remembered Fisher (1997). For example, the US baby boomers who lived through the years of protest against their government's involvement in the Vietnam War developed a mindset that reinforces questioning (and sometimes distrusting) authority. As a result, people from this generation in the United States are less likely to automatically accept orders (and agendas) than many of their colleagues from other generations and other cultures.

## Lessons learned

To . . . [lead] is not always to succeed, but it is always to learn.
It is to move forward despite the obstacles.

Krieger (1998)

## Conclusions

Given its many innovations the forum and overall change process offered many opportunities to learn. The primary lessons we learned include the following.

- *Embed global leadership development* within an overall organizational development process that focuses on systemic barriers and supports.
- *Use organizational surveys to surface gaps and catalyse change.* Surveys administered to different groups within the organization can serve as a trigger event for organizational change. Such surveys focuses attention on the differing realities and attitudes existing simultaneously within the same organization. Survey results help people realize and understand that large gaps may exist between what they believe to be true and what is actually true, thus increasing their dissatisfaction with the status quo. The most comprehensive surveys focus on factors that both promote and inhibit global leadership.
- *Involve senior leadership early in the process.* The HR department involved senior management very early on in the change initiative and planning for the forum by asking division presidents to nominate forum participants. Forum nominees were later ranked by the CSC, whose members include the most senior executives in the company. Through careful examination of the women's career progress in their divisions, this vetting process forced senior executives to become more aware of their most senior and high-potential female managers.

- *To succeed, gain top management support.* As we would expect, top management support was a critical success factor in Bestfoods's change initiative. The CEO initiated the change effort and supported it throughout the process. The visible presence of senior executives at the forum allowed them to learn about impediments and recommendations first hand, and to convey symbolically their support for developing women among the company's global leaders.
- *Explicitly link the company's global business strategy with its global diversity strategy.* The CEO sent clear messages about his goal of increasing the company's competitiveness by including the best people from all parts of the organization. Both he and Brody emphasized the strong link between Bestfoods's business strategy and a greater need for women global leaders.
- *Choose carefully between holding a women-only versus a women-and-men-together event.* Women-only versus women-and-men-together events have different advantages and disadvantages that need to be carefully considered. At Bestfoods, a combined strategy was used. The potential backlash from men that could have resulted from a women-only event seems to have been outweighed by the advantages of providing women with an opportunity to focus candidly on their issues with limited distractions, complemented by contact with senior management. Other employees were very curious about the outcomes of the forum, creating the advantage of a pull strategy for information and change from throughout the company rather than necessitating a push strategy in which employees. Post-forum company actions based on the women's recommendations that also benefited both women and men (such as flexible work hours, early-career management training) were instrumental in diminishing male backlash.
- *Expect some cautious or negative reactions when any particular group is singled out for global leadership.* Mixed reactions should be expected to announcing any program that identifies some people as potential global leaders and excludes others. HR professionals can prepare for this eventuality by considering a wide range of potential reactions and appropriate strategies for dealing with them.
- *Include target group on design team.* Had there been more time to design the forum, the designers would have used a liaison group of women from various countries to identify issues, provide ideas, and offer suggestions for the design. A virtual global design team of informal and formal leaders could have resulted in a consensus on a customized design that would have received more, and broader-based, support from participants than an event designed by support staff or consultants.
- *Understand the critical nature of the pre-forum design process.* For first-time global events such as the forum, more initial contact may be needed (for example, interviews, regional meetings, teleconferences) in some companies so that program designers can fully understand and reflect the context and needs of participants and so that participants gain a clear understanding of what to expect prior to arriving at the event.
- *Appreciate differences among women leaders.* Since women, like men, have different realities, it is more helpful to surface those realities than to expect a consensus on either "the state of women" or explanations about why women do or do not make it to the top of major companies. Participants may need to be reminded that other women have had very different experiences from their own.
- *Differentiate between complementary and sequential goals.* If there is pent-up demand to make organizational changes, some participants may prefer to focus on organizational change issues rather than leadership development activities. Designers should carefully consider whether both goals should, or can, be tackled

simultaneously. For the particular company, are the two goals complementary or sequential?

- *Use effective approaches for action learning that are already accepted as effective by the company*. The organization development portion of the forum was modelled on an action learning format already used by the company for other important issues, which gave the meeting greater legitimacy. Participants presented their recommendations and received an immediate response or a promise of future consideration from senior management. Not only did this model responsive management, but the multicultural teamwork needed to prepare the participants' recommendations was a real-life test of their global leadership competency.

- *Customize the change strategy to the particular company context*. Bestfoods created its own change strategy for increasing the number of women global leaders rather than bringing in outside experts to prescribe strategies that had worked in other settings. Bestfoods purposely relied on the women's recommendations, which, among other advantages, gave the women a voice and a sense of ownership of the process. The suggested changes fit the culture, which increases the odds of their successful implementation.

- *When possible, use inclusive strategies*. The internal change agent (Brody) used a vocabulary and a change strategy acceptable to the organization. She was careful to include other people's ideas in the change process.

- *Train cross-cultural facilitators*. The use of carefully selected participant-facilitators, chosen for their interpersonal and leadership skills, who receive cross-cultural training, contributes to positive group dynamics and provides an opportunity for the facilitators to exercise cross-cultural leadership skills. The facilitators helped other participants understand what to expect and made them feel more comfortable. By keeping the consultants informed about how each small group was functioning, it was possible to continuously customize the program in live time.

- *Coach participants on cross-cultural dynamics*. In addition to cross-cultural training for facilitators, we recommend devoting an early session in global meetings to understanding differences in cultural dimensions and communication styles. Basic training on recognizing, appreciating, and reconciling such differences is important for global leaders and allows multicultural meetings to progress more effectively.

- *Select global competencies appropriate to the organizational and industry challenges and environment*. Due to time constraints, the forum was designed using a generic model of global leadership competencies. However, many companies develop customized lists of global leadership competencies that fit their particular competitive environment. We recommend that such competency customization be done via competency studies and/or through culturally representative interviews prior to designing the development process.

## NOTES

1  For a more in-depth discussion of global women business leaders, see Adler (1997a), op.cit., and Adler, N. J. (1997b): "Global leadership: Women leaders," *Management International Review*, 37, 1, 135–43; Adler, N. J. (1999a): "Global entrepreneurs: Women, myths, and history," *Global Focus* 1, 4, 125–34; Adler, N. J. (1999b): Global leaders: Women of influence in G. Powell (ed.), *Handbook of Gender in Organizations*, Thousand Oaks, CA: Sage; and Adler, N. J. (1999c): Twenty-first century leadership: Reality beyond the myths in R. Wright (ed.), *Research in Global Strategic Management*, 7, *International Entrepreneurship: Globalization of Emerging Business*. Greenwich, CT: JAI Press.

2  For a more in-depth discussion of women political leaders, see Nancy J. Adler's (1996) Global women political leaders: An invisible history, an increasingly important future. *Leadership Quarterly* 7, 1,

133–61; Adler, N. J. (1997a): Global leaders: A dialogue with future history. *International Management*, 1, 2, 21–33; Adler, N. J. (1998a): Did you hear? Global leadership in Charity's world. *Journal of Management Inquiry*, 7, 2, 21–33; and Adler, N. J. (1998b): Societal leadership: the wisdom of peace. In S. Srivastva (ed.), *Executive Wisdom and Organizational Change*, San Francisco, CA: Jossey-Bass.

3    GM quote.

4    Kanter, Rosabeth Moss (1994): Comments on Nancy A. Nichols' *Reach for the top: Women and the changing facts of work life.* Boston: Harvard Business School Press, as reviewed by J. R. Hook in *The Academy of Management Executive*, 8, 2, 87–9.

5    Their most well-known brands were Hellmann's condiments and dressings, Knorr soups, sauces and bouillion, Skippy peanut butter, and Entenmann's baked goods (in the United States).

6    For a more detailed description of the change effort and the role of Dick Shoemate and Laura Brody, see Osland, J. S. and Adler, N. J. (2001): Women and global leadership at Bestfoods. In J. S. Osland, D. Kolb, and I. Rubin (eds), *Organizational Behavior: An Experiential Approach*, Upper Saddle River, NJ: Prentice-Hall.

7    The survey was modeled after the one used in the Catalyst report "Women in Corporate Leadership: Progress & Prospects" (Wellington, 1996). Catalyst is a well-respected research and education institute located in New York City that focuses on women in the most senior leadership and management positions in organizations.

8    For an in-depth discussion of the survey results, see Adler, Brody and Osland (2000), op.cit. and Ragins, Belle Rose, Townsend, Bickley, and Mattis (1998): Gender gap in the executive suite: CEOs and female executives report on breaking the glass ceiling. *Academy of Management Executive* 12, 1, pp. 28–42.

9    For detailed information on the agenda, see Adler, N. J., Brody, L, and Osland, J. S. (2000): The women's global leadership forum: Enhancing one company's global leadership Capability. *Human Resource Management*, 39, 2, 3, 209–25 and Adler, N. J., Brody, L. W., and Osland, J. S. (2001, in press): Advances in global leadership: The women's global leadership forum. In W. H. Mobley (ed.), *Advances in Global Research*, 2, Greenwich, CN: JAI Press.

10   According to Noel Tichy, "Development in the new era must be seen simultaneously as individual and organisational transformation." In V. Puck, N. Tichy, and C. Barnett (eds), (1993). *Globalizing Management: Creating and Leading the Competitive Organization*, New York: John Wiley.

11   For a discussion of the history of attributions on why there are so few women in management worldwide, see Adler and Izraeli (1994), op.cit.

12   Human behavior is always difficult to interpret, especially across cultures. With the help of years of anthropological and cross-cultural management research, we can make educated guesses as to the cultural dynamics operating in any given situation. However, in the process of cross-cultural interpretation, we must guard against stereotyping individuals – in this case, stereotyping particular women attending the forum.

## REFERENCES

Adler, N. J. (1997): *International Dimensions of Organizational Behavior.* Cincinnati, OH: South Western College Publishing.

Adler, N. J., Brody, L. W., and Osland, J. S. (under review): Going Beyond twentieth century leadership: A CEO develops his company's global competitiveness. *Academy of Management Executive.*

Catalyst (2000): 2000 Catalyst Census of Women Corporate Officers and Top Earners of the *Fortune* 500. New York City.

Dwyer, P., Johnston, M., and Miller, K. L. (1996): Europe's Corporate Women. *Business Week*, April 15, 40–2.

Fisher, G. (1997): *Cultural Mindsets.* Yarmouth, ME: Intercultural Press.

Gregersen, H. B., Morrison, A. J., and Black, J. S. (1998): Developing leaders for the global frontier. *Sloan Management Review*, 40, 1, 21–33.

Gudykunst, W. A. and Ting-Toomey, S. (1988): *Culture and Interpersonal Communication.* New York: Guilford.

Hall, E. T. and Hall, M. R. (1990): *Understanding Cultural Differences.* Yarmouth, ME: Intercultural Press.

Hofstede, G. (1980): *Culture's Consequences: International Differences in Work-Related Values.* Sage: Beverly Hills.

Hofstede, G. and Bond, M. (1988): The Confucius connection: From cultural roots to economic growth. *Organizational Dynamics,* 16, 4, 4–21.

Krieger, D. (1998): In F. Franck, J. Roze, and R. Connelly (eds), *What Does It Mean to Be Human?* Nyack, NY: Circumstantial Productions.

Osland, J. S. and Bird, A. (2000): Beyond sophisticated stereotyping: Cultural sensemaking in context. *Academy of Management Executive,* 13, 1.

Osland & Taylor (2001): Developing global leaders. *HR.Com.*

Phillips, M. E. and Boyacigiller, N. A. (1998): Learning culture: An integrated framework for cultural analysis. Symposium presentation at the Academy of Management Meeting, San Diego, CA.

Samovar, L. A., Porter, R. E., and Stefani, L. A. (1998): *Communication Between Cultures.* (3rd edn), Belmont, CA: Wadsworth.

Triandis, H. C., Marin, G., Lisansky, J., and Betancourt, H. (1984): Simpatia as a cultural script of hispanics. *Journal of Personality and Social Psychology,* 47, 6.

Trompenaars, F. and Hampden-Turner, C. (1998): *Riding the Waves of Culture.* New York: McGraw-Hill.

Zahra, S. A. (1998): Competitiveness and global leadership in the 21st century. *Academy of Management Executive,* 12, 4, 10–12.

# 3

# A DECADE OF DIVERSITY: STRATEGIES AIMED AT ADVANCING WOMEN BENEFIT ALL EMPLOYEES AT BANK OF MONTREAL

*Nuzhat Jafri and Katie Isbister*

Bank of Montreal's business strategy and the advancement of workplace equality are inextricably linked. The bank's commitment to an equitable workplace and a diverse workforce is grounded in its corporate vision and values, dating back to its 1990 *Corporate Strategic Plan*. As part of that plan, in the fall of 1990, Bank of Montreal launched its seminal *Task Force on the Advancement of Women* and hasn't looked back since.

The results of the *Task Force* were released in a report to all employees in November 1991. The report marked a turning point in the bank's history toward achieving an equitable workplace, a diverse workforce, and meeting the needs of a customer base that is as culturally and geographically vaired as the Canadian population itself. Bank of Montreal's commitment to workplace equality is stated as follows:

- We will create an *equitable workplace* in which all employees have an equal opportunity to enhance and advance their careers.
- We will create a *diverse workforce* that reflects, at all levels and all groups, the communities the bank serves.
- We will create a *supportive work environment* in which equality and diversity goals inform and influence all our other business goals.

This chapter will examine how the recommendations and Action Plans coming out of the *Task Force* have resulted in dramatic changes which have benefited all employees at Bank of Montreal during the past decade. These changes have earned Bank of Montreal a Catalyst Award for its efforts to advance women, an Optimas Award for its progressive policies and programs to assist employees in balancing their multiple commitments, and the 1995 and 2001 Human Resources Development Canada Annual Merit Award for achievements in employment equity.

Findings of the *Task Force on the Advancement of Women* revealed three main barriers to women's advancement at Bank of Montreal:

1   outdated assumptions and false impressions with respect to women and their ability to advance to more senior level positions
2   lack of encouragement and access to opportunities and information about senior level positions
3   the need to balance multiple commitments, including work, family, education, and community life.

The following recommendations laid the groundwork for the bank to address these barriers head on:

• *Get the facts out.* Bridge the gap between perception and reality about women's abilities, career interests and commitment.
• *Help employees get ahead.* Provide better and clearer information about – and access to – job options and career-enhancing opportunities.
• *Reduce the stress.* Implement policies to formally support women and men in balancing their multiple commitments to work, family, education, and community.
• *Make it official.* Make managers accountable for ongoing dramatic change toward workplace equity in all job families and at all levels at Bank of Montreal.

In response to the recommendations, Tony Comper, then President and Chief Operating Officer, committed the bank to dramatic and systematic change to achieve equity in the workplace. He endorsed 26 action plans presented by the *Task Force* and made a commitment to have them up and running no later than the end of 1992. The goals set out in the action plans and the changes resulting from their implementation are presented below.

## ■ Keep up the momentum ■

### Goal

Provide a focus for ongoing leadership, advocacy, accountability and support for the development and promotion of women; and make sure workplace equality remains a vital part of the *Corporate Strategic Plan.*

## Resulting change

**Leadership.** The position of Vice-President, Workplace Equality was created in January 1992. Reporting directly to the president, the vice-president and her team were to function as the catalyst and central reference point for all of the bank's workplace equality initiatives. Today, the responsibility of the vice-president has been expanded to include employee assistance programs as well as stewardship of the bank's corporate values. The vice-president has a direct reporting relationship with the chairman and the executive vice-president of Human Resources.

Also in January of 1992, a National Advisory Council on the Equitable Workplace was established to oversee bank-wide implementation of all workplace equality initiatives. The National Council's role was to support ongoing activities related to equality both in the bank and in the communities it serves. It was also meant to provide leadership, advocacy and accountability, and to sponsor additional initiatives as they became necessary. The council, whose members included the president and chief operating officer, the four vice-chairs, the senior vice-president, Human Resources, the vice-president, Workplace Equality, and six other key executives, met quarterly to review progress and to advise on what needed to be done to ensure that the bank reached its workplace equality goals. Today, Bank of Montreal's workplace equality strategy continues to be championed by the most senior individuals in the organization – the Chairman's Council on the – Equitable Workplace (CCEW). The council includes Tony Comper, the chairman and CEO of the Bank of Montreal Group of Companies, the vice-chairs of each of the lines of business, the executive vice-president of Human Resources and past presidents of the council.

**Employee involvement.** In March of 1992, workplace equality divisional advisory councils were formed. Each council had at least eight members who represented all levels of the bank and reflected the diversity of the bank's workforce. Each council reported to a senior executive and was responsible for leadership and networking at the local and divisional levels. Members served as employees' direct link to the bank's drive toward workplace equality, meeting regularly with employee groups to explain workplace equality initiatives and to assist in the resolution of problems. Since 1992, the councils have evolved to reflect the organizational changes in the bank. Today, employees across the bank are actively involved in increasing awareness and advocacy for workforce diversity and an equitable workplace. Employees are involved in numerous workplace equality sponsored community activities such as the CNIB Walk Toward Freedom and the Canadian Hearing Society's Mayfest. There are currently 12 councils and a number of affinity groups – some are geographically based, others address specific business or group concerns. Examples of such groups are given below.

- *Aboriginal sharing circles.* Aboriginal sharing circles in Calgary and Toronto include Aboriginal and non-Aboriginal employees who come together to learn about Aboriginal culture and develop strategies to enhance Aboriginal business through partnerships with Aboriginal communities and the bank's Aboriginal Banking Division.
- *People with disabilities affinity groups.* Two different affinity groups of employees have been established: one consisting of employees who are deaf and/or hard of hearing and another

one of employees who are blind or visually impaired. The groups are self-directed and have been instrumental in recommending for persons with disabilities two important initiatives that are described below.

1   Integrated Adaptive Technology Systems Support Project. In July of 2000, Workplace Equality implemented a six-month pilot project in order to identify and eliminate barriers facing employees with disabilities at Bank of Montreal with respect to the integration of adaptive technology. Key elements of the pilot included: establishing a testing lab for compatibility with adaptive technologies, and identifying systems training needs of employees with disabilities.

2   Accessibility Guidelines. In October of 2000, Workplace Equality established an initiative to examine the feasibility of accessibility guidelines beyond those required by the building code. Working with the senior partner of Accessible Housing Initiatives Inc., these guidelines aim to address both employee and customer access and may be used by Corporate Real Estate for both new and existing premises. A preliminary report and recommendations have been completed and will be tabled for the consideration by the Chairman's Council on the Equitable Workplace in April 2001.

## ■ Increase awareness ■

### Goal

Bridge the gap between perception and reality about women's abilities, career interest and commitment.

### Resulting change

**Sharing information with all employees.** The *Task Force* identified myths and misconceptions about women in the workplace as one of the key barriers to their advancement in the organization. Using facts and figures, stereotypes surrounding notions of commitment, performance, and education were irrevocably refuted. The bank ensured that each employee received a copy of this *Task Force* report. Since that time, three additional executive-sponsored task forces were established to identify and address issues dealing with the employment and advancement of people with disabilities, Aboriginal people, and members of visible minorities. The resulting reports were also released to all employees in the bank. The bank's internal magazine, *First Bank News*, regularly reports on the bank's progress and workplace equality and diversity initiatives. The workplace equality and diversity Intranet site is a popular source of information for employees. In addition, the councils and affinity groups mentioned earlier sponsor their own communication campaigns and awareness events.

**Training sessions.** To help dispel the myths and false assumptions that form invisible barriers to women's advancement, the bank developed a training program called "Women and Men as Colleagues." The one and a half-day workshop assisted women and men in coming to terms with how traditional and often unconscious attitudes distort the selection, development, and promotion of women. The program was piloted in February 1992 and implemented fully in September of the same year. Ninety percent of all of bank executives in Canada participated in the workshop. It was subsequently rolled out to the councils and senior-level employees across the organization. Since then other workshops on "Attitudes and Protocols on Working with People with Disabilities, and Managing in a Multicultural Environment" have been developed and offered to employees through the bank's Institute for Learning.

The bank's internal Employee Assistance Program (EAP) designs and provides numerous workshops, lunch-and-learns, and educational material to support the needs of all employees. EAP's "Balancing Your Life" series offers workshops on such issues as stress management, coping with change, self-awareness, communication, emotional intelligence, emotional and physical health, relationship issues, parenting, and elder-care. Participation in these seminars is completely voluntary and utilization rates have quadrupled in the past decade.

Most recently the bank has launched an Aboriginal Awareness session to educate employees and managers about Aboriginal culture and business. In the spring of 2001 a new course, "Creating and Optimizing an Inclusive Workplace Culture," will be launched at the Institute.

## ■ Develop people skills ■

### Goal

Enhance the people development skills that are necessary to create a work environment in which both women and men can and will succeed.

### Resulting change

***Managerial leadership skills.*** The bank launched a new managerial leadership curriculum in 1992 designed to help managers develop a leadership style that empha-sized coaching and teamwork. By July 31, 1993, a total of 1,511 employees had par-ticipated in the workshops. The intent was to ensure all managers participated in the program. Since then the bank's Institute for Learning has developed and offered inten-sive courses on coaching and performance management, including the very popular "Coaching for Performance." During the past couple of years managerial leadership has become a key part of the bank's strategic plan.

The bank recognizes that for its strategic vision to be realized fully, managerial lead-ership must be supported by behaviours and competencies among managers of people. To this end, an ambitious development initiative was launched in 1999. All managers of people at Bank of Montreal are required to attend "Managerial Leadership Week," a five-day residential training initiative that has taken a new approach to "managing for inclusion and managing diversity." These concepts are completely integrated into the program so that workplace equality and diversity are woven into the learning through-out the five days. In order to measure the impact of this learning, the bank measures managerial effectiveness through its Annual Employee Survey. Results are solid: a full 74 percent view Bank of Montreal as a place where people have an equal opportunity for advancement, regardless of age, disability, gender, or race. Among respondents who self-identified as a person with a disability, 81 percent are satisfied with the accommodation they receive. In some lines of business this satisfaction rate is as high as 100 percent. To build on this learning, a full managerial leadership learning system which incorporates "Managing for Inclusion/Managing Diversity" competency and behavioural scales is being developed to address learning needs of managers at all levels of the organization. The competency and behavioural scales have been recognized as "best in class" and are the basis for the new curriculum.

As the Bank of Montreal Group of Companies has grown into a truly North American enterprise, with lines of business spanning Canada and the United States, the Workplace Equality Office in Canada and the Diversity Office at Harris Bank in the United States have jointly produced a briefing book on US and Canadian laws pertinent to affirmative action, equal opportunity, employment equity and human rights issues aimed at educating managers on both sides of the border with respect to their responsibilities in these areas.

The bank offers a range of programs to support managers. Management consultation services are available from both EAP and the Human Resources Centre to provide individual coaching for managers in dealing with individual employee or team issues. Leaders' newsletters, a collaborative offering from Human Resources and EAP are published quarterly to assist leaders in developing their people management skills. Managers can also request workshop support for teams of employees dealing with transition.

## ■ Publicize opportunities and highlight personal potential ■

### Goal

Provide a bank-wide exchange of information about all management vacancies at every level, clearing the way for employees to take charge of their own careers. Enable all employees to take charge of their own careers by providing formal opportunities for meaningful discussions with managers about their goals, aspirations, and potential.

### Resulting change

*Career information network (CIN).* In March of 1993, the bank launched its Career Information Network (CIN), an easy-to-use computer system for sharing information about all job vacancies. By tapping into the CIN listings from a bank computer terminal, all employees could take the opportunity to express interest in jobs as soon as they became available. Employees could also use the system to learn about the types and range of jobs that were available to help them chart their career paths and seek the necessary training and development if they so desired. At the same time, hiring managers gained access to the widest talent pool, and thus substantially improved their chances of finding precisely the right candidates. Today CIN resides on the bank's Human Resources intranet site and continues to provide information about job opportunities in the Bank of Montreal Group of Companies. Approximately 12,000 hits are recorded on the site each month.

***Career possibilities.*** Employees told the Task Force on the Advancement of Women that they wanted increased opportunities to meet with more experienced colleagues in an informal setting – to share ideas, to learn more about different career options, and to benefit from one-on-one exposure to someone in a position to help them advance their careers. In response, the bank launched a pilot mentoring initiative, the Executive Advisor Program, which matched volunteer executives with employees who were randomly selected from senior management levels of the organization. The program, open to men and women, was highly successful. Learnings from it have helped shape many subsequent mentoring programs within the bank, including a guide to mentoring relationships which was made available through the bank's Possibilities Centre. This centre was established as a centralized resource to help employees manage their own careers and seek counseling about career possibilities within and outside the bank.

The revised Performance Planning & Review process introduced in 1992 has been specifically designed to support employees' professional growth and development. Not only does the process provide feedback on performance but it also requires employees and managers to formulate career and personal development objectives.

## ■ Expand career opportunities ■

### Goal

Provide more specific programs to help employees enhance or advance their careers.

### Resulting change

***Specialized programs.*** In 1992 the bank targeted 50 percent representation of women in the Commercial Banking Officer training program, its Management Development Program, as well as commercial credit training. The Management Development Program is still remembered fondly by female managers in the bank as one of its most effective development initiatives. An extensive workplace-based learning initiative, "Learning for Success," was launched in 1993 to all branches. This self-education series for tellers and customer service representatives incorporated self-study with on-the-job practice and coaching support. The program is still used for self-education and has proved highly effective. Since then, the bank's Institute for Learning, opened in 1994, has enabled all employees in the bank to take job-related and complementary skills training courses. The bank is committed to providing an average of five training days to each employee. The latest learning initiative targeted to all employees is an extensive e-literacy program.

## ■ Formalize flexible work ■

### Goal

Implement policies and benefits programs that formally support employees who are balancing multiple commitments to work, family, education and community.

### Resulting change

***Award-winning policies.*** The bank introduced a new policy in May 1992 intended to help reduce the stress of balancing multiple commitments and remove barriers to advancement experienced by people who, for personal reasons, prefer to work non-traditional hours or in non-traditional settings. Flex arrangements are employee initiated and manager approved. The determining factor in approving a request is whether the job can get done this new way, not on the personal reason for the request. To help ensure the successful adoption of this ground-breaking policy, the decision was made to distribute the bank's award-winning publication, *Flexing Yours Options*, to every employee in May 1993. The reader-friendly handbook supports and promotes the new flex work policy, underlines its benefits to both the bank and employees, and provides detailed information on how to propose, approve and monitor flex arrangements. The policy launched the following five options which are available to employees regardless of job, level, or group:

1   flextime
2   flexible work week
3   permanent part-time
4   job sharing
5   flexplace.

In the 2000 Annual Employee Survey, 41 percent of male and 54 percent of the female respondents indicated that they use policies and programs available to help balance their work/life commitments.

The bank has also implemented a responsive and flexible benefits program which allows employees to choose from an array of possibilities suitable for their individual needs and circumstances.

## ■ Create people care days ■

### Goal

Endorse in a formal human resources policy the practice of giving time off to employees who are balancing multiple commitments to work, family, education, and community.

## Resulting change

***People care days.*** This policy, launched in 1993, outlines a simple process for grant-ing paid time off to tend to personal matters that cannot be scheduled outside work hours. Rather than defining a set number of days, the policy is designed to be flexible. Paid time off could range from half an hour to a few days depending on the particular need. It is used by employees, at the discretion of their managers, for such things as parent – teacher interviews, writing an exam, medical appointments for self, children or aging parents, and religious or cultural holidays.

## ■ Reduce child care stress ■

### Goal

Provide expert information and advice to employees who need child care service, both ongoing and emergency, to reduce the stress of balancing responsibilities to children and work.

### Resulting change

***Childcare and eldercare.*** In 1991, Taking Care, a free, 24-hour child care tele-phone referral service, was introduced. It was one of the bank's first initiatives to help employees reduce stress related to child care. Taking Care was followed by a free Elder-care information, counseling and referral service to help employees with concerns they might have about an aging relative. Both Taking Care and Eldercare are initiatives of the bank's Employee Assistance Program. Through this program employees are able to access local day care facilities as well as locate emergency back-up child care. Over the past decade the utilization rates for the Eldercare service has risen over 100 percent as caring for aging parents has become an increasingly common challenge for employees.

## ■ Endorse leaves of absence ■

### Goal

Respond to emerging employee needs for extended time off.

### Resulting change

***Leaves of absence.*** The bank's leaves of absence policy has been revised to allow employees to take leaves of up to two years to pursue their education, family, commu-

|  | 1992 | 1993 | 1994 | 1995 | 1996 | 1997 | 1998 | 1999 | 2000 |
|---|---|---|---|---|---|---|---|---|---|
| Executives | 9.5 | 12.1 | 14.8 | 16.9 | 19.9 | 23.5 | 26.8 | 30.0 | 32.8 |
| Grades 38–40 | 8.7 | 9.5 | 11.8 | 13.7 | 17.0 | 21.1 | 25.4 | 26.6 | 28.6 |
| Grades 36–37 | 17.9 | 20.1 | 22.5 | 24.1 | 25.6 | 28.4 | 32.8 | 34.8 | 37.0 |
| Grades 34–35 | 30.2 | 31.5 | 33.6 | 35.8 | 37.7 | 41.6 | 43.2 | 45.2 | 46.9 |

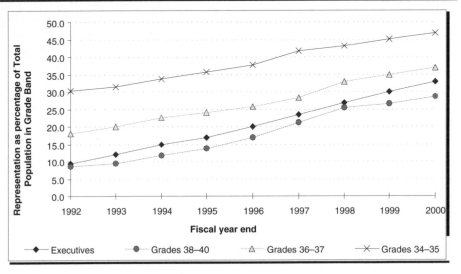

**Figure 3.1**   Representation of women as at fiscal 2000 year end
*Source*: Bank of Montreal, Workplace Equality Quarterly Reports

nity, or other interests. Pension plan rules have also been amended so that employees can pick up where they left off when they went on leave.

## ■ Set goals and monitor progress ■

### Goal

Measure our progress in achieving a balance of women and men in all job families and at all levels of the bank – particularly at more senior levels, where the imbalance is most conspicuous. (See Figure 3.1)

### Resulting change

***What gets measured, gets done!*** Since 1992, the leadership of the bank has been measuring progress toward workplace equality on a quarterly basis. Beginning in 1993, all managers' business plans included goals for hiring, retaining, and promoting women, members of visible minorities, Aboriginal people, and people with disabilities. Since that time, the bank has continued to set goals and measure its progress toward a representative workforce that mirrors the communities in which the bank does business. In 1997, Tony Comper, then president, made a public commitment to achieve gender parity in senior levels of the organization by 2007. In some parts of the bank this goal has already been realized, with women representing 50 percent of executive and senior management positions. Today, the Chairman's Council on the Equitable Workplace establishes qualitative and quantitative workplace equality goals at the beginning of each fiscal year, and measures progress toward the achievement of these goals on a quarterly basis through a comprehensive suite of reports. Recently the Chairman's Council announced a landmark decision that, beginning in 2001, achievement of qualitative and quantitative workplace equality goals will be taken into consideration in the calculation of executive incentive compensation.

## ■ Beyond the task forces and action plans ■

### Celebrating and recognizing equality champions

Beyond measuring our success in implementing workplace equality, the bank has adopted a strategy of celebrating and recognizing individuals whose behaviours and attitudes contribute to the Bank of Montreal's success in the financial services industry, and its leadership role in workplace equality and diversity. During the past three years, at gala events and conferences, 211 individuals from across the enterprise have been honoured as Equality Champions by Tony Comper, Chairman and CEO of the Bank of Montreal Group of Companies. These champions were selected by their peers from over 2,000 nominations. The Equality Champions campaigns created a heightened awareness throughout the organization about behaviours that make workplace equality come to life in employees' daily lives. The Champions' accomplishments and stories were shared with all employees through video and employee news magazines.

Over time the bank has introduced numerous initiatives that continue to benefit its diverse employees as well as the community at large. The following are a few examples of some of these initiatives.

*Aboriginal educational initiatives.* Bank of Montreal deeply understands the need for and is committed to providing educational opportunities for Aboriginal youth. The bank provides annual scholarships to Aboriginal youth aged 13 to 18 through the Foundation for the Advancement of Aboriginal Youth and sponsors several youth conferences throughout Calgary, Edmonton, and Vancouver. Of particular note is Bank of Montreal's 1999 involvement in the Treaty 7 Education Conference. In addition to sponsoring this event, the bank spoke on the benefits of Aboriginal youth staying in school to all Treaty 7 educators (approximately 300) attending this event. This presentation complements the numerous sessions facilitated by the bank in support of the Junior Achievement – Aboriginal Economics of Staying in School Program.

Bank of Montreal is a founding sponsor of the Aboriginal MBA program at the University of Saskatchewan. This program is focused on Aboriginal business and economic development. Our senior vice president of Aboriginal Banking is an honoured member of the Circle of Founders. In partnership with the Saskatchewan Indian Federated College and the University of Regina, the bank is a sponsor of a bachelor of administration degree program providing Aboriginal and non-Aboriginal students with the opportunity to explore issues of common concern.

***Possibilities program.*** The bank continues to expand its award-winning flagship Possibilities – Youth Internship Scholarship Program, a result of the Task Force on the Advancement of Visible Minorities. The program, which was originally designed to target visible minority youth in Montreal, has been expanded to include Toronto, Halifax, Winnipeg, Calgary, Edmonton, Vancouver, Saskatoon, and Lethbridge, and was extended to Aboriginal students and students with disabilities. Students in their final year of high school are selected for internships at the bank and receive a $1,000 scholarship toward their post-secondary education. These exceptional young people work as interns at the bank one day per week during the school year, and, depending on the availability of jobs and the students' ability and interest, obtain summer employment with the bank.

***Career edge internship program.*** This internship initiative is a private-sector response to provide meaningful job experiences to new graduates. At Bank of Montreal, the program is used exclusively to provide internships in support of its workplace equality goals. The bank, along with the other major banks in the country, has also participated in the Canadian Bankers Association's (CBA) Ability Edge Program. This program, co-sponsored by Career Edge and the CBA, is designed to provide graduates with disabilities meaningful work experience in a variety of jobs within the financial services sector. Last year Bank of Montreal won the Career Edge Vision Award for its focus on diversity.

***Advancement of women.*** In 1997 Bank of Montreal was a major sponsor and key advisor to a landmark study conducted by The Conference Board of Canada and Catalyst, titled "Closing the Gap: Women's Advancement in Corporate and Professional Canada." This research was the first to systemically identify the issues that are inhibiting the advancement of women into senior management in Canada from the perspectives of both chief executives and senior women. Since 1998 the bank has been the key sponsor of Junior Achievement's annual young women's conferences designed to attract girls in Grade 10 to non-traditional occupations, including professional careers in the financial services sector.

## Conclusion

The Bank of Montreal Group of Companies is committed to creating an equitable workplace, a diverse workforce and a supportive work environment. The bank's commitment is embedded in the recently published *Corporate Values*, which includes the statements: "We draw our strength from the diversity of our people and our business," and "We insist upon respect for every one and encourage all to have a voice." Enterprise standards for an equitable workplace and a diverse workforce, including the *Corporate Values*, have been established for the entire enterprise regardless of jurisdiction, so that employees across North America enjoy an environment built for their success. The dynamic body of work that was begun by Bank of Montreal in the 1990s has successfully laid the foundation for the enterprise to meet new challenges as an equitable workplace becomes table stakes in the war for talent and the face of diversity continues to evolve in the first decade of the new millennium.

# CHALLENGES

# 4

# THE BLACK AND ETHNIC MINORITY WOMAN MANAGER

*Marilyn J. Davidson*

Until relatively recently, research addressing the issues of black and ethnic minority male and female managers has been almost exclusively American (predominantly black African-American) and the amount of total published research is, according to a review by Cox and Nkomo (1990), "small, relative to the importance of the topic" (p. 419). Indeed, Bell et al. (1993) and Betters-Reed and Moore (1995) emphasized that studies of African-American and professional "women of color," especially in corporate settings, are virtually excluded from the growing body of research on women in management. The assumption has been that "women in management" refers to "white" women in management.

It is important to note that there are currently differing opinions and inconsistencies regarding descriptive terminology used when describing "non-white" women and men. In the US for example, while Asian, Indian, Hispanic, Native American, and African-American women would be referred to collectively as "women of color," only the African-American group tends to be referred to as "black" (Hite, 1996). A number of prominent British researchers, such as Mirza (1992) and Bhavnani (1994) used the term "black" to include women from African, Asian and Caribbean ethnic backgrounds, as well as from mixed ethnicity backgrounds.

What is evident from the limited research literature to date is that black and ethnic minority women managers often face a double jeopardy of sexual and racial discrimination which secures their position at the very bottom of the managerial pyramid (Bell

Parts of this chapter are taken with permission of Paul Chapman Publishing, a SAGE Publications Company, from *The Black and Ethnic Minority Woman Manager: Cracking the Concrete Ceiling* by Marilyn J. Davidson (London: Chapman/Sage Publishers, 1997).

and Nkomo, 2000; Davidson, 1997). Therefore, the aim of this chapter is to first describe the position of black and ethnic minority women managers and then to review the present literature pertaining to the major problems, pressures and barriers faced by these women.

## ■ The position of the black and ethnic minority woman manager ■

Numerous cross-cultural studies have concluded that, compared to their white male counterparts, white managerial women experience more career advancement barriers (that is, glass ceilings and glass walls) and more external discriminatory-based pressures including strains of coping with discrimination, prejudice, and sex stereotyping; lack of role models and feelings of isolation; burdens of coping with the role of "token woman"; and higher work/home conflict pressures (Greenglass, 1995; Devanna, 1987; Davidson and Cooper, 1992; Davidson and Fielden, 1999).

American research confirms that African-American and other ethnic minority managers, particularly women, are doubly disadvantaged in terms of upward mobility, and high levels of work and home pressures (Bell, 1990; Greenhaus et al., 1990; Dickens and Dickens, 1991; Hite, 1996). Indeed, according to Iles and Auluck (1991) "such findings in American studies of black managers resemble those often reported for white women managers in Britain." In the US, the number of African-American employees occupying managerial positions has increased from 3.6 percent of the national total in 1977 to 5.2 percent in 1982, to 6 percent of all managers in 1986 (Greenhaus et al., 1990). In 1988, 72 percent of all managers in American companies employing more than 100 people were white men, 23 percent white women, 3 percent African-American men and 2 percent African-American women (Reskin and Padovic, 1994). By 1994, in the category of executive, administrative, and managerial occupations, white women held 38 percent of the positions, while women "of color" represented only 5 percent (Hite, 1996).

In the UK, by 1998 the percentage of women managers was 18 percent with women making up 33 percent of those in managerial and administrative posts, and 40 percent of those in professional occupations (EOC, 1999; Davidson and Burke, 2000). However, while the long-term trends indicate women are entering management-graded jobs in increasing numbers, Bhavnani and Coyle (2000) suggest that the types of new management jobs being created through restructuring are different from those previously taken by men. These authors point out that these are predominantly in public and private service sectors, where women predominate in low-paid managerial positions.

According to the British Labour Force Survey, 9 percent of ethnic minority females in the UK are found in the category – Professional Manager, Employer, Employees, and Managers – large establishments, compared to 11 percent of white females (Davidson, 1997). It should be noted, however, that the high percentage of ethnic minority women in the "professional" category may be misleading since this also includes nursing – a profession which attracts almost a quarter of all employed black-Caribbean women compared to 9 percent of white women (Holdsworth and Dale, 1996). While there has been a small overall rise in the proportion of black and ethnic minority British women in managerial and skilled manual jobs, Bhavnani and Coyle (2000) suggest that they have actually experienced a deterioration of their position relative to white women. Compared to the late 1970s, they account for a smaller proportion of women in professional jobs, and a higher proportion of women in management. Of the general managerial and administrators' jobs held by women in "national/local government, large companies and organizations" in the UK in 1991, 1.4 percent were filled by Afro-Caribbean women. Moreover, only 1.3 percent of women in "other managers and administrators" category were Afro-Caribbean, as were 0.7 percent of women who were "specialist managers" and "managers in transport and storing," and 0.6 percent of women who were "financial institutions and office managers, and civil service executive officers" (African and Caribbean Finance Forum et al., 1996).

There is limited information relating to the numbers of ethnic minority female entrepreneurs. British researchers Bhavnani and Coyle (2000) maintain that as "managers," they are more likely to be self-employed owner-managers of very small units, where employment is badly remunerated compared to being a "manager" in a large public or private sector organization (Bruegel, 1994). In the UK, between 1979 and 1984 ethnic minority female small business owners constituted 5.7 percent of all female business owners. Furthermore, between 1987 and 1989 more than 34,000 ethnic minority women in the UK were self-employed, of which 12,000 had employees (Bakshi, 1992; Bhavnani, 1994). This compares with 5.2 percent of all male small business owners being made up of ethnic minority males. As well, some minority communities such as South Asians, Cypriots, and Chinese, have secured significant presence in certain local economies and sectors. Asians, for example, are reputed to control over half of Britain's retail trade (Aziz, 1995).

## ■ Role conflict–living in a bicultural world ■

Research literature has highlighted particular problems linked with the roles black and ethnic minority women managers play in their work and non-work environments. This includes the role conflicts related to the complexities involved in living in a bicultural world, and the role of the token black and ethnic minority women.

In her study of 71 career-orientated African-American women, Bell (1990) revealed that these women perceived themselves as living in two specific cultural contexts, one black and the other white. In order to cope with these bicultural dimensions, the women tended to compartmentalize the different components of their lives. This kind of split personality role stress was also often highlighted by Davidson (1997) in her study of 30 British black and ethnic minority female managers. Both these studies concluded that these women professionals experienced role stress due to the persistent "push and pull" between the varying cultural contexts in their lives. The expectations, values, and norms of the predominantly white male dominated organizations in which they work are very dissimilar to other black and ethnic minority experiences/cultures. Bravette's (1994) participating action research with British black and ethnic minority women managers also emphasized the conflict involved in the pressure to deny one's cultural heritage and the particular vulnerability of British-born black female managers.

Interestingly, Davidson (1997) found that bicultural role stress appeared to be a particularly pronounced problem for a number of Indian women managers, where the assigned status in the work environment was significantly higher than their home and community status. This could be due to ethnic issues related to caste, position in the family hierarchy, marital status, the role of women generally, and whether they had "provided" sons.

Reid (1984) posed the important question as to why there appeared to be the constant need for black women to reaffirm their commitment to equal rights for all people. Certainly, this can result in role conflict regarding service to their ethnic community versus career commitment. Simpson (1984), for example, revealed that African-American female lawyers often spoke about feeling a sense of guilt and having "sold out" when they left the public service for the corporate world. Similarly, in their study of predominantly black African-American male managers, Dickens and Dickens (1991) reported this sense of having deserted the black community and "sold out" to the whites. This was found to be particularly the case with successful black managers who were very much in the minority at that seniority of management and/or those who were the first black to be promoted to that particular position.

## ■ The role of the token black and ethnic minority woman manager ■

More than two decades ago, Kanter (1977) argued that when women comprise less than 15 percent of a total category in an organization, they can be labeled "tokens", as they would be viewed as symbols of their group rather than as individuals. Black and ethnic minority women managers are not only more likely to constitute an even lower percentage of managers compared to their white female counterparts, but face the double burden of being seen as symbols of both their race and their gender. These women are much more likely to experience intensified negative effects associated with their tokenism and to have to cope with the double negatives associated with both racism and sexism. In the author's study of 30 black and ethnic minority women managers in the UK, the majority viewed their colour as being a greater barrier/problem than their gender. In addition, many of the major problems were linked to their role of the token black woman, and related to performance pressure, racial stereotyping, isolation and lack of same-colour role models, visibility, tokenism, and ghettoization; and to being a test case for future black women (Davidson, 1997).

Certainly, these findings have been replicated in other studies. Williams (1989), in her study of African-American female college administrators for example, highlighted performance pressure. The majority of the sample felt that a black female administrator had to work twice as hard as her male counterparts. Moreover, American studies on black and ethnic minority female managers suggest that this sort of pressure is even more intensive, that these women have to be bright and more talented than either their white or black male counterparts, and that they do not get the same promotional opportunities as white women managers (Essed, 1991).

In relation to racial stereotyping, Gilkes (1990) investigated childhood, educational, occupational, and cultural experiences of 25 UK black and ethnic minority women community workers in a northern city by in-depth interviews. She concluded that all her interviewees spoke of a feeling of victimization originating from isolation, inequality, and the status degradation fostered by negative images and stereotypes.

Stereotyping is the process of categorizing an individual into a particular group, and attributing a set of characteristics to the individual on the basis of the group membership. Sex role stereotypes related to management seem to evolve from the common views of males as more independent, task oriented, objective, and generally better able than females to handle managerial responsibilities. Davidson and Cooper (1992) reported that the majority of white female managers at all levels of the hierarchy are often pressurized into adopting certain sex stereotyped roles at work. These include the "mother earth role," becoming "one of the boys," the "pet," the "sex-object", and so on.

Schein's research has consistently reaffirmed that male managers continue to hold the same stereotypical views of the managerial job requirements, that is, "to think manager–think male" (Schein and Davidson, 1993; Schein, 1994). However, analysis of the author's interviews with 30 black and ethnic minority UK female managers consistently revealed that this stereotypical phrase should change to "think manager – think *white* male" (Davidson, 1997). Interestingly, the majority of the sample, when questioned about both gender and racial role stereotyping alignment at work, commonly complained of role imposition based primarily on the stereotypical image of females of their *specific ethnic origin*. For example, Afro-Caribbean and African women managers often complained of the role expectation linked to the stereotypical image of the "aggressive, black female mama." Conversely, many of the Asian women interviewees commonly complained of being treated paternalistically and patronizingly, and being expected to conform to the stereotypical "female, timid Asian flower" role alignment.

When reviewing the comparative American research literature, Cleveland, Stockdale, and Murphy (2000) conclude that while class and race do affect gender stereotypes, gender stereotypes emerge beyond these variables. According to these authors:

> There is some evidence that the feminine stereotype in the United States largely reflects views of white, middle-class females. Although Black and white middle- and working-class women are rated similarly on the female stereotype, stereotypical descriptions differ significantly by race and social class. Black and white women are described similarly on traits including ambitious, competent, intelligent, self-confident, and hostile, but white women are described more similarly to the traditional feminine stereotype (e.g., higher on characteristics such as dependent, emotional, and passive). (p. 51)

Compared with white women, black and ethnic minority women managers in token positions are even less likely to have role models they can emulate and turn to for support and guidance (Bell and Nkomo, 2000; Davidson, 1997; Essed, 1991). As a consequence, they are more likely to complain of feeling isolated and missing support from black peers. Essed (1991) viewed lack of black and ethnic minority role models and isolation from other ethnic women, as major structural problems related to securing and keeping jobs for these women in higher education. In her study of black and ethnic minority women community workers in the UK, Gilkes (1990) found that many of these women discussed their feelings of isolation which tended to encourage them to develop an interdependent approach to their problems. This isolation, however, has also been linked to being omitted from important support networks which could help enhance one's professional skills. Furthermore, a number of Davidson's (1997) female ethnic minority managers in the UK also highlighted feelings to isolation at work due to cultural differences related to dress, communication, interests, and verbal, and non-verbal behaviour. Certainly, for Asian women managers in particular, their Muslim religion, which prohibits alcohol, was often viewed as a factor facilitating isolation from white colleagues where socializing over drinks was an important career development and network strategy.

American research literature indicates that black and ethnic minority female professionals and managers often tend to quote important role models as being someone not associated with their work environment. Williams's (1989) sample of African-American female college administrators all identified black role models from their youth with whom they had formed a strong identification. These included teachers, a parent, a relative, and in some cases black sororities such as Alpha Kappa Alpha and Delta Sigma Theta. In Davidson's (1997) study, like their American counterparts, many of the women quoted important role models from outside their work environment, and the mother-provider figure as role model was particularly common for the Afro-Caribbean women managers.

Linked to lack of black role models are also the difficulties related to finding suitable sponsors/mentors. Dickens and Dickens (1991) assert that seeking sponsors/mentors is an important progression for black and ethnic minority managers, particularly in the planned growth phase of career development, but is often fraught with difficulties. Bell (1990) supports this argument and suggests that African-American managers, particularly female managers, are more likely than their white counterparts to encounter difficulties finding mentors to provide guidance for moving up the organizational hierarchy.

Certainly, there is some evidence in the literature (for example, Herbert, 1989; Thomas, 1989), that black and ethnic minority managers are less likely than white managers to report having even had a mentor. When Davidson's (1997) sample of British black and ethnic minority women managers were asked whether they had ever had a mentor, only 43 percent reported experiencing a mentoring relationship. This is in sharp contrast with previous studies of British white female managers in which between 87 percent (White, Cox, and Cooper, 1992) and 94 percent (Clutterbuck and Devine, 1987) reported having had at least one mentor. Thomas (1989) viewed sex and race taboos, combined also with the black Americans' history of slavery, as critically shaping the dynamics of cross-race relationships. For Thomas (1989), racial differences, and sex and race taboos, can significantly hamper feelings of closeness and identification between blacks and whites. He also suggests that identification with the protégé by the mentor reduces the uncertainty and risk in terms of the protégé's performance. He found that 63 percent of black American managers he studied formed their mentoring relationships with whites but same-race relationships provided significantly more psychosocial support than cross-race relationships. This is of particular relevance for black and ethnic minority women managers, taking into account previous studies on white managers, which suggests the importance of psychosocial support for female white protégés (Arnold and Davidson, 1990; White, Cox, and Cooper, 1992).

Token women are also subject to three "peripheral tendencies" associated with unsuitability, contrast, and assimilation (Kanter, 1977). Indeed, being female in management and being from an ethnic minority exposes these female executives to extremes of high visibility (Iles and Auluck, 1991). Almost all the women managers interviewed by Davidson (1997) viewed themselves as highly visible in their organization, much more so than their white female counterparts. For some, this brought disadvantages such as loss of privacy, mistakes being highlighted, and getting attention for their "discrepant" sex and ethnic characteristics rather than for their skills. This often resulted in their having to put extra effort into getting taken seriously. A number of women also complained that while they often wanted to discuss racial issues (including in reference to themselves), white colleagues and superiors usually evaded the issue and preferred "not to discuss such things as they obviously felt highly uncomfortable – a taboo topic" (Davidson, 1997).

Nevertheless, high visibility need not always be a negative factor. All of the 31 African-American female lawyers interviewed by Epstein (1973) felt that their colour and being female enhanced their career aspirations and gave them opportunities they may well not have had, had they been "only women" or "only black." Being black and female gave these attorneys a unique status combination making them extremely visible and ensuring that news of "good performances" spread speedily throughout the law fraternity.

Numerous research studies on white women managers have isolated a particular burden associated with being token women: the pressures related to being a test case for the employment of future women in the company at management level (Harnett and Novarra, 1979; Davidson and Cooper, 1992). Bell (1990) points out that compared to white women managers, black women are much more likely to be the first of their race and gender to have held a middle or upper-level management position in the organization.

It should also be noted that Iles and Auluck (1991) mentioned that black and ethnic minority professionals in Britain are often steered away from the main career tracks and sidelined into routine "token," "showcase", or "black" jobs in areas such as personnel, welfare, dealing with black staff, customers or clients, or in equal opportunity units. Bhavnani (1994) has also highlighted that horizontal and vertical segregation are both racialized and gendered. Black doctors, for example, tend to be concentrated in the more unpopular specialities, and to have had inferior training opportunities. Both American and Dutch research has found that black and ethnic minority women in the higher-skilled jobs are often steered into "ethnic" work (Essed, 1991). Bhavnani and Coyle (2000) suggest that in the social services, there is more and more evidence that black British women are working with predominantly black clients and mainly in "specialist" areas, that is, they are being racially ghettoized. These authors also assert that despite the lack of national data on black women's pay in Britain, the evidence suggests a pay differential between black and ethnic minority and white women.

Certainly, the limited studies assessing the pay of black and ethnic minority women managers and professionals highlight pay differentials between their white and black and ethnic minority male counterparts. Essed (1991) compared the job opportunities for highly educated American black women and those of black men, and concluded that black women are more likely to end up in the lower-paying jobs. More than half of the black and ethnic minority women managers interviewed by the author maintained they were being paid less than their white counterparts (Davidson, 1997). When each of the women managers was asked whether they thought they would be doing a different job with higher pay and status if they had been born a white woman, more than half believed they would. An even higher 80 percent believed they would have been in a more highly paid, higher-status position if they had been born a white man. While 57 percent of Davidson's (1997) interviewees maintained they faced blocked promotion and career progression at the entry phase of career progression, half of the women described incidents in the past in which they strongly believed that racial discrimination was the main reason for their not getting a particular job or promotion. These findings have also been substantiated by other British research, and according to Kirton and Greene (2000), high-level qualifications or work experience do not protect these women against the effects of employer discrimination.

> For example, a National Service report (EOR, 1996) found that black nurses were less likely than white staff with similar personal profiles to be in the higher grades. A Commission for Racial Equality (CRE) report on the graduate labour market found that minority ethnic groups made more job applications, but received fewer job offers (Brennan and McGeevor, 1990). The same study also found evidence suggesting that fewer Black Caribbean graduates were in jobs that had long-term career prospects. (p. 23)

## ■ Occupational stress and the black and ethnic minority woman manager ■

Despite the fact that the proportion of minority group members in the total workforce in the UK and the USA is increasing, and projected to continue to do so, little research has examined work stress among minority employees (James, 1994; James, Lovato, and Khoo, 1994). Indeed, Cleveland, Stockdale, and Murphy (2000) maintain it is even more important than ever to ascertain whether organizational and individual antecedents of stress vary for minority and non-minority employees.

While numerous cross-cultural studies conclude that white managerial women experience unique sources of stress related to their minority status and gender compared to their white male counterparts (for example, Devanna, 1987; Davidson and Cooper, 1983, 1987, 1992; Fielden and Davidson, 2000), research also confirms that black and ethnic minority managers (particularly women) are doubly disadvantaged in terms of upward mobility and high levels of work, and have additional pressures (Bell, 1990; Greenhaus et al., 1990; Davidson, 1997; Bell and Nkomo, 2000).

Research investigating the main sources of stress intrinsic to the job that seem to affect white women managers have isolated: work overload; feeling undervalued; "being the boss"; having to acquire male managerial skills; being assertive and confident; and attending or being unable to attend training (Fielden and Davidson, 2000). When Davidson's (1997) 30 black and ethnic minority British women managers were asked to reveal what they viewed as work stressors for them, similar sources were isolated. The most commonly cited stressor was performance pressures followed by work overload/deadlines/time pressures, feeling undervalued/under-utilized, feelings of powerlessness, needing to be qualified, and delegation. However, what made these stressors different from those of their white female counterparts is that the sources of these stressors were often linked to the double bind, that is, sexism *and* racism. When the sample were asked to state which particular stressors they found *most* stressful, many were again linked to racial and gender factors. Work overload and performance pressure were isolated as leading major stressors, followed by home–work conflicts, job insecurity, and coping with racism without much support (Davidson, 1997). Cleveland, Stockdale, and Murphy (2000) also present empirical evidence that perceived discrimination and prejudice in the work environment contribute to minority group members' stress (for example, Guitieres, Sqenz, and Green, 1992). These authors also emphasize the performance pressures and bicultural stressors experienced by black managers by quoting other researchers as illustrated by the following two quotations:

> When employed, especially at higher levels in an organisation, African-Americans may experience heightened career stress resulting from attempts to demonstrate their competence by excessively working. Mutual feelings of distrust between Black managers, peers, and superiors, and participation in organisational policies that are not in the best interests of blacks also contribute to stress. (Latack, 1989)

> The literature on African-Americans suggests that minority experiences at work may be largely bicultural, in the sense that the dominant culture in the workplace is likely to reflect the experiences, preferences, and biases of white employees. Stress is experienced when one moves back and forth between one's own culture and the dominant culture. (Bell, 1986). (Cleveland, Stockdale, and Murphy, 2000, p. 350)

American researchers such as Frone et al. (1990) and James et al. (1994) have found that perceived prejudice and discrimination in Euro-American organizations were unique sources of stress for ethnic minority workers above and beyond other work stressors. James (1994) and James et al. (1994) very much emphasize the importance of social identity and minority workers' health, and view social identities as an important source of stress and having an impact on stress coping ability. These authors have pinpointed six variables involved in social identity processes in organizations which have been previously correlated with minority workers' health. These include individual expressiveness, levels of perceived prejudice and discrimination experienced on the job, perceived differences in values between minority and majority organization members addressed separately for supervisors and for peers, and levels of self- and collective, ethnic-group based esteem (James et al., 1994). Certainly, good self-esteem is linked with a strong believe in self and good self-confidence. The author found that 60 percent of her British female black and ethnic minority women managers were satisfied with their feelings of confidence, and over three-quarters with their independence (Davidson, 1997). This staff sufficiency-independence seems to substantiate previous American research. Epstein (1973), for example, found black and ethnic minority women professionals had acquired a sense of confidence in their competence and abilities and proposed that this was probably reinforced as they overcame each obstacle on the way to the top. Simpson (1984), on the other hand, refers to Watson's (1974) thesis of ego formation of black and ethnic minority women, drawn upon theories based on the process of symbolic interaction. This assumes that the self-concept (how one feels about oneself) is a flexible, structural process which is not static, and, rather than being a passive recipient, the woman can be active in shaping her self-image. Interestingly, for the 40 percent of Davidson's (1997) interviewees who felt they lacked confidence, this was blamed either on lack of qualifications, lack of assertiveness, their individual personality, and/or their colour, that is, "self-defence" rather than "self" creation.

Certainly, the aforementioned stressors linked to perceived discrimination and prejudice have contributed to minority group members' negative stress outcomes. Cleveland, Stockdale, and Murphy (2000), for example, quote American research which has associated racial discrimination at work with increased blood pressure (James, et al., 1984), and physiological symptoms, work distress and depression among African-American workers (Erlich and Larcum, 1992; Frone, et al., 1990). The vast majority, that is, 83 percent of Davidson's (1997) British black and ethnic minority women managers reported negative stress manifestations: psychological, physical and behavioural. The most commonly reported symptoms were depression/stress/anxiety; job dissatisfaction; exhaustion; sleeping problems; and physical ill-health. When probed as to whether these stress reactions were instigated by negative factors linked to race, gender, and/or other, stressors linked to racial issues were the most prominent (Davidson, 1997).

One of the few comparative studies investigating occupational stress, social support, and depression among black and ethnic minority and white American professional-managerial women was carried out by Snapp (1992). She found that for both black and white women, of the occupational stressors, only "trouble with boss or subordinates" was significantly related to levels of depression. Moreover, race was a significant predictor of both levels of social support and occupational stress. The black and ethnic minority women reported lower levels of co-worker support, workload, and trouble with subordinates or boss than the white women. Compared to middle-class black women, white women and black women from working-class backgrounds reported lower levels of family support (Snapp, 1992). James et al. (1994) also found that relations with supervisors affect minority workers' circumstances, including their health, more than relations with non-minority peers.

## Conclusion

From the research studies reviewed in this chapter, what is clear is that black and ethnic minority managers tend to be underrepresented in the majority of American and British organizations, particularly at middle and higher managerial levels of the organizational hierarchy, and for them, the glass ceiling is even harder to shatter. In her study of the development of black nurses in the British National Health Service, Mayor (1996) suggests that black men and women experience a series of "cold spots," or smoked-glass ceilings in their career progress. She concludes that the threshold of the glass ceiling for black professionals is set lower than the level experienced by white women managers. In another British report addressing the position of Afro-Caribbean people in management, the glass ceiling concept is transformed into "the cement roof" (African and Caribbean Finance Forum et al., 1996).

In a recent review by Bhavnani and Coyle (2000), they conclude that in the UK, while more black and ethnic minority women have entered management positions, they have not experienced social mobility and there has been a re-segregation of the labour market in terms of both race and gender. Furthermore, their research indicates that unless positive action training for black and ethnic minority women is part of a wider strategy of organizational development and change, it can actually reinforce racialized notions of differences. According to Bhavnani and Coyle (2000), Research in the future may need to examine in depth how far we are witnessing the re-racializing and re-gendering of labour markets. The role of organizations in promoting equality needs to be re-examined as equal opportunities policies increasingly look ineffective and out of date (p. 233).

Clearly, one must recognize that the multiplicity of experience and discrimination encountered by black and ethnic minority women managers is complex and varied, and dependent on gender, culture, class, and specific ethnic origin. This view was recently reinforced by Ferdman (1999) in his statement in which he concludes:

A focus on ethnicity and race highlights the cultural, ethnic, and racial specificity of gendered interactions. Theorists and researchers interested in gender must be more precise about the ethnic, racial and cultural context for their work and the identities of their participants. I believe that the time has come for the study of gender in organizations to fully incorporate and attend to race, ethnicity, and culture. (p. 34)

## REFERENCES

African and Caribbean Finance Forum, Foundation for Management Education and The Wainwright Trust (1996): *The Cement Roof: Afro-Caribbean People in Management*. London: Midland Bank.

Arnold, V. and Davidson, M. J. (1990): Adopt a Mentor – The New Way Ahead for Women Managers. *Women in Management Review and Abstracts*, 5(1), 10–18.

Aziz, S. (1995): The Global Entrepreneur. Paper presented to the Researching Asian Entrepreneurship Conference, 9 November.

Bakshi, P. (1992): *Small Business Intervention Strategies and Ethnic Minority/Migrant Women*. Birmingham: School of Continuing Studies, University of Birmingham.

Bell, E. L. (1986): The Power Within: Bicultural life structures and stress among black women, unpublished doctoral dissertation, Case Western Reserve University, Cleveland, OH, USA.

Bell, E. L. (1990): The Bicultural Life Experience of Career-Oriented Black Women. *Journal of Organizational Behaviour*, 11(6):, 459–78.

Bell E. L., Denton, T., and Nkomo, S. (1993): Women of Colour in Management: Toward an Inclusive Analysis. In E. Fagenson (ed.), *Women in Management: Trends, Issues and Challenges in Managerial Diversity, Vol. 4, Women and Work: A Research Policy Series*, Newbury Park, CA: Sage, 105–30.

Bell, E. L. and Nkomo, S. (2000): Refracted lives: Sources of disconnection between Black and White women. In M. J. Davidson and R. J. Burke (eds), *Women in Management: Current Research Issues Volume II*, London: Sage, 205–22.

Betters-Reed, B. and Moore, L. (1995): Shifting the Management Development Paradigm for Women. *Journal of Management Development*, 14(2), 24–38.

Bhavnani, R. (1994): *Black Women in The Labour Market – A Research Review*. Manchester: Equal Opportunities Commission.

Bhavnani, R. and Coyle (2000): Black and ethnic minority women managers in the UK – Continuity or change? In M. J. Davidson and R. J. Burke (eds), *Women in Management: Current Research Issues Volume II*, London: Sage, 223–35.

Bravette, G. (1994): *Black Women Managers and Participating Action Research*. Published Conference Paper in World Congress on American Learning, Action Research and Process Management, University of Bath.

Brennan, J. and McGeevor, P. (1990): *Ethnic Minorities and the Graduate Labour Market*. London: Commission for Racial Equality.

Bruegel, I. (1994): Labour market prospects for women from ethnic minorities. In Institute for Employment Research (ed.), *Labour Market Structures and Prospects for Women*, Institute for Employment Research/Equal Opportunities Commission, Warwick University.

Cleveland, J. N., Stockdale, M., and Murphy, K. R. (2000): *Women and Men in Organizations – Sex and Gender Issues at Work*, London: LEA.

Clutterbuck, D. and Devine, M. (eds), (1987): *Business Women – Present and Future*. London: Macmillan.

Cox, T. and Nkomo, S. M. (1990): Invisible Men and Women: A Status Report on Race as a Variable in Organization Behaviour Research. *Journal of Organizational Behaviour*, 11(6), 419–32.

CRE (1995): *Racial Equality Means Business – A Standard for Racial Equality for Employers*. London: CRE.

Davidson, M. J. (1997): *The Black and Ethnic Minority Woman Manager: Cracking the Concrete Ceiling*. London: Paul Chapman.

Davidson, M. J. and Burke, R. (eds), (2000): *Women in Management: Current Research Issues Vol. II*, London: Sage.

Davidson, M. J. and Cooper, C. L. (1983): *Stress and The Woman Manager*. Oxford: Martin Robertson.

Davidson, M. J. and Cooper, C. L. (1987): Female Managers in Britain – A Comparative Review. *Human Resource Management*, 26, 217–42.

Davidson, M. J. and Cooper, C. L. (1992): *Shattering The Glass Ceiling – The Woman Manager*. London: Paul Chapman.

Davidson, M. J. and Fielden, S. (1999): Stress and the working woman. In G. N. Powell (ed.), *Handbook of Gender and Work*, New York: Sage, 413–26.

Devanna, M. A. (1987): Women in Management: Progress and Promise. *Human Resource Management*, 26, 409–81.

Dickens, F. and Dickens, J. B. (1991): *The Black Manager – Making It In The Corporate World*. New York: American Management Association.

EOC (Equal Opportunities Commission) (1999): *The Fact About Women Is*. Manchester: EOC.

EOR (Equal Opportunities Review) (1996): Racial Harassment in NHS. *Equal Opportunities Review*, 65, January–August, 20–28.

Epstein, C. F. (1973): Positive Effects of the Multiple Negative: Explaining the Success of Black Professional Women. *American Journal of Sociology*, 78(4), 912–35.

Erlich, H. J. and Larcum, B. E. K. (1992): *The effects of prejudice and ethnoviolence on workers' health*. Paper presented at the 2nd American Psychological Association/National Institute of Occupational Safety and Health Conference on Work Stress and Health, November, Washington DC.

Essed, P. (1991): *Understanding Everyday Racism – An Interdisciplinary Theory*. London: Sage.

Ferdman, B. M. (1999): The color and culture of gender in organizations: Attending to race and ethnicity. In G. N. Powell (ed.), *Handbook of Gender & Work*, London: Sage, 17–34.

Fielden, S. and Davidson, M. J. (2000): Stress and the Woman Manager. In J. Dunham (ed.), *Stress in Occupations: Past, Present and Future*. London: Colin Whurr.

Frone, M. R., Russell, M., and Cooper, M. L. (1990): *Occupational Stressors, Psychological Resources and Psychological Distress: A Comparison of Black and White Workers*. Paper presented at the Annual Meeting of the Academy of Management, San Francisco.

Gilkes, C. T. (1990): Liberated to Work Like Dogs: Labelling Black Women and their work. In H. Y. Grossman and N. L. Chester (eds), *The Experience and Meaning of Work in Women's Lives*, London: Lawrence Erlbaum, 165–88.

Greenglass, E. R. (1995): An interactional perspective on job related stress in managerial women. *The Southern Psychologist*, 21, 42–8.

Greenhaus, J. H., Parasuraman, S., and Wormley, W. M. (1990): Effects of Race on Organizational Experiences, Job Performance Evaluations and Career Outcomes. *Academy of Management Journal*, 33(1), 64–86.

Guitieres, S. E., Sqenz, D., and Green, B. (1992): *Occupational stress and health among Anglo and ethnic minority university employees*. Paper presented at the 2nd American Psychological Association, National Institute of Occupational Safety and Health Conference on Work Stress and Health, November, Washington DC.

Harnett, O. and Novarra, V. (1979): Facilitating the Entry of Women into Management Posts. Paper presented at Association of Teachers of Management Conference, The Training and Development Needs of Women Managers, November: London.

Herbert, J. (1989): *Black Entrepreneurs and Adult Development*. New York: Praeger Press.

Hite, L. M. (1996): Black Women Managers and Administrators: Experiences and Implications. *Women in Management Review*, 11(6), 11–17.

Holdsworth, C. and Dale, A. (1996): *Modelling ethnic group differences in women's employment*. Paper presented at conference on The Research Value of the SARs, Manchester Business School, 13–14 March.

Iles, P. and Auluck, R. (1991): The Experience of Black Workers. In M. Davidson and J. Earnshaw (eds), *Vulnerable Workers – Psychological and Legal Issues*, London: Wiley, 297–322.

James, K. (1994): Social Identity, Work Stress, and Minority Workers' Health. In G. P. Keita and J. J. Hurrell (eds), *Job Stress in A Changing Workforce – Investigating Gender, Diversity and Family Issues*, Washington: American Psychological Association, 127–46.

James, K., Lovato, C., and Khoo, G. (1994): Social Identity Correlates of Minority Workers Health. *Academy of Management Journal*, 37(2), 383–91.

James, S. A., La Croix, A. Z., Kleinbaum, D. G., and Strogatz, D. S. (1984): John Henryism and blood pressure differences among Black men: II – The role of occupational stressors. *Journal of Behavioral Medicine*, 7, 259–75.

Kanter, R. (1977): *Men and Women of the Corporation*. New York: Basic Books.

Kirton, G. and Greene, A. (2000): *The Dynamics of Managing Diversity – A Critical Approach*. Oxford: Butterworth–Heinemann.

Labour Force Survey (1995): London: HMSO.

Latack, J. C. (1989): Work, stress and careers: A preventative approach to maintaining organizational health. In M. B. Arthur, D. T. Hall, and B. S. Lawrence (eds), *Handbook of Career Theory*, Cambridge: Cambridge University Press, 252–74.

Mayor, V. (1996): Investing in People: Personal and Professional Development of Black Nurses. *Health Visitor*, 69(1), January, 20–3.

Mirza, H. S. (1992): *Young, Female and Black*. London: Routledge.

Reid, T. P. (1984): Feminism Versus Minority Group Identity: Not For Black Women Only. *Sex Roles*, 10(3/4), 247–55.

Reskin, B. and Padovic, I. (1994): *Women and Men at Work*. Pine: Forge Press.

Schein, V. E. (1994): Managerial Sex Typing: A Persistent and Pervasive Barrier to Women's Opportunities. In M. J. Davidson and R. J. Burke (eds), *Women in Management – Current Research Issues*, London: Paul Chapman, 41–52.

Schein, V. E. and Davidson, M. J. (1993): Think Manager – Think Male. *Management Development Review*, 6(3), 24–8.

Simpson, G. (1984): The Daughters of Charlotte Ray: The Career Development Process During the Exploratory and Establishment Stages of Black Women Attorneys. *Sex Roles*, 11(1/2), 113–38.

Snapp, M. B. (1992): Occupational Stress, Social Support and Depression Among Black and White Professional–Managerial Women. *Women and Health*, 18(1), 41–79.

Thomas, D. A. (1989): Mentoring and Irrationality: The Role of Racial Taboos. *Human Resource Management*, 28(2), 279–90.

White, B., Cox, C., and Cooper, C. L. (1992): *Women's Career Development – A Study of High Flyers*. Oxford: Blackwell.

Williams, A. (1989): Research on Black Women College Administrators: Descriptive and Interview Data. *Sex Roles*, 21(1/2), 99–112.

# 5

# WORK AND FAMILY ISSUES: OLD AND NEW

*Suzan Lewis*

It has long been assumed that women's advancement in corporate management is hampered by their domestic roles and responsibilities, and that the development of corporate work–family[1] policies to enable both women and men to manage work and family roles could contribute to significant change in this respect. Research on work and family, however, indicates that the process of change is much more complex and uneven than this suggests. The growing awareness of work–family issues has undoubtedly contributed to some change in corporations (Fletcher and Rapoport, 1996) but these changes are often marginal rather than mainstream (Hochschild, 1997; Lewis, 1997) and there is little empirical evidence that they have any substantial positive impact on women's careers. Rather, policies such as part-time work, if not equally valued with standard forms of work (Raabe, 1996), can perpetuate women's economic disadvantage relative to men, often with lifelong consequences (Ward, Dale, and Joshi, 1996). Furthermore, developments in work–life practice, and in the social and economic context in which corporations operate, frequently generate new work–life issues and problems (Lewis and Cooper, 1999), so corporate policies and practices need to be constantly revisited. This chapter traces some developments in work–family research and considers some significant contemporary and emerging issues facing women and men in today's families and corporations.

## ■ Developments in work–family research and practice ■

Research on the work–family interface has reflected and developed alongside dramatic social and workplace changes (Lewis and Cooper, 1999). The early research was initially a response to the influx of women, including those with young children and other family obligations, into the labor force; a trend which escalated in the US and most European states in the 1960s (Hayghe, 1997; Henwood, Rimmer, and Wicks, 1987).

Research focused on the family, especially dual-career couples, which were regarded as a new social phenomenon, and examined the experience and equity of gender roles (for example, Rapoport and Rapoport, 1969, 1971). This research was important in high-lighting issues within the family with implications for women's career development, but most of the studies in this period constructed the issues emerging as "individual", and especially women's issues, rather than "organizational" problems. The focus was on role conflicts, identity dilemmas, attitudes to traditional role expectations, and ambivalence about emerging degendered roles, particularly among middle-class couples (for example, Epstein, 1971; Rapoport and Rapoport, 1971).

Women's dual roles and the growing recognition that many men could no longer expect the support of a full-time wife at home also led to a focus on the interdependence of work and family, or what Kanter (1977) described as the "myth of separate worlds". The "male model of work", which assumes continuous employment from the end of education to retirement, and separation of work and family roles was challenged (Pleck, 1977). Nevertheless, most research in this period focused on the impact of women's rising employment on well-being, often reflecting gendered assumptions. Research questions such as what is the impact of women's employment on children, on hus-bands, on marital satisfaction and on women's own well-being (for example, Hoffman, 1979; Staines et al., 1978; Welch and Booth, 1977) belied the underlying assumption that women were deviating from their expected roles, with possible negative conse-quences for all. This was reflected in the scarcity hypothesis (Sieber, 1974) which assumes that time and energy are finite and that multiple roles will inevitably have adverse effects on well-being, implicitly questioning women's abilities to sustain full career and family roles This was juxtaposed with the role expansion hypothesis, that time and energy expand to meet the demands of multiple roles (Marks, 1977). Never-theless, the role scarcity model informed many of the earlier studies. It was primarily women who were regarded as having multiple roles and this was considered to be a powerful contributor to the gender gap in corporate advancement.

The 1980s was a period of increased competitiveness and a time when "stress" and "burnout" became concepts in the everyday vocabulary of many working people (Cartwright and Cooper, 1997). Questions about stress and conflict among those with dual responsibilities in work and family domains became a particular area of research interest and concern. The impact of women's dual roles on themselves and their families continued to be examined, but it became increasingly clear that multiple roles offered potential multiple sources of satisfaction to women, and can have positive impacts on well-being (Crosby, 1987). The focus also began to shift somewhat to acknowledge that men as well as women engage in multiple roles (for example, Barling, 1986). This period saw a burgeoning of research on work–family conflict and stress among employed women, and in dual earner couples (for example, Greenhaus and Beutell, 1985; Lewis and Cooper, 1987, 1988), and on the nature of the links between experiences of stress and also satisfaction across work–family boundaries (for example, Crouter, 1984; Staines, 1980). Later this developed into increasingly sophisticated research examining the nature of work–family linkages. Research explored the antecedents and consequences of work–family conflict and stress, recognizing the mul-tiplicity of variables impacting on individual well-being (Greenhaus and Parasuraman, 1999). It became clear that extensive conflict can produce distress within both work and family domains, and that work interfering with family or family interfering with work are separate processes that need to be distinguished in research (for example, Frone et al., 1997). Gender differences in these effects continue to be investigated and evidence of different outcomes of different forms of work–family interference or conflict for women and men demonstrates that women still retain a greater psychological and behavioral involvement in family work (see Greenhaus and Parasuraman, 1999). Increasingly it has been recognized, too, that experiences in work and family not only spill over between domains, but also cross over to affect other family members (for example, Jones and Fletcher, 1992; Westman and Etzion, 1995), and again the effects are largely gendered (women are affected by their partners' stress more than men). Research questions of the 1970s and 1980s on the impact of maternal employment on children, initially based on assumptions about women's roles and young children's needs, have gradually been replaced by concern about the impact of parents' experiences of pressurized work on children and other family members.

Evidence that work–family stress and conflict can impact on employee well-being, but that stress is not an inevitable consequence of multiple roles, led many researchers in the 1980s to call for organizations to change in recognition of employees' complex lives (for example, Sekaran, 1986; Lewis and Cooper, 1987). The call for workplaces to change intensified in the late 1980s and early 1990s, often based on a cost-benefit or business case, focusing particularly on recruitment and retention issues (Metcalfe and Leighton, 1989; Galinsky and Johnson, 1998; Bevan et al., 1999). The desired changes have largely been conceptualized in terms of introducing family-friendly or work–life policies such as flexible working arrangements (for example, part time, reduced hours or job sharing, flexitime, and parental or other leaves) and dependent care support (including childcare and eldercare). A developing literature has documented the nature and extent of strategies adopted by companies to respond to work–family issues (for example, Kammerman and Kahn, 1987; Berry-Lound, 1990; Hogg and Harker, 1992; Forth et al., 1996), while other research evaluates the impact of family-friendly initiatives (Galinsky and Stein, 1990; Lewis, 1997), especially the impact on productivity and related organizational outcomes (see Kossek and Ozeki, 1999 for a review). Other research examines processes for bringing about changes in organizational cultures (for example, Milliken et al., 1990; Milliken et al., 1998; Fletcher and Rapoport, 1996).

Recent research indicates that work–family policies are increasingly prevalent, especially in larger corporations (Forth et al., 1996; Milliken et al., 1990), and there is evidence that if well implemented, these policies can help individual employees to reconcile work and family (Thomas and Ganster, 1995; Kossek and Oseki, 1999). For example, there is evidence that flexible schedules, together with supportive supervisors, can enhance employees' sense of control over work and family demands, which in turn reduces work–family conflict and stress (Thomas and Ganster, 1995). What is more contentious is the question of whether such policies actually alter organizational values and assumptions which both determine and reflect what is the socially constructed "ideal worker," and consequently affect the take-up of work–family initiatives, as well as the ways in which those who do make use of these provisions are perceived within the organization. There is often a gap between policy and practice, or policies are implemented half-heartedly (Burke, 1997; Lewis, 1997; Lewis et al., 1999), and workplace culture remains a potent barrier to take up, particularly by men (Haas and Hwang,

1995; Hochschild, 1997). A long-hours culture, for example, can result in those who are unwilling or unable to put in long hours (whether or not these are productive) being stigmatized as uncommitted, and often obscures the positive impact of flexible forms of work (Lewis, 1997; Lewis and Taylor, 1996). Many women and most men fear that to be seen to be accommodating work for family will be career limiting, while others, pre-dominantly women, take up so-called family-friendly provisions but accept that they will pay a price in career terms (Lewis, 1997; Lewis et al., 2000).

Thus work–family research has progressed from a focus on employed women and families to a growing recognition that women and men need to manage multiple roles, and from a focus on work–family issues as individual, and especially women's issues, to an examination of the ways in which corporations can change to take account of employees' work–family needs, and barriers to such change. Research has also begun to take account of changing social and economic contexts and values, and to look at the ways in which these are changing the work–family equations.

## ■ The current situation, and issues of fairness and entitlement ■

There have been dramatic shifts in families and workplaces in the last few decades. Traditional provider–homemaker families have now given way to dual-earner families as the norm for married and cohabiting couples. Yet the gender gap in promotions and earnings persists as family members struggle with ever more complex strategies for managing family and the growing complexity of employment. There is also a decline in marriage and fertility rates among younger generations, and a growth in single-person households (see, for example, Young, 1999; Lewis et al., 1998). The corporate world is also changing dramatically, with work becoming more intense, flexible, and unstable (Burchall et al., 1999). The proliferation of contracting out, temporary con-tracts, and other new forms of work, which increase flexibility from the employers' per-spective, transferring risk and uncertainty from employers to employees, has created a growing peripheral or contingent workforce to whom family-oriented policies often do not apply.

These changes have given rise to a number of new and emerging issues in relation to the work–family interface. Many of these can be conceptualized as issues of perceived justice or fairness. Within families, judgments about what are fair or equitable strate-gies for managing work and family are closely bound up with ideologies of gender and gender entitlements. Notions of what men and women feel entitled to expect also influ-ence behavior in organizations, especially expectations of support for work and family and perceived entitlement to take up any work–family supports available. Within work-places notions of organizational justice, that is perceived fairness of organizational procedures and rewards, also influence experiences of work and family, directly or indirectly.

Theories of social and organizational justice provide a useful framework for explor-ing new and emergent work–family issues. An important element of social justice theory is the concept of sense of entitlement, which is used to denote a set of beliefs and feelings about deservingness and about what individuals can legitimately expect in social exchanges, based on what is perceived to be fair and equitable (Major, 1993; Blysma and Major, 1994; Lewis, 1996). This influences family members' notions of what is a fair and equitable division of family roles and responsibilities (Lewis, 1996; Lewis and Lewis, 1997). Social justice theory suggests that sense of entitlement is determined by social comparison processes (Lerner, 1987), influenced by social context and ideology (Lewis, 1996), and constructed on the basis of social, normative, and feasibility comparisons (Major, 1987, 1993; Lewis and Lewis, 1997). Thus judgments about what is fair or equitable are made on the basis of normative comparisons with others who are assumed to be similar to oneself (Major, 1993; Bylsma and Major, 1994). For example, women's reporting of relative satisfaction with an unequal division of family labor has been explained by their tendency to compare themselves with other women rather than with their male partners (Major, 1993). These comparisons will determine what alternative strategies appear to be normative and feasible, and reinforce sense of entitlement. Sense of entitlement is gendered in the family and also in workplaces. For example, there is evidence that many women have a lower sense of entitlement than men in terms of equal rewards for work and may expect less pay or work longer hours or more efficiently than men for the same pay (Major 1987; Byslma and Major, 1994·).

Within corporations, organizational justice theory, which focuses on processes whereby people make judgments about what is fair in an organizational context, provides a further framework for examining work–family issues. Three forms of organizational justice are described in the literature: distributive, procedural, and interpersonal justice, relating to the, perceived fairness of outcomes, processes, and interpersonal treatment (Deutsch, 1985; Thibault and Walker, 1975; Greenberg, 1990; Young, 1999). These have different individual and organizational outcomes. For example, perceptions of distributive justice are related to satisfaction with outcomes (Folger and Konovsky, 1989) while perceived procedural justice or injustice predicts feeling about the organizations, such as commitment (Schappe, 1996). Organizational justice theory has identified three principles which may be used to reach judgments about what is fair: equity, equality, and need, which may be invoked by different individuals and in different contexts. The equality principle is the assumption that everybody should be treated the same regardless of performance or need ( for example, everyone should have equal access to flexible work). The equity principle relates outcomes to input such that people should be treated according to merit (for example, flexible working options should be available to those with a good performance record). The need principle argues that people should be treated according to needs (for example, parents have greater need for flexibility). Disagreements can occur when people use different justice principles to judge fairness (Young, 1999).

The remainder of this chapter considers some of the contemporary and emerging work and family issues and developments which are facing women and men in today"s families and corporations, in relation to notions of entitlement and justice.

# ■ Work–family strategies ■

There has been much debate about whether dual earner partners seek equality (equal sharing of the same roles and entitlements) or equity (fairness which can include different but equal roles) (for example, Rapoport and Rapoport, 1969). Recent studies examining processes influencing family decision making within households throw some light on these debates by highlighting the heterogeneity of families and the factors influencing decisions about partners' work–family strategies.

Barnett et al. (1999) operationalize work–family strategies as workers' plans for optimizing their own work and non-work needs as well as those of other member of their work–family social system. A number of typologies of work–family strategies have been described. For example, Hertz (1997) describes three approaches to child care which determine work–family household strategies: the mothering approach; the market approach; and the new parenting approach. The mothering approach is rooted in a central belief in the mother as the best person to raise and care for children. Motherhood is the pivotal status around which all the mothers' other possible statuses are organized (Hertz, 1997) so families organize to optimize time for mothering. Mothers do not want, expect, or feel entitled to equal sharing of the parental role, nor do fathers feel entitled to make much accommodation to their work for parenting. The market approach includes the acceptability of delegating considerable child care to paid help, and can enable both parents to prioritize employment. The new parenting approach is exemplified by the belief that family and work should be organized around children, with both parents highly involved, so work–family strategies include creating time for fathering as well as mothering. A variant on this typology is developed by Lewis et al. (2000, forthcoming) based on a study of British dual-earner families with disabled children. They identified four work–family strategies. Most families managed to sustain a one-and-a-half earner and some a full-time dual-earner strategy, both of which are common among parents in Britain. However, two new strategies specific to these families emerged: a modified single-earner strategy and a flexible dual-earner pattern. The modified single-earner pattern reflects the mothering approach as described by Hertz (1999). Mothers take on minimal paid work so that they are available for almost full time mothering, and fathers work full-time and inflexibly to meet their provider responsibilities. Alternatives based on a parenting approach are not even considered because of the taken-for-granted nature of mothers' responsibilities. The flexible dual-earner pattern reflects a parenting approach where both parents make adjustments to their work schedules so that shared parenting is possible.

Work–family decisions and strategies are influenced by a complex multiplicity of factors. Workplace flexibility is important, but decisions still have to be made about whether this will be taken up and by which partner(s) (Barnett and Lundgren, 1998). Without workplace flexibility, flexible work–family strategies are impossible (Hertz and Ferguson, 1998; Lewis et al., 2000), but this interacts with a number of other occupational, economic, and ideological determinants. In terms of occupational status, Hertz (1999) found that middle managers and professionals were able to use flexibility to co-parent while senior managers with more authority and responsibility for others were less likely to do so. Other research also suggests that professional women are better able to combine flexible work and sustain career development than those in managerial-type jobs (Crompton and Harris, 1998). Economic factors also impact on household work–family strategies but not always in a straightforward way. Reduced working-time schedules are often not perceived as an option for those on lower incomes, although some parents with very low incomes and strong ideological commitment to mothering nevertheless adopt strategies involving loss of mothers' income (Lewis et al., 2000). In these cases mothers may have a low sense of entitlement to sustain full-time or longer schedules because of strong ideologies of gender and caring, despite great economic and psychological need for employment above the minimum (Lewis et al., 2000).

Job loss or insecurity can act as a catalyst to co-parenting, with wives taking over as main breadwinner and increasing fathers' involvement in parenting, albeit initially for practical rather than ideological reasons (Hertz, 1999). However, in our study of parents of disabled children, we found that economic factors were perceived through a gender lens (Lewis et al., 2000). Among families with weaker attachment to traditional gender roles and a parenting approach to child care, men's job loss was constructed as an opportunity to adopt a non-gendered flexible work–family strategy, while among those with traditional gender roles and a mothering approach to child care, it became a reason for prioritizing men's new jobs at all costs, so that women were underemployed and men worked long hours. While men's job loss or underemployment was a factor influencing some of the dual-earner families adopting a new parenting approach in Hertz's study, shifting gender ideology influenced another subset of families adopting this approach. This group emphasize, "men have historically been short-changed as nurturers. Husbands talked about achieving parity with their wives." (Hertz, 1999, p. 20). Thus men in this subgroup compare themselves with women rather than other men, and feel entitled to expect to adopt strategies which give then time for nurturing. For change in roles and expectations to take place it is important to articulate gender beliefs in order to challenge them, but this is not always easy to achieve, even among egalitarian families (Zvonkovic et al., 1997).

The consequences of work–family strategies adopted are wide ranging. They can reproduce or challenge inequalities, maximize or minimize earning potential and career development, act as a force for workplace change or perpetuate the status quo (Lewis et al., 2000; Hertz, 1999; Zvonkovik et al., 1997). They can raise expectations and sense of entitlement to flexible, non-gendered solutions, but if these expectations are thwarted, because of family or workplace barriers, the subsequent lack of fit between desired and actual strategies can have negative effects on well-being. For example, Barnett et al. (1999), in a study of physicians working voluntarily reduced hours, found those who worked more or less than they would have preferred were more disengaged and distracted than those working their preferred schedules.

New forms of work can provide new opportunities and challenges for work–family strategies. For example, the growth of trends such as home-based teleworking, hot desking and distributed work (Wikstrom et al., 1998), that is, working part of the week at a central workplace and other days at home or in another non-central location, contribute to a blurring of physical and psychological boundaries between work and family (Sullivan and Lewis, forthcoming). Where home-based work is voluntarily chosen it may be for a number of reasons, not all of which are related to work–family strategies. However, a desire to ease child care or elder care by reducing distance and commuting, and by increasing flexibility and autonomy over schedules, is one often-reported reason (Standen et al., 1999; Sullivan and Lewis, forthcoming). Unlike more traditional home-working, computer-mediated teleworking is undertaken by both men and women, and thus may have the potential to support work–family strategies based on a non-gendered

approach to caring. In fact, there are two schools of thought about the impact of telework on gendered family roles. One model proposes that these changes will lead to a
reallocation of unpaid work and will equalize gender roles in the home by providing
greater flexibility and liberating men as well as women to spend more time with family
(Dooley, 1996; Hill et al., 1996), suggesting a greater sense of entitlement to non-
gendered roles. A second model proposes that home-based working will perpetuate
gender inequalities both in the workforce and at home (Hadden and Silverstone, 1993)
because employers will provide poorer conditions for home-based workers, women will
use flexibility to integrate paid and unpaid work, and men will maintain boundaries
between the two domains. The evidence for these two views is mixed. Certainly home-
based work, performed by men and women, can be associated with a more egalitarian
division of domestic labor and even role reversal in some cases, but this is by no means
inevitable (Huws et al., 1996). It may enable men to spend more time with their families but can also threaten gender identity and cause them to cling to traditional behaviors (Huws et al., 1996). Outcomes appear to depend primarily on previous division of
labour and sexual politics within families (Huws et al., 1996; Hadden and Silverstone,
1993; Hill et al., 1996; Sullivan and Lewis, forthcoming), and may also differ according to type of work, level of autonomy, skills and rate of pay, rather than the effects of
home-based working *per se*. If teleworking is chosen by families with a mothering
approach to child care, it enables women to care, but if the father is the teleworker it
has little impact on the division of labor (Sullivan and Lewis, forthcoming). Only in
those families with non-traditional gender orientations is home-based work for men a
strategy to enable both parents to work and care. In the more traditional families men
feel entitled to shut themselves away, and often work harder or longer than they would
at a central workplace. Few women feel entitled to impose such discrete boundaries
between work and family. Relatedly, conflict can also arise over gendered entitlements
to and use of space within the home, which may serve to further disadvantage women
(Sullivan, 2000).

Thus sense of entitlement to support for managing work and family, as expressed via
work–family strategies adopted by family units, is closely tied up with ideologies of
gender. Even the advantages or challenges of new forms of working appear to depend
on beliefs about gender and entitlement.

## ■ Changes in organizations ■

Workplaces in the twenty-first century are very different from those in earlier decades
when work–family research was first developing. Downsizing, delayering, restructuring, and a growth in what was once considered "atypical" forms of work such as
subcontracting, outworking, part-time, casual, and non-permanent work in most
advanced industrialized societies (ILO, 1995) have all contributed to widespread perceived job insecurity and to an intensification of work (Burchall et al., 1999; Lewis and
Cooper, 1999 ). Fewer people are expected to do more work in jobs that are no longer
lifelong. Many workers are spending long hours in the workplace (Bureau of Labor
Statistics, 1999; Employment in Europe, 1999) in response to job insecurity, workplace
demands, perceived career needs, financial pressures, and, as Hochschild (1997) has

suggested, often to escape from the tensions at home created by these long working hours. In organizations with a long-hours culture, workers feel they need to put in substantial "face time" to demonstrate their commitment (Bailyn, 1993; Lewis, 1997), while many in low-wage occupations do more than one job. So time for family is squeezed and many workers do not feel entitled to take the time they need to be with family members (Daly, 1997). The drive for so-called family-friendly practices continues among all these changes, supported by state policies and legislation in some contexts (Fagnani, 1998; Lewis and Lewis, 1997) and by corporate policies, mostly in large organizations. But in practice many of these provisions can only be enjoyed by the dwindling numbers of employees in relatively secure jobs. In reality, it is largely the employee who must take responsibility for managing multiple demands.

## ■ Experiences of younger-generation workers ■

The contemporary context raises a number of issues for young workers entering the labor market in this post job-security era. A study of 18 to 30 year olds in five European countries (Lewis et al., 1998) suggests that many are reluctant to put in the long hours and effort that they see older workers expending. Rather, they talk about wanting to achieve a balance between work and other areas of their lives. Most participants in the study were not yet parents. In fact, when asked to think ahead to possible future work and family scenarios they found this very difficult to envisage. A common theme across all the countries was that it is difficult to plan for future family without some degree of security and certainty in their lives, qualities which they feel are currently lacking. These young adults are caught within an "extended present" (Lewis, et al., 1999; Nilsen, 1998). They accept and even enjoy lack of certainty in the present but feel unable to move forward to plan for a future that involves relationships and children.

Participants in the study were also asked about what support they might expect from employers to enable them to reconcile future work and family life. In all five countries there was a limited sense of entitlement to workplace support. Expectations that employers should be flexible were highest in Sweden and Norway where there is considerable statutory support for reconciling work and family, such as paid and flexible parental leave, although this was undermined in Sweden by the growth of precarious work. In Britain, sense of entitlement to employer support was not automatic but appeared to depend on being able to articulate a business case: those who believed that it was in employers' interests to, for example, introduce child care or flexible working felt entitled to expect such support, while those who constructed these provisions as benefits and as costs to employers did not consider it feasible to expect such support.

## ■ Backlash ■

Experiences of work and family depend partly on personnel policies and the ways in which they are implemented. Management attitudes and support are important factors determining sense of control which is crucial for work–life balance (Thomas and

Ganster, 1995). When provisions are subject to management discretion and therefore constructed as rewards which have to be earned, rather than being viewed as entitlements, they do not enhance sense of entitlement or control. The attitudes of co-workers are also crucial in this process, and there is evidence that this may be increasingly problematic.

Employees with family responsibilities often report that colleagues are supportive if they need to accommodate work for family needs. For example, there is some evidence from Danish research that colleague support may be available but gendered; female-dominated workplaces are more supportive of the use of informal flexibility to support colleagues' family needs, while male-dominated workplaces were more likely to be supportive of accommodations made to work because of a second job or other, more stereo-typically male, non-family reasons (Holt and Thaulow, 1996). In a study of parental leave in the UK, Grover, 1991 shows that colleagues who are more similar in terms of current needs, or who view themselves as possibly having similar needs in the future, are the most likely to be supportive of colleagues taking up leave. Thus colleague's attitudes appear to be determined by their ability to empathize with the person using informal or formal flexibility to fit in family demands. Conversely, in contexts where co-workers do not have similar non-work demands, and do not plan to have children or take on other responsibilities, it can create resentment if colleagues feel that parents are receiving special treatment.

The initial focus on the needs of employed women with young children in work–family research has been largely reflected in corporate responses. Initially at least, work–family policies were targeted, explicitly or implicitly, at parents, particularly mothers. Despite growing awareness of elder care and other issues, it was, and to a large extent still is, considered more legitimate for parents than other employees to take up work–family provisions (Young, 1999), although not necessarily to be able to combine this with career progression (Lewis, 1997). Moreover, there is evidence that parents are also the most likely to actually take up such benefits (Young, 1999). But new demographic trends, especially the falling fertility rate in most Western countries, the growth in single-person households, and aging of the populations, contribute to a workforce where, overall, parents of young children are a minority (Young, 1999; Lewis et al., 1998).

One consequence of the growth of work–family policies in large corporations, particularly if they are perceived to be targeted at and taken up by parents, along with diverse workforces in which parents are a minority, is the growth of what has been termed work–family backlash (Young, 1999). Described by Young (1999) as a controversy over the fundamental issues of what is "fair", this backlash has been described in a number of studies (Young, 1999; Lewis, 1991; *Management Today*, 2000), For example, in a recent survey of 1,855 British managers, more than half reported that childless workers felt resentful when colleagues left the workplace to spend time with children (*Management Today*, 2000). Qualitative research attests to similar reactions elsewhere (Young, 1999; Lewis et al., 1998). This is particularly the case if childless colleagues feel that they have to do extra work to cover for parents. Clearly this is a management issue, and flexible work should not impinge on others' workloads, but if it does, resentment and lower morale are likely consequences. Notably, this backlash has been witnessed between women as well as men (Lewis, 1991; Young, 1999). While female-dominated organizations may be more supportive of informal flexibility for families (Holt and Thaulow, 1996), many childless career women working in male-dominated organizations may be as hostile as men to what may be perceived as parental privileges (Lewis, 1991).

There is some debate about the extent of work–family backlash. For example, in a survey of 78 US companies, 75 percent said childless employees carried more of the work, but 74 percent believed that concerns about backlash were exaggerated (Parkinson, 1996). Responses may vary according to how questions are phrased. However, it clearly does exist to some extent, and can be understood in terms of organizational justice perceptions. Indeed, Young (1999) argues that organizational justice theory helps to understand deep assumptions underpinning both corporate work–family policies and employees' perceptions of their fairness. The first employer assumption, according to Young (1999), is that most employees are married or living with a partner and raising children, a view which is increasingly out of touch with current trends. There is growing evidence that child care is only one of many reasons for work/non-work conflict (for example, Campbell and Koblenz, 1997). For the younger generation particularly, but also other workers, the desire is simply to "have a life" (Lewis et al., 1999).

Judgments about whether work–family policies and practices are fair are likely to vary according to perceptions of outcomes (distributive justice) and perceived fairness of processes (procedural justice). Childless employees who feel they are expected to do more work are likely to perceive distributive injustice, and this may be compounded by perceived procedural injustice if they are not consulted on this. Perceived justice is also influenced by the justice principles invoked, that is, equity, equality, or need principles (Deutsch, 1985; Thibaut and Walker, 1975). If work–family policies are perceived to be targeted only at parents, the justice principle would be one of need, but colleagues are just as likely to use equality or equity principles in deciding what is fair. If they use equality principles there will be an expectation that everyone should have access to the same or equivalent benefits. Equity principles will draw on notions of fairness based on input and outcomes. This can be illustrated by a woman accountant who felt that women who take breaks for maternity leave should not receive rewards commensurate with those whose working lives have been unbroken: "I felt really annoyed that Janet was promoted at the same time as me. We both started together, but she had two lots of maternity leave. I feel there is no recognition of my commitment to the firm. I have never taken time off" (Lewis, 1991).

A problem is that these principles are not always clearly articulated and employees may not all invoke the same principle, leading to perceptions of unfairness. This can exacerbate work–family issues for those with family responsibilities, and has important implications for employer policies and the ways in which they are introduced.

## ■ Reduced hours, rewards and entitlements ■

Other possible issues of injustice in relation to work and family are not articulated because of low expectations and feelings of entitlement. Policies and practices of reduced working hours illustrate this issue. It has been argued that reduced hours strategies may meet organizational, professional, individual, and family needs (Lund-gren and Barnett, 2000). In Britain, some leading-edge employers have introduced reduced hours schemes whereby employees, including those in senior management, are permitted to work less than full time in order to fulfill dependent care or other obliga-tions. This is usually more than part time; for example, four days a week or one hour a day less than the standard. Pay is reduced accordingly but benefits and, in the best cases, promotion are unaffected (Lewis, 2001; Stamworth, 1999). Qualitative research, however, demonstrates that senior people working in this way tend to accom-plish the same amount of work as they did when working full time, as illustrated by the chief accountant quoted below.

> There's things like not talking, not going off and making several cups of coffee. I can go through a whole day without having a cup of coffee if I don't have the time to think about getting up. I tend to steam through meetings, I organise meetings carefully. There's an agenda, we go through it and I also tend to wind it up a bit faster so I think that's where the 7 hours has gone in the organisation aspect of it. (Lewis, 2001)

Thus the long-hours culture, or the valuing of face time rather than output, reduces sense of entitlement to receive full pay among those who complete work in a shorter time. Put another way, other colleagues are rewarded for working inefficiently. Many employees working reduced hours recognize this irony but do not feel entitled to chal-lenge it because of the pervasiveness of cultural assumptions about face time (Lewis, 2001). Although reduced hours schemes are taken up by both men and women it is women who are most likely to use this option (Ludgren and Barnett, 2000; Pupo and Duffy, 2000), and hence women will be most affected by this trend.

## Conclusions

As families and workplaces change over time new work–family issues arise, many of which reflect, in one way or another, issues of justice and fairness. Ideologies of gender and organizational values influence individual sense of entitlement to work–family support at home and at work. Some families are reconstructing gender but the processes involved are complex and many still struggle with old and new ideologies. Some organizations are responding to work–family needs by developing a range of policies and practices. However, issues of social and organizational justice will have to be addressed to avoid creating new problems for employees with family responsibilities and the corporations which employ them. Unless these issues are addressed, parents, and disproportionately mothers, will con-tinue to be disadvantaged in corporations.

### Note

1   The literature also refers to these as work–life policies, with the intention of highlighting the range of non-work scenarios covered, and as family friendly policies, although this term has been contested because the complexity of families is not always acknowledged and because it implies favors rather than entitlements (Lewis and Cooper, 1995).

## REFERENCES

Bailyn, L. (1993): *Breaking the Mold. Women, Men and Time in the New Corporate World.* New York: Free Press.

Barling, J. (1986): Interrole conflict and marital functioning amongst employed fathers. *Journal of Occupational Behaviour*, 12, 39–53.

Barnett, R., Gareis, K., and Brennan, R. (1999): Fit as a mediator of the relationship between work hours and burnout. *Journal of Occupational Health Psychology*, 4(4), 307–17.

Berry-Lound, D. (1990): *Work and the Family. Carer the Friendly Employment Practices.* London. Institute of Personnel Management.

Barnett, R. and Lundgren, L. (1998): Dual-earner couples and the decision to work less. *Community, Work and Family*, 1(3), 273–95.

Bevan, S., Dench, S., Tamkin, P., and Cummings, A. (1999): *Family-friendly Employment: The Business Case.* London: Department for Education and Employment.

Byslma, W. H. and Major, B. (1994): Social comparisons and contentment: Exploring the psychological costs of the gender wage gap. *Psychology of Women Quarterly*, 18, 241–9.

Burchall, B., Day, D., Hudson, M., Lapido, D., Nolan, J., Reed, H., Wichert, I., and Wilkinson, E. (1999): *Job Insecurity and Work Intensification. Flexibility and the Changing Boundaries of Work.* York: Joseph Rowntree Foundation.

Bureau of Labor Statistics (1999): *Household Data.* April 2nd.

Burke, R. (1997): Culture's consequences: organisational values, family friendliness and a level playing field. *Women in Management Review*, 12(6), 222–7.

Campbell, A. and Koblenz, M. (1997): *The Work and Life Pyramid of Needs.* Deerfield, IL: Baxter Health Care.

Cartwright, S. and Cooper, C. L. (1997): *Managing Mergers, Acquisitions and Strategic Alliances.* Oxford: Butterworth Heinmann.

Crompton, R. and Harris, F. (1998): Explaining women's employment patterns: "Orientations to work" revisited *British Journal of Sociology*, 49(1), 118–36.

Crosby, F. J. (ed.) (1987): *Spouse, Parent, Worker: Gender and Multiple Roles.* New Haven, CT: Yale University Press.

Crouter, A. C. (1984): Spillover from family to work: The neglected side of the work–family interface. *Human Relations*, 37, 425–42.

Daly, K. J. (1997): *Families and Time.* Thousand Oaks: Sage.

Deutsch, M. (1985): Equity, equality and need: what determines which values will be used as the basis for distributive justice? *Journal of Social Issues*, 31(3), 137–49.

Dooley, B. (1996): At work away from home. *The Psychologist*, 9(4), 155–8.

Employment in Europe (1999): Brussels: European Commission.

Epstein, C. (1971): Law partners and marital partners. *Human Relations*, 24, 549–64.

Fagnani, J. (1998): Helping mothers to combine paid and unpaid work – or fighting unemployment. *Community, Work and Family*, 1, 3.

Fletcher, J. and Rapoport, R. (1996): Work–Family Issues as a Catalyst for Organizational Change. In S. Lewis and J. Lewis (eds). *The Work–Family Challenge*, London: Sage.

Folger, R. and Konovsky, M. (1989): Effects of procedural and distributive justice on reactions to pay increase decisions. *Academy of Management Journal*, 32(1), 115–30.

Forth, J., Lissenburgh, S., Callender C., and Millward N. (1997): *Family friendly working arrangements in Britain 1996.* Research Report No. 16. Policy Studies Institute, Department for Education and Employment.

Frone, M., Yardley, J., and Markel, K. (1997): Developing and testing an integrative model of the work–family interface. *Journal of Vocational Behaviour*, 50, 145–67.

Galinsky, E. and Johnson, A. A. (1998): *Reframing the Business Case for Work–Life Initiatives*. New York: Families and Work Institute.

Galinsky, E. and Stein, P. J. (1990): The impact of human resource policies on employees: Balancing work and family life. *Journal of Family Issues*, 11, 368–83.

Greenberg, J. (1990): Organisational justice: yesterday, today and tomorrow. *Journal of Management*, 16, 399–432.

Greenhaus, J. H. and Beutell, N. J. (1985): Sources of conflict between work and family roles. *Academy of Management Review*, 10, 76–88.

Greenhaus, J. and Parasuraman, S. (1999 in press): Research on work, family and gender: current status and future directions. In G. N. Powell (ed.), *Handbook of Gender in Organizations*, Newbury Park, CA: Sage.

Grover, S. L. (1991): Predicting the perceived fairness of parental leave policies. *Journal of Applied Psychology*, 76, 247–55.

Haas, L. and Hwang, P. (1995): *Company culture and men's usage of family leave benefits in Sweden*. Family Relations, 44, 28–36.

Hadden, L. and Silverstone, R. (1993): *Teleworking in the 1990s: a view from the home*. SPRU CICT Report No. 10 CICT, SPRU, University of Sussex.

Hayghe, H. (1997): Developments in Women's Labour Force Participation. *Monthly Labor Review*, September, 41–6.

Henwood, M., Rimmer, L., and Wicks, M. (1987): *Inside the Family: Changing Roles of Men and Women*. London: Family Policy Studies Centre.

Hertz, R. (1997): A typology of approaches to child care: the centrepiece of organising family life for dual-earner couples. *Journal of Family Issues*, 18(4), 355–85.

Hertz, R. (1999): Working to place family at the centre of life: dual-earner and single parent strategies. *Annals of the American Academy of Political Science*, 562, 15–31.

Hertz, R. and Ferguson, F. (1998): Only one pair of hands. Ways that single mothers stretch work and family resources. *Community, Work and Family*, 1(1), 13–37.

Hill, E. J., Hawkins, A. J., and Miller, B. C. (1996): Work and family in the virtual office. Perceived influences of mobile telework. *Family Relations*, 45(3), 293–301.

Hochschild, A. (1997): *The Time Bind. When Work Becomes Home and Home Becomes Work*. New York: Henry Holt.

Hoffman, L. W. (1979): Maternal employment. *American Psychologist*, 34(910), 859–65.

Hogg, C. and Harker, L. (1992): *The Family-friendly Employer. Some Examples from Europe*. London: Daycare Trust.

Holt, H. and Thaulow, I. (1996): Formal and informal flexibility in the workplace. In S. Lewis and J. Lewis (eds), *The Work Family Challenge. Rethinking Employment*. London: Sage.

Huws, U., Podro, S., Gunnarsson, E., Weijers, T., Arvanitaki, K., and Trova, V. (1996): *Teleworking and Gender*. Brighton, UK: Institute of Employment Studies.

ILO (International Labour Organisation) (1995): *World Employment 1995*. Geneva: International Labour Office.

Jones, F. and Fletcher, B. (1993): An empirical study of occupational stress transmission in working couples. *Human Relations*, 46(7), 881–903.

Kammerman, S. and Kahn, A. (1987): *The Responsive Workplace. Employers and a Changing Labor Force*. New York: Columbia University Press.

Kanter, R. M. (1997): *Work and Family in the United States: a critical review and agenda for research and policy*. New York: Russell Sage Foundation.

Kossek, E. E. and Ozeki, C. (1999): Bridging the work–family policy and productivity gap: A literature review. *Community, Work and Family*, 2(1), 7–32.

Lerner, M. J. (1987): Integrating societal and psychological rules of entitlement: implications for comparable worth. *Social Justice Research*. 1, 107–25.

Lewis, S. (1991): Motherhood and/or Employment: the Impact of Social and Organizational Values. In A. Phoenix, A. Woollett, and E. Lloyd (eds), *Motherhood, Meanings, Practices and Ideologies*. London Sage.

Lewis, S. (1996): Sense of entitlement, family friendly policies and gender. In H. Holt and I. Thaulow (eds), *The Role of Companies in Reconciling Work and Family Life*, Copenhagen: Danish National Institute of Social Research.

Lewis, forthcoming Restructuring workplace cultures. The ultimate work–family challenge? *Women in Management Review*.

Lewis, S. (1997): Family friendly organizational policies: a route to organizational change or playing about at the margins. *Gender, Work and Organisation*, 4, 13–23.

Lewis, S. (2001): Restructuring workplace cultures: the ultimate work-family challenge? *Women in Management Review*, 16, 1, 21–9.

Lewis, S. and Cooper, C. L. (1987): Stress in two earner couples and stage in the life cycle. *Journal of Occupational Psychology*, 60, 289–303.

Lewis, S. and Cooper, C. L. (1988): The transition to parenthood in two earner couples. *Psychological Medicine*, 18, 477–86.

Lewis, S. and Cooper, C. (1995): Balancing the work–family interface. A European perspective. *Human Resource Management Review*, 5, 289–305.

Lewis, S. and Cooper, C. L. (1999): The work–family research agenda in changing contexts. *Journal of Occupational Health Psychology*, 4(4), 382–93.

Lewis, S., Kagan, C., and Heaton, P. (1999): Economic and psychological benefits from employment. The experiences of mothers of disabled children. *Disability and Society*, 14(4), 561–75.

Lewis, S., Kagan, C., and Heaton, P. (2000): Dual earner parents with disabled children: Patterns for working and caring. *Journal of Family Issues*, 21, 1031–60.

Lewis, S. and Lewis, J. (1997): Work, family and well being. Can the law help? *Legal and Criminological Psychology*, 2, 155–67.

Lewis, S., Smithson, J., Brannen, J., Das Dores Guerreiro, M., Kugelberg, C., Nilsen, A, and O'Connor, P. (1998): *Futures on Hold. Young Europeans Talk about Combining Work and Family*. London: Work–Life Research Centre.

Lewis, S., Smithson, J. and Brannen, J. (1999): Young Europeans' orientations to families and work. *Annals of the American Academy of Political Science*, 562, 83–97.

Lewis, S. and Taylor, K. (1996): Evaluating the Impact of Employer Family Friendly Policies. A Case Study. In S. Lewis and J. Lewis (eds), *The Work Family Challenge*. London: Sage.

Lundgren, L. and Barnett, R. (2000): Reduced-hours careers in medicine: a strategy for the professional community and the family. *Community, Work and Family*, 3(1), 65–80.

Major, J. (1987): Gender, Justice and the Psychology of Entitlement. In P. Shaver and C. Hendrick (eds). *Review of Personality and Social Psychology*, 7, 124–48. Newbury Park, CA: Sage.

Major, B. (1993): Gender, entitlement and the distribution of family labour. *Journal of Social Issues*, 3, 141–59.

*Management Today* (2000): Age of the flex exec. August 1–6 London: Management Publications.

Marks, S. R. (1977): Multiple roles and role strain: some notes on human energy, time and commitment. *American Sociological Review*, 42, 244–54.

Metcalfe, H. and Leighton, P. (1989): *Underutilization of women in the workforce*. Brighton, England: Institute of Management Studies.

Milliken, F. J., Dutton, J. E., and Buyer, J. M. (1990): Understanding organizational adaptation to change: the case of work–family issues. *Human Resource Planning*, 3, 91–107.

Milliken, F. J., Martins, L. L., and Morgan, H. (1998): Explaining Organizational Responsiveness to Work–Family Issues: The Role of Human Resource Executives as Issue Interpreters. *Academy of Management Journal*, 41(5), 580–92.

Nilsen, A. (1998): Forever Young (*Jovens para sempre?*), *Sociologia: Problemas e Practicas*, 27, 59–78.

Parkinson, D. (1996): *Work–family roundtable. The childless employee*. New York: Conference Board.

Pleck, J. (1977): The work–family role system, *Social Problems*, 24, 417–27.

Pupo, N. and Duffy, A. (2000): Canadian part time work into the Millennium. On the cusp of change. *Community, Work and Family*, 3(1), 81–102.

Raabe, P. (1996): Constructing pluralistic work and career arrangements. In S. Lewis and J. Lewis (eds), *The Work–Family Challenge. Rethinking Employment*. London: Sage.

Rapoport, R. and Rapoport, R. N. (1969): The dual career family: a variant pattern and social change. *Human Relations*, 22, 3–30.

Rapoport, R. and Rapoport, R. N. (1971): *Dual Career Families*. London: Penguin.

Schappe, S. (1996): Bridging the gap between procedural knowledge and positive employee attitudes. *Group and Organizational Management*, 337–64.

Sekaran, U. (1986): *Dual Career Families*. San Francisco: Jossey Bass.

Sieber, S. D. (1974): Towards a theory of role accumulation. *American Sociological Review*, 39, 567–78.

Staines, G. L. (1980): Spillover versus compensation: a review of the literature on the relationships between work and nonwork. *Human Relations*, 33, 111–29.

Staines, G. L., Pleck, J. H., Shephard, C. J., and O'Connor, J. (1978): Wife's employment status and marital adjustment – yet another look. *Psychology of Women Quarterly*, 3(1), 90–120.

Stamworth, C. M. (1999): A best case scenario? Non manual part time work and job sharing in UK local government in the 1990s. *Community, Work and Family*, 2(3), 295–310.

Standen, P., Daniels, K., and Lamond, D. (1999): The home as a workplace: work–family interaction and psychological well-being in telework. *Journal of Occupational Health Psychology*, 4(4), 368–81.

Sullivan, C. (2000): Space and the intersection of work and family in homeworking households. *Community, Work and Family*, 3(2), 185–204.

Sullivan, C. and Lewis, S. (forthcoming): Home based telework, gender and the synchronisation of work and family. *Gender, Work and Organisation*.

Thibaut, J. and Walker, L. (1975): *Procedural Justice: A Psychological Analysisi*. Hillsdale, NJ: Lawrence Erlbaum.

Thomas, L. and Ganster, D. (1995): Impact of family supportive work variables on work–family conflict and strain: A control perspective. *Journal of Applied Psychology*, 80, 6–15.

Ward, C., Dale, A., and Joshi, H. (1996): Combining employment with childcare: an escape from dependence. *Journal of Social Policy*, 25(2), 223–47.

Welch, S. and Booth, A. (1977): Employment and health among married women with children. *Sex Roles*, 3, 385–97.

Westman, M. and Etzion, D. (1995): Crossover of stress, strain and resources from one spouse to another. *Journal of Organizational Behaviour*, 16, 169–81.

Wikstrom, T., Palm Linden, K., and Michelson, M. (1998): *Hub of Events or Splendid Isolation: Teleworkers and the Home*. Stockholm NUTEK.

Young, M. (1999): Work–family backlash. Begging the question, what's fair? *Annals of the American Academy of Political Science*, 562, 32–46.

Zvonkovik, A. M., Greaves, K. M., Schmiege, J., and Hall, L. D. (1996): The marital construction of gender through work and family decisions: A qualitative analysis. *Journal of Marriage and the Family*, 58(1), 91–100.

# 6

# SEXUAL HARASSMENT AND WOMEN'S ADVANCEMENT: ISSUES, CHALLENGES, AND DIRECTIONS

*Myrtle P. Bell and Mary E. McLaughlin*

More than two decades have passed since the United States's Equal Employment Opportunity Commission (EEOC, 1980) originally published its guidelines on sexual harassment. These guidelines defined sexual harassment and clarified its illegality as a form of sex discrimination prohibited by Title VII of the Civil Rights Act of 1964. In the past twenty years a considerable amount of research on the costs, antecedents, and consequences of sexual harassment has been published. Indeed, the severity and pervasiveness of the problem is now widely acknowledged (for example, Fitzgerald, 1993; Gutek, 1985; USMSPB, 1981, 1988). Sexual harassment remains a significant problem for working women in the US and around the world.

Estimates suggest that about half of all working women in the US will experience sexual harassment at some time during their careers (Gutek, 1985; USMSPB, 1981, 1988), though some research suggests this figure may be even higher (for example, Gutek, 1993; Martindale, 1990), particularly in environments that have typically been dominated by men (Fitzgerald and Shullman, 1993; Piotrkowski, 1998). Further, although researchers acknowledge that men may be targets of sexual harassment and that same-sex harassment occurs, sexual harassment is most commonly perpetrated by men against women (Fitzgerald and Shullman, 1993). Each year, in the US, more than 15,000 sexual harassment charges are filed with the EEOC – the agency responsible for handling initial claims (Buhler, 1999). When the large numbers of formal complaints filed are coupled with large estimates of those who are harassed but do not file formal complaints (for example, Gutek and Koss, 1993), it appears that sexual harassment may affect the majority of women workers. Studies conducted in Austria, Brazil, China,

Canada, India, Israel, and the United Kingdom suggest that the prevalence of sexual harassment in various regions around the world is comparable to that in the US (for example, Barak, 1997; Can, 1994; Gelfand, Fitzgerald, and Drasgow, 1995; Gruber, 1997; Pryor et al., 1997; Shaffer et al., 2000). In addition to similarity in prevalence, researchers have demonstrated the similarity of sexual harassment constructs in various countries (for example, Barak, 1997; Gelfand et al., 1995; Shaffer et al., 2000).

Negative consequences for women who are harassed are also widely acknowledged (for example, Crull, 1982; Hanisch, 1996; Fitzgerald, Drasgow, Hulin, Gelfand, and Magley, 1997). Women who are sexually harassed may experience various negative physical, psychological, and motivation-related outcomes. For example, women who have been harassed have reported higher stress (Crull, 1982; Piotrkowski, 1998; Shaffer et al., 2000), lowered job satisfaction (O'Farrell and Harlan, 1982; Piotrkowski, 1998), and increased intentions to quit (Shaffer et al., 2000). Women who are harassed may also experience career stagnation, decline, or even job loss. More than 20 percent of the women in Gutek's 1985 study reported losing or leaving a job because of sexual harassment, and nearly 20 percent of the women in the later USMSPB (1988) study reported taking leave after being sexually harassed. Tangri, Burt, and Johnson (1982, p. 40) have argued that sexual harassment serves to "maintain male dominance occupationally and therefore economically, by intimidating, discouraging, or precipitating removal of women from work." More recently, Gutek and Koss (1993, p. 31) have suggested that "sexual harassment can derail a career or lead or force a woman into an occupation which pays less well and/or offers fewer opportunities for advancement," thus hindering advancement. Somewhat less obvious is the converse: pay and advancement opportunities are negatively related to sexual harassment. Indeed, research has found that women who are harassed are more likely to be lower in status and pay than women who are not harassed, and that women who are higher in status and pay are less likely to be harassed (Fain and Anderton, 1987; Gruber, 1998).

In this chapter we focus on the relationship between sexual harassment and women's opportunities and advancement in organizations, arguing that the very nature of sexual harassment makes it inextricable from women's opportunities and advancement and thus requires interventions designed to affect them both. We first present a brief history of sexual harassment in the US, including prominent legal cases and decisions, and recent US Supreme Court decisions particularly relevant to efforts to prevent sexual harassment. We then discuss determinants of sexual harassment and their relationships with women's (lack of) advancement. Finally, we make recommendations for reducing sexual harassment in the twenty-first century in the fabric of advancing women in management.

## ■ Definitional and historical issues ■

### Quid pro quo and hostile environment sexual harassment

The US EEOC and US courts have recognized two forms of sexual harassment, characterized as "quid pro quo" and "hostile environment" harassment. Sexual harassment upon which some job-related benefit is contingent is characterized as quid pro quo or "this for that" sexual harassment. This type of harassment involves employment-related bribery or threat (promotions, raises, sometimes employment itself or mainte-nance of a job) to obtain sexual cooperation. Quid pro quo harassment is more easily recognized, and less common than is the hostile environment form of harassment (for example, Gruber and Bjorn, 1982; Munson, Hulin, and Drasgow, 2000; O'Hare and O'Donohue, 1998). Hostile environment harassment has "the purpose or effect of unreasonably interfering with an individual's work performance or creating an intimi-dating, hostile, or offensive" work environment (EEOC, 1980, p. 74677). Hostile envi-ronment harassment may occur when vulgar or sexually explicit graffiti, pornographic photographs, cartoons, calendars, or literature are posted in the workplace (Conte, 1997). Quid pro quo sexual harassment is more likely to be perpetrated by managers or supervisors while hostile environment harassment may be perpetrated by co-workers as well as managers and supervisors.

Quid pro quo and hostile environment harassment are the two forms of sexual harassment recognized in legal arenas. Psychological dimensions of sexual harass-ment include gender harassment, unwanted sexual attention, and sexual coercion (Fitzgerald, Hulin, and Drasgow, 1995; Gelfand et al., 1995). Gender harassment includes a broad range of verbal and non-verbal behaviors designed to convey nega-tive, degrading, insulting, and/or threatening attitudes toward women and is deemed the most widespread form of harassment (Fitzgerald et al., 1995). Unwanted sexual attention consists of various offensive, unwanted, and unreciprocated behaviors including repeated requests for dates, telephone calls, or letters, or unwanted touching or assault (Gelfand et al., 1995). Gender harassment and unwanted sexual attention can both contribute to hostile environment harassment, while sexual coercion, which makes some job-related benefit (for example, continued employment or promotion) contingent upon sexual cooperation, is considered quid pro quo harassment.

One of the earliest and most prominent cases of sexual harassment to reach the US Supreme Court involved Michelle Vinson and Meritor Savings Bank (*Meritor Savings Bank v. Vinson*, 1986) and clarified employer liability for a hostile working environment. Vinson was hired as a teller in 1974 by Sidney Taylor, the bank vice-president. Over the four years in which she worked for Meritor, Vinson was subjected to severe sexual harass-ment by Taylor. Vinson stated that she first refused his advances, but eventually relented because she feared losing her job, eventually having intercourse with Taylor forty to fifty times. Vinson also stated that Taylor had raped her on several occasions, followed her into the women's rest room, fondled her in front of other employees, and exposed himself to her. After Vinson was fired in 1978 for excessive use of sick time,[1] she filed suit against Meritor alleging continued sexual harassment during her employment at Meritor. Meritor's arguments centered around the "voluntariness" of the relationship, Vinson's failure to suffer tangible or economic losses because of the harassment, and her failure to use the bank's complaint procedure. Though the behaviors exhibited by Taylor appear to be at least partially representative of quid pro quo harassment (at least from Vinson's reported fear of losing her job unless she relented), after various appeals through lower courts the Supreme Court ruled on the illegality of the "hostile or offensive" working environment created by Taylor's behaviors. The ruling also clarified the importance of the "unwelcomeness" of the behaviors, rather than requiring proof of tangible loss or harm, or focusing on the employee's failure to complain.

## Affirmative defense

In decisions since Meritor (for example, *Harris* v. *Forklift Systems*, 1993; *Highlander* v. *K. F. C. National Management Co.*, 1986), ambiguity regarding employer liability and the determination of unwelcomeness, severity, and pervasiveness remained (Paetzold and O'Leary-Kelly, 1996).[2] Two important decisions were rendered by the US Supreme Court in 1998 that clarified some of these remaining questions. Specifically, in *Burlington Industries* v. *Ellerth* (1998) and *Faragher* v. *City of Boca Raton* (1998), the US Supreme Court provided clear answers as to whether organizations could be found liable regardless of whether they "knew or should have known" about harassment. These rulings gave employers specific means to avoid liability in cases of harassment provided they had exercised "reasonable care" to prevent and promptly correct harassment *and* provided that the complainant had "unreasonably" failed to utilize preventive or corrective measures provided by the employer.

As part of the exercise of reasonable care, employers should widely communicate intolerance of sexual harassment. Policies against harassment should be communicated clearly and regularly to employees at all levels and should include clarification of what constitutes harassment, avenues for complaint, and the penalties for harassment. Targets and witnesses should be encouraged to report incidences of sexual harassment by ensuring confidentiality, providing protection against retaliation, and responding to complaints with appropriate remedial action. If an instance of sexual harassment is reported, the employer should investigate promptly and thoroughly, and take immediate and appropriate action to: end the harassment, prevent its recurrence, administer sanctions to the harasser based on explicit disciplinary policy and the seriousness of the offense, and make follow-up inquiries to make sure the harassment has not resumed and the target has not suffered retaliation (EEOC, 1995).

These guidelines provide employers with a strong incentive and impetus to ensure harassment does not occur and to remedy it if it does. Implementation of these guidelines also imply the employer's *genuine* commitment to a harassment-free organization. In the following sections we present reasons why the actions necessary for an employer to mount an affirmative defense are related to women's opportunities, status, and position in organizations.

## ■ Relationships between women's advancement and sexual harassment ■

Researchers attempting to explain the occurrence of sexual harassment have considered biological, organizational, and sociocultural explanations and combinations of these explanations, yet no model fully explains these dysfunctional, harmful behaviors (O'Hare and O'Donohue, 1998). Sexual harassment of women is a complex phenomenon, with interrelationships between women's status and power being integral to its manifestation (Welsh, 1999). Riger (1991, p. 503) has argued that organizational promotion of "equal opportunities for women" may be the most important factor in reducing sexual harassment. Similarly, Piotrkowski (1997, p. 34.28) has stated that "an end to sexual harassment requires that men and women reach social and economic equality and full integration in all occupations and workplaces." In this regard, there are numerous, complex causes of sexual harassment. In this chapter we focus on three factors that are clearly related to both sexual harassment and to women's opportunities and advancement: 1) women's organizational power and status; 2) the male to female ratio of employees; and 3) the professionalism or sexualization of the working environment. Welsh (1999) has characterized these three factors as "organizational-level explanations" for sexual harassment. After a discussion of these factors, we provide suggestions for organizational-level initiatives focused on creating an organizational environment of gender equity and intolerance of harassment. We also argue that such an environment would create and be enhanced by opportunities for women and their advancement.

## Women's organizational power and status

Research in the field of women's studies and cross-disciplinary research on gender and diversity has long documented women's relatively lower organizational status and power relative to men's (for example, Luhman and Gilman, 1980; Muli, 1995; Nagy and Rich, 2001). Women who are younger, have lower status, authority, and power, and who earn significantly less than men are more likely to be sexually harassed (Gruber, 1998; Gruber and Bjorn, 1982). Brown (1987, p. 146) noted that in 1981 about 30 percent of working women were employed in occupations involving domestic duties such as cleaning, cooking and serving food, sewing, teaching children, and doing clerical work. These jobs and responsibilities are assigned little or no status in society, and are positions of low pay, prestige, and power (Luhman and Gilman, 1980). More recently, women have had some success in entering first-line and other low-level management positions, but the higher the organizational position the fewer the numbers of women holding those positions (FGCC, 1997). In the US, men hold about 95 percent of senior management positions (FGCC, 1997; Rice, 1994) and about 70 percent of all salaried manager positions (Bose and Whaley, 2001) – jobs that are generally associated with high status and other perks.

In addition, when men and women are working together, women are far more likely to be supervised or managed by men than men are to be supervised or managed by women (Gutek and Morasch, 1982; Nieva and Gutek, 1981). A male doctor with a female nurse, a male dentist and a female hygienist, and a male executive with a female secretary are a few obvious examples. In 1991, women were about 99 percent of all secretaries, 95 percent of all registered nurses, and 80 percent of administrative support workers (Fagenson and Jackson, 1993) – all positions that are likely to be supervised by or in support of the work of men, making them more likely targets for quid pro quo harassment. As most sexual harassment is perpetrated by co-workers rather than supervisors (Gutek and Morasch, 1982), however, status and power differences alone are not sufficient to explain it.

Gender harassment or unwanted sexual attention may be perpetrated by supervisors, managers, or co-workers, particularly in work environments that are male-dominated. Further, supervisor gender may influence perceived tolerance of and existence of sexual harassment (Gutek, 1985; Hulin et al., 1996; Piotrkowski, 1998). Hulin et al.'s (1996) study at a public utility found that women who reported to a male supervisor viewed the organization as being more tolerant of harassment than did women who reported to a female supervisor. Gutek (1985) found that women who had a male supervisor were more likely to be harassed – though not necessarily by the supervisor; most of the harassment was perpetrated by their male co-workers who may have perceived tolerance for harassment by the male supervisor. In a field study of women office workers (performing support roles in male-dominated environments), Piotrkowski (1998) found that more frequent gender harassment was reported by women whose supervisors were men whom they perceived as being biased against women. Piotrkowski also found that women whose supervisors were men reported experiencing more frequent gender harassment than did women with female supervisors.

## Sex ratio

Sex ratio refers to the relative numbers of men and women working in an organization and/or in a particular job. In conjunction with women's status and power, it is a determinant of sexual harassment. As noted above, women working in female-dominated work environments, but supervised by men, may be subjected to quid pro quo harassment, while women who are working in male-dominated environments and supervised by men may be subjected to hostile environment harassment by their co-workers as well as quid pro quo harassment by their supervisor. Gutek and Morasch (1982) have argued that in environments dominated by men or by women, sex differences become salient, and expectations for performance of expected sex roles may dominate interactions (for example, "sex-role spillover," Gutek and Morasch, 1982).

Women employed in occupations traditionally held primarily by men are more likely to experience harassment by their peer co-workers than are other women (Gruber and Bjorn, 1982; Gutek, Cohen, and Konrad, 1990; Gutek and Morasch, 1982; LaFontaine and Tredeau, 1986; Mansfield et al., 1991; O'Farrell and Harlan, 1992; Rosenberg, Perstadt, and Phillips, 1993; Yoder and Aniakudo, 1996). Mansfield et al. (1991) found that women working in blue-collar trade and transit positions (both male dominated) were more likely to be harassed (by their male co-workers) than were women working as secretaries. They expressed particular concern at the level of harassment of the tradeswomen (greater than that of the transit workers), because their "skills usually are acquired during apprenticeships or on the job" thus making them "dependent on the help and support" of their (harassing) co-workers (Mansfield et al., 1991, p. 76); clearly such harassment has implications for performance and advancement of the tradeswomen and implications for other women in similar situations as well. Mansfield et al. (1991) noted that there were relatively more women working in transit occupations than in blue-collar trade positions and that women had been in those transit occupations for a much longer period of time. They suggested that the entrance of women into an historically male-dominated job may serve to break down sexist barriers and hostile environments gradually, over time. As the proportion of women in these positions steadily increases, hostility and harassment should be ameliorated, either by the gradual acceptance of and adjustment to women co-workers by men, and/or by the explicit demonstration of an intolerance of sexual harassment by those in supervisory positions committed to cessation of harassment.

## Professionalism or sexualization of the working environment

The final set of factors that we discuss as linked to both sexual harassment and women's advancement is the professionalism or sexualization of the working environment. Professionalism refers to implicit or explicit communication of and employee adherence to norms for appropriate appearance, dress, and treatment of others with courtesy and respect. Sexualization refers to employee communication, dress, displays, or other behaviors of a sexual or erotic nature. Research has supported the links between professionalism, sexualization, and sexual harassment.

Using a stratified random sample of over 1,200 working men and women in Los Angeles, CA, Gutek et al. (1990) found that sexualization of the work environment was associated with sexually harassing behaviors. They described a sexualized work environment as one in which "sexual jokes, comments, innuendos, and sexual or seductive dress are tolerated, condoned, or encouraged" (Gutek et al., 1990, p. 565). In O'Hare and O'Donohue's (1998) sample of faculty, staff, and students, at a large Midwestern university, an unprofessional work environment (in which employees are generally treated disrespectfully, are expected to perform activities that are not formally a part of their jobs, or in which there is drinking or cursing on the job) was a strong predictor of sexual harassment. Work environments that are sexualized or unprofessional clearly would appear to increase the opportunity for sexual harassment and other harmful behaviors, regardless of the overall sex-ratio of the environment. O'Hare and O'Donohue (1998) found that an unprofessional environment, a sexist atmosphere, and women's lack of knowledge about the organization's sexual harassment procedures were the risk factors most strongly associated with sexual harassment.

Each of these risk factors can be changed through organizational interventions, such as establishing, communicating, and enforcing rules regarding appropriate and inappropriate speech, dress, and other behaviors regarding sexualization and professionalism in the workplace. In addition, in order to reduce sexual harassment more directly and to mount an affirmative defense against potential sexual harassment charges, sexual harassment policies must be established, communicated, and enforced. Such policies are discussed below, along with other initiatives to reduce sexual harassment.

## ■ Reducing sexual harassment: policies, assessment, and equity ■

We have conceptualized an intertwined and recursive relationship between women's advancement and sexual harassment based on empirically supported links with three interrelated factors: women's organizational power and status; sex-ratio; and professionalism or sexualization of the work environment. Though by no means exhaustive, these three interrelated factors are specifically important to both women's advancement and sexual harassment. Past research has demonstrated the viability and effectiveness of proactive organizational efforts to reduce workplace aggression, such as sexual harassment (Keyton, 1996; O'Leary-Kelly et al., 1996). We suggest that 1) sexual harassment policies; 2) regular organizational assessments and directed training; and 3) organizational support of gender equity are three such proactive organizational efforts that will reduce sexual harassment and increase women's advancement. Sexual harassment policies are an important first step in prevention of sexual harassment (Bell, Cycyota, and Quick, in press). Regular organizational assessments and directed training naturally follow implementation of a sexual harassment policy and will work directly to encourage a professional working environment. Finally, organizational support of gender equity will affect women's power and status within the organization and the sex-ratios of jobs within the organization. These three initiatives are detailed below.

## Sexual harassment policies

The existence of strong, formal sexual harassment policies is proposed by many researchers as a means of reducing sexual harassment in organizations (Dekker and Barling, 1998; Gruber and Smith, 1995; Pryor, LaVite, and Stoller, 1993) and is required as part of the affirmative defense strategy. Research has found support for the effect of policies on harassment, with stronger policies and sanctions against harassment being associated with fewer reports of sexual harassment (Dekker and Barling, 1998; Grundmann, O'Donohue, and Peterson, 1997; Pryor et al., 1993). Hulin et al. (1996) argued that employees in organizations that do not have harassment policies or sanctions for harassment may regard this as evidence of tolerance for the dominance of men over women. Having a strong sexual harassment policy is a necessary, but not sufficient, step in the reduction of sexual harassment, however (Bell et al., in press).

In *Faragher* v. *Boca Raton* (1998), the city of Boca Raton's policy had not been widely disseminated, thus its existence was of little effect in prevention or reporting of harassment, or in absolving the city of Boca Raton from responsibility for the harassment. O'Hare and O'Donohue (1998) found that women's lack of knowledge about the organization's harassment procedures, and steps to take if harassed, were strongly associated with sexual harassment. As discussed earlier, clarification of what constitutes harassment and steps to be taken if harassment occurs are also requirements of the affirmative defense strategy. Employees also must be sure they will be protected from retaliation if they report harassment. Finally, formal disciplinary procedures must be followed when harassment occurs. A single demonstration of the policy (perhaps through suspension or termination of a harassment perpetrator) should deter other harassers, thus reducing the likelihood of future harassment.

## Organizational assessments and training

Organizational attitude surveys are used to assess employee perceptions about such issues as pay, job security, opportunities for advancement, and similar areas of importance. They are also used to investigate sources of problems (such as high turnover) and effectiveness of changes implemented to address problems. We suggest that measures of sexual harassment should be included in regular attitude surveys to assess the existence of sexually harassing behaviors, the level of sexualization of the work environment, and the level of organizational tolerance for sexual harassment. Hulin et al. (1996) developed an inventory to assess the latter. Their *Organizational Tolerance for Sexual Harassment Inventory* measures perceptions that complaints would be taken seriously, that harassers would be sanctioned, and perceptions of the risk of retaliation. As did Hulin et al. (1996), we recommend such measures be included along with other measures (for example, withdrawal, job satisfaction, etc.) in anonymous surveys. Employees should be asked if they have experienced harassing behaviors or witnessed others being harassed. In addition to providing information on the level of harassment and organizational tolerance for harassment, inclusion of such measures in regular surveys would indicate to employees (both men and women) that sexual harassment is perceived similarly to withdrawal, job satisfaction, and other such important work-related issues. Rather than being a one-shot training issue, measurement of issues related to sexual harassment in regular surveys would provide a recurring signal of its importance as well as information useful for affecting change. Over time, as regular surveys are conducted and changes implemented, it is expected that the organizational tolerance for harassment and reports of harassing behaviors will both decline.

Once information is obtained on organizational tolerance for harassment and the existence of harassing behaviors, organizations must implement steps to change the environment where warranted. As well as regular training on what constitutes harassment and how to recognize and address it, interventions and training based on organization-specific problems that were identified should be designed (Burley and Lessig, 1999; Sahl, 1999).

## Organizational support of gender equity

Organizational support of gender equity would be demonstrated by having women in non-stereotyped positions, in decision-making and supervisory positions, and earning pay comparable to men. Are women generally managed by men but few men managed by women in the organization? Are pay disparities based on job-related factors? Have charges of other forms of discrimination (which may be associated with sexual harassment – for example, Yoder and Aniakudo, 1996) been leveled?

Organizational efforts should be made to change skewed gender ratios and power imbalances as well as creating a culture of intolerance for harassment. Grundmann et al. (1997, p. 177) argued that efforts to prevent sexual harassment would include equal numbers of women and men in various levels of authority, and clearly communicated job roles with expected duties and limits. On the other hand, not having women in decision-making and supervisory positions, and the existence of glass ceilings and walls may be indicative of a lack of organizational support of gender equality, and may facilitate sexual harassment. Where organizational structures retard the operation of sexism and harassment, support for inter-gender diversity and equality are more apparent (Tomaskovic-Devey, 1993).

## ■ Summary ■

Women now comprise nearly half the workforce in the US and one-third of the workforce worldwide (Johnston, 1991) and at least half of them may experience sexual harassment during their work lives. As discussed earlier, women comprise the great majority of harassment targets, but rarely perpetrate harassment. The mere presence of more women managers would thus necessarily reduce quid pro quo harassment. As discussed previously, this might also serve to reduce perceptions of, and actual organizational tolerance for, harassment of any kind.

In addition, the documented relationship between women's higher power and status and lower incidences of sexual harassment should provide greater motivation to increase women's status as employees and as managers overall. One suggestion from research was that "women will benefit from greater integration throughout all levels" of organizations (Gutek and Morasch, 1982, p. 73); women working in integrated settings, with ratios relatively balanced, report lowest levels of sexual harassment (for example, Gutek and Morasch, 1982; Piotrkowski, 1998; Sheffey and Tindale, 1992). The potential for increased initial harassment as women begin to increase as a percentage of the workforce should not be ignored; given this possibility, interventions to prevent sexual harassment should be implemented. These interventions can ensure that the opportunities for harassment do not result in harassment, due to support of gender equity, and intolerance of and negative sanctions for harassment. As organizations become gender balanced, harassment can be expected to decline.

## Conclusion

In this chapter we have clarified and elaborated on the inter-relationships between sexual harassment and women's advancement in organizations. This represents an important contribution to the literature on women's employment issues and on sexual harassment in organizations. Arguments and empirical evidence were presented supporting the impact of sexual harassment on women's advancement, as well as the impact of women's advancement on sexual harassment in the workplace. Clearly, these two constructs are inextricably linked in complex ways. Such a rich set of complex relationships is supported only in part by research evidence, leaving much of this topic ripe for further study and elucidation.

Although many questions remain, enough is now known to implement organizational policies and procedures to reduce sexual harassment and improve women's status. Suggestions were provided for both, with a focus on developing and maintaining an organizational environment of support for gender equity and intolerance for sexual harassment.

The outlook for eliminating sexual harassment and advancing women in organizations is optimistic as long as employers increasingly implement and enforce sexual harassment policies and prevention programs, and women progressively advance to higher-level positions within organizations.

## NOTES

1 Use of sick time or annual leave or other withdrawal behaviors may be common responses of women who are sexually harassed, possibly in attempt to avoid the harasser (see Hanisch, 1996, for a discussion).
2 Readers are referred to Paetzold and O' Leary-Kelly (1996) for discussions of these decisions through 1993.

## REFERENCES

Barak, A. (1997): Cross-cultural perspectives on sexual harassment. In W. O'Donohue (ed.), *Sexual Harassment: Theory, Research, and Treatment*, Boston: Allyn and Bacon.

Bell, M. P., Cycyota, C., and Quick, J. C. (2001, in press): Affirmative defense: The prevention of sexual harassment. In D. L. Nelson and R. J. Burke (eds), *Gender, Work, Stress, and Health: Current Research Issues*, Washington, DC: American Psychological Association.

Bose, C. E. and Whaley, R. B. (2001): Sex segregation in the U.S. labor force. In D. Vannoy (ed.), *Gender Mosaics: Social Perspectives (Original Readings)*, Los Angeles, CA: Roxbury Publishing.

Brown, C. A. (1987): The new patriarchy. In C. Bose, R. Feldberg, N. Sokoloff with the Women and Work Research Group (eds), *Hidden Aspects of Women's Work*, New York: Praeger.

Buhler, P. M. (1999): The manager's role in preventing sexual harassment. *Supervision*, 60, 4, 16–18.

Burley, K. M., Jr. and Lessig, L. R. (1999): Supervisors, employees, and harassment. *Human Resource Professional*, Sept/Oct 28–32.

*Burlington Industries* v. *Ellerth*, 524, U.S. 742 (1998).

Can, T. (1994): Sexual harassment in China. *Chinese Education and Society*, 27, July/Aug 39–48.

Conte, A. (1997): Legal theories of sexual harassment. In W. O'Donohue (ed.), *Sexual Harassment: Theory, Research, and Treatment*, Boston: Allyn and Bacon.

Crull, P. (1982): Stress effects of sexual harassment on the job: Implications for counseling. *American Journal of Orthopsychiatry*, 52: 539–44.

Dekker, I. and Barling, J. (1998): Personal and organizational predictors of workplace sexual harassment of women by men. *Journal of Occupational Health Psychology*, 31, 7–18.

EEOC (Equal Employment Opportunity Commission) (1980): Guidelines on discrimination because of sex. *Federal Register*, 45, 74676–7.

EEOC (Equal Employment Opportunity Commission) (1995): *Guidelines on Discrimination Because of Sex*, 29, C.F.R. Sex. 1604.11.

Fagenson, E. A. and Jackson, J. J. (1993): The status of women managers in the United States. *International Studies of Management and Organizations*, 23, 93–112.

Fain, T. C. and Anderton, D. L. (1987): Sexual harassment: Organizational context and diffuse status. *Sex Roles*, 5, 6, 291–311.

*Faragher* v. *City of Boca Raton*, 524, U.S. 775 (1998).

FGCC (Federal Glass Ceiling Commission) (1997): The glass ceiling. In D. Dunn (ed.), *Workplace/women's place: an anthology*, Los Angeles, CA: Roxbury Publishing.

Fitzgerald, L. F. (1993): Sexual harassment: Violence against women in the workplace. *American Psychologist*, 48, 1070–6.

Fitzgerald, L. F., Drasgow, R., Hulin, C. L., Gelfand, M. J., and Magley, V. J. (1997): Antecedents and consequences of sexual harassment in organizations: A test of an integrated model. *Journal of Applied Psychology*, 82, 578–89.

Fitzgerald, L. F., Hulin, C. L., and Drasgow, R. (1995): The antecedents and consequences of sexual harassment in organizations: An integrated model. In G. P. Keita and J. J. Hurrell, Jr. (eds), *Job stress in a changing workforce: Investigating gender, diversity, and family issues*, Washington, DC: American Psychological Association.

Fitzgerald, L. F. and Shullman, S. L. (1993): Sexual harassment: A research analysis and agenda for the 1990s. *Journal of Vocational Behavior*, 42, 5–27.

Gelfand, M. J., Fitzgerald, L. F., and Drasgow, F. (1995): The structure of sexual harassment: A confirmatory analysis across cultures and settings. *Journal of Vocational Behavior*, 47, 164–77.

Gruber, J. E. (1997): An epidemiology of sexual harassment: Evidence from North America and Europe. In W. O'Donohue (ed.), *Sexual Harassment: Theory, Research, and Treatment*, Boston: Allyn and Bacon.

Gruber, J. E. (1998): The impact of male work environments and organizational policies on women's experiences of sexual harassment. *Gender and Society*, 12, 301–20.

Gruber, J. E. and Bjorn, L. (1982): Blue-collar blues: The sexual harassment of women auto-workers. *Work and Occupations*, 93, 271–98.

Gruber, J. E. and Smith, M. E. (1995): Women's responses to sexual harassment: A multivariate analysis. *Basic and Applied Social Psychology*, 17, 543–62.

Grundmann, E. O., O'Donohue, W., and Peterson, S. H. (1997): The prevention of sexual harassment. In W. O'Donohue (ed.), *Sexual Harassment: Theory, Research, and Treatment*, Allyn and Bacon: Boston.

Gutek, B. A. (1985): *Sex and the Workplace*. San Francisco: Jossey-Bass.

Gutek, B. A. (1993): Responses to sexual harassment. In S. Oskamp and M. Costanzo (eds), *Gender issues in social psychology: The Claremont symposium on applied social psychology*, Newbury Park, CA: Sage.

Gutek, B. A., Cohen, A. G., and Konrad, A. M. (1990): Predicting social-sexual behavior at work: A contact hypothesis. *Academy of Management Journal*, 33, 560–77.

Gutek, B. A. and Koss, M. P. (1993): Changed women and changed organizations: Consequences of and coping with sexual harassment. *Journal of Vocational Behavior*, 42, 28–48.

Gutek, B. A. and Morasch, B. (1982): Sex-ratios, sex–role spillover, and sexual harassment of women at work. *Journal of Social Issues*, 38(4), 55–74.

Hanisch, K. A. (1996): An integrated framework for studying the outcomes of sexual harassment: Consequences for individuals and organizations. In M. S. Stockdale (ed.), *Sexual harassment in the workplace*, Vol. 5, Thousand Oaks, CA: Sage.

*Harris v. Forklift Systems, Inc.*, 114 S. Ct. 367 (1993).

*Highlander v. K. F. C. National Management Co.*, 805 F. 2d 644 (65h Cir. 1986).

Hulin, C. L., Fitzgerald, L. F., and Drasgow, F. (1996): Organizational influences on sexual harassment. In M. S. Stockdale (ed.), *Sexual harassment in the workplace*, Vol. 5, Thousand Oaks, CA: Sage.

Johnston, W. B. (1991): Global workforce 2000: The new world labor market. Reprinted in M. C. Gentile (1996), *Managerial Excellence Through Diversity*, Prospect Heights, IL: Waveland Press.

Keyton, J. (1996): Sexual harassment: A multidisciplinary synthesis and critique. In B. R. Burleson (ed.), *Communication Yearbook*, Vol. 19, 92–155. Thousand Oaks, CA: Sage Publications.

LaFontaine, E. and Tredeau, L. (1986): The frequency, sources, and correlates of sexual harassment among women in traditional male occupations. *Sex Roles*, 15, 433–42.

Luhman, R. and Gilman, S. (1980): *Race and ethnic relations: The social and political experience of minority groups*. Belmont, CA: Wadsworth Publishing.

Mansfield, P. K., Koch, P. B., Henderson, J., Vicary, J. R., Cohn, M., and Young, E. W. (1991): The job climate for women in traditionally male blue-collar occupations. *Sex Roles*, 25, 63–79.

Martindale, M. (1990): *Sexual harassment in the military: 1988*. Arlington, VA: Defense Manpower Data Center.

*Meritor Savings Bank* v. *Vinson* (1986): 477 U.S. 57, 40 FEP Cases 1822.

Muli, K. 1995. "Help me balance the Load": Gender discrimination in Kenya. In J. Peters and A. Wolper (eds), *Women's rights, human rights: International feminist perspectives*. London: Routledge.

Munson, L. J., Hulin, C., and Dragsow, F. (2000): Longitudinal analysis of dispositional influences and sexual harassment: Effects on job and psychological outcomes. *Personnel Psychology*, 53, 21–46.

Nagy, D. M. and Rich, A. R. (2001): Constitutional law and public policy: Gender equity. In D. Vannoy (ed.), *Gender Mosaics: Social Perspectives (Original Readings)*, Los Angeles, CA: Roxbury Publishing.

Nieva, V. F. and Gutek, B. A. (1981): *Women and work: A psychological perspective*. New York: Praeger.

O'Farrell, B. and Harlan, S. L. (1982): Craftworkers and clerks: The effects of male coworker hostility on women's satisfaction with nontraditional jobs. *Social Problems*, 29, 252–64.

O'Hare, E. A. and O'Donohue, W. (1998): Sexual harassment: Identifying risk factors. *Archives of Sexual Behavior*, 27, 561–80.

O'Leary-Kelly, A. M., Paetzold, R. L., and Griffin, R. W. (2000): Sexual harassment as aggressive behavior: An actor based perspective. *The Academy of Management Review*, 25, 372–88.

Paetzold, R. L. and O'Leary-Kelly, A. M. (1996): The implications of U.S. Supreme Court and Circuit Court Decisions for Hostile Environment Sexual Harassment Cases. In M. S. Stockdale (ed.), *Sexual harassment in the workplace*, Vol. 5, Thousand Oaks, CA: Sage.

Piotrkowski, C. S. (1997): Sexual harassment. In S. L. Sauter and L. Levi (eds), "Part I. Hazards on the Job/ Section 4: Psychosocial and Organizational Factors." In J. M. Stellman (ed.), *ILO Encyclopaedia of Occupational Health and Safety*, 34.28–34.29. Geneva, Switzerland: International Labour Office, and Chicago: Rand McNally.

Piotrkowski, C. S. (1998): Gender harassment, job satisfaction, and distress among employed white and minority women. *Journal of Occupational Health Psychology*, 3, 33–43.

Pryor, J. B., DeSouza, E. R., Fitness, J., Hutz, C., Kumpf, M., Lubbert, K., Pesonen, O., and Erber, M. (1997): Gender differences in the interpretation of social-sexual behavior: A cross-cultural perspective on sexual harassment. *Journal of Cross-Cultural Psychology*, 28, 509–34.

Pryor, J. B., LaVite, C. M., and Stoller, L. M. (1993): A social psychological analysis of sexual harassment: The person/situation interaction. *Journal of Vocational Behavior*, 42, 68–83.

Rice, F. (1994): How to make diversity pay. *Fortune*, August 8.

Riger, S. (1991): Gender dilemmas in sexual harassment policies and procedures. *American Psychologist*, 46, 497–507.

Rosenberg, J., Perlstadt, H., and Philips, W. R. (1993): Now that we are here: Discrimination, disparagement, and harassment at work and the experience of women lawyers. *Gender and Society*, 7, 415–33.

Sahl, R. J. (1999): Creating a company-specific attitude survey. *Human Resources Professional*, 12, 5, Sept/Oct 23–7.

Shaffer, M. A., Joplin, J. R. W., Bell, M. P., Lau, T., and Oguz, C. (2000): Gender discrimination and job-related outcomes: A cross-cultural comparison of working women in the United States and China. *Journal of Vocational Behavior*, 57, 4, 395–427.

Sheffey, S. and Tindale, R. S. (1992): Perceptions of sexual harassment in the workplace. *Journal of Applied Social Psychology*, 22, 1502–20.

Tangri, S., Burt, M., and Johnson, L. (1982): Sexual harassment at work: Three explanatory models. *Journal of Social Issues*, 38, 4, 33–54.

Tomaskovic-Devey, D. (1993): The gender and race composition of jobs and the male/female, White/Black pay gaps. *Social Forces*, 72, 1, 45–76.

U.S. Merit Systems Protection Board (1981): *Sexual harassment in the Federal workplace: Is it a problem?* Washington, DC, US Government Printing Office.

U.S. Merit Systems Protection Board (1988): *Sexual harassment in the Federal workplace: An Update.* Washington, DC, US Government Printing Office.

Welsh, S. (1999): Gender and sexual harassment. *Annual Review of Sociology*, 25, 169–90.

Yoder, J. D. and Aniakudo, P. (1996): When pranks become harassment: The case of African American women firefighters. *Sex Roles*, 35, 253–70.

# 7

# GENDER DIFFERENCES IN EXPLANATIONS FOR RELOCATING OR CHANGING ORGANIZATIONS FOR ADVANCEMENT

*Phyllis Tharenou*

Women managers and executives appear to be leaving organizations apparently unfriendly to their advancement (Brett and Stroh, 1994; Buttner and Moore, 1997; Caudron, 1998; Lawlor, 1994; Russell and Burgess, 1998). Indeed, women executives report that they had to change organizations to overcome obstacles or they would not have got ahead (Korn/Ferry International, 1993; Riley and White, 1994) but men did not report having to do so (Davies-Netzley, 1998). For women to advance to high levels they may have to change jobs more than men, although Brett and Stroh (1999) concluded that women gain few benefits from using an external labor-market strategy. The aim of this study was to examine if women do change jobs to advance more than men because of obstacles. Two types of job change were considered: changing organizations to advance, and relocating to advance. The first is what most of the executive women said they had to do. The second is important to increasing women's managerial advancement, more so than to men's (Brett, Stroh, and Reilly, 1992a).

Why is this topic important? Women should be able to advance to high levels in their organizations as much as men, and not have to leave to advance. If women have to change jobs more than men to advance, barriers to their managerial advancement are being masked. In addition, examining why women leave to advance can help organizations identify the factors to address to reduce women's turnover for advancement.

Unlike prior studies, this study assesses the relative importance of the three major explanations proposed for why women leave organizations (Brett and Stroh, 1994). No systematic study has been done of all explanations. Brett and Stroh (1994) proposed that women leave organizations because of structural and systemic discrimination embedded in organizational policies, practices, and culture. Second, they proposed that women leave for family reasons; for example, to stay home and take care of their families. Third, they proposed that women leave for better career opportunities in organizations that are friendlier to women. Past studies of women's and men's turnover (Brett and Stroh, 1994; Nicholson and West, 1988; Stroh and Reilly, 1997; Rosin and Korabik, 1990, 1992) have not examined these major explanations simultaneously. Greenhaus et al. (1997) found that women left public accounting because of work experiences and not family responsibilities, as did men, not helping to explain why the women left more than the men.

To examine the reasons for gender differences in job change, actual job change needs to be examined. Prior studies mostly examined intentions to leave (Burke and McKeen, 1996; Korabik and Rosin, 1995; McKeen and Burke, 1994; Miller and Wheeler, 1992; Rosin and Korabik, 1991, 1995; Stroh, Brett, and Reilly, 1996). But intent only explains about one-tenth to one quarter of actually leaving (Hom and Griffeth, 1995; Maertz and Campion, 1998). Future job change needs to be predicted, unlike the prior cross-sectional multivariate studies of actual job change (Rosin and Korabik, 1990, 1992), to allow stronger conclusions about why women leave to advance. Prior longitudinal studies of actual job change have not examined the relative importance of the several explanations for why women leave (Brett and Stroh, 1994; Nicholson and West, 1988; Stroh and Reilly, 1997). Prior studies used samples of middle and upper managers, executives and CEOs in quantitative (Brett and Stroh, 1994; Nicholson and West, 1988; Stroh and Reilly, 1997) and qualitative (Davies-Netzley, 1998; Riley and White, 1994) studies. This study surveys employees at chiefly low and middle levels at early and middle career stages to capture the reasons for job change to advance when it is happening, rather than from the recollections of those already advanced to high levels. The study also extends chiefly US evidence through use of a sample of Australian managers and professionals.

## ■ Why do women leave to advance? ■

The first question of interest in this study is: Do women change jobs to advance when they are in male-dominated environments? Brett and Stroh (1994) argued that women leave organizations because of structural and systemic discrimination embedded in organizational policies, practices, and culture. Such discrimination would result in male-dominated organizations, having mostly male managerial hierarchies and few women managers. Prior multivariate studies have not predicted women's turnover by male-dominated environments. The lack of investigation is despite male managerial hierarchies being related to women's intentions to leave (Burke and McKeen, 1996; Rosin and Korabik, 1991), and women executives' reports that they changed employers during their careers because they were excluded from the all-male networks needed to advance, and were dissimilar from male colleagues and peers, who felt uncomfortable with them and created obstacles for their advancement (Davies-Netzley, 1998;

Marshall, 1995; Riley and White, 1994). The present study therefore addresses an important gap in prior research.

Similarity-attraction theory (Byrne, 1971) helps explain why. According to the theory, those who make advancement decisions are attracted to and prefer individuals similar to themselves (Baron and Pfeffer, 1994). Women are an anomaly in male managerial hierarchies and therefore, according to the theory, would not be preferred or advanced like men. So women can reasonably expect that, to advance, they need to leave environments more friendly to men. Male-dominated situations are reflected not only in the lack of women managers but also is policies relevant to women's advancement, including equal employment opportunity (EEO). EEO should discourage similarity-attraction processes, encouraging women to stay to advance. Hence hypothesis 7.1 proposes:

*H7.1: Male-dominated environments (male hierarchy, not working with women managers, lack of use of EEO) will predict women changing organizations and relocating to advance more than men.*

Second, do women change jobs more than men to advance because they lack career advancement opportunities (Brett and Stroh, 1994)? Multivariate studies show that women managers and professionals intend to leave more than men because of perceived lack of advancement opportunities (Miller and Wheeler, 1992; Stroh et al., 1996; Stroh and Reilly, 1997). The advancement opportunities were in general, rather than in relation to opportunity structures. Baron, Davis-Blake, and Bielby (1986) argued that job ladders provide promotion paths that are more helpful to men than women. Advancement occurs in job ladders more when they are long with few jobs dead-ended at the top, and when selection practices are formal and open to all in the organization (Bielby et al., 1986). Men are likely to have longer, more formal and open ladders than women, and so advance more. Job ladders also arise more in managerial and production occupations than professional, technical, clerical, and sales and service occupations, because the former provide more incremental skill acquisition and internal promotions than the latter (Baron et al., 1986; Markham, Harlan, and Hackett, 1987). Women are more likely than men to be more in the latter occupations than the former. Hence, hypothesis 7.2 proposes:

*H7.2: Less favorable promotion ladders for advancement (shorter promotion ladders; informal, less open selection practices; lower occupation types) will predict women changing organizations and relocating to advance more than men.*

Third, are family circumstances the reason for gender differences in job change for advancement? Executive women say they did not leave, nor intend to leave, their organizations for family reasons, but their male CEOs thought they did (Davies-Netzley, 1998; Griffith, MacBride-King, and Townsend, 1997). Family circumstances need to be more comprehensively examined than previously. In some studies, women managers' and professionals' intentions to leave have not been found related to their being married, having children, being single or having dual-earner status any more than men's (Rosin and Korabik, 1995; Stroh et al., 1996). By contrast, Dalton, Hill, and Ramsay (1997) found that women accountants left their organizations for others more than men because of problems with work–family balance. Work interference in family life was important. Although prior evidence is limited and inconsistent, family roles with substantial responsibilities (marriage, a baby, teenage children) and work interference in non-work life may be leaving organizations in which family factors reduce their chance of advancement, and seeking others, in order to advance. hypothesis 7.3 proposes:

**H7.3: Family roles and responsibilities (marriage, child care) and work interference in non-work will predict women changing organizations to advance more than men.**

Relocation for work is usually a family decision. Role theory explains how women and men are socialized to view relocation for work differently (Coser, 1975; Markham, 1987). Markham (1987) explained how geographic mobility for work implies freedom from social control and a strong commitment to personal advancement. Women are socialized to view such mobility as inappropriate because it threatens male dominance and traditional family roles. Therefore, women are likely to suffer role conflict and social pressure when considering relocating for work, and should be more likely to relocate to advance when they are single rather than married.

On the other hand, relocating for work is consistent with men's socialized role as family provider. Men are expected to give higher priority to work obligations and lower priority to family than women (Markham, 1987). Yet men's relocation does seem to depend on their wife's employment, especially if she has a career. Bird and Bird (1985) found that, when the husband's income and provider role were the most important of the couple's, his job offer was the most related to any espoused future mobility. By contrast, the more the wife had a career, which was measured by her salary and employment status, the less likely her husband was found to have relocated (Bird and Bird, 1985; Rives and West, 1993). Reed and Reed (1993) found that male public servants in dual-career families relocated less than those in dual-earner families, but the latter did not relocate less than men in single-earner families. Therefore, when investigating relocation, the spouse's work as a career, and not just an income, needs to be assessed. Hence, hypotheses 7.4 and 7.5 test:

**H7.4: Women will relocate to advance more than men when single rather than married.**

**H7.5: Men who are primary providers (that is, single-earner couple) and who have spouses where work is less likely to be a career (that is, lower salaries and managerial levels) will relocate and change organizations to advance more than women.**

Finally, does the willingness to be mobile explain gender differences in job change for advancement? This is an individual difference related to whether people want to relocate or change organizations to advance. Men should need to change jobs less to advance than women, because they have fewer obstacles to doing so (for example, Schneer and Reitman, 1995). But women, because of the circumstances they face (for example, male managerial hierarchies), may have to change jobs to advance more than men, as argued by Nicholson and West (1988), and their willingness to do so may be especially important to that. Hence, hypothesis 7.6 proposes:

**H7.6: Willingness to relocate or to change organizations for advancement will predict women's relocation and organization change, respectively, more than men's.**

## ■ Method ■

### Respondents and data collection

**Data collection.** In order to survey employees where advancement was possible, respondents were sought at lower and middle hierarchical levels and in early and mid-career stages. Both the public and private sectors were chosen as they may vary in the conditions related to advancement (for example, EEO, Shenhav, 1992) and thus perhaps job change for advancement. The Australian Public Service (APS) provided the public-sector sample of full-time managers and administrators, professionals, and clerks. To obtain private-sector employees in comparable occupations to the APS, full-time white-collar employees were sampled from chiefly the finance, property, and business services industry (for example, banks). The sample surveyed in this study was asked to participate as part of a study into Australians' careers, and this study was part of that larger study.

Because about 25 percent of Australian managers and administrators are women (Australian Bureau of Statistics, 1996), a stratified sampling procedure was used within organizations to select men and women by their grade level for mailing. A total of 10,820 surveys were mailed overall by organizations to their staff. The Time 1 return rate, in prepaid envelopes, was 52 percent ($n = 5,627$; 2,614 women, 3,013 men). On the first mail-out, respondents could supply their names and addresses if they wished to participate in a longitudinal study. Data were collected twice more, each a year apart. At Time 1, 83 percent (4,670) volunteered for the longitudinal study. Of these, 323 persons were lost to the Time 2 mailing through incorrect addresses, ineligibility from having left employment permanently (for example, retired), or from having left for other reasons (for example, now unemployed, went part-time, maternity leave, started own business). The Time 2 response from the 4,347 able or eligible to participate was 79 percent (3,434): 1,593 women and 1,841 men. On the third mail-out, 123 respondents were lost for similar reasons to Time 2. The Time 3 response was 87 percent, resulting in 2,880 respondents.

Only the Time 1 and Time 3 data were used because a year (that is, by Time 2) gave too few job changers for analysis. By Time 2, 13 percent had changed organizations and 10 percent had relocated for advancement since Time 1. By Time 3, two years later, the figures were 16 percent and 20 percent respectively. As well, only supervisors, managers, and professionals were selected for this study, because they were most likely to be able to advance. These respondents comprised 73 percent of the 5,627 Time 1 respondents ($n = 4,112$) and 79 percent of the Time 3 respondents ($n = 2,266$). In addition, 55 individuals had to be excluded because they rated the number of times overall that they had changed organizations or relocated as lower at Time 3 than Time 1, reducing the Time 3 sample to 2,211 (1,020 women, 1,191 men). They did not differ on demographic characteristics from the rest of the sample.

*The sample.* In the final Time 1 sample (4,112), most respondents were from 25 to 44 years old; 60 percent were younger than 39. On average, they had worked in their organizations from five to ten years; 39 percent had fewer than five years and 25 percent had from five to ten years. They had on average worked full time from 10 to 15 years. About 70 percent had spouses of whom 23 percent were not employed outside the home (80 percent were wives). About 55 percent had children; of that total 19 percent had a child under 18 months (75 percent were men). In Australia, all organizations must offer 12 months unpaid maternity leave (and only five days unpaid paternity leave), and women may not work more than men when they have babies. More than two-thirds of the respondents were lower managers or below: subordinates (19 percent), first-line supervisors (30 percent), lower managers (19 percent), middle managers (21 percent), upper managers (7 percent), and executives (4 percent). About 60 percent were public servants or in the community sector. About 39 percent worked in organizations of more than 8,000 employees and 34 percent in organizations of fewer than 1,000.

*Non-response.* Chi-square tests of the Time 1 data showed that those who did not respond at Time 3 differed from those who did. The non-respondents, at Time 1, were younger, less educated, had fewer workforce years, were more likely single, lower in managerial level and occupational type, and were in the private more than public sector and in larger more than smaller organizations. The Australian Bureau of Statistics (1998) provides data that show that employees who change employers and relocate are somewhat younger, single, in lower occupation types, and with fewer years company tenure than others. Therefore, the characteristics of the non-respondents suggest that they could have changed jobs more than the respondents. This should result in the underestimation of the prediction of job change because possible job changers are lost to the sample. Gender was not related to non-response. So the results for gender are likely unaffected, and thus the testing of hypotheses unaffected.

Family variables may have caused women to drop out of the study. Hence, the link between family variables and non-response was examined. Chi-square tests of the Time 1 data showed that the number and age of children, presence of a baby, and the extent of financial responsibility for the family, child-minding ease, and dependent assistance (three single items) were not related either to women or men responding or not responding at Time 3. Both men and women were more likely not to respond than respond when single than married at Time 1. Overall, therefore, non-sresponse due to gender and family variables should not affect the testing of the hypotheses. I also assessed by analysis of variance if relocating versus not relocating, or changing organizations versus not changing organizations, was related to a change in marital status, the number or age of children, having a baby, or spouse employment status from Time 1 to 3. There were no significant effects.

## Measures

***Job change.*** The number of relocations was measured by asking respondents how many times overall they had relocated their residence geographically to advance to a higher-level position than their current one. Number of organizational changes was measured by asking how many times respondents had changed organizations to advance to a higher-level position than their current one. Responses for both items were from 1, never; to 5, four or more times. The single-item format and frequency format are similar to those used elsewhere (for example, Dougherty, Dreher, and Whitely, 1993; Stroh, Brett, and Reilly, 1992). The items were reliable (see table 7.1 for test-retest correlations). The Time 1 scores were correlated with Time 3 scores: 0.87 for relocation, 0.77 for organization change.

***Male dominance.*** Two items examined the dominance by men of management roles. They were from Tharenou, Latimer, and Conroy (1994) who provided the items and evidence for their construct validity and discriminant validity. Male hierarchy was measured by the proportion of men in the managerial hierarchy in the respondent's local organization (1, all women; 2, a majority of women and a minority of men; 3, about 50 percent women and 50 percent men; 4, a majority of men and a minority of women; and 5, all men). Presence of women managers was assessed by the length of time the respondent had worked closely with a woman manager in their organization (from 1, not at all; to 5, 4 or more years).

***Equal employment opportunity.*** A single item asked the length of time the organization had had an EEO policy, from 1, does not have one; to 5, 11 or more years.

***Length of promotion ladders.*** Based on Baron et al. (1986), length of promotion ladder was the number of positions available to the respondent for promotion within their organizations. It was a distinct factor from factor analysis of structure items in another sample (Tharenou et al., 1994). The factor also emerged as a distinct factor in analyses of the Times 1, 2 and 3 data here, supporting construct validity. The five, 7-point items averaged were the number of positions above the respondent that they could apply/be selected for promotion in the same, or in a different, occupational category (two items); the number of broad levels of positions in their organization, or above them, for which they could eventually apply for promotion (two items); and organization size. The alphas at Times 1, 2, and 3 of 0.73, 0.74, and 0.73 indicated reliable scores.

***Selection practices.*** Based on Baron et al. (1986), two items measured open and formal selection practices linked to promotion ladders. The items assessed the extent that selection procedures were based on informal methods (for example, invitations to take up positions; reversed) and open (self-nomination, job posting, vacancy gazetting) rather than secret. Responses were from 1, strongly disagree; to 7, strongly agree.

**Occupation type.**  Occupation type averaged the codes for both the respondents' positions and occupations using the Australian Standard Classification of Occupations' single-digit codes (Department of Employment and Industrial Relations, 1987): 1, managers and administrators; 2, professionals; 3, paraprofessionals; 4, tradespersons; 5, clerks; 6, sales or personal service; 7, plant or machine operators or drivers; and 8, laborers or related workers. The single-digit codes are numerically graduated from high (1) to low (8) based on the skill requirements of occupations (from education, on-the-job experience, and training). The alpha coefficients at Times 1, 2, and 3 were 0.88, 0.90, and 0.78, indicating reliable scores.

**Marital status.**  Marital status was coded as 1, spouse (married, cohabiting); and 2, no spouse (single, separated, widowed, divorced).

**Child care.**  Number of children was measured from 1, none; to 7, six or more. Baby was assessed as whether the respondent's youngest child was from less than six months (coded 1) to having no child under 18 months (coded 4). Respondents were asked if they had (coded 2) or did not have (coded 1) teenage children.

**Work interference in nonwork.**  The extent to which work interfered with non-work life was Kopelman, Greenhaus, and Connoly's (1983) 4, 5-point item scale, whose alpha was 0.81 (Gutek, Searle, and Klepa, 1991). The alphas at Times 1, 2, and 3 were 0.75, 0.72, and 0.72. An example item is, "My work takes up time that I'd like to spend with family/friends."

**Single- versus dual-earner status.**  The item asked if the respondent's spouse worked currently full time (1), part-time (2), or was not employed (3) (that is, single-earner status).

**Spouse career.**  The extent to which the spouse's work was a career was measured, as previously (for example, Bird and Bird, 1985), by spouse salary (from 1, under $15,000 Australian to 10, over $95,000), and managerial level (from 1, subordinates to 8, CEOs).

**Mobility attitudes.**  Two items asked how willing respondents were to relocate, or to change organizations, for a higher-level position than their current one, from 1, very unwilling; to 5, very willing. The format is similar to other measures of willingness (for example, Baker, Markham, Bonjean, and Corder, 1988; Markham, 1987). Some stability but also change was shown by the test-retest stabilities (willingness to relocate, 0.61; to change organizations, 0.53).

**Gender.**  Gender was coded 1, men; and 2, women.

**Control variables.**  To ensure men and women were comparable, control variables were partialed in the multivariate analysis that were related to employees' job change

(Australian Bureau of Statistics, 1998). The controls were: age (from 1, less than 19; to 11, over 65), education level (from 1, some secondary school; to 11, doctorate), years of organization tenure (1, up to five years; to 8, 35 or greater years), managerial level (1, subordinate; to 8, CEO), location (1, regional; 2, urban), and employment sector (1, public; 2, private). Employment disruption averaged standardized scores for two items measuring continuity of full-time work (1, yes; 2, no) and years of breaks (from 1, none; to 5, 10 or more years) since full-time education (Tharenou, 1999). The measure emerged as a distinct factor in factor analyses. The alphas at Times 1, 2, and 3 of 0.84, 0.83 and 0.82 indicated reliable scores.

# ■ Results ■

Table 7.1 gives the means and standard deviations for the men and women, the correlations between all variables for the total sample, and test-retest correlations (Time 1 and 3). Men and women significantly differed (tested by $t$-tests) on the control variables. Therefore the control variables were entered as Step 1 in analyses.

Moderated hierarchical regression analysis was used to test Hypotheses 1 to 5. The dependent variables were Time 3 relocation or changing organizations for advancement. Step 1 entered the Time 1 measures of relocation and organization change for advancement in order to predict only their change from Time 1 to Time 3. Step 2 entered the control variables to partial out their effects. Then the main effects were entered, in blocks 3 to 6, and gender in the seventh step. The eighth block entered the interactions between each of the main effect variables in Steps 3 to 6. In order to allow the largest sample to be retained each time when testing the family variables, four different equations were repeated. Always included in the family variable sets were the number of children and work interference in non-work life. The first set also included marital status (table 7.2), the second set also included single-versus dual-earner status (table 7.3), the third set also included spouse salary and managerial level (table 7.4), and, the fourth set also included the presence of a baby and teenagers. The regressions were also run separately for men and women to help interpret the significant two-way interactions between gender and the main effects.

Pairwise deletion was used for missing data. Potential violations of assumptions underlying regression analysis, including multivariate multicollinearity, were checked and none found. Because multiple tests were being conducted, I reduced the significance level to $p < 0.01$ to reduce experiment-wide error and to have significant effects account for a greater proportion of variance. In order to ensure that the employment sector did not affect the results found, I also entered three-way interactions with sector when significant two-way interactions arose. Only one test was significant. In addition, willingness to relocate for advancement or change organizations for advancement could have been a mediator of the effects of the situational variables on actual job change, so rendering the hierarchical regressions mis-specified. A mediator needs to have significant relationships with the independent variables (and the dependent variable). The correlations of willingness with the independent variables (for example, 0.00 to 0.15, table 7.1) show that willingness could not be a mediator with these data.

Table 7.2 provides the results for the total sample. In Step 1, Time 1 relocation and organization change strongly predicted their Time 3 counterparts, in which they were

**Table 7.1**　Means, standard deviations, test-retest correlations, and intercorrelations for all variables

| Variables | Women Mean | Women SD | Men Mean | Men SD | $r_{13}$ | 1 | 2 | 3 | 4 | 5 | 6 | 7 | 8 | 9 |
|---|---|---|---|---|---|---|---|---|---|---|---|---|---|---|
| 1. Relocated Time 3 | 1.65 | 1.03 | 2.37 | 1.51 | — | | | | | | | | | |
| 2. Changed Time 3 | 2.23 | 1.40 | 2.02 | 1.33 | — | 14 | | | | | | | | |
| 3. Relocated Time 1 | 1.64 | 1.04 | 2.34 | 1.54 | 87 | 87 | 11 | | | | | | | |
| 4. Changed Time 1 | 1.99 | 1.31 | 1.88 | 1.27 | 77 | 13 | 77 | 11 | | | | | | |
| 5. Location | 1.89 | 0.31 | 1.84 | 0.36 | 82 | −26 | 12 | −26 | 10 | | | | | |
| 6. Age | 4.52 | 1.73 | 4.97 | 1.79 | 99 | 20 | 19 | 22 | 24 | −03 | | | | |
| 7. Years organization | 1.90 | 1.09 | 2.76 | 1.82 | 87 | 19 | −30 | 24 | −29 | −14 | 44 | | | |
| 8. Disruption | 0.31 | 1.07 | −0.24 | 0.71 | 78 | −17 | 06 | −16 | 09 | 03 | 19 | −23 | | |
| 9. Education | 5.22 | 2.46 | 4.69 | 2.37 | 96 | −08 | 18 | −09 | 21 | 19 | −05 | −34 | 05 | |
| 10. Male hierarchy | 3.69 | 0.83 | 3.89 | 0.77 | 59 | 10 | −01 | 09 | −03 | −03 | −05 | 09 | −15 | 00 |
| 11. Woman manager | 2.31 | 1.30 | 2.35 | 1.40 | 61 | −11 | −01 | −11 | 05 | 09 | 12 | 02 | 07 | 05 |
| 12. EEO | 4.18 | 1.28 | 4.33 | 1.32 | 52 | −02 | −18 | −01 | −18 | −03 | −03 | 12 | −02 | −10 |
| 13. Sector | 1.27 | 0.44 | 1.47 | 0.50 | 89 | 29 | −07 | 28 | −14 | −16 | −06 | 20 | −24 | −21 |
| 14. Spouse | 1.36 | 0.48 | 1.25 | 0.44 | 79 | −09 | −06 | −12 | −05 | 09 | −26 | −18 | −02 | 08 |
| 15. Children | 1.58 | 0.92 | 2.13 | 1.23 | 86 | 11 | 04 | 15 | 08 | −08 | 31 | 22 | 05 | −06 |
| 16. No baby | 3.91 | 0.43 | 3.75 | 0.72 | 56 | −02 | 03 | −05 | 02 | 08 | 07 | −00 | 05 | 02 |
| 17. Single earner | 1.18 | 0.52 | 1.96 | 0.85 | 73 | 23 | −08 | 28 | −05 | −14 | 17 | 26 | −16 | −10 |
| 18. Work interferes | 3.04 | 0.84 | 3.03 | 0.84 | 55 | 08 | 07 | 14 | 05 | −06 | 06 | 08 | −00 | 01 |
| 19. Teenagers | 1.17 | 0.38 | 1.27 | 0.44 | 76 | 13 | 05 | 15 | 09 | −03 | 36 | 21 | 08 | −06 |
| 20. Spouse salary | 3.94 | 1.80 | 2.36 | 1.49 | 76 | −19 | 18 | −19 | 14 | 18 | −03 | −25 | 19 | 24 |
| 21. Spouse level | 3.05 | 1.98 | 1.98 | 1.49 | 68 | −10 | 18 | −07 | 17 | 12 | 09 | −13 | 16 | 17 |
| 22. Managerial level | 2.73 | 1.45 | 2.94 | 1.53 | 76 | 17 | 24 | 17 | 27 | −00 | 37 | 17 | −06 | 07 |
| 23. Occupation type | 2.48 | 1.37 | 2.44 | 1.43 | 51 | 01 | −20 | −00 | −22 | −12 | −22 | 01 | −04 | −27 |
| 24. Length ladder | 3.94 | 1.36 | 4.23 | 1.43 | 66 | 04 | −21 | 07 | −22 | −07 | −16 | 17 | −06 | −13 |
| 25. Formal selection | 5.49 | 1.65 | 5.31 | 1.77 | 61 | −04 | −15 | −03 | −14 | −03 | 03 | 10 | 02 | −09 |
| 26. Open selection | 5.29 | 1.92 | 4.58 | 2.28 | 71 | −30 | −12 | −29 | 21 | 17 | 06 | −29 | 22 | 22 |
| 27. Will relocate | 2.48 | 1.30 | 2.80 | 1.37 | 61 | 27 | −00 | 24 | −01 | −11 | −20 | −08 | −11 | 03 |
| 28. Will change | 3.27 | 1.24 | 3.14 | 1.24 | 53 | −06 | 32 | −08 | 29 | 13 | −12 | −35 | 06 | 23 |
| 29. Gender | 1.00 | 0.50 | 2.00 | 0.50 | 1.00 | −26 | 08 | −25 | 04 | 07 | −13 | −26 | 30 | 11 |

*Decimal points have been omitted from correlations. For the total sample (n = 2,211), correlations greater than 0.04 are significant at p < 0.05, at 0.05 are significant at p < 0.01, and at 0.07 are significant at p < 0.001. EEO = equal employment opportunity. For correlations with sample with spouses, n = 1,623. For correlations with sample with employed spouses, n = 1,480. t-tests showed significant gender differences on all variables but woman manager, work interferes, and occupation type. Disruption averaged standardized scores.*

included. Of the 74.9 percent of the variance explained in Time 3 relocation by the predictor set, including both Time 1 relocation and organization changes, 74.8 percent was by Time relocation. Of the 59.1 percent of the variance explained in Time 3 organization change by the predictor set, including both Time 1 measures, 58.0 percent was predicted by Time 1 organization change. So Time 3 relocation was not predicted by Time 1 organizational change, nor Time 3 organizational change by Time 1 relocation. The measures were therefore separate and non-overlapping, supporting the interpretation that they measure only their specific constructs.

As shown in tables 7.2 to 7.4, the interactions with gender (Step 8) added a significant amount (about 1 percent) to the variance predicted in change in relocation and organization change from Time 1 to 3 by Steps 1 to 7. The variance added was low. This was because only the change in relocation and organizational change was predicted

| | | | | | | | | | Correlations | | | | | | | | | | |
|---|---|---|---|---|---|---|---|---|---|---|---|---|---|---|---|---|---|---|---|
| 10 | 11 | 12 | 13 | 14 | 15 | 16 | 17 | 18 | 19 | 20 | 21 | 22 | 23 | 24 | 25 | 26 | 27 | 28 | 29 |
| −36 | | | | | | | | | | | | | | | | | | | |
| −05 | 07 | | | | | | | | | | | | | | | | | | |
| 21 | −29 | −08 | | | | | | | | | | | | | | | | | |
| −02 | −02 | 01 | −06 | | | | | | | | | | | | | | | | |
| 04 | 01 | −00 | 04 | −39 | | | | | | | | | | | | | | | |
| −03 | 01 | −00 | −04 | 18 | −23 | | | | | | | | | | | | | | |
| 08 | −02 | 03 | 22 | −03 | 34 | −24 | | | | | | | | | | | | | |
| 04 | −03 | −11 | 19 | −11 | 12 | −03 | 09 | | | | | | | | | | | | |
| 02 | 00 | 00 | 00 | −21 | 56 | 10 | 06 | 07 | | | | | | | | | | | |
| −07 | 03 | −06 | −15 | 06 | −22 | 12 | −56 | −01 | −06 | | | | | | | | | | |
| −09 | 07 | −08 | −07 | 01 | −07 | 08 | −24 | 02 | −03 | 56 | | | | | | | | | |
| −03 | 13 | −12 | 09 | −17 | 19 | −01 | 08 | 16 | 18 | 05 | 21 | | | | | | | | |
| 05 | −16 | 08 | 24 | 10 | −14 | 01 | −05 | −04 | −11 | −09 | −10 | −30 | | | | | | | |
| 03 | 02 | 24 | −07 | 03 | −01 | −02 | 05 | −04 | −04 | −10 | −12 | −17 | 16 | | | | | | |
| −06 | 06 | 13 | −26 | −01 | 00 | 00 | −04 | −11 | 02 | −04 | −07 | −02 | 05 | 26 | | | | | |
| −20 | 27 | 04 | −57 | 05 | −04 | 04 | −19 | −20 | −01 | 15 | 10 | 03 | −31 | −10 | 14 | | | | |
| 08 | −09 | −00 | 14 | 13 | −09 | 03 | 14 | 00 | −11 | −10 | −05 | 01 | 05 | 11 | −04 | −25 | | | |
| 00 | −01 | −11 | −15 | 11 | −08 | 01 | −10 | −01 | −05 | 11 | 10 | 01 | −07 | −08 | −06 | −14 | 25 | | |
| −13 | −01 | −06 | −21 | 12 | −24 | 13 | −46 | 01 | −12 | 43 | 29 | −07 | 01 | −10 | −10 | 14 | −12 | 05 | — |

(the stabilities were partialed) and relocation and organization change were initially low-frequency behaviors.

As shown in table 7.2, not supporting Hypothesis 7.1, no significant interactions arose between male hierarchy and gender. Supporting Hypothesis 7.1, not working with a woman manager predicted women relocating and changing organizations to advance two years later more than men; for men, having worked with a woman manager predicted their relocating. Supporting Hypothesis 1, the less time their organization had an EEO policy, the more women changed organizations to advance two years later than men. As shown by the only significant three-way interaction with employment sector ($B = 0.04$, $p = 0.003$), this was more in the private than public sector. Overall, hypothesis 7.1 gained partial support.

Hypothesis 7.2 gained little support for advancement opportunities. Gender did not significantly interact with the length of promotion ladders or open selection practices. The significant interactions found differed for the two types of job change. Supporting hypothesis 2 (table 7.2), women in organizations with more informal than formal selection methods changed organizations two years later than men, and women in lower- rather than higher-level occupations relocated more two years later than men.

**Table 7.2** Regression analysis predicting Time 3 relocation and organizational change from Time 1 variables for total sample

| Step Time 1 variables | Relocation | | | Changing organizations | | | |
|---|---|---|---|---|---|---|---|
| | $R^2$ | $\Delta R^2$ | B | $R^2$ | $\Delta R^2$ | B | df |
| 1. Job change | 0.749 | 0.749** | | 0.591 | 0.591** | | 2,2105 |
| 2. Controls | 0.756 | 0.007** | | 0.608 | 0.018** | | 7,2098 |
| 3. Mobility attitudes | 0.761 | 0.005** | | 0.618 | 0.010** | | 2,2096 |
| 4. Family | 0.764 | 0.003** | | 0.620 | 0.002* | | 3,2093 |
| 5. Advancement | 0.766 | 0.002* | | 0.624 | 0.004** | | 4,2089 |
| 6. Male dominated | 0.766 | 0.000 | | 0.626 | 0.002 | | 3,2086 |
| 7. Gender | 0.768 | 0.002** | −0.04** | 0.628 | 0.002** | 0.07** | 1,2085 |
| 8. Interactions with gender | 0.775 | 0.008** | | 0.642 | 0.014** | | 12,2073 |
| Willing relocate x gender | | | 0.03* | | | 0.03 | |
| Willing change x gender | | | −0.02 | | | 0.04* | |
| Marital status x gender | | | 0.04* | | | −0.02 | |
| Children x gender | | | 0.01 | | | 0.04 | |
| Work interferes x gender | | | 0.02 | | | 0.04* | |
| Occupation x gender | | | 0.03* | | | −0.01 | |
| Length ladder x gender | | | −0.02 | | | 0.01 | |
| Formal selection x gender | | | 0.01 | | | −0.05** | |
| Open selection x gender | | | −0.01 | | | −0.01 | |
| Male hierarchy x gender | | | −0.02 | | | −0.02 | |
| Woman manager x gender | | | −0.05** | | | −0.05** | |
| EEO x gender | | | −0.01 | | | −0.04* | |

EEO = equal employment opportunity; * $p < 0.01$; ** $p < 0.001$.

**Table 7.3** Regression analysis predicting Time 3 relocation and organizational change from Time 1 variables for respondents with spouses

| Step 3 Time 1 variables | Relocation | | | Changing organizations | | | |
|---|---|---|---|---|---|---|---|
| | $R^2$ | $\Delta R^2$ | B | $R^2$ | $\Delta R^2$ | B | df |
| 1. Job change | 0.749 | 0.749** | | 0.591 | 0.591** | | 2,1620 |
| 2. Controls | 0.756 | 0.007** | | 0.608 | 0.018** | | 7,1613 |
| 3. Mobility attitudes | 0.761 | 0.005** | | 0.618 | 0.010** | | 2,1611 |
| 4. Family | 0.764 | 0.004** | | 0.621 | 0.002 | | 3,1608 |
| 5. Advancement | 0.766 | 0.002 | | 0.625 | 0.004* | | 4,1604 |
| 6. Male dominated | 0.766 | 0.000 | | 0.626 | 0.001 | | 3,1601 |
| 7. Gender | 0.769 | 0.002** | −0.05* | 0.627 | 0.001 | 0.04 | 1,1600 |
| 8. Interactions with gender | 0.775 | 0.007** | | 0.642 | 0.014** | | 12,1588 |
| Willing relocate x gender | | | 0.04* | | | 0.03 | |
| Willing change x gender | | | −0.01 | | | 0.04* | |
| Children x gender | | | 0.01* | | | 0.04 | |
| Single-earner x gender | | | 0.01 | | | 0.04 | |
| Work interferes x gender | | | 0.02 | | | 0.04* | |
| Occupation x gender | | | 0.03* | | | −0.01 | |
| Length ladder x gender | | | −0.02 | | | 0.00 | |
| Formal selection x gender | | | 0.01 | | | −0.05* | |
| Open selection x gender | | | −0.01 | | | −0.01 | |
| Male hierarchy x gender | | | −0.02 | | | −0.02 | |
| Woman manager x gender | | | −0.05** | | | −0.04* | |
| EEO x gender | | | −0.01 | | | −0.04* | |

EEO = equal employment opportunity; * $p < 0.01$, ** $p < 0.001$.

**Table 7.4** Overall equation predicting Time 3 relocation and organizational change from Time 1 variables for respondents with employed spouses

| Step | Relocation | | | Changing organizations | | | |
|---|---|---|---|---|---|---|---|
| Time 1 variables | $R^2$ | $\Delta R^2$ | B | $R^2$ | $\Delta R^2$ | B | df |
| 1. Job change | 0.749 | 0.749** | | 0.591 | 0.591** | | 2,1477 |
| 2. Controls | 0.756 | 0.007** | | 0.608 | 0.018** | | 7,1471 |
| 3. Mobility attitudes | 0.761 | 0.005** | | 0.618 | 0.010** | | 2,1469 |
| 4. Family | 0.766 | 0.005** | | 0.623 | 0.005** | | 4,1466 |
| 5. Advancement | 0.768 | 0.002 | | 0.627 | 0.004* | | 4,1462 |
| 6. Male dominated | 0.768 | 0.000 | | 0.628 | 0.001 | | 3,1459 |
| 7. Gender | 0.769 | 0.001 | −0.03 | 0.629 | 0.001 | 0.05* | 1,1458 |
| 8. Interactions with gender | 0.777 | 0.008** | | 0.642 | 0.013** | | 13,1445 |
| Willing relocate x gender | | | 0.03** | | | 0.03 | |
| Willing change x gender | | | −0.01 | | | 0.04* | |
| Children x gender | | | −0.01 | | | 0.03 | |
| Spouse salary x gender | | | −0.05** | | | −0.02 | |
| Spouse level x gender | | | 0.01 | | | 0.02 | |
| Work interferes x gender | | | 0.02 | | | 0.04 | |
| Occupation x gender | | | 0.03 | | | 0.01 | |
| Length ladder x gender | | | −0.02 | | | −0.01 | |
| Formal selection x gender | | | 0.00 | | | −0.05* | |
| Open selection x gender | | | −0.01 | | | −0.01 | |
| Male hierarchy x gender | | | −0.02 | | | −0.02 | |
| Woman manager x gender | | | −0.05** | | | −0.04* | |
| EEO x gender | | | −0.02 | | | −0.04* | |

*EEO = equal employment opportunity;* * $p < 0.01$, ** $p < 0.001$.

Overall, hypothesis 3 for family variables gained little support. As shown in table 7.2, not supporting Hypothesis 3, women did not change organizations more when they had more family roles and responsibilities – as indicated by the non-significant interactions of gender with marital status and number of children. When children's age (having a baby, teenage children) was entered in the family set, there were no significant interactions with gender. However, supporting Hypothesis 3, work interference in non-work life predicted women changing organizations two years later more than men.

Hypothesis 7.4 was supported. Single as opposed to married women relocated more than men two years later (table 7.2).

Hypothesis 5 for spouse employment gained little support. Table 7.3 provides the regression results when single- versus dual-earner status was entered in the family variable set, reducing the sample to couples. As shown, not supporting hypothesis 5, being a single-earner rather than dual-earner family did not predict men relocating more than women. Table 7.4 provides the regression results in which the family variable set included spouse salary and managerial level, reducing the sample to those with employed spouses. Supporting Hypothesis 7.5, women whose spouses had higher salaries relocated less than two years later whereas men whose spouses had lower salaries relocated more. However, gender did not interact with spouse managerial level. Therefore, overall, little support arose for hypothesis 7.5. Men did not relocate more than women when they were the primary providers or their spouses did not have a career as indicated by their managerial level, but did relocate more when their spouses had lower salaries.

Supporting hypothesis 7.6 (table 7.2), women who were willing to relocate or change organizations to advance relocated and changed organizations more two years later than men.

## ■ Discussion ■

The aim of this study was to examine the relative importance of explanations for why women change jobs to advance. The results suggest that women are likely to change jobs more than men to advance when they are in environments less friendly to women and when they are willing to be more mobile. Most support arises for Brett and Stroh's (1994) explanation of systemic factors acting to cause women to leave. Women change jobs to advance more than men when they do not work with women managers and when they work in environments that do not use EEO or have had EEO fewer years. In addition, extending the explanations offered by Brett and Stroh (1994), women who are more willing to relocate or change organizations to advance do so more than men, suggesting that women may need to leave to advance more than men. Family factors and advancement opportunities are not as explanatory for this sample as work factors and attitudes for why women change jobs more than men to advance, consistent with Greenhaus et al.'s (1997) results. The results of this study extend the recollections of women CEOs about why they needed to leave organizations in early and mid career to advance (Davies-Netzley, 1998; Riley and White, 1994) to the decisions actually being made in early and mid career by more junior employees.

Admittedly, the amount of explanation by gender-linked effects in this study is very low. However, scholars show that gender-linked effects of 1 or 2 percent have substantial effects in practice on women (Brett et al., 1992a; Haberfeld, 1992; Stroh et al., 1992). Even after taking into account the substantial explanation by respondents' prior job changes and the explanations due to their age, education, tenure, managerial level, location, sector, and employment disruption, women still changed jobs to advance for different reasons than men. The interactions suggest that aspects of the work environment are explanatory.

This study is the first to examine if male-dominated environments are an explanation for women changing jobs to advance. The key variable for the women of this sample is working with women managers, not the proportion of men in the hierarchy, which may be more distant to women than the managers with whom they work closely. When women do not work with women managers, they likely expect that they will not advance as much as men. So, women are more likely to leave to advance than men. In this study, the women also change organizations to advance more than men when EEO policy is not used or has operated for less time in the organization. Perhaps those organizations are less equity conscious in selection than others, enabling similarity-attraction processes and homosocial reproduction to operate. However, other explanations than similarity-attraction theory may also explain the results. When women have close ties with women managers, scholars suggest that they gain advice and encouragement from role models facing similar obstacles to themselves, and that this advice and encouragement help them advance (Davies-Netzley, 1998; Ibarra, 1997; Riley and White, 1994; Tharenou, 1995). When women do not work with women managers they may lack advice and encouragement, perhaps resulting in their leaving to advance.

Women's attitudes to mobility also help explain their leaving to advance. Women's willingness to relocate or change organizations to advance predicts their leaving two years later more than men's. This is surprising because women are less willing to relocate than men (table 7.1). Women appear to be choosing to change jobs more than men, as Nicholson and West (1988) explained. Men do not need to select to be mobile as much as women because their environments are "male friendly." So men can stay, unlike women who have more obstacles and need to leave to get ahead (Nicholson and West, 1988). As found by Brett et al. (1992a), women appear to be using a free-agency career pattern more than men.

Supporting women having more obstacles to advancement than men, women leave more than men to advance when their organizations have more informal than formal selection practices and when they are in lower occupation types. Informal selection practices may allow gender discrimination to take place. Heilman (1997) argued, in sex-role stereotyping theory, that under more unstructured (for example, informal selection practices) than structured (for example, formal selection practices) decision-making conditions, gender stereotypes arise more strongly that women do not fit management roles. So women may leave to advance more when their organizations have informal selection practices.

Despite the views of male CEOs (Davies-Netzley, 1997; Griffith et al., 1997), for these respondents, women's family roles and responsibilities are not as important as their work experiences and attitudes to their changing jobs to advance. The result is consistent with other studies of job change, although they did not predict the relative importance of family factors for women's actual job change for advancement (Griffith et al., 1997; Nicholson and West, 1988; Rosin and Korabik, 1995; Stroh et al., 1996). Overall, the women in this sample do not change organizations to advance because of family responsibilities. However, only a third of the women were mothers and only 5 percent had babies. Hence, the impact of family responsibilities may be underestimated. Women with very young children are likely to have dropped out of the workforce already to care for children, although they did not drop out of this sample more than others. Rather than actual roles and responsibilities, it is problems arising with work–family balance, as found (Dalton et al., 1997) and proposed (Brett and Stroh, 1994) that predict women changing organizations to advance more than men. When work interferes in non-work life, the employing organizations may not provide practices that allow for work–family balance, and this is may interfere with advancement. So women leave.

Unexpectedly, few gender differences arose in the factors predicting relocation. The women of this sample relocate more than men when single than married, consistent with role theory (Markham, 1987). Single women have less pressure to conform to gender roles by putting family before career than married women, and do not have spouses to consider when making relocation decisions. So less role conflict and social pressure arises for single than married women.

Men's relocations appear not to be explained by their wives' employment, but by how much their wives earn. The men do not relocate more when they are the single family provider than when they are dual earners, suggesting men's relocation is not linked to their wives being employed *per se*. Yet relocation appears to be a joint decision for the family. The men of this sample relocate more when their spouses have lower salaries, consistent with the view that relocation is more likely when wives' employment is less likely to constitute a career (Bird and Bird, 1985; Reed and Reed, 1993). The results are also consistent with family power theory (Brett et al., 1992a). The spouse with low salary has the least power to affect relocation decisions; so when men have spouses with lower salaries, men relocate more. Also supporting family power theory, the women of this sample relocate less than men when their spouses have higher salaries. Presumably, the higher the husband's income, the more power he has over relocation decisions of the family caused by his wife's work.

## ■ Limitations and future research ■

A major limitation of the way this study was conducted is that the information was self-report. The measures are therefore subjective and subject to inaccuracies, especially when measuring the environment. The measures of job change may not have been as accurate as objectively gathered data. Although respondents were asked for the number of times they relocated or changed organizations for advancement, they may have included times they did so for other reasons. The study did not measure both job changes for advancement and job changes not for advancement (for example, spouse relocation, unemployment). It may be that the gender differences found in the explanations for job change for advancement may have happened in general for any type of job change. Hence, future research needs to specifically include items that separate out relocation and organization change for advancement from job change for other reasons.

From these results, it is also obvious that other reasons exist for gender differences in job change than those examined here. In particular, future research needs to examine employer choices. Employers appear to choose women to relocate to advance less than men (Brett and Stroh, 1999; Brett, Stroh, and Reilly, 1992b), as found for married women (Eby, Allen, and Douthitt, 1999). Men may be chosen for promotions that require relocation. Moreover, the processes by which gender differences in job change arise were not examined in this study. Although the willingness to change jobs appears not to be a mediator, other mediators may operate. For example, does the presence of women managers result in women gaining advice and encouragement that then lead to their staying, unlike men? Do informal selection methods lead to increased bias against women's fit to management roles which then leads to their leaving, unlike men?

A limitation of this study was that women are presumed to be leaving to escape organizations because of a lack of women managers, lack of use of EEO, use of informal selection practices, and problems with work interference in family. Future research needs to examine if women do actually leave to go to organizations or locations that are more women friendly (for example, more women managers, use of EEO, formal selection practices, practices to reduce work interference in non-work) than those they are in?

## Conclusions

The results of this study have several practical implications for helping organizations reduce women leaving to advance more than men. Organizations need to ensure women work with women managers, and use, and persist with, EEO policies and practices. If women are not to leave to advance, organizations need to ensure that selection methods for advancement are formal so that the bias that may arise in informal practices is reduced. To help women advance, organizations need to institute practices to help deal with work interference in non-work life (for example, flexible work arrangements, leave, work hours) or women will leave for other organizations to advance. Organizations also need to take note of the frequency of women's prior job changes and take note of their expressions of willingness to change jobs if they are to retain women managers and professionals. Women who have previously changed jobs are likely do so again, and women's expressions of willingness to change jobs are likely to bear fruit in their actually changing jobs, made worse if the obstacles in women's work environments are not ameliorated.

### REFERENCES

Australian Bureau of Statistics (1996): *Labour force Australia.* (Cat. No. 6203.0), Canberra: Australian Government Publishing Service.

Australian Bureau of Statistics (1998): *Labour mobility.* (Cat. No. 6209.0), Canberra: Australian Government Publishing Service.

Baker, P. M., Markham, W. T., Bonjean, C. M., and Corder, J. (1988): Promotion interest and willingness to sacrifice for promotion in a government agency. *The Journal of Applied Behavioral Science,* 24, 61–80.

Baron, J. N., Davis-Blake, A., and Bielby, W. T. (1986): The structure of opportunity. *Administrative Science Quarterly,* 31, 248–73.

Baron, J. N. and Pfeffer, J. (1994): The social psychology of organizations and inequality. *Social Psychology Quarterly,* 57, 190–209.

Bird, G. A. and Bird, G. W. (1985): Determinants of mobility in two-earner families: Does the wife's income count? *Journal of Marriage and the Family,* 147, 753–8.

Brett, J. M. and Stroh, L. K. (1994): Turnover of female managers. In M. J. Davidson and R. Burke (eds), *Women in management,* London: Paul Chapman Publishing.

Brett, J. M. and Stroh, L. K. (1999): How far have we come and what needs to be done as we approach 2000? *Journal of Management Inquiry,* 8, 392–8.

Brett, J. M., Stroh, L. K., and Reilly, A. H. (1992a): Job transfer. In C. L. Cooper and I. T. Robertson (eds), *International Review of Industrial and Organizational Psychology,* New York: Wiley.

Brett, J. M., Stroh, L. K., and Reilly, A. H. (1992b): What is it like being a dual career manager in the 1990s? In S. Zedeck (ed.), *Work, families and organizations,* San Francisco: Jossey-Bass.

Burke, R. J. and McKeen, C. A. (1996): Do women at the top make a difference? *Human Relations,* 49, 1093–104.

Buttner, E. H. and Moore, D. P. (1997): Women's organizational exodus to entrepreneurship. *Journal of Small Business Management,* 38, 34–46.

Byrne, D. (1971): *The attraction paradigm.* New York: Academic Press.

Caudron, S. (1998): Fleeing corporate America for more meaningful jobs. *Workforce,* 77, 10, 23–6.

Coser, R. L. (1975): Stay home with little sheba. *Social Problems,* 22, 470–80.

Dalton, D. R., Hill, J. W., and Ramsay, R. J. (1997): Women as managers and partners. *Auditing,* 16, 1, 29–50.

Davies-Netzley, S. A. (1998): Women above the glass ceiling. *Gender and Society*, 12, 339–55.

Department of Employment and Industrial Relations (1987): *Australian standard classification of occupations*. Canberra: Australian Government Publishing Service.

Dougherty, T. W., Dreher, G. F., and Whitely, W. (1993): The MBA as careerist: An analysis of early career job change. *Journal of Management*, 19, 535–48.

Eby, L. T., Allen, T. D., and Douthitt, S. S. (1999): The role of nonperformance factors on job-related relocation opportunities: A field study and laboratory experiment. *Organizational Behavior and Human Decision Processes*, 79, 29–55.

Greenhaus, J. H., Collins, K. M., Singh, R., and Parasuraman, S. (1997): Work and family influences on departure from public accounting. *Journal of Vocational Behavior*, 50, 249–70.

Griffith, P. G., MacBride-King, J. L., and Townsend, B. (1997): *Closing the gap*. Canada: The Conference Board of Canada and Catalyst.

Gutek, B. A., Searle, S., and Klepa, L. (1991): Rational versus gender-role work–family conflict. *Journal of Applied Psychology*, 76, 560–8.

Haberfeld, Y. (1992): Employment discrimination: An organizational model. *Academy of Management Journal*, 35, 161–80.

Heilman, M. E. (1997): Sex discrimination and the affirmative action remedy: The role of sex stereotypes. *Journal of Business Ethics*, 16, 877–89.

Hom, P. W. and Griffeth, R. W. (1995): *Employee turnover*. Cincinnati, OH: South-Western Publishing Company.

Ibarra, H. (1997): Paving an alternative route. *Social Psychology Quarterly*, 60, 91–102.

Kopelman, R. E., Greenhaus, J. J., and Connoly, T. F. (1983): A model of work, family, and inter-role conflict. *Organizational Behavior and Human Performance*, 32, 198–215.

Korabik, K. and Rosin, H. (1995): The impact of children on women managers' career behavior and organizational commitment. *Human Resource Management*, 34, 513–28.

Korn/Ferry International (1993): *Decade of the executive woman*. LA: Korn-Ferry.

Lawlor, J. (1994): Exodus. *Working Woman*, November, 39–41, 80–7.

Maertz, C. P. and Campion, M. A. (1998): 25 years of voluntary turnover research. In C. L. Cooper and I. T. Robertson (eds), *International Review of Industrial and Organizational Psychology*. New York: Wiley.

Markham, W. T. (1987): Sex, relocation, and occupational advancement. In A. Stromberg, L. Larwood, and B. A. Gutek (eds), *Women and work*, Beverly Hills, CA: Sage.

Markham, W. T., Harlan, S. L., and Hackett, E. J. (1987): Promotion opportunity in organizations. *Research in Personnel and Human Resources Management*, New York: JAI Press.

Marshall, J. (1995): *Women managers moving on*. London: Routledge.

McKeen, C. A. and Burke, R. J. (1994): An exploratory study of gender proportions of the experiences of managerial and professional women. *The International Journal of Organizational Analysis*, 2, 280–94.

Miller, J. G. and Wheeler, K. G. (1992): Unraveling the mysteries of gender differences in intentions to leave the organization. *Journal of Organizational Behavior*, 13, 465–78.

Nicholson, N. and West, M. (1988): *Managerial job change: Men and women in transition*. Cambridge, England: Cambridge University Press.

Reed, C. M. and Reed, B. J. (1993): The impact of dual-career marriages on occupational mobility in the local government management profession. *American Review of Public Administration*, 23, 141–54.

Riley, K. A. and White, J. (1994): Pathways to leadership: Issues for women chief executives. *Public Money and Management*, 4, 39–43.

Rives, J. M. and West, J. M. (1993): Wife's employment and worker relocation behavior. *The Journal of Socio-Economics*, 22, 13–22.

Rosin, H. and Korabik, K. (1990): Marital and family correlates of women managers' attrition from organizations. *Journal of Vocational Behavior*, 37, 104–20.

Rosin, H. and Korabik, K. (1991): Workplace variables, affective reasons, and intentions to leave among women managers. *Journal of Occupational Psychology*, 64, 317–30.

Rosin, H. and Korabik, K. (1992): Corporate flight of women managers. *Women in Management Review*, 7, 31–5.

Rosin, H. and Korabik, K. (1995): Organizational experiences and propensity to leave. *Journal of Vocational Behavior*, 46, 1–16.

Russell, J. E. A. and Burgess, J. R. D. (1998): Success and women's career adjustment. *Journal of Career Assessment*, 6, 365–87.

Schneer, J. A. and Reitman, F. (1995): The impact of gender as managerial careers unfold. *Journal of Vocational Behavior*, 47, 290–315.

Shenhav, Y. (1992): Entrance of blacks and women into managerial positions in scientific and engineering occupations. *Academy of Management Journal*, 35, 889–901.

Stroh, L. K., Brett, J. M., and Reilly, A. H. (1992): All the right stuff: A comparison of female and male managers' career progression. *Journal of Applied Psychology*, 77, 251–60.

Stroh, L. K., Brett, J. M., and Reilly, A. H. (1996): Family structure, glass ceiling, and traditional explanations for the differential rate of turnover of female and male managers. *Journal of Vocational Behavior*, 49, 99–118.

Stroh, L. K. and Reilly, A. H. (1997): Rekindling organizational loyalty. *Journal of Career Development*, 24, 1, 39–54.

Tharenou, P. (1995): Correlates of women's chief executive status. *Journal of Career Development*, 21, 201–12.

Tharenou, P. (1999): Is there a link between family structures and women's and men's managerial advancement? *Journal of Organizational Behavior*, 20, 837–63.

Tharenou, P., Latimer, S., and Conroy, D. K. (1994): How do you make it to the top? *Academy of Management Journal*, 37, 899–931.

# OPPORTUNITIES

# 8

# TRAINING AND DEVELOPMENT: CREATING THE RIGHT ENVIRONMENT TO HELP WOMEN SUCCEED IN CORPORATE MANAGEMENT

*Viki Holton*

There is no doubt that training and development is key in helping women succeed in corporate management. A great deal of what is needed to build a career is to do with having the "right" training and development opportunities. Senior managers, men and women alike, often talk about this when describing what helped them to progress with comments such as, "having a good mentor helped me gain a broad strategic view of the company" or, "taking part in our fast track development program." The mirror image of this is that women often highlight unequal access to career development or training opportunities when talking about barriers in the organization. These issues invariably cut across regional, national, and sector boundaries.

IBM's chief executive Thomas Watson, speaking in the 1930s, described his ideal company as one where: "men and women will do the same kind of work for equal pay. They will have the same treatment, the same responsibilities and the same opportunities for advancement." Seventy years later it is clear that women do not always experience the same training and development opportunities as men. This chapter outlines some of the problems and sets out a corporate response. The response, a strategic plan for training and development (see Keys for success) is likely to create tangible benefits, namely:

- a more effective and better skilled workforce
- higher levels of morale from increased levels of career and job satisfaction

- reduced turnover levels
- improved company image as a recruiter, more likely to appeal as a "best-in-class" employer to high calibre graduates.

These benefits make it evident that adopting such a plan to help women will also improve the general situation and therefore benefit all staff, men and women alike.

Training and development is only one aspect of equal opportunity and diversity change. A broader model of change, developed by Opportunity NOW, a UK equal opportunity campaign, offers greater benefits. See the campaign's annual report for more information (Opportunity 2000, 1995). Before focusing on training and development let me first describe some aspects of the current situation for women.

## ■ Improvements mask a slow pace of change ■

Despite various improvements the pace of change for women managers in the UK is slow. Women now hold three times as many managerial jobs as they did a decade ago. This may sound like a significant step forward, but still women hold less than one-quarter of all management jobs. Table 8.1 shows how the number of women managers has risen from a base of 8.6 percent in 1990 up to 22 percent in the year 2000 (Institute of Management). Women's share of the top jobs is a lot lower than men's and has yet to move into double figures. Marjorie Scardino, at publishing group Pearsons, is a solitary woman chief executive among the top 100 UK companies, the FTSE 100 (The Financial Times Stock Exchange). This scarcity of women was evident in earlier Ashridge surveys (Holton, Rabbetts, and Scrivener, 1993). The surveys found that external, non-executive, appointments of women directors far outnumbered executive directors appointed from within organizations. "Single" appointments were the norm, only one woman rather than two or more being selected. We also found evidence of clear sector trends. The majority of banks, building societies and retail stores in 1997 had appointed a woman director; this was not the case in engineering and investment trusts.

Changes in higher education are more positive. The number of women graduates has steadily increased during the 1990s. Figures from Oxford reveal that for the first time in 1999 the number of women applying to study is greater than the number of men. Just over 50 percent (4,679) of applications came from women, men accounted for 4,661 applications (Oxford University). Similar improvements elsewhere mean that a major increase has occurred from the early 1960s when women made up only one-quarter of undergraduates (EOC 1999, 2000).

**Table 8.1**   Women managers in the UK, 1990–2000

| Responsibility level | 1990 | 1995 | 1996 | 1997 % | 1998 | 1999 | 2000 |
|---|---|---|---|---|---|---|---|
| Director | 1.6 | 3.0 | 3.3 | 4.5 | 3.6 | 6.1 | 9.6 |
| Function head | 4.4 | 5.8 | 6.5 | 8.3 | 10.7 | 11.0 | 15.0 |
| Department head | 7.8 | 9.7 | 12.2 | 14.0 | 16.2 | 16.9 | 19.0 |
| Section leader | 13.3 | 14.2 | 14.4 | 18.2 | 21.9 | 24.9 | 26.5 |
| **Total** | **8.6** | **10.7** | **12.3** | **15.2** | **18.0** | **19.9** | **22.1** |

**Source:** *Institute of Management (2000).*

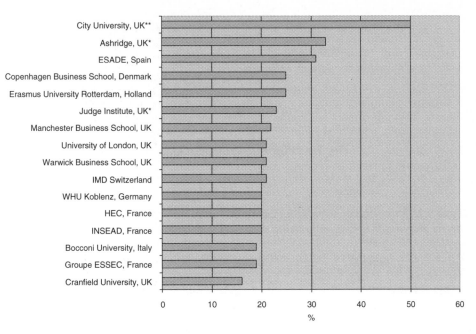

**Figure 8.1** Women MBA students in Europe
*Source*: www.businessweek.com Business School Profiles, downloaded 27.10.00

MBAs (Master of Business Administration) are another important measure of change as these have become a sought-after executive qualification in many organizations. The news here is less encouraging. Women MBAs remain a minority group and in fact numbers have now plateaued. The USA figures have hardly changed in the past decade (Jampol, 1999; Reingold, 2000). MBA programmes are renowned for requiring long hours, a 16-hour day is a typical workload. Combining this with the fact that "30-something," the average age of an MBA student, is a time when women are likely to start or already have families may go some way to explain the difficulties women face. The number of women MBAs is around 1 in 3, 30 percent in North America but is lower, only 1 in 4, in Europe (Jampol, 1999). Figure 8.1 shows the European data. Women are only 16 percent of the MBA group at Cranfield. This rises somewhat higher to around one-third at ESADE in Spain and at Ashridge. The highest figure, however, is at City University in the UK which has an equal number of men and women MBA students. Women's share on part-time MBA programmes is somewhat lower. Figure 8.2 shows that women are only 10 percent of students at Erasmus through to the highest figure, 25 percent, at University College, Dublin.

The number of women attending business schools for general training programmes is somewhat lower than the proportion of women studying for MBAs. Women are just over one-fifth of delegates attending Ashridge Centre for Business and Society. In 1984 a small pioneer group of 182 women came to Ashridge; the most recent data from 1999 reveals that this has grown to 1,075. Up until 1998 there had been a steady year-on-

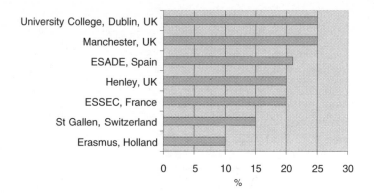

**Figure 8.2**   Women part-time MBA students in Europe
*Source*: Business Week www.businessweek.com Downloaded 20.11.00

**Table 8.2**   Women participants at Ashridge, 1984–2000

| 2000 | 1999 | 1998 | 1997 | 1996 % | 1995 | 1994 | 1993 | 1992 |
|------|------|------|------|--------|------|------|------|------|
| 21 | 21 | 21 | 19 | 18 | 17 | 14 | 17 | 14 |

| 1991 | 1990 | 1989 | 1988 | 1987 | 1986 | 1985 | 1984 |
|------|------|------|------|------|------|------|------|
| 15 | 14 | 13 | 10 | 9 | 7 | 6 | 5 |

year increase but 1998, 1999, and 2000 data suggest that the number of women delegates has plateaued (see table 8.2). Ashridge ran a women's business leadership program between 1987 and 2000, and this may partly explain the growing number of women during the 1990s.

Finally, what is happening to women who work in the business schools? The data shows that, as for women MBAs, there is a larger pool of women in the USA. *Business Week*'s (2000) figures in table 8.3 reveal that the situation for women professors in non-USA business schools trails quite a long way behind the USA. The number of tenured women professors in non-USA business schools starts from a low base figure – 1 percent – and only rises up to 11 percent at IMD, Switzerland. The USA start point at 10 percent is much higher and the figure rises much higher, up to 24 percent at Duke where women hold nearly one-quarter of all professorships. It is a very small survey group but it appears to indicate a significant international divide.

These then are some of the current trends for women. The rest of this chapter focuses on the situation for women with regard to training and development issues.

## ■ Training and development ■

Training and development is a sizable item in most corporate budgets. Data from the American Society for Training and Development (ASTD) indicates a high average training budget. Expenditure varies little between countries and is 1.2 percent of

**Table 8.3**   Percentage of women professors in US and non-US business schools

| US business schools | Women Professors % |
|---|---|
| Duke (Fuqua) | 24 |
| Michigan | 16 |
| Harvard | 15 |
| North Western (Kellogg) | 14 |
| Columbia | 11 |
| Pennsylvania (Wharton) | 11 |
| MIT (Sloan) | 10 |

| Non-US business schools | Women Professors % |
|---|---|
| IMD, Switzerland | 11 |
| IESE, Spain | 10 |
| Toronto (Rotman) Canada | 7 |
| London Business School | 5 |
| INSEAD France | 2 |
| Western Ontario (Ivey) Canada | 1 |
| Erasmus (Rotterdam) Holland | Not available |

*Source: Business Week* Survey of Business Schools, November 2000 *www.businessweek.com:/bschools/00/index.html*

payroll in Japan, 2 percent among USA organizations and slightly higher, 3.2 percent, in Europe.

A few years ago Deloitte & Touche realized that simply recruiting women did not necessarily mean they gradually progressed into senior management jobs. The organization considered the reasons for the lack of progress and one of the key issues was the male-dominated culture; the lack of flexible work practices was another. Another problem concerned women's lack of access to career advancement and training opportunities (Capowski, 1996). These experiences are typical of what has happened in many organizations. Three training and development issues that are barriers for women are:

1   "sign-posting" and access to development and training opportunities
2   work–life balance
3   organizational culture.

The issues are not listed in order of importance. Ruth Simpson's research into the career barriers found that culture, namely the "men's club network," was the single most important barrier highlighted by women. Culture is a key issue but many employers have also brought about a good deal of change for women by improving "sign-posting" – the access to career development and training opportunities – issue 1 on the list above. Together with a review of culture and work–life integration this helps create an environment that "includes" rather than "excludes" women. Avon Cosmetics is a good example of this type of approach (Roosevelt Thomas, 1991). Each issue is discussed below.

## "Sign-posting" and access to development and training opportunities

Better sign-posting of information and improving access to career development and training opportunities are important ways to help women. It is obvious that if you don't know what is available, you cannot take part. It is also important to ensure women receive the same opportunities as men. Organizations need to keep a watching brief on this. Few monitor promotion rates among women and men. Fewer still collect data on women's share of training and career development opportunities. Boxes 8.1 and 8.2 show two exceptions.

---

### BOX 8.1  INLAND REVENUE

Between 1975 through to 1985 the Inland Revenue in the UK tracked the careers of 400 men and women. The analysis revealed differences, for example that men joining in 1975 progressed at a faster rate than women. Research into the reasons why, and ways to address the issue, have helped improve the situation for women.

---

### BOX 8.2  MAKING SURE WOMEN ARE AMONG THE HIGH POTENTIALS

A major employer reviewing the list of candidates for its high-potential program found there were few women in the group. Talented women existed just beyond the group selected but the concern was that these were not likely to be included in any targeted career development in the foreseeable future. The organization looked at ways to include this group in certain stages of the training process. This helped ensure women were able to develop the key skills required.

---

Staff in large organizations often say that it is hard to find out about career choices available, and to identify key training or development opportunities that will help them develop their career in the right direction. Hewlett Packard and Shell are among an increasing number of employers using electronic job posting to open up this process. The scale of the problem is evident from a survey of some 500 managers. While most, 81 percent, believed that promotions were fairly handled, only just over half the group said the processes involved in promotions were clear (Handy, Holton, and Wilson, 1997).

It is unfortunate that women-only programmes have attracted so much controversy. They can be extremely helpful in certain scenarios. The first instance is whether there are key skill gaps, say leadership, or experience, or confidence building, for women

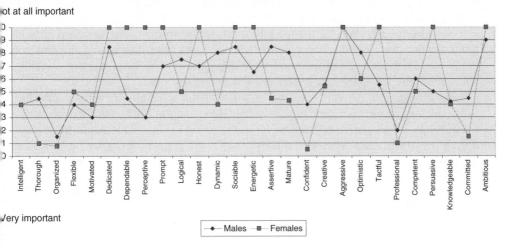

ot at all important

Very important

Males — Females

**Figure 8.3** The impact of gender on performance attributes of men and women managers
*Source*: IMS Survey, 1992

generally? Second, would women-only programmes (and/or women's networks) help build a training and support infrastructure that would help women? However, you do not have to use a "women only" approach. The same results can be achieved using a mixture of different initiatives.

Another problem for women arises from the use of informal training processes. In many organizations the line manager is responsible for identifying high-potential staff or nominating who will be included in succession planning. The evidence shows such informal processes, without objective checks and balances in place, often disadvantage and exclude women. Evidence indicates, for example, that women are not as likely as men to nominate themselves for training or promotion opportunities.

Managers sometimes value different attributes in men and women, an issue that impacts on performance-related pay, 360-degree feedback and other career selection processes (Bevan and Thompson, 1992). Figure 8.3 indicates the dramatic impact of gender on a group of men and women in one organization. Mentoring is an important career tool, and one that has proved especially helpful for women (Roosevelt Thomas, 1991; Deutsche Jugendinstitut, 1995; West, 2000). One aspect of inequality is the finding that women are less likely to be mentored. Ashridge work found men were twice as likely as women to be mentored (Handy, Holton and Wilson, 1997). Other research, looking at the careers of some three hundred senior managers, revealed that women were also less likely than men to have personal development plans (Holton, Rabbetts and Stone, 1993).

Women and men may receive the same development opportunity but experience it differently. Ragins and Cotton's (1999) research is one of a number of studies that found women in formal mentoring programmes received less support from their mentors than was the case among men. Similar gender differences have been tracked for assessment and development centres and in psychometric and selection tests (McHenry, 1997; Pearn et al., 1987). Responses to this have included auditing procedures and material to check for possible gender bias. Another is to include women as assessors. The Crown Prosecution Service, for example, ensured that women were included on senior promotion interview boards.

Collecting the key skills for the top jobs is crucial for women. Top jobs often require a significantly deeper and broader skill set and in recent years downsizing and delayering of management levels means some wide skill gaps have opened up between middle and senior jobs, and particularly between senior and top jobs.

Pitney Bowes and AB Volvo are two among a cluster of employers using mentoring to help women move through to top jobs. Trygg Hansa, one of the largest Swedish insurance groups, is now part of SE Banken. It sponsored a very successful mentoring project during the 1990s. Senior women managers at Trygg Hansa were paired with senior managers and board members. This helped women understand core management and leadership skills; it also enabled the transfer of skills that often are hard to learn such as organizational politics and networking. Specific training programmes as developed at Merrill Lynch (box 8.3) can also help.

---

## BOX 8.3   WOMEN'S LEADERSHIP AT MERILL LYNCH

In response to feedback from women staff Merill Lynch developed a women's leadership program. In conjunction with the Center for Creative Leadership and the University of North Carolina the 1999 program ran with 41 participants, vice-presidents and director level women.

---

Job shadowing is another tool to help women gain specific leadership skills. A recent UK project matched a woman director at one small company with a chief executive at a larger printing organization. This proved to be a good development opportunity. Spending time with someone more experienced provided the woman with a chance to appreciate the breadth, skills, and scope of a more senior job (James and Holton, 2000).

Training provision also should take account of differing management styles. The majority of managers say there is a difference in management styles between men and women (Holton, Rabbetts and Stone, 1993). Women's-people orientated skills were emphasized, contrasting with the task-based approach of men.

## Work–life balance (24/7) and training

The tension between business life and work–life balance is well documented in the media and business press (Scheibl and Dex, 1988; Rice, 2000; Martino, Lineham, and Walsh). The response from major employers such as Merrill Lynch and PriceWaterhouseCoopers has been to offer work–life programmes. These aim is to help staff combine personal life with the long-hours culture, or "24/7" – 24 hours a day and 7 days a week, as it has been recently been dubbed. The long-hours culture is a general block for women in the UK and in other countries, such as Japan (Hutton, 2000); it also impacts on training.

During the 1950s and 1960s when a number of leading business schools launched their training programmes, the needs of working parents and young children were not high on the agenda. Most delegates, and academics involved in the teaching, were male. Travelling and staying away for a training program of a few days or sometimes a few weeks became part of the accepted norm for many organizations. It still is in many cases.

Formal management development is a central part of most training programmes and a good deal still is offered off-site in packages of days or maybe weeks. Fast-track leadership and graduate programmes may be international programmes run across a number of different countries and/or sites. This involves staying away from home, something that is not always easy for someone juggling a management career with family responsibilities.

Creating a more family-friendly model is proving to be a slow process. One major UK employer incorporated family facilities into the design of a major new training facility. Another exception is Shell UK where considerable effort has been placed on family-friendly issues. Shell offers child care advice for staff along with site facilities such as a child care nursery at Shell Expro in Aberdeen.

A few business schools have also responded positively including Cranfield and IMD where an on-site crèche or kindergarten is available. It is difficult to find out what help is provided. An on-line search among the seven top non-USA schools in *Business Week*'s 2000 survey[1] revealed little information. Toronto (Rotman) is an exception, offering a family care office to help advise students and staff.

## Organizational culture and training

The third training and development issue concerns the organizational culture. Women, especially those in technical roles and at more senior management levels, may feel isolated. It is quite likely that women managers will be a minority of those attending in-house training events, particularly likely for more senior programmes.

A survey of some 1,600 MBA students asked why more women do not pursue MBAs (Catalyst, 2000a). The key reason given by just over half the women concerned was a lack of female role models. Another issue that needs to be addressed by business schools and employers is the lack of encouragement from employers, mentioned by 42 percent. The incompatibility of a business career with work–life balance (47 percent) was high-lighted and nearly as many cite a lack of confidence in analytical/maths skills.

Traditional stereotypes and assumptions are an aspect of culture that can cause difficulties for women. Typical comments heard in organizations include: "someone working part-time isn't interested in a career" and "it's a dual career marriage so he will take first place for any career decisions made; she'll take the number 2 slot." Misconceptions about women's abilities to handle international assignments and their willingness to accept these assignments are the issues highlighted as to why such a small number of women managers in US companies are selected for international assignments (Catalyst, 2000b).

Some attitudes appear deeply ingrained. Research with UK chief executives found that certain jobs, such as directing operations, were considered more suited to men. Buying, marketing and sales were regarded as "areas were women could excel" (EOC,

1999). One of the BBC Northern Ireland's aims a few years ago was to "break down the traditional notion that certain jobs can be done only by men and others by women" (Opportunity 2000, 1995).

The retail group Boots employs over 56,000 staff and is one of a number of major UK employers to look closely at such issues. Boots developed objective selection procedures including a manual for senior non-store managers to improve consistency of personnel practice across the business. Avon Cosmetics in the UK decided to introduce a computerized job evaluation system to eliminate gender bias.

## Company action: a strategic plan

There are number of practical ways organizations can adopt to ensure women are as likely as men to access and benefit from training and career development opportunities. Creating a company strategic plan of action to respond to the issues described above is relatively simple. There are three separate stages. First, the diagnosis; second, action; and finally measurement. Each stage is briefly outlined below. Figure 8.4 illustrates this as a simple, linear model.

The time taken to complete the cycle varies, some organizations take a year or so, others are far quicker, reaching the end of stage 2 within a matter of a few weeks. There is no time limit, but the value of a fast turnaround is that it keeps the topic close at the top of the list. As with any other business issue, too long over the diagnosis and data collection in stage 1 may mean the spotlight has moved elsewhere.

The plan is not intended to be a one-off initiative, designed, implemented, and then filed away in a desk drawer somewhere. There is more value in applying the model in a continuous circle as shown in figure 8.4. Working through the three separate steps in sequence is important, but returning to stages 1 and 2 – diagnosis and action – on a

| Diagnosis: stage 1 | Action: stage 2 | Measurement: stage 3 |
|---|---|---|
| • Review existing practices<br><br>• Survey women managers<br><br>• Set up company-wide working groups on different topics, eg: combining parenting with a career | • Decide on a few key issues and develop initiatives<br>• Agree measures and key responsibilities for action<br><br>**Create individual champions for each initiative** | • Measure progress at regular intervals and collect qualitative and quantitative data<br><br>• Celebrate and reward success |
| **Output** | **Output** | **Output** |
| Presentation to board of directors and CEO<br><br>Report (including pdf file for intranet company site.) | Company-wide announcement on action | Regular articles or reports on progress |

**Figure 8.4**  A strategic plan for women's training and development

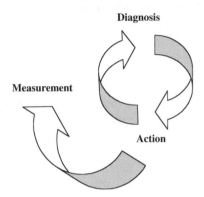

**Figure 8.5**　The strategic cycle

regular basis make it more likely that the plan will be embedded into the organization's core training and development values.

***Stage 1. Diagnosis.***　Where to begin? Spending a little time to analyze where the organization is can be useful, especially if it is a new topic, Appendix 1 has 12 basic questions to help provide such a benchmark.

The value of diagnosis can be easily overlooked especially if specialist equal opportunity or HR/personnel staff feel close to the issues. An HR manager may feel that already they have a good knowledge of the issues for women and how to address these. Data collection by someone outside of the organization often helps make the process more objective and independent; not only is this person seen as "objective" but career topics are often sensitive and staff often feel able to talk more openly with someone outside the company.

In one organization where this approach was taken the HR manager observed that "it was extremely powerful to be able to present the facts to our board of directors. The data held no surprises for me, I knew where we were going wrong and I'd heard the feedback from women managers over the years. However, it was new information for some of the senior managers sitting round the table, and packed quite a punch." Hearing the findings from an independent source was important: "If I'd said these things it might have have been questioned; someone outside, with no preconceived ideas, made a stronger impression on the board than I could have done."

Three separate strands of work are required in the diagnosis:

1　a review of existing training and career development practices (see appendix 2 for topics)
2　a survey of women managers (see appendix 3 for questions to use)
3　working groups to review specific topics, for example, a higher turnover among women graduates, issues for working parents.

All three are important. There is little point in reviewing existing training and career development policy and practices without talking to women managers. Likewise, a survey alone will reveal some issues but working groups mean that more knowledge can be gathered. The working groups are also useful way to gather interest and energy for different topics.

***Stage 2. Action.*** The action stage is worth spending time and effort on. Deciding what action should be taken is important for two reasons. First of all there is likely to be a list to choose from and it is important to select something that is challenging but achievable. There is no point in saying that the number of women chemists recruited next year will double if the pool of possible recruits includes few women.

Resist the temptation to try to create a plan to address every issue that has emerged. It is more valuable, and practical, to select a few key issues. Supporting and developing women for top jobs may be a critical part of the action plan. An initiative adopted by the UK National Health Service (NHS) was a career development register held at Ashridge (see box 8.4). The project operated as an internal head-hunting service for the NHS and was one of a series of different approaches to improve the situation for women. The register helped senior women compete on an equal basis for more senior appointments.

---

## Box 8.4   The National Health Service Career Development Register

The register targeted senior women above certain salary or budget levels. During the last year of the project the register was also opened to help men at senior levels. One-to-one career coaching was used to help with individual development needs. A series of meetings, workshops and development centres were provided to help improve women's skills.

Assistance was provided to help women apply and prepare for the selection process. The project was funded from a central budget, separately from local training initiatives. It was enthusiastically supported at senior levels within the NHS. Over 250 of the 600 or so women on the register were promoted.

---

Some organizations stop at this point – stage 2. Another common error is that, having made the diagnosis process very public, little is said to employees about the next steps. If a women-only program is planned (see box 8.5) the idea may be controversial. Company-wide announcements, via a variety of electronic, paper, and line-management routes, can help diffuse this. A good communication policy also keeps staff up-to-date on progress.

***Stage 3. Measurement.*** Measurement and evaluation of training also play a part in success. If there are no measures of progress then it is likely that the topic won't be regarded as a serious business issue. Collecting quantitative data is useful, but qualitative material also can help show progress. Interviewing women achievers are an example of this. A feature in the company newsletter with women MBAs can act as a

## Box 8.5  Career Planning at Deloitte & Touche

Formal three- to five-year career plans have been developed for the majority of women partners and senior managers. These are discussed with their practice manager.

| Policy | Provision |
|---|---|
| People | Positive encouragement |

**Figure 8.6**  Four principles of change

useful role model for other, younger women. Profiles of working mothers featured on the company intranet are another example.

## Keys for success

It is all too easy to describe what an organization could or should do without talking about the size of the challenge. There are significant difficulties in creating this type of change. Large corporates, for the most part, are not noted for being nimble or quick to create change. Another issue is the gap that often exists with regard to equal opportunity and diversity change between spoken and espoused values. The public company voice may say such ideas are "good", but unless there are clear internal processes and structures of action, change is unlikely to happen. Even programmes with senior management interest and a significant resource may fail to progress. Change of any sort requires a lot of concerted effort and energy. Equal opportunity and diversity change requires a further degree of commitment. It may be that the action proposed is not regarded as a proper business issue. Line managers, rightly or wrongly, will therefore regard it as optional. Applying four key principles can help ensure change does happen. Figure 8.6 the four principles or Ps.

1   *Policy.* It is important to have a policy that is clear to staff within the organization. A policy that is made clear to those outside of the company creates a stronger message of the importance of what is happening to those within the organisation.
2   *People.* Identify people who will take responsibility for implementing policy.
3   *Provision.* Policy will count for little unless there is a good structure of training and development provision.
4   *Positive encouragement.* Change also is likely to be slow unless the organization (and top management) creates an atmosphere of positive encouragement. A chief executive who acts as a mentor or one who regularly hosts women's training and development events leads the way for the rest of the organization, especially for his or her own management team.

I have already described some of the issues that block women. Those likely to trip the organization up and block change are noted in box 8.6 "Women's training and career development initiatives: barriers and gateways", together with some responses drawn from company experience. As with any business issue, the key is to think ahead about what might help and what could hinder the action plan.

# BOX 8.6   TRAINING AND CAREER DEVELOPMENT INITIATIVES FOR WOMEN: BARRIERS AND GATEWAYS

1   One barrier for a large organization may be a diverse collection of HR initiatives, e.g. one multi-national found eight competency frameworks operating across the company. Such multiplicity makes it hard to have a single framework and understanding of what the key skills are

*Response. Develop structured network exchange between HR staff in different parts of the company and find ways to share different frameworks, e.g. annual HR conference on women's training and development*

2   An approach that looks broadly at diversity rather than focusing on women's issues may make it harder to help women. Some issues are similar between different diversity groups, but some will be women-only problems

*Response. If a diversity approach operates, an audit of women's issues and what specific action is needed to address these. Hewlett-Packard's mentoring program at Roseville, California was offered to women and people of colour. The program partnered staff on a 1:1 basis with a more experienced or skilled employee*

3   Training decisions are made locally, this means there are few opportunities to develop a strategic, company-wide approach to helping women

*Response. Centrally fund (or ring-fence) some of the training budget and/or places on key training programmes. BT for example has for a number of years run a leadership program for senior women managers resourced from central rather than local budgets*

4   It is often hard to find an inclusive initiative, one that will be regarded as relevant by women at all levels of the company, not only managers

*Response.* *One academic institution, faced with such a problem, developed a women's mentoring scheme open to staff at all levels*

5 A related issue is the fear that men may resent a women-only approach. Women also may be concerned at receiving remedial or "special" treatment not being offered to men.

*Response.* *One multi-national designed a women's mentoring scheme; this was also offered to men who wished to take part. Others have used information campaigns to inform staff about what is happening and why a women-only approach is helpful*

6 Recent downsizing has created big gaps between different levels in some organizations. This may make it more difficult for women to move up into the next level

*Response.* *Job shadowing and job exchange schemes help women gain knowledge at the next level. Tailored training programmes also can help*

7 Isolated pockets of good practice. Commissioned by a major UK employer to review "family-friendly" issues, Ashridge found some good schemes operating in local business areas

*Response.* *Feature such schemes in company newsletter and/or on the intranet. Alternatively, set up an intranet bulletin board and/or give a co-ordinator role to someone in HR*

*A "gemelli" or twin approach can also help. Once a scheme has been successfully set up in one part of the organization, target another area/line manager/business department as its twin and get both groups of staff to work together*

## Future trends in training and development

Training is undergoing a good deal of change and certain trends seem set to alter existing frameworks beyond recognition. Some trends may help women, others may create more barriers. Outsourcing, for example, is altering the way training is delivered and monitored. On-line delivery is another growth area. A recent survey of the finance sector found that between 30 to 80 percent of training material was delivered in this way (Holton and Robinson, 2000). Xerox Europe's goal for the end of 2001 is a training delivery ratio of 50:50 between classroom and virtual/distance learning. This means a substantial investment in virtual delivery as the 1998 ratio is 88 percent class and only 12 percent delivered via virtual/distance learning (Ashridge, 2000).

Some future trends and the impact these might have on women are briefly noted in box 8.7.

## Box 8.7 Future Trends in Training and Development and the Impact on Women

- *The increasing role of the line manager in human resource (HR) activities* such as identifying talented and high potential staff. Some organizations have found that women and men are judged differently. A simple example of this is that what might in a male candidate be described as assertive could become more negative, as bossy, in a female candidate. A number of organizations have implemented specialist equal opportunity and diversity training to ensure that assessors are aware of such issues, and that men and women are judged equally.

- *Training budgets and/or provision moving from central to local/business levels (also the outsourcing of training.)* One organization used personal development plans for all staff but kept this information at local levels and did not co-ordinate it centrally. This makes it harder to track the development needs for women generally. It is also harder to track what is happening company-wide to women compared with their male colleagues.
- *The increasing trend toward individual responsibility for career development.* Effort on the part of the organization is required to make sure that individual responsibility for career development is managed centrally, and women's issues are monitored.
- *Corporate universities.* At best corporate universities offer a co-ordinated strategy for organizational learning. At worst they may provide an *ad hoc* training facility that means company-wide issues for women are submerged.
- *On-line training and company-wide training intranets.* Whether interest and take-up rates of on-line training are affected by gender is not yet clear. Training providers should check program development and design for possible gender bias. Organizations should be aware of such possibilities and keep a watching brief.

## Conclusion

There are a number of key players who could take more responsibility to help change the situation for women:

- employers
- government
- business schools.

The employer's role is likely to continue to be significant in helping create change, developing a positive attitude helping to ensure that women succeed. There are some employer-led campaigns but there is certainly room for more, a employer-led multinational campaign could, for instances create an influential international campaign. Finding more ways to celebrate women's achievements is also important. A recent international development is the agreement in 1999 between UNESCO and pharmaceutical giant L'Oréal on a series of awards to recognize the achievements of women scientists worldwide. A UK debate on women in science, held in October 2000, was a direct result of this collaboration. The meeting was hosted by the Royal Institution (*www.ri.ac.uk*), an important professional institution.

Government, at regional, national, international, and European Union level, is another key player. It is easy for example to see ways that national governments could do more. Maybe by partnering and encouraging the major employers in different regions and/or sectors, or the work by the Canadian Government campaign, "2000 @ 2000", to create change in the public sector. The UK Government's Department of Trade and Industry has a website site and staff dedicated to help small to medium-sized employers. Why not a similar push to help women?

Business schools are a third lever for change. INSEAD in France, for instance, has a women's MBA network *www.insead.edu/alumni/womensnetwork/index.htm* Harvard's women's network *www.hbsnwa.org* has branches in Boston, Washington, Chicago, San Francisco and New York, and further afield in Hong Kong. London Business School hosted a Breaking the Mould conference to put the spotlight on women who have broken the mould in today's global economy. An event sponsored by Andersen Consulting and Chubb, Henley in the UK had a similar conference in June 2001.

There have also been certain initiatives and awards to help encourage women. IMD in Switzerland offers a women's MBA scholarship sponsored by Nestlé.

These pockets of good practice appear a fragmented response. Business schools could achieve far more if they pooled resources and built a more strategic approach. The INSEAD/ESSEC Programme for Women Managers in France, the IMD/LBS International Conference for Women Leaders, or the Harvard/Stanford Women's Initiative are suggestions. Similarly, a series of Leadership and Strategy summer schools, an MBA entry coaching and mini-MBA weekend courses could be sponsored in each country by national business schools.

There is still more that could, and should, be done to create the right training and development environment for women. If the key players pick up the challenge and find ways to help women succeed, then Thomas Watson's ideal may finally come true for all women working in corporate management.

## NOTE

1   *www.businessweek.com:/bschools/00/index.html* The seven top non-USA business schools in rank order: INSEAD, France; London Business School, UK; IESE, Spain; IMD, Switzerland; Western Ontario, Canada; Erasmus (Rotterdam), Holland; and Toronto (Rotman), Canada.

## REFERENCES

Ashridge Newsletter Communique (2000): *Xerox Aims to Educate Through Virtual Learning*, spring/summer.

Bevan, S. and Thompson, Marc. (1992): *Merit Pay, Performance Appraisal and Attitudes to Women's Work*. Institute of Manpower Studies.

Business Week (2000): Survey of Business Schools.
    *www.businessweek.com:/bschools/00/index.html*

Catalyst (2000a): *Women and the MBA: Gateway to Opportunity. www.catalystwomen.org*

Catalyst (2000b): *Passport to Opportunity: US Women in Global Business*. Catalyst.

Capowski, G. (1996): Where have all the Women Gone? One firm Asks. *Management Review*, 85, 5, 7.

Deutsche Jugendinstitut e.V. (1999): *Mentoring for Women in Europe: A Strategy for the Professional Support of Women*. European Commission.

EOC (Equal Opportunities Commission) (2000): *Women and Men in Britain. 1999/2000*. EOC.

EOC (1999): *Women in Senior Management in Wales*. EOC.

Fondas N. and Sassalos, S. (2000): A Different Voice in the Boardroom. *Global Focus*, 12, 2, 13–22.

Handy, L., Holton V., and Wilson, A. (1997): *Ashridge Management Index, 1997: A Survey of Management and Organisational Change*. Ashridge.

Holton, V. and Rabbetts, J. (1997): *Women on the Boards of Britain's Top 200 Companies*. Ashridge.

Holton, V., Rabbetts, J., and Scrivener, S. (1993): *Women on the Boards of Britain's Top 200 Companies*. Ashridge.

Holton, V., Rabbetts, J., and Stone, R. (1993): *Women on the Boards of Britain's Top 200 Companies: A Progress Report*. Ashridge.

Holton, V. and Robinson, S. (2000): *Staff Training in Preparation for the European Monetary Union: A Guide to Training Initiatives in the Finance Sector*. The Banks and Building Societies National Training Organisation, UK.

Hutton, B. (2000): "Working Mothers with a Yen for Family Life," *Financial Times*, 2 Nov. 22.

Institute of Management (2000): *Annual Salary Survey*. Remuneration Economics, Kingston-upon-Thames, UK.

Institute of Employment Studies (2000): *Family Friendly Employment: The Business Case Report*. Institute of Employment Studies.

James, P. and Holton, V. (2000): *Creating more Effective Print Companies*. The Print and Graphic Communications National Training Organisation, UK.

Jampol, J. (1999): Women and the MBA, 3rd Edition of Directory of MBAs. Edward More O'Ferrall in conjunction with the European Foundation for Management Development (EFMD), 12–14.

Lineham, M. and Walsh, J. (2000): Work–Family Conflict and the Senior Female International Manager. *British Journal of Management*, 11, Sept., 49–58.

McHenry, R. (1997): Tried and Tested, *People Management*, 23 Jan., 32–7.

Martino, J. M. (1999): *Work-Life Initiatives in a Global Context*. The Conference Board, June.

Opportunity (2000): *4th Year Summary of Goals and Action Plans of Campaign Organisations*. Opportunity NOW, 15 Nov.

Opportunity NOW (2000): *Benchmarking Report 2000*. www.opportunitynow.org.uk Opportunity NOW.

Oxford University, November 1999, *www.ox.ac.uk/aboutoxford/women.shtml*

Pearn, M., Kandola, R., and Mottram, R. (1987): *Selection Tests and Sex Bias: The Impact on Selection Testing on the Employment Opportunities of Women and Men*. EOC.

Ragins, B. R. and Cotton, J. L. (1999): Mentor Functions and Outcomes: A Comparison of Men and Women in Formal and Informal Mentoring Relationships. *The Journal of Applied Psychology*, 84, 4, 529–49.

Reingold, J. (2000): It's Still a Guy Thing: Female MBA Enrollment hasn't Budged in a Decade, *Business Week*, 22 May.

Rice, M. (2000): Age of the Flex Exec, *Management Today*, August.

Jr Roosevelt Thomas, R. (1991): *Beyond Race and Gender: Unleashing the Power of your Total Workforce by Managing Diversity*. American Management Association.

Scheibl, F. and Dex, S. (1998): Should We Have More Family-Friendly Policies? *European Management Journal*, 16, 5, 586–99.

Simpson, R. (2000): Winners and Losers: Who Benefits most from the MBA? *Management Learning*, 31, 3, 331–51.

Van Buren, M. and King, S. (2000): The 2000 ASTD Annual Accounting of Worldwide Patterns in Employer-Provided Training. *The American Society for Training and Development*.

West, D. (2000): Pharma Companies for Women. *Pharmaceutical Executive*, June.

## APPENDIX 8.1. TRAINING AND DEVELOPMENT FOR WOMEN: COMPANY BENCHMARK

How well is your organization doing with regard to creating the right training and career development environment for women?

1    The organisation – and senior management – is committed to providing a level playing field for women.

2 We know what the issues are with regard to training and development, for example have run discussion groups with women new entrants, working mothers, technical specialists and senior managers.

3 We have on-going communication systems to hear about any training and career development issues that women wish to raise, for example a CEO e-forum, "Training, Career Development and Women," www information. Shell UK's web-site has a section on "promoting diversity in employment" (*www.shell.com*).

4 We have commissioned an independent review of training and development – in-house provision and external programmes – to check out any inequalities or bias; to look at how "women friendly" it is.

5 All staff involved in training and career development (including such activities as appraisals) have received equal opportunity/diversity training.

6 We have a clear idea of what we want to achieve and know what needs to change.

7 Our training and career development structure is clearly defined.

8 Women are included in the informal as well as the formal training and career development initiatives.

9 Career development structures are clearly defined.

10 Goals have been set for women with regard to accessing key aspects of training and career development.

11 Individuals have ownership for achieving these goals, and systems are in place to monitor progress on a regular basis, for example regular reports to senior management.

12 We have taken an active interest in creating change outside the organization.

## APPENDIX 8.2. A TRAINING AND CAREER DEVELOPMENT AUDIT

As well as looking at training and career development approaches generally (Appendix 8.1), it is also important to consider in detail specific training and career development initiatives. The following list is not exhaustive and should be adapted to what is offered company-wide or in different business units.

| | |
|---|---|
| Appraisal process/annual performance reviews | Succession planning |
| Competency profiles/frameworks | High-potential lists |
| Identifying high-potential staff | 360 degree feedback |
| Graduate recruitment | Graduate programs |
| Assessment/development centers | Career planning |
| Psychometric tests/skill profiles | Personal development plans |
| Job advertising | Career plans |
| External adverts | Coaching |
| Internal processes | Mentoring |
| Interview processes | Educational leave, e.g. MBAs |
| External candidates | Job secondments |
| Internal candidates | Job shadowing |
| Creating shortlists of candidates | 1:1 career counselling |
| Equal opportunity or diversity training | Job exchanges |

## APPENDIX 8.3. SURVEYING WOMEN ABOUT CAREER DEVELOPMENT

The following questions will provide a useful database of information about women managers. It could be used either company-wide or for a small group of women.

1 *Current appointment*
   - How did you get your current job?
   - What are your main responsibilities?
   - What would help you to do a better job? If training, what sort of skills or experience would be important? If better knowledge about the business is important how could you obtain this?
   - How are you judged? Who is responsible for the process and what has happened in recent discussions?

2 *Career to date*
   - What has helped you advance your career?
   - Looking back over the jobs you've held in the past, why did you change and were there any critical steps or changes?
   - Have you faced any particular barriers to progress?
   - What has helped you develop your career?

3 *Training and career development*
   - Think about training and career development issues? What is provided by the organization that is helpful? Is there anything else that the organization could do?
   - What are the characteristics of successful people in your organization? What type of experience and/or skills are valued and rewarded? Are men and women judged in the same way?
   - Are there structures or career guidance that could help other women in your organization?

4 *The holistic view*
   - What is the balance between work and your personal life? Is it satisfactory or is there something that you would like to change?

# 9

# CAREER DEVELOPMENT OF MANAGERIAL WOMEN

*Ronald J. Burke*

During the past two decades, dramatic increases in the numbers of women entering the workforce and pursuing professional and managerial careers has had a major impact on the workplace (Burke and McKeen, 1992). Although armed with appropriate education, training, and years of experience, managerial and professional women have not made much progress in entering the ranks of senior management (Powell, 1999). They encounter what some have termed a "glass ceiling" (Morrison, White, and Van Velsor, 1987). Because women are now a significant component of the workforce, their recruitment and development is increasingly seen as a bottom-line issue related to corporate success (Schwartz, 1992).

This chapter provides a selective review of content areas reported to have positive influences on the career development of professional and managerial women, and considers issues raised by these findings. It also reports new results examining the relationship of work experiences and career outcomes in a large sample of Canadian managerial and professional women. Specific topics covered include:

- work experiences and career development
- developmental job experiences
- developmental relationships
- models of career development
- different models of career development for women and men
- alternative work arrangements
- organizational initiatives
- implications.

Preparation of this chapter was supported in part by the School of Business, York University. Sandra Osti prepared the manuscript. Carol McKeen and Cobi Wolpin contributed to some of the research projects discussed in the chapter.

## ■  Work experiences and career development  ■

Some light has been shed on the types of work experiences likely to be associated with women's career development. Morrison, White, and Van Velsor (1987), in a three-year study of top female executives, identified six factors that contributed to women's career success. These were: help from above, a track record of achievements, a desire to succeed, an ability to manage subordinates, a willingness to take career risks, and an ability to be tough, decisive, and demanding. Three derailment factors were common in explaining the failure of some female managers to achieve expected levels. These were: inability to adapt, wanting too much (for oneself or other women), and performance problems.

Furthermore, to be successful, women more than men needed help from above, needed to be easy to be with, and to be able to adapt. These factors related to developing good relationships with men in a male-dominated environment (also see Ragins, Townsend, and Mattis, 1998). Women, more than men, were also required to take career risks, be tough, have strong desires to succeed, and have an impressive presence. These factors could be argued to be necessary to overcome the traditional stereotypes of women, such as being risk averse, weak, and afraid of success. Unfortunately, the narrow band of acceptable behavior for women contained some contradictions, the most obvious being take risks but be consistently successful, be tough but easy to get along with, be ambitious but do not expect equal treatment, and take responsibility but be open to the advice of others, that is more senior men. These findings suggest that additional criteria for success were applied to women so that women had to have more assets and fewer liabilities than men.

As part of the same study, Morrison et al. (1987) also examined the experiences of women who had advanced to levels of general management. They identified four critical work experiences: being accepted by their organizations, receiving support and encouragement, being given training and developmental opportunities, and being offered challenging work and visible assignments. In speculating about their future success, these career-successful women perceived that there were even more constraints and less support now than in lower-level positions. Many reported exhaustion and talked about their futures involving doing something very different from what they were currently doing. In a series of follow-up interviews, Morrison, White, and Van Velsor (1992) obtained information from approximately one-third of their original sample and found that although some women had made progress, many were still stuck.

The literature on work experiences and career development can be organized within a framework proposed by Morrison (1992). Her model for successful career development includes three elements which interact over time to spur and sustain development. These elements are challenge, recognition, and support. This model is based on research with women in managerial practice and is consistent with Morrison's earlier work with McCall and Lombardo (McCall, Lombardo, and Morrison, 1988), which identified three work experiences with developmental value – specific jobs, other people, and hardships. These can be recast as challenge, the presence or absence of recognition, and support. McCall et al. (1988) studied the kinds of experiences that developed managers and what made them developmental. They found that five broad categories of experience had developmental potential (challenging jobs, other people particularly bosses, hardships, course work, off-the job experiences) but that it was also important for the individual to have learned lessons from them. Learning was made possible, but not guaranteed, by these experiences.

Morrison (1992) defines the components of her model as follows. The *challenge* of new situations and difficult goals prompts managers to learn lessons and skills that will help them perform well at higher levels. *Recognition* includes acknowledgment and rewards for achievement and the resources to continue achieving in the form of promotions, salary increases, and awards. *Support* involves acceptance and understanding along with values that help managers incorporate their career into rich and rewarding lives. This model assumes that all three elements must be present in the same relative proportions over time – balanced – to permit and sustain development.

Morrison (1992) proposes that, for women, an imbalance typically occurs such that the level of challenge exceeds the other two components. Her research shows that aspects of assignments and day-to-day life which constitute challenge are often overlooked, recognition may be slow, and traditional support systems may fall short. Common barriers to advancement (stereotypes, prejudices, male discomfort) contribute to this imbalance, and as a consequence managerial women become exhausted, experience failure, and may "bail out" of this frustrating work situation.

An important method for preparing individuals for executive jobs is to plan a sequence of assignments that provide continued challenge, for example changing or rotating jobs every year or two. New assignments require the learning of new or better skills, broaden one's perspective, stretch the individual to develop, and also serve as "tests" by which individuals are rewarded and/or promoted.

An interesting question is whether or not managerial and professional women experience the same developmental job demands and learn similar skills from them. One possible explanation for the glass ceiling is that women are afforded different developmental opportunities than men over the course of their careers. McCall, Lombardo, and Morrison (1988) and Horgan (1989), suggest that certain types of job assignments and challenging experiences are less available to women. For example, women may be offered staff, not line jobs, and jobs that are not high profile or challenging.

Some of these suggestions were supported by Ohlott, Ruderman, and McCauley (1990) when they looked at the demands of managerial jobs and factors that may complicate learning from the job. They found that women experienced very different demands from managerial jobs and they had to work harder to prove themselves, but women were also learning about managerial work from a greater variety of sources than were men. Horgan (1989) also suggests that what is learned from a given set of developmental experiences may differ between men and women.

Although some sources of challenge are common to all managers (high stakes, adverse business conditions, dealing with difficult staff members) women may experience additional challenges such as prejudice, isolation, or conflict between career and personal life, and may also face higher performance standards, more adverse conditions (resentment and hostility of male staff), more scrutiny, and more "second-shift" work (Hochschild, 1989). Despite these things, limiting challenge is dangerous for the career advancement of women, since giving women less important jobs and not considering them for key assignments blocks their advancement by denying them important business experiences. Morrison (1992) advocates not reducing the level of job challenge but reducing demands from other sources – by reducing prejudice, promoting other women, using the same performance standards – and providing commensurate recognition and support so that the critical balance of these three items is retained.

Education, training, and development can be conceived of as being either or both challenge and support. To the extent that they may provide technical training, coaching and key assignments, they represent challenge and a chance to improve/prove oneself. To the extent that they may involve training geared to women, for example assisting women with issues unique to being women in male-dominated organizations or industries, or providing career pathing or mentoring, they could be viewed as support activities. Some activities, for example mentoring, clearly involve aspects of challenge and support.

Recognition involves acknowledging and adjusting to the additional challenges faced by women in organizations because they are women. Equal performance by men and women in a male-dominated organization may mean that women have overcome more and this must be recognized. Furthermore, when contemplating a challenge such as a new task or promotion, women may seem less keen because they are aware of the additional challenge of being a women performing that new task. The reward system must account for this. Morrison concludes that expected rewards fall short for women when one considers additional demands and sacrifices needed. Women are more likely to have the title "acting" and do the job before getting it than are male colleagues, and receive fewer promotions and benefits, and less pay than men (Morrison and Von Glinow, 1990). The forms that recognition takes include pay, promotion, prerequisites, inclusion in decision making, respect and credibility, and faith (Morrison, 1992). Statistics that indicate the continuing presence of a glass ceiling are evidence that recognition in the form of promotion has not been forthcoming for women.

Support is necessary to help women cope with the additional demands, and the absence of acceptance and colleagueship contributes to the isolation and discouragement that women feel (Morrison, White, and Van Velsor, 1987). Sources of support include features of the work environment such as mentors, sponsors, information feedback, and networks as well as organizational and societal support for dual-career couples. Women may face additional unique challenges because of the scarcity of female role models, difficulty in getting feedback, and a lack of acceptance and support (Morrison, White, and Van Velsor, 1987).

■ **Developmental job experiences** ■

Some progress has also been made in identifying specific developmental properties of jobs. Ohlott, Ruderman, and McCauley (1990, 1994) compared male and female managers" experiences of developmental job demands and examined managerial skills learned from them. Their findings indicated that female mangers were experiencing job demands to a greater extent than were male mangers and that female managers were learning more from their experiences. One hundred and six managerial women and 146 managerial men completed the Job Challenge Profile. Women scored higher than men on six scales (lack of top management support, lack of strategic direction, conflict with boss, downsizing/reorganization, achieving goals through personal influence, and establishing personal credibility). Men scored significantly higher than women on only one scale, supportive boss. Women also scored significantly higher than men on five of the seven "complicating factors" (for example, not part of the organization's "old boy" network); men scored higher on one (no one higher in the organization was looking out for their careers). Interestingly women seemed to be learning more from their experiences than were men.

Van Velsor and Hughes (1990), in an interview study of 189 managerial men and 78 managerial women, also observed that women and men learned different things. Women were focused on discovering who they were as individuals in their organizations, on finding their niche, and on integrating self with their business and working environments. Men focused on the acquisition and mastery of more specific business skills. This difference in emphasis may result from women having had less organizational experience. A number of factors (greater isolation, ambiguous criteria of what a good manager is) may also contribute to the more complex working environment women face producing more "personal" development.

## ■ Developmental relationships ■

The literature on careers suggests that mentors play a crucial role in career development and that they may be even more critical to the career success of women than of men (Kanter, 1977; Hennig and Jardim, 1977; Morrison, White, and Van Velsor, 1987). The literature reports that more women than men who advance to corporate management have mentors, and women who fail to reach these levels cite the absence of mentors as critical to their failure. Persons with mentors have been found to have more organizational policy influence, access to important people and resources (Fagenson, 1989), and higher promotion rates, income, and income satisfaction (Dreher and Ash, 1990).

Although mentors are critical to the success of women, there is evidence that there may be a smaller supply of mentors available to women than to men (Murrell, Crosby, and Ely, 1995). Women may have trouble finding mentors because they are different from men in more senior positions, they occupy a token status, and there may be potential discomfort in cross-gender relationships (Ragins, 1989). Noe (1988) identified six potential barriers to mentoring relationships involving women. These included lack of contact with potential mentors, high visibility of women as protégés due to their small numbers (tokenism), negative stereotypes making women unattractive as protégés, behavioural differences between men and women, women's use of non-male influence strategies, and cultural and organizational biases with respect to cross-gender relationships. Mentor relationships that cross gender lines must be concerned about managing actual closeness and intimacy in the relationship, as well as the perception of those things by others in the organization (Clawson and Kram, 1984). This was highlighted in Bowen's (1985) study which found that resentment of co-workers was a problem in cross-gender mentoring relationships; however, both mentors and protégés felt that the positive benefits more than offset the problem. In a study of male mentors and their protégés, Kram (1985) found that female protégés were more likely to experience greater social distance, discomfort, and overprotectiveness than male protégés.

In addition to their role in career success, mentoring relationships may have a special role in improving the quality of organizational life for women. The literature suggests that one of the moderating variables which may influence the effect of stress on professional women is mentoring. Mentoring relationships have the potential to alleviate women's stress by increasing their self-confidence, forewarning them about career stress and suggesting ways to deal with it. In addition, female mentors provide unique role models for female protégés because they can more easily relate to the stresses that young women face – discrimination, stereotyping, family/work interface, and social isolation (Nelson and Quick, 1985).

At the present time there are not sufficient women at senior levels in organizations for them to be able to provide all of the mentoring needs of younger women. Ragins and Cotton (1991) found that women and men do have equal intentions to mentor; however, women perceived more drawbacks to engaging in that role. The drawbacks cited were time and request overload. We must remember that the women exist in organizations in which they may not have an appropriate balance of challenge, recognition, and support. If they experience the typical imbalance that Morrison (1999) anticipates, they will have inadequate support for the amount of challenge. This will influence their perception of the difficulty of the challenge of being a mentor, given their inadequate level of support.

An additional source of organizational support may be peer relationships and interpersonal networks. Such networks may also be a source of challenging work and recognition; however, this discussion will focus on their role in support. It has been suggested that women lack access to informal networks with male colleagues – the "old boy network" (Ragins and Sundstrom, 1989; Ibarra, 1993). This may result for several reasons. Women may not be aware of informal networks and their importance and potential usefulness, they may not be as skilled as men in building informal networks, and they may prefer to communicate with others similar to themselves. Men, being the dominant group, may want to maintain their dominance by excluding women from informal interactions. If women are excluded from male networks, they may be missing several ingredients important for career success such as information, resources, support, advice, influence, power, allies, mentors, sponsors, and privilege.

Kram and Isabella (1985) examined the role of peer relationships and found they provided a range of developmental supports for personal and professional growth at all career stages. These functions were similar to those obtained from mentors. Although some peer relationships provided only one career function, others provided several career and psychosocial functions. Peer relationships, unlike mentor relationships, were characterized by mutuality, with both individuals experienced at being the giver as well as the receiver of various functions.

There have been relatively few studies of women's and men's networks in organizations. Brass (1984, 1985) examined interaction patterns of men and women in one organization and the effects of these patterns on perceptions of influence and actual promotions. Women were generally rated less influential than men but were similar to men on many other measures. Women and men were not well integrated into one another's networks. Promotions were found to be related to centrality in department, men's, and dominant coalition interaction networks. Interestingly, women's networks more closely resembled men's when their immediate work group included both women and men.

Ibarra (1992) used an intergroup perspective to investigate differences in men's and women's access to informal networks at work. Results indicated that men had greater centrality and homophily (relationships with same-sex others) in their network relationships than women. Women's networks were differentiated in that social support was sought from women and instrumental access was sought from men. Men gained centrality through background characteristics such as work experience and professional activities; women gained centrality but added to men's. Women belonging to subgroups with a higher proportion of women had more ties with women but less centrality; however, the gender composition of men's groups did not affect their network patterns.

## ■ Models of career development ■

Most researchers have taken the position that general models of career development should fit women as well as men, particularly if women are entering the same occupations and are similar to men in abilities and ambitions. Issues of child rearing and family have been given little attention and it has been assumed that women would have successful careers by following the male model and by sharing child and home responsibilities with their partners. For dual-career families with children, two people now attempt to do the work of two careers and one homemaker role. Earlier in this century, before the influx of women into the workforce, two people managed one career and one home. Although some work in the home can be purchased by dual-career couples, research by Hochschild (1989) indicates that, in such couples, women perform 30 extra 24-hour days per year of "second shift" work, compared to their male partners. Clearly, not all of the traditional homemaker's work can be or is purchased. The dual-career couple has much left to do, and women do the bulk of it.

This difference, as well as findings from literature on the psychology of women, indicates that career development for women may be different from career development for men (Phillips and Imkoff, 1997; Stroh and Reilly, 1999). For example, work on the early career experiences of MBA graduates by Rosen, Templeton, and Kinchline (1981) and by Cox and Harquail (1991), found that career motivation and the need for challenging work were similar for men and women, but women had fewer opportunities to share ideas and receive feedback by interacting with their supervisors. Bailyn (1989) reported, in a closely matched sample of male and female engineers, that women experienced their careers very differently from men, even though in external aspects they were similar. Women engineers reported less self-confidence and a less integrated view of their work and non-work lives.

Gallos (1989) contends that career theories have typically been built on male models of success and work in which there is an assumption of the centrality of work to one's identity and the notion that maturity involves separation from others. For women, attachment to others, not separation, is an important source of both identify and maturity, and their development emphasizes the centrality of relationships, attachments, and caring. These affect how women view the world around them and how they choose to live their lives. The success of a woman's career complements, rather than replaces, close interpersonal relations. Gallos believes that women express their professional selves over a lifetime, with commitment to accomplishment and a desire for a fair treatment and rewards for their efforts, rather than the ongoing organizational affiliation and life choices that put occupational progress first. Phases of development, for women, may not have the linear and predictable character of men's, and women may use a broader range of criteria for evaluating their choices than men (Bardwick, 1980).

To overcome the exclusion of family in the male model of career research, Lee (1993) has argued for a new approach to understanding women's careers which includes the diversity of women's experiences in the workforce and in the family. She proposes six alternative models of women's careers to describe the most common ways women integrate commitment to work and family over the lifespan. Some sequence work and family, one first then the other; others try to combine high commitment to both; still others choose a particular type of work or family situation that makes combining the two easier. She also discusses the costs and benefits of each model for women themselves, the family, organizations, and society. These various models of women's career development show great variety and diversity. It is important to appreciate and legitimize the different patterns that characterize women's commitment to occupation and family over the lifespan. One must consider the lifespan perspective because many women change their levels of involvement and participation in employment and family (Gordon and Whelan, 1998).

Powell and Mainero (1992) offer an approach to the understanding of women's careers that is significantly different from traditional models of men's careers. Their approach incorporates four unique elements: (1) it includes both non-work and work issues; (2) it uses both objective and subjective measures of career success; (3) it includes the influence of personal, organizational, and societal factors on women's choices and outcomes; and (4) it does not assume that women's careers go through a predictable sequence of stages over time.

In conclusion, several writers (Phillips and Imkoff, 1997; Powell and Mainero, 1992; White, 2000) note that women's career and life development involve a variety of choices and constraints, with balance, connectedness, and interdependence as well as achievement and separation issues coming into play. This raises the possibility of unique models of career advancement for women and men.

## ■ Different models of career advancement ■

There is accumulating resaerch evidence supporting the notion of different models of career advancement for women and men. Kirchmeyer (1998), in a study of 292 mid-career managers, examined potential differential effects of four types of career success determinants among women and men. The four career success determinants were: human capital variables, gender roles, supportive relationships, and family status variables. Both subjective and objective measures of career success were included (income, organizational-level and self-reported success). She hypothesized that the effects of human capital and interpersonal support would be stronger for men, the effects of gender roles would be stronger for women, and the effects of family status would be opposite for women and men in predicting objective career success indicators. She predicted, for perceived career success, that human capital measures would have stronger effects for men, gender role would have stronger effects for women, and that interpersonal and family status measures would have similar effects for women and men. Kirchmeyer found support for all hypothesized relationships with the exceptions of the family status measure which was found to have similar effects for women and men.

Kirchmeyer (1998) reported that men and women indicated generally similar levels on the career determinants. Men and women indicated similar perceptions of career success as well. Women did have more career interruptions, fewer children, were less likely to be married, were less likely to have a non-employed spouse, and earned less money. Kirchmeyer was also able to explain more variance in men's career success than in women's.

Kirchmeyer (1999) later compared the career progression of men and women mid-career managers using a longitudinal research design. The groups of men and women were selected to have similar education and experience profiles. There was evidence that women's careers unfolded differently than men's, with gaps in income and number of promotions widening over time. Kirchmeyer measured change in progression from time of MBA graduation to the present and then change over the following four years. Three career success indicators were used: income, promotion, and a subjective indicator of perceived career success. Five determinants of career success indicators were considered simultaneously: human capital, individual, interpersonal, relational demography, and family. Although women and men earned the same incomes in the year of graduation, women reported less income progression since MBA graduation and less income change in the four years between these two measurement periods, as well as less likelihood of promotion. Perceived success at the two measurements showed no gender differences.

Kirchmeyer found that certain determinants of managerial success affected men and women differently. Training was associated with greater income for men and job tenure had a positive effect on perceived success only for men. Women reported a lower payoff from education and experience than did men. Having a mentor had a positive effect only on men's income progression. Children lowered women's perceptions of success at both measurement points while they increased men's perception of success. Children also tended to have a positive effect on men's income change and a negative effect on women's. Kirchmeyer concludes, along with others (Gallos, 1989; Powell and Mainero, 1992; Tharenou, 1990), that gender-specific career models are needed – trying to understand women's careers using the traditional male model is "a case of comparing apples and oranges."

Tharenou, Latimer, and Conroy (1994), in a sample of Australian managers, also concluded that career models tended to be gender-specific, and they explained more variance for men's career progression than for women's. Four categories of determinants of career success have been considered in most of this work. *Human capital* determinants refer to personal investments one makes to increase one's value in the workplace (education, job tenure). *Individual* determinants include personality, levels of motivation, and sex roles. *Interpersonal* determinants include supportive relationships (mentors, peers). *Family* determinants include family status variables that can effect careers (marital, parental).

Tharenou (undated manuscript) specifically tested gender-specific models of managerial advancement using a sample of 1,682 female and 1,763 male Australian mangers. Four categories of determinants of career advancement were considered. Individual (age, education), interpersonal (for example, interpersonal support), organizational (for example, training) and home influences (for example, children, family interference with work). Tharenou used salary and managerial level in combination to reflect managerial advancement. Her model is comprehensive, containing relationships among variables common to women and men, and relationships between some measures that are hypothesized to be different between women and men.

Her results showed that gender-specific models were required. More specifically, women's education was found to lead to greater managerial advancement than men's, both directly and through increased training. Women's training, however, led to fewer promotions than men's. Children were shown to reduce women's work experience and increase men's, and work experiences led to more promotions but less managerial advancement of women than men. Women's promotion was found to lead to less managerial advancement than men's.

Tharenou (undated manuscript) provides one of the few tests of an integrated model of women's career advancement. She suggests a sequenced interaction between individual male-typed traits, level of education, work experiences, and responsibilities for children, and organizational career encouragement, training, and promotion. Women had lower managerial advancement than men because of their lower human capital inputs of training and work experience, structural barriers in regard to promotion and training, and the multiple roles of manager and mother.

Finally, Stroh, Brett, and Reilly studied the career progression of male and female managers employed by 20 *Fortune* 500 companies. All respondents had been geographically transferred for career advancement during the two years preceding the study. Women managers lagged behind men in both salary progression and frequency of job transfers. The women "had all the right stuff" in terms of levels of education, similar levels of family power, working in similar industries, similar career gaps or exits, and willingness to make geographic moves. But those factors were not enough to equalize salary progression and numbers of geographic moves. Having the "right stuff" (Stroh, Brett, and Reilly, 1992) ended up being more useful for men than for women. Stroh et al. (1982) conclude there is little more that women can do. The responsibility and leverage for equalizing returns/benefits from having the "right stuff" must rest with employers (see also Powell, 1990, Tharenou and Conroy, 1994).

## ■  New research findings  ■

To empirically examine some of the hypotheses reported above, we undertook an investigation of the work experiences and career success of managerial and professional women. (McKeen and Burke, 1991). A total of 792 women business school graduates completed questionnaires, a 55 percent response rate. The sample tended to be in early career (1–10 years work experience), fairly young (average age about 30), married (about 66 percent), but childless (about 66 percent). In order to collect a variety of data, three versions of the questionnaire were developed, with each having common and unique measures. Each version was randomly sent to one-third of the female business graduates. About 270 women completed each version. As expected, there were no differences on the common measures across the three subsamples. Each version of the questionnaire examined different work and career experiences but included the same measures of career success.

McKeen and Burke (1991) reported the results of women's participation in 14 different education, training, and development activities (number, usefulness) and their self-reported career success. Professional and managerial women who participated in a greater number of education, training, and development activities were more job satisfied, more career satisfied, more job involved, and held more optimistic future career prospects. Similarly, women who rated their education, training, and development activities more *useful* reported all of the above and were also less likely to intend to quit their organizations.

McKeen and Burke (1991) also examined the relationship of five work experiences with measures of career success and career progress in a large sample of Canadian managerial and professional women. Four of these experiences constituted types of support: (1) support and encouragement by one's organization; (2) training and development opportunities; (3) feeling accepted; (4) an absence of tension from overload and ambiguity from being woman. Women who reported more positive work experiences in these areas also reported greater job and career satisfaction, job involvement, and career optimism, and lower intentions to quit. These work experiences were most strongly related to job and career satisfaction and less strongly related to job involvement and future career prospects.

We have since undertaken more sophisticated analyses of our data to more systematically and comprehensively understand relationships of various work experiences and career outcomes. We first developed a model which considered the use of career strategies and levels of supervisor support as exogenous variables, career satisfaction and job satisfaction as endogenous variables, and future career prospects and intent to quit as outcome measures. LISREL analyses (see figure 9.1) indicated that the data provided a very good fit to the model.

The following comments are offered in summary. First, use of career strategies had direct effects on levels of career satisfaction and future career prospects, and indirect effects on future career prospects through career satisfaction. Second, supervisor support had direct effects on career and job satisfaction, and indirect effects on job satisfaction through career satisfaction, and on intent to quit through job satisfaction. Third, both job satisfaction and future career prospects had direct effects on intentions to quit. Fourth, supervisor support had an indirect effect on intent to quit through job satisfaction. Fifth, use of career strategies had an indirect effect on intentions to quit through career satisfaction, and through career satisfaction and future career prospects.

We then developed a research model which considered work stress and levels of job challenge as exogenous variables, emotional exhaustion and job satisfaction as endogenous variables, and self-reported psychosomatic symptoms and intent to quit as out-

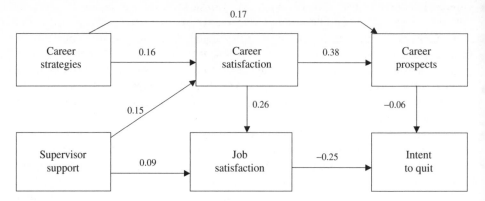

**Figure 9.1** Work experiences, satisfactions, and career outcomes

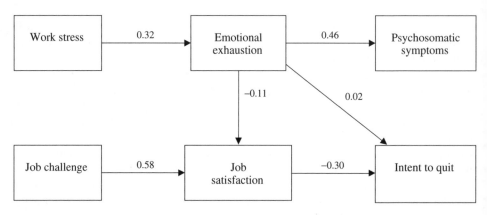

**Figure 9.2** Work experiences, satisfaction, and well-being

comes. LISREL analyses indicated that the data provided a good fit to the model (see figure 9.2).

The following comments are offered in summary. First, work stress had direct effects on emotional exhaustion and job satisfaction. Second, job challenge had a direct effect on job satisfaction. Third, emotional exhaustion had direct effects on psychosomatic symptoms, job satisfaction, and intent to quit. Fourth, job satisfaction had a direct effect on intent to quit. Fifth, job challenge had an indirect effect on intent to quit through job satisfaction. Sixth, work stress had on indirect effect on psychosomatic symptoms through emotional exhaustion. Sixth, work stress had indirect effects on intent to quit through emotional exhaustion, and through both emotional exhaustion and job satisfaction. Emotional exhaustion had an indirect effect on intent to quit through job satisfaction.

We also developed a more comprehensive research model to examine the relationship of participation in training and development activities (number, usefulness) and other variables. Number and usefulness of training and development activities were

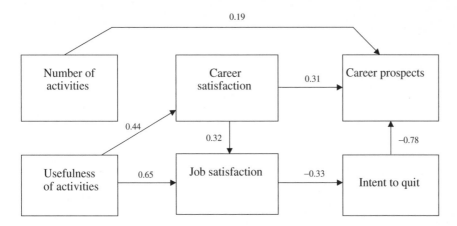

**Figure 9.3**   Training and development, career satisfaction, and career outcomes

exogenous variables, career and job satisfaction served as endogenous variables, and future career prospects and intent to quit were indicators of career success. LISREL analyses (see figure 9.3) indicated that the data provided a good fit to the model.

The following direct and indirect effects were observed. First, participation in a greater number of training and development activities had a direct positive relationship with future career prospects. Second, usefulness of training and development activities had direct effects on both career satisfaction and job satisfaction, career satisfaction in turn having direct effects on both career prospects and job satisfaction. Third, job satisfaction had a direct effect on intentions to quit. Fourth, intentions to quit had a direct negative effect on future career prospects. Fifth, usefulness of training and development activities had indirect effects on future career prospects through career satisfaction and through the career satisfaction–job satisfaction–intention to quit path.

Finally, a comprehensive research model was developed to consider specific work experiences proposed by Morrison, White, and Van Velsor (1987) and career outcomes. These were examined in a preliminary way by McKeen and Burke (1991). In this model, four work experiences served as exogenous variables (support and encouragement, training and development opportunities, challenging and visible assignments, acceptance) job and career satisfaction serving as endogenous variables and two career outcomes (future career prospects, intent to quit) serving as dependent variables. LISREL analyses (see figure 9.4) indicated a good fit of the data to the model.

The following direct and indirect relationships were observed. First, support and encouragement and career satisfaction had direct effects on future career prospects. Second, acceptance and job satisfaction had direct effects on intent to quit. Third, both training and development opportunities, and challenging and visible assignments, had direct effects on self-reported career satisfaction. Fourth, challenging and visible assignments also had a direct effect on job satisfaction. Fifth, training and development opportunities, and challenging and visible assignments, had indirect effects on career prospects through career satisfaction. Sixth, challenging and visible assignments, and training and development opportunities, had indirect effects on intent to quit through career and job satisfaction, and job satisfaction, respectively.

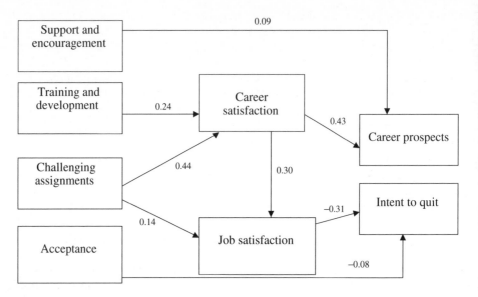

**Figure 9.4** Work experiences, career satisfactions, and career outcomes

These analyses provide empirical support for the role of particular work experiences (Morrison, White, and Van Velsor, 1987; Morrison, 1992) in the career development and success of managerial and professional women. The specific findings highlight work experiences that can be fastened for managerial women as part of broader organizational efforts to support women's advancement (Morrison, 1992).

■ **Alternative work arrangements** ■

It has been suggested that providing greater flexibility in how, when, and where work gets done for short periods of time may be one way that organizations can support women's career advancement (Adams, 1995; Schwartz, 1992). Part-time work arrangements are one such option that has received increasing research attention.

MacDermid, Lee, Buck, and Williams (2000) examined part-time work arrangements among 78 women professionals and mangers to learn more about their implications for career development. Women today, rather than following the typical male pattern of working steadily full time for the same employer for an entire career, are using alternative work arrangements such as telecommuting, sharing jobs, and reduced workload arrangements for significant periods of time (Catalyst, 1997). Women have always had more diverse career patterns than men (Lee, 1993). Women are more likely to leave and re-enter the labour force and to work part-time. Historically, low status and poorly compensated job incumbents have exhibited these patterns, often involuntarily. Today more high-level women are working this way.

MacDermid et al. (2000) examined 78 cases of women professionals and managers working on a reduced workload basis (RWL) for family or personal reasons. RWL was defined as voluntarily working 90 FTE with an accompanying reduction in pay. Interviews were conducted with the person working less, as well as other relevant stakeholders (senior manager, a co-worker, an HR representative, spouses, or partners). Respondents worked in 44 different North American employing organizations, most being large in size. Most respondents were married and parents of young children. On average, the RWL had been ongoing for 4.4 years and represented a 0.72 FTE. The reduced hours per week averaged 32, about 17 hours less than worked on full-time basis. The average salary was $80,000.

How successful were these arrangements? Global ratings of success were made by the researchers on a 1–9 scale (1 = consistently negative outcomes across stakeholders; 9 = consistently positive outcomes). The average rating was 6.8. Direct reports ratings of these managers and professionals effectiveness was 7.2.

What were the expected and actual implications of these RWL arrangements? Most of the managers and professionals were satisfied with their jobs. Most (about two-thirds) felt that the quality of their performance had been maintained or improved by working a RWL, and in most cases their managers agreed. About 20 percent of the senior managers were rated by the researchers as supportive of the RWL arrangement.

Most of the managers and about half of the professionals were satisfied with the likely career implications of the RWL arrangement. Many thought they had given up some short-term advancements but were happy with the trade-off. About one-third of the sample had been promoted while working RWL.

Senior managers indicated three concerns about RWL arrangements: (1) how to support continuous professional growth and advancement of individuals who continue on RWL; (2) what to do if an increasing number of people want to work RWL – would this become unmanageable?; (3) some jobs above a certain level in the structure are not "do-able" on a RWL basis.

There were some common factors that distinguished the low success cases. First, these individuals felt underemployed and their advancement was "on hold" until they worked full time. Second, individuals had difficulty, for a variety of reasons, in making the RWL manageable. Third, women in less successful RWL arrangements felt that they were viewed differently by others and felt uncomfortable when comparing themselves to others.

Some factors distinguished the most and least successful RWL arrangments as well. These included: external support (least successful RWL arrangements had disinterested managers and unsupportive corporate cultures) – a supportive manager was the single most important factor critical for success of the RWL; a supportive corporate culture was also in the top five factors important to RWL success; women in less successful RWL arrangements were more concerned about their slower career progress – they were less happy with the trade-off and less sure about how to make career progress; women in both successful and less successful RWL arrangements shared common career development concerns as well – these included missing out on professional networking, being seen as less committed, hesitating to ask for more training, and having less time for professional development.

Individual characteristics emerged as the most important success factors in making RWL arrangements work. Chief among them were flexibility, a strong performance record, and high levels of hard work and commitment. Individual women shouldered tremendous responsibility for their progress under these arrangements. It was clear, however, that RWL arrangements, if properly managed, need not be a career liability.

## ■ Organizational values, work satisfactions and career advancement ■

Thompson, Beauvais, and Lyness (1999) developed a measure of work–family culture and examined its relationship to work–family benefit utilization, organizational attachment, and work–family conflict. Work–family culture consisted of shared assumptions, benefits, and values regarding the extent to which an organization supports and values the integration of employees work and family lives. Three dimensions of work–family culture emerged in their measures: managerial support for work–family balance, career consequences associated with utilizing work–family benefits, and organizational time expectations that may interfere with family responsibilities. Data were obtained using questionnaires from 276 women and men MBA graduates. Perceptions of a supportive work–family culture were related to employees use of work–family benefits. Both work–family benefit availability and supportive work–family culture were positively related to organizational and commitment, and negatively related to work–family conflict and intention to quit.

Burke (2000) examined the relationship of managerial and professional men's perception of organizational values supporting work–personal life balance in their workplace and their work experiences, indicators of work and life satisfaction, and psychological well-being. Data were collected from 283 men using anonymous questionnaires. Managerial men reporting organizational values more supportive of work–personal life balance also reported, less job stress, greater joy in work, lower intentions to quit, greater job career and life satisfaction, fewer psychosomatic symptoms, and more positive emotional and physical well-being. An identical study involving 257 managerial and professional women produced similar findings but fewer statistically significant relationships. It appeared that men may have more consistent benefits from organizational values supporting work–personal life balance. Was this still another example of greater rewards to men from work environment factors? Were women less influenced by organizational values supporting work–personal life balance because of greater demands at work or at home?

## ■ Organizational initiatives ■

The last ten years have been characterized by increased research attention being dedicated to examining women in management issues, an increasing awareness of the glass ceiling in the popular press and media, and yet only slow, hardly visible, change in the number of women reaching positions of executive leadership.

Breaking the glass ceiling requires three types of information (Ragins, Townsend, and Mattis, 1998). First, it is vital to understand the obstacles women face in their advancement. Second, it is helpful to understand the career strategies used by success-ful women. Third, it is central that CEOs have an accurate and complete understand-ing of the obstacles and cultures experienced by their female employees.

Ragins, Townsend, and Mattis (1998) report findings from a national survey of *Fortune* 1,000 CEOs and the highest ranking, most successful women in their com-panies, on the barriers to advancement women faced in their firms and the key career strategies women need to pursue to advance their careers. They report vastly different perspectives between the *Fortune* 1,000 CEOs and the managerial women of organiza-tional and environmental barriers faced by women and of their companies, progress in advancing women.

How do women break the glass ceiling? Ragins, Townsend, and Mattis found that nine career strategies were central to the advancement of these successful women exec-utives, four standing out. These were: consistently exceeding performance expectations; developing a style with which men are comfortable; seeking difficult or high-visibility assignments, and having an influential mentor.

These women had to repeatedly prove their ability by exceeding performance expec-tations. They also had to develop a managerial style acceptable to men that was not too masculine or feminine. They also reported having challenging and highly visible job assignments, such assignments providing both growth and learning challenges. Finally, mentoring was identified as an important element in the career advancement of these successful women.

The CEOs revealed considerable consensus in their views as to what prevents women from advancing. The most common was women's lack of general management or line experience, followed by women not being in the pipeline long enough. The executive women had as their first factor male stereotyping and preconceptions, followed by exclusion from influence networks. The CEOs and executive women had significantly different views on what was holding women back. CEOs say the problem is the women themselves; women saw it as a problem of corporate culture.

This disparity may result from the fact that two environments co-exist in organiza-tions – one for men which explains their advancement, and one for women that has subtle barriers to their advancement. This disparity is important, however, since men are powerful agents of change in most organizations, and the way in which men frame the problem will define potential solutions.

These findings have implications for both organizations and the managerial and professional women they recruit, hire, utilize, and develop. Organizations must realize that managerial and professional women, like men, are not homogeneous (Goffee and Nicholson, 1994). In addition, they must be more sensitive to work and family demands which, together, may be reducing the energy and time available for a single-minded career commitment and in fact adding to the challenge faced by women. Consideration must be given to the possibility of alternative career models in which commitment and energy over one's career may follow a different pattern for employees with primary responsibility for family and children (Gordon and Whelan, 1998). For example, early career commitment when women are single and childless may shift with the as-yet unshared burdens of marriage and children, but re-emerge as children become less dependent. Perhaps organizations need to envision a restructured model in which people with primary family/child responsibility contribute later in their lives what others contribute earlier. At the present time these people are women whose life expectancy is several years greater than that of men in North America. This differential longevity would, for example, permit a different career model in which interested women resume and continue career commitment later in their lives than men.

Other initiatives by organizations to rebalance the challenge–recognition–support model must specifically address the needs of women, and remove the barriers which contribute to the imbalance. Women need active organizational assistance and support in managing their careers. It has been found (Lee, 1993) that more, and more varied, patterns exist in the careers of women than of men. Women face more choices when it comes to investments in work, investments in family, and the timing of children. Men are influenced by these choices, too, but women still experience more dislocation from particular events and usually undertake more second-shift work. Women's choices need to be legitimized and assisted by organizations. It is clear that this second-shift work is not done by free choice in most cases. To say that women choose the "mommy track" or "choose" more flexibility over career development activities, is to avoid discussion of the environment in which this choice occurs. We do not know how women would feel about a variety of career development activities if they could make that decision in an environment of at least equally shared second-shift work. If they had the flexibility they wanted/needed, and we asked them again about career development activities, how would they respond? What employees bring to the workplace is dramatically influenced by their personal circumstances. Situational characteristics are relevant in attitudes to, and energy for, work, and we know from the work of Hochschild (1989) and others that the situational characteristics of women with families are dramatically different from those of men. How organizations respond to these different realities will determine how successful they are in assessing what educated women have to offer at various times in their lives. Organizations with long-run views of their relationships with their employees need to consider the present and future realities of their employees" lives, and to respond creatively and with their employees" input.

What can organizations do to develop such work–life balance values? The most common approach is to create workplace policies that promote them. Accumulating evidence suggests that the presence of such policies has produced inconsistent benefits (Bailyn, 1994; Schwartz, 1992). In some cases these policies have brought about value, attitude and behavior changes; in other cases these policies have existed only on paper. These latter organizations have only paid lip-service to the existence of their policies.

More recently several researchers have begun to describe and evaluate more intensive collaborative projects with organizations interested in addressing work–family concerns. These projects make an explicit link between employees' personal needs (for example, family responsibilities) and business objectives, with the intention of changing work practices so that both the organization and the employees benefit (Rapaport, Bailyn, Kolb, and Fletcher, 1998). The work of Bailyn et al. (1997) describe several "collaborative action research projects" in which researchers work jointly with companies to bring about change in the work culture and the organization of work that will facilitate work–family integration in a meaningful way (Bailyn, Fletcher, and Kolb, 1997; Fletcher and Bailyn, 1996; Fletcher and Rapaport, 1996).

# Conclusions

We believe that the field of women in management has both research and practical relevance. Because this area has only gained research attention within the past ten years, many research questions remain unanswered or have been only partially addressed (Lobel, 1999). In addition, supporting the career aspirations of managerial women has practical implications for women, men, families, organizations, and social policy (see Burke and Davidson, 1994).

Let us now move to the practical agenda. These areas, involving action research projects in field settings, are equally important because the topic of women in management has obvious practical implications. All research in this area does not have to have immediate practical value – though this might be desirable – but some of our research needs to have usefulness. A pressing need in this regard is to document efforts by organizations to develop the talent of women managers and professionals. This will serve to identify what works and does not work, and why. In addition, the successful efforts of some organizations will provide a blueprint for others in their own efforts. Some contributions of this type would include: Adams (1995), Schwartz (1995), Totta and Burke (1995), Mattis (1994, 1995), Christie (1997), Townsend (1997), McAllister (1997), and Catalyst (1998). Efforts by organizations in this area will be more credible to senior corporate leaders. It is also important to have successful CEOs committed to full partnership for women at senior ranks, so that they can influence others at those levels.

We have achieved some understanding of the challenges and obstacles women face in the workplace (and home front) as they pursue their career journeys. We have also gotten a clearer sense of the types of work and career experiences that are likely to be associated with women's advancement (many of which are also likely to be associated with men's advancement as well). We have begun to document "best practice" initiatives among corporations interested in utilizing the talents of all employees, but more attention and effort must be placed here.

A clear gap in the research literature is the limited attention paid to interventions. Although there is substantial agreement on the problems and challenges women face in the development of their careers, there are few descriptions and evaluations of initiatives designed to support the career development of professional and managerial women over the lifespan.

Another gap in the research is the limited knowledge of "what happens" when women at work exhibit changes and transition as they grapple with multiple life roles. More attention has been paid to supporting women's advancement (for example, Catalyst, 1998) resulting in less attention being devoted to understanding how women prepare for the variety of choices they make in navigating the challenges of organizational life and various life roles. Women's lives, even more than men's, are complex (Powell and Mainero, 1992).

REFERENCES

Adams, S. M. (1995): Part-time work: Models that work. *Women in Management Review*, 10, 21–30.

Bailyn, L. (1989): Understanding individual experiences at work: comments on the theory and practice of careers. In M. B. Arthur, D. T. Hall, and B. S. Lawrence (eds), *Handbook of Career Theory*, New York: Cambridge University Press, 477–89.

Bailyn, L. (1994): *Breaking the mold*. New York: The Free Press.

Bailyn, L., Fletcher, J. K., and Kolb, D. (1997): Unexpected connections: considering employees' personal lives can revitalize your business. *Sloan Management Review*, 38, 11–20.

Bardwick, J. (1980): The seasons of a woman's life. In D. McGuigan (ed.), *Women's Lives: New Theory, Research and Policy*, Ann Arbor, MI: University of Michigan Center for Continuing Education of Women, 35–55.

Bowen, D. D. (1985): Were men meant to mentor women? *Training and Development Journal*, 39, 30–4.

Brass, D. J. (1984): Being in the right place: a structural analysis of individual influence in an organization. *Administrative Science Quarterly*, 29, 518–39.

Brass, D. J. (1985): Men's and women's networks: a study of interaction patterns and influence in an organization. *Academy of Management Journal*, 32, 662–9.

Burke, R. J. (2000): Do managerial men benefit from organizational values supporting work–personal life balance? *Women in Management Review*, 15, 81–9.

Burke, R. J. and Davidson, M. J. (1994): Women in management: Current research issues. In M. J. Davidson and R. J. Burke (eds), *Women in management – Current research issues*. London: Paul Chapman Publishing, 1–8.

Burke, R. J. and McKeen, C. A. (1992): Women in management. In C. L. Cooper and I. T. Robertson (eds), *International Review of Industrial and Organizational Psychology*, New York: John Wiley, 245–83.

Catalyst (1997): *A new approach to flexibility: Managing the work/time equation*. New York: Catalyst.

Catalyst (1998): *Advancing women in business: The Catalyst guide*. San Francisco, CA: Jossey-Bass.

Christie, K. (1997): Deloitte & Touche takes an integrated approach to the advancement of women. *Equal Opportunities International*, 16, 14–22.

Clawson, J. G. and Kram, K. E. (1984): Managing cross-gender mentoring. *Business Horizons*, 17, 22–32.

Cox, T. H. and Harquail, C. V. (1991): Career paths and career success in the early career stage of male and female MBA. *Journal of Vocational Behavior*, 29, 54–75.

Dreher, G. F. and Ash, R. A. (1990): A comparative study of mentoring among men and women in managerial, professional and technical positions. *Journal of Applied Psychology*, 75, 539–46.

Fagenson, E. A. (1989): The mentor advantage: perceived career/job experiences of proteges versus non-proteges. *Journal of Organizational Behavior*, 10, 309–20.

Fletcher, J. K. and Bailyn, L. (1996): Challenging the last boundary: Re-connecting work and family. In M. B. Arthur and D. M. Rousseau (eds), *Boundaryless careers*. Oxford: Oxford University Press.

Fletcher, J. K. and Rapaport, R. (1996): Work family issues as a catalyst for change. In S. Lewis and J. Lewis (eds), *Rethinking employment: The work family challenge*. London: Sage Publications.

Gallos, J. V. (1989): Exploring women's development: implications for career theory, practice and research. In M. B. Arthur, D. T. Hall, and B. S. Lawrence (eds), *Handbook of Career Theory*, New York: Cambridge University Press, 110–32.

Goffee, R. and Nicholson, N. (1994): Career development in male and female managers – convergence or collapse? In M. J. Davidson and R. J. Burke (eds), *Women in management*, London: Paul Chapman, 80–92.

Gordon, J. R. and Whelan, K. S. (1998): Successful professional women in mid-life: How organizations can more effectively understand and respond to the challenges. *Academy of Management Executive*, 12, 8–24.

Hennig, M. and Jardim, A. (1977): *The Managerial Woman*. New York: Anchor Press/Doubleday.

Hochschild, A. (1989): *The Second Shift*. New York: Avon Books.

Horgan, D. D. (1989): A cognitive learning perspective in women becoming expert managers. *Journal of Business and Psychology*, 3, 299–313.

Ibarra, H. (1992): Homophily and differential returns: sex differences in network structure and access in an advertising firm. *Administrative Sciences Quarterly*, 37, 422–47.

Ibarra, H. (1993): Personal networks of women and minorities in management. *Academy of Management Review*, 18, 56–87.

Kanter, R. M. (1977): *Men and Women of the Corporation*. New York: Basic Books.

Kinsley, M. J. (1993): A pragmatic approach to workplace equality. *Business and the Contemporary World*, 5, 171–84.

Kirchmeyer, C. (1998): Determinants of managerial career success: Evidence and explanation of male/female differences. *Journal of Management*, 24, 673–92.

Kirchmeyer, C. (1999): Women's vs men's managerial careers: Is this a case of comparing apples and oranges? Paper presented at the 1999 Annual Meeting of the Academy of Management, Chicago, August.

Kram, K. E. (1985): *Mentors in Organizations*. Chicago: Scott, Foresman.

Kram, K. E. and Isabella, L. (1985): Mentoring alternatives: the role of peer relationships in career development. *Academy of Management Journal*, 28, 110–32.

Lobel, S. A. (1999): Impacts of diversity and work–life initiatives in organizations. In G. N. Powell (ed.), *Handbook of gender and work*. Thousand Oaks, CA: Sage Publications, 453–75.

Lee, M. D. (1993): Women's involvement in professional careers and family life: themes and variations. *Business in the Contemporary World*, 5, 106–27.

MacDermid, S. M., Lee, M. D., Buck, M., and Williams, M. L. (2001): Alternative work arrangements among professionals and managers: Rethinking career development and success. *Journal of Management Development*, 20, 305–17.

Mattis, M. C. (1994): Organizational initiatives in the USA for advancing managerial women. In M. J. Davidson and R. J. Burke (eds), *Women in management*. London: Paul Chapman, 261–76.

Mattis, M. C. (1995): Corporate initiatives for advancing women. *Women in Management Review*, 10, 5–14.

McAllister, M. (1997): Profiting from diversity: Westpac Banking Corporation. *Equal Opportunities International*, 16, 23–33.

McCall, M. W., Lombardo, M. M., and Morrison, A. M. (1988): *The Lessons of Experience*. New York: Lexington Books.

McKeen, C. A. and Burke, R. J. (1991): Work experiences and career success of managerial and professional women: study design and preliminary findings. *Canadian Journal of Administrative Sciences*, 8, 251–8.

Morrison, A. M. (1992): *The New Leaders*. San Francisco, CA: Jossey-Bass Publishers.

Morrison, A. M. and Von Glinow, M. A. (1990): Women and minorities in management. *American Psychologist*, 45, 200–8.

Morrison, A. M., White, R. P., and Van Velsor, E. (1987): *Breaking the Glass Ceiling*, Reading, MA: Addison-Wesley.

Morrison, A. M., White, R. P., and Van Velsor, E. (1992): *Breaking the glass ceiling*. Updated edition. Reading, MA: Addison-Wesley.

Murrell, A. J., Crosby, F. J., and Ely, R. J. (1995): *Mentoring dilemmas: Developmental relationships within multi-cultural organizations*. Mahwah, NJ: Lawrence Erlbaum Associates, Inc.

Nelson, D. L. and Quick, J. D. (1985): Professional women: are distress and disease inevitable? *Academy of Management Review*, 10, 206–18.

Noe, R. A. (1988): Women and mentoring: A review and research agenda. *Academy of Management Review*, 13, 65–78.

Ohlott, P. J., Ruderman, M. N., and McCauley, C. D. (1990): Women and men: equal opportunity for development? Paper presented at the Annual Meeting of the Academy of Management, August, San Francisco.

Ohlott, P. J., Ruderman, M. N., and McCauley, C. D. (1994): Gender differences in manager's developmental job experiences. *Academy of Management Journal*, 37, 46–67.

Phillips, S. D. and Imkoff, A. R. (1997): Women and career development. *Annual Review of Psychology*, 48, 31–59.

Powell, G. N. (1990): One more time: do male and female managers differ? *Academy of Management Executive*, 4, 68–75.

Powell, G. N. (1999): Reflections on the glass ceiling: Recent trends and future prospects. In G. N. Powell (ed.), *Handbook of gender and work.* Thousand Oaks, CA: Sage Publications, 325–46.

Powell, G. N. and Mainero, L. A. (1992): Cross-currents in the river of time: Conceptualizing the complexities of women's careers. *Journal of Management,* 18, 215–37.

Ragins, B. R. (1989): Barriers to mentoring: the female manager's dilemma. *Human Relations,* 42, 1–22.

Ragins, B. R. and Cotton, J. C. (1991): Easier said than done: gender differences in perceived barriers to gaining a mentor. *Academy of Management Journal,* 34, 939–51.

Ragins, B. R. and Sundstrom, E. (1989): Gender and power in organizations: a longitudinal perspective. *Psycholgical Bulletin,* 105, 51–88.

Ragins, B. R., Townsend, B., and Mattis, M. (1998): Gender gap in the executive suite: CEOs and female executives report on breaking the glass ceiling. *Academy of Management Executive,* 12, 28–42.

Rapaport, R., Bailyn, L., Kolb, D., and Fletcher, J. K. (1998): *Rethinking life and work.* Waltham, MA: Pegasus Communications.

Rosen, B., Templeton, M. E., and Kirchline, K. (1981): The first few years on the job: women in management. *Business Horizons,* 24, 26–9.

Schwartz, D. B. (1995): The impact of work–family policies on women's career development: boon or bust? *Women in Management Review,* 10, 31–45.

Schwartz, F. N. (1992): *Breaking with Tradition,* New York: Time-Warner Books.

Stroh, L. K., Brett, J. M., and Reilly, A. H. (1992): All the right stuff: A comparison of male and female managers. *Journal of Applied Psychology,* 77, 251–60.

Stroh, L. K. and Reilly, A. H. (1999): Gender and careers: Present experiences and emerging trends. In G. N. Powell (ed.), *Handbook of gender and work.* Thousand Oaks, CA: Sage Publications, 307–24.

Tharenou, P. (1990): Psychological approach for investigating women's career advancement. *Australian Journal of Management,* 15, 363–78.

Tharenou, P. (undated manuscript): Managerial advancement: A confirmatory test of gender-specific models. School of Business and Economics, Monash University, Melbourne, Australia.

Tharenou, P. and Conroy, D. (1994): Men and women managers advancement: Personal or situational determinants. *Applied Psychology: An International Review,* 43, 5–31.

Tharenou, P., Latimer, S., and Conroy, D. (1994): How do you make it to the top? An examination of influences on women's and men's managerial advancement. *Academy of Management Journal,* 37, 899–931.

Thompson, C. A., Beauvais, L. L., and Lyness, K. S. (1999): When work–family benefits are not enough: The influence of work–family culture on benefit utilization, organizational attachment and work–family conflict. *Journal of Vocational Behavior,* 54, 392–415.

Totta, J. and Burke, R. J. (1995): Integrating diversity and equality into the fabric of the organization. *Women in Management Review,* 10, 46–53.

Townsend, B. (1997): Breaking through: The glass ceiling revisited. *Equal Opportunities International,* 16, 4–13.

Van Velsor, E. and Hughes, M. W. (1990): Gender differences in the development of managers: How women managers learn from experience. Technical Report 145, Greensboro, NC: Center for Creative Leadership.

White, B. (2000): Lessons from the careers of successful women. In M. J. Davidson and R. J. Burke (eds), *Women in management.* Thousand Oaks, CA: Sage Publications, 164–76.

# 10

# MENTORING AND DEVELOPMENTAL RELATIONSHIPS

*Terri A. Scandura and S. Gayle Baugh*

It has long been recognized that women are not represented in the managerial ranks of companies proportionally to their representation in the full-time, paid workforce. The absence of women in the upper ranks of organizations is particularly noticeable. The proportion of women at the highest levels of organizations has not shown substantial increases over the past twenty years, which suggests that women have not advanced to the extent that one might expect, given their greater educational preparation and increasing levels of experience (Ragins, Townsend, and Mattis, 1998).

The reasons for this state of affairs are not immediately obvious. This chapter draws upon role theory as one approach to understanding the absence of women at the upper levels of management in organizations. Roles and role theory offer an important perspective to understanding the issues facing women in management. Role theory can also present a useful vantage point for exploring developmental relationships, one of the mechanisms suggested to women for overcoming the barriers they face in advancing into upper levels of management (Noe, 1988; Ragins, 1989).

Theory and research on role negotiation and role making offers significant new insight into the mentoring process. Improved understanding of the mentoring process will provide the basis for useful prescriptions for women to maximize the benefits of mentoring to achieve upward mobility in organizations. In the discussion that follows, a role theory perspective is used to examine the extent to which existing definitions of work and gender roles serve as a key deterrent to the effective development of mentoring relationships. We will then highlight several areas for future research on gender roles and mentoring.

The authors would like to acknowledge the contributions of Kim A. Stewart to an earlier version of this chapter.

# ■ Role theory: an overview ■

Historically, the concept of role was taken from early Greek and Roman theater. In this context, a role referred to an actor's portrayal within a dramatic presentation. More recently, Shaw and Costanzo (1970) defined a role as "the functions a person performs when occupying a particular characterization (position) within a particular social context" (p. 326). The social context is an important component of this definition. Part of the social context involves the milieu of other actors and their roles in relation to a focal actor in the situation. Thus, an individual's role is interdependent with the roles of related others in the social context.

It is obvious from the interdependence of roles just described that roles are enacted within a social context. As a result of the social nature of roles, there are other actors who have an interest in a particular individual's role portrayal. Roles are therefore significant to both incumbents and others within the social context in terms of role expectations, role performance, role evaluation, and role sanctions (Biddle and Thomas, 1966). Those in a focal person's role set have a vested interest in socializing the person to behave in a manner that results in little or no change in their own role definition. This interest stems from the need to preserve one's own role within a complex social structure. Thus, very clear messages are usually sent to a role incumbent regarding what behavior is appropriate and inappropriate within that role. These messages are based upon the expectations that the other actors in the social context hold for the focal actor.

Role expectations are beliefs held by others who regularly interact with the role incumbent regarding appropriate behaviors for the role incumbent. For example, in the work context, supervisors will hold expectations for those who report to them. Coworkers, too, will have expectations, some of which may be different from, or even contradictory to, those of the supervisor. Role performance consists of behaviors displayed by the incumbent in the course of enacting the role. Role evaluations are the positive or negative judgments made by others within the social context concerning a role incumbent's performance. For example, performance evaluations are conducted by supervisors on various aspects of an employee's performance, such as the quality and quantity of their work. Coworkers also will evaluate performance, even though they are not always asked to a formal evaluation. They will simply assess how well the focal individual's behavior fits with their own role in the work unit. Role sanctions are actions by others directed toward bringing the incumbent's role performance in line with role expectations. This is accomplished by positively reinforcing appropriate role behaviors and/or disapproving of objectionable role behaviors. Following the above example, a supervisor might write a letter to the personnel file in order to sanction an employee who is consistently tardy for work. Coworkers might use teasing or other verbal sanctions to correct the same behavior.

Clearly, the sanctions applied, based on the expectations among the role set, will influence the way in which the focal individual chooses to enact his or her role in the future, which will, in turn, affect the role set's evaluation of and sanctions directed toward the role incumbent. The role incumbent may also attempt to influence the role set, especially if the incumbent is subjected to contradictory sets of expectations from different members of the role set. Over time, the group will develop a relatively stable set of interlocked behaviors. It is not necessarily the case that all of the individuals involved will be equally satisfied with the stasis achieved, however. Dissatisfaction may occur if a the role set reacts to a focal individual's behavior based on something other than expectations resulting from something other than the individual's work role – her gender role, for example.

## Gender role effects in the workplace

Work roles are obvious in the workplace, and are often formalized in a written job description. The formal, written job description is only a rough outline of the role, however (Graen, 1976). As indicated previously, the details of the work role are further elaborated by the individuals with whom the worker must interact in the course of doing the job. Role expectations of the individuals in the role set influence the manner in which the worker enacts the work role. Thus, roles and role theory are important in understanding workplace behavior. Workplace behavior can also be influenced by other roles, both ascribed and attained, that the worker occupies. Gender roles at work have thus been the subject of much theory and research over the last few decades.

Gender roles are among the most pervasive in our society and influence behavior in a wide range of settings, including the workplace (Deaux, 1985; Deaux and Kite, 1993; Kessler and McKenna, 1978). While one might argue that gender roles are not relevant at work, one's gender role is not easily ignored or discarded at the factory or office door. They influence both the behavior of the worker and the expectations of the worker's role set. There is clear research evidence that gender role expectations influence a number of important processes at work, such as the evaluation of leader effectiveness (Eagly and Johnson, 1990), the experience of work–family conflict (Greenhaus and Parasuraman, 1999), evaluation of job applicants (Graves and Powell, 1988; Heilman, Martell, and Simon, 1988) and mentoring (Ragins, 1989; Scandura and Ragins, 1993).

The influence of gender roles on work role expectations can be easily discerned. Role expectations for managers, and certainly for executives, are still largely based on a male gender role model. These role expectations include decisiveness, rationality, the absence of emotion, and willingness to take risks (Heilman, Block, Martell, and Simon, 1989). This model of the manager is quite opposite to how women are generally characterized – that is, indecisive, emotional, and conventional, or risk averse (Eagly and Johnson, 1990; Freedman and Phillips, 1988; Powell and Butterfield, 1989). Hence, work role stereotypes and gender role stereotypes are congruent for men, but conflicting for women (Gutek, 1988).

The conflict between work role expectations and gender role expectations has been institutionalized in the form of sex role segregation at work (Jacobs, 1999). As a result, women often work in peripheral areas such as personnel management, clerical positions, administrative posts, and other staff functions in which role expectations are more congruent with gender role expectations than in line positions (for example, factory supervisor). Line positions offer better opportunities for upward mobility; however, they are less consistent with the female gender role (Larwood and Gattiker,

1987). As a result, there are few women in senior line positions. The absence of women in key positions may place constraints on the professional mobility of women as a group, because there are few women with the potential to serve as mentors and role models and to encourage more women to work in line positions (Morrison, White, and Van Velsor, 1987). Thus, there is a noticeable degree of gender-based segregation based on position centrality in organizations, with women relegated to the periphery.

Occupational segregation based on gender occurs as well. Gender role expectations have also influenced industry differences in the employment and upward mobility of women. Service occupations offer work roles that are more in line with female gender roles; hence, more women are employed in banking, financial services, and hotel/restaurant management. Yet industries and positions which are more congruent with the female gender role offer lower salaries and fewer promotional opportunities (Gutek, 1988). Clearly, gender and gender roles have an impact on the experience of both men and women in the workplace.

This spillover of gender roles into the workplace affects many workplace phenomena, but it is especially influential with regard to interpersonal interactions in the workplace. Developmental relationships such as mentoring have been suggested as an antidote to workplace segregation and discrimination, but they have not yet proven to be effective in ensuring true equal employment opportunity. Role theory offers an explanation for why the role expectations held by both men and women regarding the appropriate and acceptable role of women at work may impact the cross-gender mentoring process.

## Role conflicts for women

As a result of the discrepancy between managerial roles and gender roles, women experience role conflict in the workplace to a greater extent than men do (Greenhaus and Parasuraman, 1999). The conflict between work role and gender role makes role performance more difficult for women than for men. Women must decide which role to enact, or how to integrate the manager role and the gender role effectively.

Women who are seen as passive and emotional fit the female stereotype and role expectations, but stereotypical feminine behavior is contrary to role expectations for a manager. Managerial women who act according to their gender role may have a difficult time gaining acceptance by male colleagues (Eagly and Johnson, 1990). Women who behave in accordance with the managerial role engage in behavior that is contradictory to that prescribed for their gender role. They are frequently seen as too aggressive, and are evaluated negatively for being too masculine (Fiske, Bersoff, Borgida, Deaux, and Heilman, 1991; Gutek and Larwood, 1987). From a role theory perspective, women who choose to accept either gender role or managerial role as primary are subject to sanctions from their role set due to the failure to effectively enact the other (contradictory) role. These sanctions may take the form of lack of mentoring or mentoring that is designed more to help the woman accept her situation in the workplace than to enhance her career progress. Thus, women are left searching for an effective solution to conflicts presented by their work role and gender role.

■  **Mentoring and role conflict**  ■

A balance of masculine and feminine behaviors may be the optimal approach to the role performance of female managers, and may be particularly advantageous for women seeking a mentor (Scandura and Ragins, 1993). This balance of gender-typed behaviors has been referred to as an androgynous gender role orientation (Spence, 1984). Determining the exact nature of that balance is not a simple issue, however. As a result, women experience more difficulty in role enactment within the context of mentoring relationships than men do, as female protégées struggle to determine what constitutes appropriate role performance in the eyes of their mentor (Clawson and Kram, 1984; Cook, 1979).

Even if they determine the appropriate definition of the expected role, some women may have difficulty in enacting the role. The appropriate role for a female manager may involve some behaviors that are associated with the female gender role (for example, allowing participation) and others that are associated with the managerial role (for example, being decisive). Women may be inexperienced with and feel uncomfortable exhibiting some of the more stereotypically masculine behaviors that are included in the managerial role. They may fail to enact those portions of the role, or enact them less ineffectively. Most men do not have the additional burden of enacting a role for which they are relatively unprepared because acceptable role performance for the managerial role is congruent with their prescribed gender role (for example, Heilman et al., 1989; Schein, 1973, 1975).

Given the difficulties that women experience in role performance in the managerial role, mentoring might offer an approach to learning to manage the inherent conflicts between managerial roles and gender roles. That is, a mentor can model the appropriate mix of behaviors appropriate to each role. In addition, the mentor can offer the opportunity for the female protégée to learn to enact those behaviors effectively. Mentoring, then, would seem to be an equalizing factor with respect to career progression for women and men. However, research has indicated that while women are just as likely as men to report having a mentor, they are not realizing the same benefits in terms of promotions and salary (Dreher and Ash, 1990).

As a result of the differences in benefits accruing to men and women, mentoring is imperfect as a system for providing equal opportunity. Despite the fact that women are just as likely as men to report having a mentor, and experience the same level of mentoring functions (career support, psychosocial support, and role modeling) as men do, representation of women in top-level management positions is still extremely limited (Ragins, 1997; Ragins et al., 1998). The argument that women have not been in the workforce long enough to have reached high level positions might have been convincing in the 1970s; however, it sounds hollow at the start of the twenty-first century. Role theory, however, may offer some new insight into the reasons why women have not progressed in large numbers to higher ranks in organizations, despite the mentoring they report receiving.

Role evaluation and sanctions may explain why women are not benefiting from mentoring to the extent that men do (Dreher and Ash, 1990). While women may become adept at integrating managerial roles and gender roles, their performance in the managerial role will necessarily deviate somewhat from norms and expectations, due to necessity to enact both the managerial role and the female gender role simultaneously. Their role performance will be evaluated negatively because they are perceived to violate both role expectations and required role performance for a top-level executive. Women pose an alteration of the existing male-oriented role of top executive. As noted above, a key aspect of role theory is that roles are defined in relation to one another: A change in one role implies a change in all others. The need to maintain this important web of interlocking role relationships may pose yet another critical barrier to advancement for women. This barrier may be difficult to overcome even with the support which a mentor can provide.

If women are to be mentored into the upper echelons of organizations, men's roles must change as well. In order to interact effectively with women as executives, men must accept and enact behavioral changes in their own managerial roles. However, role theory suggests that actors within role systems strive to maintain highly valued roles, with any deviation from role expectations for these prestigious roles presenting a threat to the existing role structure (Biddle and Thomas, 1966). It is reasonable to expect, then, that any deviation from the existing, male-oriented role of top executive would be subject to a number of sanctions. As noted by Terborg (1977), in his discussion of the socialization of women as newcomers into management:

> Coworkers who have an interest in, and dependency on, the newcomer communicate prescriptions and proscriptions for job behavior. Over time, evaluations are made concerning the adequacy of the newcomer's behavior and performance. Deviations from the expected pattern may result in additional pressures on the newcomer to conform, alterations in the content of the communications or some combination of both. (p. 651)

This group-sanctioning behavior explains a number of the intergroup processes observed in the literature on mentoring, such as exclusion from power networks (Ragins, 1997; Ibarra, 1993). Although these intergroup processes have been documented in the literature on women in management, role theory offers some new insight into these social psychological processes. Role theory links identity group behaviors to one another and to structural effects based on role expectations and role performances which are negatively evaluated due to a desire to maintain the existing role definition of a top-level executive. Therefore, exclusion from networks of powerful individuals, such as top managers, despite the backing of a mentor, may be seen as a sanction imposed upon women who wish to advance in the organization. From a role theory perspective, this sanction is necessary in order to maintain the current, stable system of role behaviors among men in the organization, and particularly among men at the top levels of the organization.

Role theory also offers a research agenda for changing the role definitions within mentoring relationships (Ragins and McFarlin, 1990). Ragins (1992) specified a role theory approach to the development of mentoring relationships, utilizing concepts of role conflict and role ambiguity (Kahn, Wolfe, Quinn, and Snoek, 1964). In this framework, mentor and protégée gender influence role expectations in mentoring relationships due to sex-role spillover (Nieva and Gutek, 1981). In cross-gender mentor–

protégée relationships, these expectations result in higher levels of role conflict and role ambiguity. Outcomes in the Ragins's (1992) model include career satisfaction, job performance, relationship satisfaction, and organizational commitment. We will next build upon Ragins's framework by discussing the social–psychological processes through which roles are enacted within cross-gender mentoring relationships.

## ■ A role-making approach ■

Given that role theory offers a theoretical perspective on the development of mentoring relationships, the approach also offers some directions for research on cross-gender mentoring. In the following sections, we draw upon the work of Graen (1976), who presented a role-making perspective on behavior in complex organizations which is grounded in role theory. According to Graen:

> Role-making systems are those processes whereby the participant in the organization: (a) acquires knowledge about the content of the constraints and demands placed upon his behavior and the sources of those constraints and demands; (b) receives and sends persuasive communications regarding his behavior in the role; (c) accepts a particular pattern of behavior, and (d) modifies this pattern over time. (p. 1202)

Hence, role making can be viewed as a set of processes through which work roles (which can be fluid and flexible) are renegotiated over time as circumstances and situational demands change. Although much of the research on role making has been conducted on superior–subordinate relationships (Graen and Scandura, 1987), the framework has demonstrated usefulness in other areas, such as the development of work teams (Seers, 1989). This approach suggests that women managers must renegotiate their roles within their role set, recognizing that these changes will alter the roles of male executives. This renegotiation process must start with the mentor. If successful, the mentor will then become the woman's ally in changing the entrenched role behaviors among male executives in the organization. Graen and Scandura (1987) provide a three-phase role negotiation model which can be followed by the protégée in her role-making process.

The first step in the process involves role taking, in which an "iterative testing sequence" (Graen and Scandura, 1987, p. 180) is employed to determine the abilities and motivations of the role incumbent. For the female protégée, the sanctions previously discussed may be seen as tests of her resolve and resourcefulness in dealing with the role performance requirements of the next level. The current status of women at work suggests that few women have moved beyond the role-taking stage because so much confusion exists regarding the appropriate role behaviors of a woman manager (Schein, 1973; Freedman and Phillips, 1988). In the role-taking stage, the work role must be viewed as primary and gender roles as secondary. Thus, the women should focus on obtaining a clear understanding of the job demands and then on enacting the appropriate behaviors (Nieva and Gutek, 1981). Women may have to overcome some discomfort with enacting behaviors that are more stereotypically associated with the male gender role, and with which they have less experience. If the focus on the work role as primary is maintained, however, the discomfort may be lessened, because the association of the requisite behaviors with the male gender role is de-emphasized.

"Role making" is the next phase in the role negotiation model. In this process, involving mutual adjustment by both parties, the mentor and protégée determine over time how each will behave in a variety of situations. Any perceived sanctions that are attributed to gender or stereotypes must be clarified and renegotiated as necessary. For example, inappropriate remarks regarding women's qualifications for upper-level management must be overtly addressed and made part of the negotiations by the female protégée (for example, "If I am to continue to be your trusted and loyal ally, please refrain from making derogatory comments about women's abilities"). This process may be slow, and is not without risk; however, the research on role making suggests that, once stable patterns of role behavior are established, they have long-term implications for upward career mobility (Wakabayashi and Graen, 1984).

The role-making phase results in sets of interlocked behaviors and mutual understandings regarding the protégée's role in relation to the role of the mentor. In this "role routinization" phase, the mentor and protégée develop shared understandings, share personal and positional resources, and establish norms of mutual trust. When role routinization occurs, role performance should be evaluated without reliance on stereotypes or threats to the male mentor's role, because the role-making process also redefines the male role in a manner that is acceptable to both female and male executives. Kram (1985) referred to this as the "cultivation" phase of mentoring relationships. Baker (1991) refers to this process as "reciprocal accommodation," a collaborative process in which women gain power by assertive communication, and those in power acknowledge women's right to do so. After roles are routinized, renegotiation can occur but it is far less frequent than during the role-making phase.

The mentor–protégée dyad has now established a stable system of interlocked behavior, but the dyad does not exist in isolation from other organizational members. This dyad, with its redefined sets of behaviors, will start to influence the expectations and evaluations of other individuals in powerful networks in the organization. The mentor–protégée dyad, which includes a more powerful member in the mentor position and a less powerful member in the protégée position, has a greater opportunity to begin to change entrenched role behavior among the role set than the protégée alone would have.

The protégée understands in what ways behavior among male executives needs to change in order for her to function effectively at high levels in the organization. The mentor, as the more powerful member of the dyad, has a greater likelihood of gaining cooperation of his male peers. As a result, the likelihood of bringing about a change in behaviors at the highest levels of management in organizations, is greater when the mentor-protégée dyad works together. However, the woman's need for a mentor at the highest levels of organizations may mean that women must enact the role of the protégée longer than men do. The likelihood of successful entry and establishment within the top management team, with concomitant changes in role enactment within the team, is enhanced if the woman enters the team as a protégée rather than as a peer equal in status with the male team members. The risk, of course, is that the woman may be viewed, and may never view herself, as never truly "owning" a place on the team.

In the mentoring literature, the last phase of the mentoring relationship is termed the "redefinition" phase. In this phase, the mentor–protégée relationship, which is unequal in status, evolves to a more peer-like relationship, which entails equality in status. If mentoring relationships are instrumental in bringing women into the top levels of management, then it is hoped that the redefinition stage of that relationship will result in a redefinition of relationships within the team as a whole, resulting in the former protégée taking her place as a peer equal in status. This suggestion is speculative, however, as is much of the discussion in this chapter, and awaits empirical verification. We turn our attention next to identifying the areas of research that will support more prescriptive models of behavior in organizations.

## ■ The role-based perspective: some future research directions ■

### Role expectations and norms

Role expectations and norms explain why women still do not benefit from mentoring relationships to the extent that men do (Dreher and Ash, 1990; Ragins, 1997). Future research should explore the impact of role expectations and norms upon the development of mentoring and the benefits that accrue to women as compared with men. Role expectations may also influence role performance and evaluation. The role of female manager lacks clear definition and the prevailing role definition of top executive is male, which results in negative evaluations of females in male-typed top executive roles. Future research should investigate whether men and women differ in their definitions of the female executive role and how discrepancies in these definitions may contribute to women managers being excluded from networks of powerful individuals (Ibarra, 1994). Also, the role ambiguity resulting from a lack of female role models and inappropriate stereotyping of female managers is an area worthy of future research.

### Role performance

Research on performance evaluations of men and women indicates that gender bias against women exists (Eagly and Johnson, 1990; Graves and Powell, 1988; Heilman and Martell, 1986). From a role theory perspective, this bias may be reflected in negative role performance evaluations, which may be related to difficulty in access to mentors or difficulties in the development of the relationship. The discrepancy between the role incumbent's gender and role expectations (that is, a woman in a "man's" job) may be more influential in the role development process than the incumbent's actual performance. Hence, another direction for future research would be to examine how changes in the managerial role itself affect evaluations of role performance. For example, job descriptions might be altered in experimental settings to reflect more feminine or androgynous role requirements (Powell and Butterfield, 1989) and the resulting impact on role performance evaluations could be assessed. Future research could also explore whether a gender–role interaction bias exists in male mentor–female protégée pairings. Mentors may actually impede the role performance of female protégées if they hold stereotypes of women that result in communicating biased performance expectations and evaluations to the protégée.

## Role evaluation and sanctions

Negative evaluations of female protégées may also be related to perceived threats to the male executive role. According to role theory, high-status roles such as the male executive role must be maintained to preserve the existing informal and formal role structure. Research should explore whether barriers to mentoring for women (Ragins, 1989) are sanctions for women who occupy roles in which they are seen as a threat to the existing norms of managerial roles. Women may not be mentored because to do so would offer them legitimacy within the existing system of roles. The inclusion of women with legitimate status would introduce the likelihood of change in the existing system of roles, currently held almost exclusively by men. Indeed, the existing role structure must change, if women become part of powerful networks within organizations. Research is needed to uncover the types of sanctions that are imposed and what the career-related impact of these sanctions might be. Empirical attention should also be directed to the degree of masculinity or femininity triggers sanctioned by other role incumbents in the social context. Minority women are even less likely to reach top executive ranks (Morrison and Von Glinow, 1990). The role theory concepts of role evaluation and sanctions may also explain why women who are also minorities (for example, Blacks, Hispanics) are even slower to gain access to mentoring. Therefore, examination of role expectations, evaluations and sanctions for women who are also minorities is clearly a direction for future research.

## Role making

The literature on role making between superiors and subordinates (Graen and Scandura, 1987) offers a potentially fruitful framework for future research on mentoring (Scandura and Schriesheim, 1994). Samples of female executives might be interviewed or surveyed to identify how roles are effectively renegotiated and routinized and whether role making and routinization contributed to the emergence of mentoring. Given that the mentoring process has been shown to progress through stages of initiation, cultivation, separation, and redefinition (Kram, 1985), the redefinition phase is of particular interest. Research might examine the process through which a female executive must redefine her role from protégée to one of a top executive who may be a mentor to others. Research is also need on the effect of the redefinition of mentor and protégée roles on the network of role relationships in which the mentoring dyad is included.

# Summary

Following a brief review of some key definitions from role theory, we developed a framework for analyzing gender role influences on the mentor-protégée relationship. Building upon the prior theoretical and empirical work of Ragins and McFarlin (1991) and Ragins (1992), we examined several aspects of the role development process from the perspective of Graen's (1976) role-making theory. From this theoretical stance, several areas for future research were highlighted, including role expectations and norms, role performance, role evaluation and sanctions, and role-making. These four areas are key points of departure for future research on gender roles in mentoring. It is time to begin to question why more women have not made it into the upper echelons of management, given the number of years that women have been participating in the workforce. There are numerous possible explanations for this phenomenon. However, we believe that role theory offers some directions for future research that may help explain why women are not reaping the same career benefits from mentoring as men do. Future research should examine the expectations of women within mentoring relationships, how their roles are evaluated and sanctioned by those in power, and the process through which the managerial role is negotiated. When we begin to understand the complex interlockings of role relationships, we may begin to better understand why some role relationships are so resistant to change.

## REFERENCES

Baker, M. A. (1991): Reciprocal accommodation: A model for reducing gender bias in managerial communication. *Journal of Business Communication*, 28, 113–30.

Biddle, B. J. and Thomas, E. J. (1966): *Role theory: Concepts and research.* New York: John Wiley & Sons.

Clawson, J. G. and Kram, K. E. (1984): Managing cross-gender mentoring. *Business Horizons*, 27, 22–32.

Cook, M. F. (1979): Is the mentor relationship primarily a male experience? *The Personnel Administrator*, 24, 82–6.

Deaux, K. (1985): Sex and gender. *Annual Review of Psychology*, 36, 49–81.

Deaux, K. and Kite, M. E. (1993): Gender stereotypes. In F. L. Denmark and M. A. Paludi (eds), *Psychology of women: A handbook of issues and theories*, New York: Greenwood Press.

Dreher, G. F. and Ash, R. A. (1990): A comparative study of mentoring among men and women in managerial, professional and technical positions. *Journal of Applied Psychology*, 75, 539–46.

Eagly, A. and Johnson, B. T. (1990): Gender and leadership style: A meta-analysis. *Psychological Bulletin*, 108, 233–56.

Fiske, S. T., Bersoff, D. N., Borgida, E., Deaux, K., and Heilman, M. E. (1991): Social Science research on trial: Use of sex stereotyping research in *Price Waterhouse v. Hopkins*. *American Psychologist*, 46, 1049–60.

Freedman, S. M. and Phillips, J. S. (1988): The changing nature of research on women at work. *Journal of Management*, 14, 231–50.

Graen, G. B. (1976): Role-making processes within complex organizations. In M. D. Dunnette (ed.), *Handbook of industrial/organizational psychology*, Chicago: Rand-McNally, 1201–45.

Graen, G. B. and Scandura, T. A. (1987): Toward a psychology of dyadic organizing. In L. L. Cummings and B. Staw (eds), *Research in organizational behavior*, 9, Greenwich, CT: JAI Press.

Graves, L. M. and Powell, G. N. (1988): An investigation of sex discrimination in recruiters' evaluations of actual applicants. *Journal of Applied Psychology*, 73, 20–29.

Greenhaus, J. H. and Parasuraman, S. (1999): Research on work, family, and gender: Current status and future directions. In G. N. Powell (ed.), *Handbook of gender and work*. Thousand Oaks, CA: Sage.

Gutek, B. A. (1988): Sex segregation and women at work: A selective review. *Applied Psychology: An International Review*, 37, 103–20.

Gutek, B. A. and Larwood, L. (1987): Introduction: Women's careers are important and different. In B. A. Gutek and L. Larwood (eds), *Women's career development*, Newbury Park: Sage.

Heilman, M. E., Block, C. J., Martell, R. F., and Simon, M. C. (1989): Has anything changed? Current characterizations of men, women, and managers. *Journal of Applied Psychology*, 74, 935–42.

Heilman, M. E. and Martell, R. F. (1986): Exposure to successful women: Antidote to sex discrimination in applicant screening decisions? *Organizational Behavior and Human Decision Processes*, 37, 376–90.

Heilman, M. E., Martell, R. F., and Simon, M. C. (1988): The vagaries of sex bias: Conditions regulating the undervaluation, equivaluation, and overvaluation of female job applicants. *Organizational Behavior and Organizational Behavior and Human Decision Processes*, 41, 98–110.

Ibarra, H. (1993): Personal networks of women and minorities in management: A conceptual framework. *Academy of Management Review*, 18, 56–87.

Ibarra, H. (1994): *The structure of mentoring: A network perspective on race and gender differences in developmental relationships*. Paper presented at the annual Academy of Management meeting, Dallas, TX.

Jacobs, J. A. (1999): The sex segregation of occupations: Prospects for the 21st century. In G. N. Powell (ed.), *Handbook of gender and work*, Thousand Oaks, IL: Sage.

Kahn, R. L., Wolfe, D. M., Quinn, R. P., and Snoek, J. D. (1964): *Organizational stress: Studies in role conflict and ambiguity*. New York: John Wiley.

Kessler, S. J. and McKenna, W. (1978): *Gender: An ethnomethodology approach*. New York: Wiley.

Kram, K. E. (1985): *Mentoring at work*. New York: Goodyear.

Larwood, L. and Gattiker, U. E. (1987): A comparison of the career paths used by successful women and men. In B. A. Gutek and L. Larwood (eds), *Women's Career Development*. Thousand Oaks, CA: Sage.

Morrison, A. M. and Von Glinow, M. A. (1990): Women and minorities in management. *American Psychologist*, 45, 200–08.

Morrison, A. M., White, R. P., and Van Velsor, E. (1987): *Breaking the glass ceiling: Can women reach the top of America's largest corporations?* Reading, MA: Addison-Wesley.

Nieva, V. F. and Gutek, B. A. (1980): Sex effects on evaluation. *Academy of Management Review*, 5, 267–76.

Noe, R. A. (1988): Women and mentoring: A review and research agenda. *Academy of Management Review*, 13, 65–78.

Powell, G. N. and Butterfield, D. A. (1989): The "good manager": Did androgyny fare better in the 1980s? *Group and Organization Management*, 14, 216–33.

Ragins, B. R. (1989): Barriers to mentoring: The female manager's dilemma. *Human Relations*, 42, 1–22.

Ragins, B. R. (1992): An application of role theory to gender and mentorship. Paper presented at the Diversity in Mentoring Conference, Chicago, IL.

Ragins, B. R. (1997): Diversified mentoring relationships: A power perspective. *Academy of Management Review*, 22, 482–521.

Ragins, B. R. and McFarlin, D. (1990): Perception of mentor roles in cross-gender relationships. *Journal of Vocational Behavior*, 37, 957–71.

Ragins, B. R., Townsend, B., and Mattis, M. (1998): Gender gap in the executive suite: CEOs and female executives report on breaking the glass ceiling. *Academy of Management Executive*, 12, 28–42.

Scandura, T. A. and Ragins, B. R. (1993): The effects of sex and gender role orientation on mentorship in male-dominated occupations. *Journal of Vocational Behavior*, 43, 251–65.

Scandura, T. A. and Schriesheim, C. A. (1994): Leader-member exchange and supervisory career mentoring as complementary constructs in leadership research. *Academy of Management Journal*, 37, 1588–602.

Schein, V. E. (1973): The relationship between sex role stereotypes and requisite management characteristics. *Journal of Applied Psychology*, 57, 95–100.

Schein, V. E. (1975): Relationships between sex-role stereotypes and requisite management characteristics among female managers. *Journal of Applied Psychology*, 60, 340–44.

Seers, A. (1989): Team-member exchange quality: A new construct for role-making research. *Organizational Behavior and Human Decision Processes*, 43, 118–35.

Shaw, M. E. and Costanzo, P. R. (1970): *Theories of social psychology*. New York: McGraw-Hill.

Spence, J. T. (1984): Gender identity and its implications for the concepts of masculinity and femininity. *Nebraska Symposium on Motivation*, 32, 59–95.

Terborg, J. R. (1977): Women in management: A research review. *Journal of Applied Psychology*, 62, 647–64.

Wakabayashi, M. and Graen, G. B. (1984): The Japanese career progress study: A 7-year follow-up. *Journal of Applied Psychology*, 69, 603–14.

# 11

# EXPLORING THE BOUNDARIES IN PROFESSIONAL CAREERS: REDUCED-LOAD WORK ARRANGEMENTS IN LAW, MEDICINE, AND ACCOUNTING

*Mary Dean Lee, Lori Engler, and Leanne Wright*

The growth of part-time work in North America over the past two decades has been well documented, as has the increase in contract-based rather than permanent employment-based relationships between individuals and organizations (Arthur and Rousseau, 1996; Blossfeld and Hakim, 1997; Catalyst, 1997; Parks and Kidder, 1994). Increased use of part-time and contractual workers has generally been viewed as having primarily negative consequences for individuals and positive consequences for organizations. Part-time work has been traditionally associated with low-status jobs and hourly pay; in addition, part-time employment has been found to be associated with decreased upward mobility and overall life-time earnings (Adams, 1995). Yet reports are emerging which indicate that part-time or reduced-load work is increasing in popularity in professional-level jobs, and not as a result of company initiatives but of individual initiatives (Bond, Galinsky, and Swanberg, 1998; Buck, Lee, MacDermid, and Smith, 2000; Frank, 1994; Meiksins and Whalley, 1995). Such initiatives are puzzling on the one hand, because they challenge existing assumptions about what it means to be a professional, that is, having a strong commitment to a "calling," for example, working long hours, going beyond the call of duty to serve client needs. On the other hand, such initiatives are not surprising given the well-documented dual-career family "crunch", in which two full-time professionals (who are also parents) find the 60 hours a week each puts in at the office leaves inadequate time and energy for an enjoyable and meaningful family life (Lee, 1993; Moen, 1999).

The phenomenon of reduced-load or part-time work in professional-level jobs has been greeted with considerable suspicion in the academic community, perhaps because most of those experimenting with these alternative work arrangements are women trying to balance career and family. Indeed, some view part-time work among professionals as simply a new manifestation of society's persistence in relegating primary responsibility for child raising to women (Seron and Ferris, 1995). Others are concerned that if women pursue career paths which are divergent from the typical male career pattern, they will fail to rise to the top or break through the glass ceiling, thereby damaging not only their own careers but also those of all women who follow in their footsteps. Part-time work in the professions, if undertaken mostly by women, could be viewed as a threat to the goal of gender equality in the workplace. On the other hand, some writers propose that it is misguided to assume that the only way for women to achieve equality is to emulate typical male career patterns (Gallos, 1989). Several authors have recently described the different kinds of careers women are forging (Bateson, 1989; Brett and Stroh, 1994; Lee, 1994). Others go even further in suggesting that we need to rethink what it means to have a professional career, because the traditional model for these careers was based on a traditional family structure with men as the primary breadwinners and women staying at home. Now that for the most part men and women no longer play these traditional roles, the career structures are no longer viable (Bailyn, 1994). From this perspective, reduced-load work may be viewed as a harbinger of change or as part of a more general upheaval in the ways we think about "units" of work.

The purpose of the research project reported here was to investigate reduced-load work in three professions – law, medicine, and accounting – in order to gain further understanding of this phenomenon. The findings described below are based on an exploratory pilot study, focused on these specific occupations because there was substantial empirical documentation of the availability and utilization of less than full-time work arrangements in these fields. There were three main objectives of the study: (1) to learn about the variety of reduced-load work arrangements in these fields, and under what circumstances they are being negotiated; (2) to further our understanding of the costs and benefits of reduced-load work – from the perspective of individual professionals, their families, and their employers; and (3) to examine occupational characteristics which may explain the relatively high level of experimentation with alternative work arrangements in the fields of law, medicine, and accounting.

According to professional association reports, as well as research reported in scholarly journals, "alternative work arrangements" are widely available within the three professions of law, medicine, and accounting. The term "alternative work arrangements" generally includes flexible hours, telecommuting, and part-time or reduced-load work. However, the focus here is specifically on part-time or reduced-load work arrangements. In the legal field, evidence of the increase in alternative work arrangements lies in the widespread existence of part-time formal and informal policies and practices among private firms (Epstein, Seron, Oglensky, and Saute, 1999). In 1994, The National Association for Law Placement (NALP) conducted a study based on data from the National Directory of Legal Employers, which consists of predominantly large-firm listings including information from 995 individual law offices representing about 600 firms and 80,000 attorneys. According to NALP, part-time options are widely available in large law firms in major centres in the United States. In New York, San Francisco, Washington, Los Angeles, and Chicago, a substantial majority of law firms make part-time schedules available either as part of affirmative action policies or on a case-by-case basis (NALP, 1995). Both the American Bar Association and the Canadian Bar Association have model part-time policies they recommend (ABA, 1990; CBA, 1993). A survey of Ontario lawyers in 1990 found 24 percent reported part-time arrangements available in their firms or offices (Hagan and Kay, 1993).

Several studies have also pointed out that lawyers with heavy family responsibilities pursue strategies other than alternative work arrangements for lightening their career workload. For example, the CBA (1993) has documented that women are more likely than men to practice family law, juvenile law, labour law, and worker's compensation, while men are more likely to be involved in general practice, civil litigation, criminal law, personal injury, and real estate. The latter are considered more time-consuming with unpredictable time demands. Some lawyers also set up their own practices so that they can opt to work part time (Seron and Ferris, 1995). Machlowitz (1988) found a large number of women leaving private law firms early in their careers to join corporate legal departments, where the hours were more contained and predictable, and there was relief from billable hours pressure. Indeed, in Canada women are overrepresented in the corporate sector of legal work relative to their numbers (CBA, 1993). Several surveys also suggest that lawyers pursue jobs in the public sector as a strategy for balancing career and family. A CBA (1993) study showed a higher proportion of women than men employed in government legal departments, where there are more flexible work arrangements as well as more extensive family-related benefits, like parental leave. A Canadian survey found that women lawyers who take maternity leave from large law firms often opt for government employment upon their return to the workforce (Hagan and Kay, 1993).

In accounting there has also been a well-documented increase in the number of firms with formal or informal part-time policies. Kuechler and Buszha (1994) showed that the number of part-time accountants has increased by 50 percent in the past ten years. Part-time work includes a variety of alternatives, such as working a reduced load throughout the year, or working full-time nine months of the year with three months off in the summer, or working full-time during the peak tax season but reduced load the remainder of the year. The 1994 Survey on Women's Status and Work/Family Initiatives in Public Accounting found that approximately 65 percent of US firms, including all of the "Big Six" accounting firms, now offer some form of part-time professional employment (Hooks and Cheramy, 1994). A survey of the prevalence of part-time opportunities in accounting firms in New York, Pennsylvania, and New Jersey indicated that 66 percent currently use part-time professional staff (Kuechler and Buszha, 1994). Furthermore, a CPA professional association survey of 4,300 members showed that 85 percent of managers who had allowed an employee to use an alternative work schedule said that they would permit it again (Hooks, 1990). This supports the idea that employees on alternative work schedules are able to fulfill work-related objectives without sacrificing service quality. Many firms also have part-time partners (Kalands, 1993; Stewart, Belcourt, Sherman, Bohlander, and Snell, 2000), and it is widely recognized that firms must offer alternative work arrangements in order to remain competitive in recruiting and keeping the top talent in the field. For example, a 1990 survey done by the Women's Society of CPAs revealed that 60 percent of respondents stated that availability of alternative work schedules would be a factor in selecting a new position. In a 1993 study of female CAs in Quebec, part-time work arrangements and flexible scheduling were ranked first in importance (above extended maternity leaves and compressed work weeks) as the most sought-after firm policies. Most notable in the accounting profession is that researchers are now proceeding to document the financial benefits to firms of offering part-time options and to examine the consequences of alternative career path structures being implemented in cutting-edge firms (Levy, Flynn, and Kellogg, 1998; Mingle, 1994).

The concept of part-time or reduced-load work arrangements takes on a slightly different meaning in medicine than in the other professions, because physicians are more likely to work on a contract basis and be self-employed. The extent and content of their workload is therefore more likely to be discretionary. Furthermore, because they routinely work in different locations, (for example, private practice or clinic, hospital, and so on), their actual total professional workload is difficult to discern. However, for those who work for a single employer such as a hospital or other health care organization, reduced-load arrangements similar to those in law and accounting are found. Robinson (1993) reported job sharing, flex-time, and part-time positions as being chosen more and more among physicians. Surveys of physicians indicate that part-time is more prevalent among women than men. A 1990 Canadian study found that 20.8 percent of all female physicians worked part time, compared to 2.7 percent of male physicians. A 1986 survey found that among family physicians in Canada 37 percent of the women reported working part time (*Canadian Family Physician*, 1986). Cejka (1994) points out that hospitals and other health care facilities have found they must offer flexibility and other family-friendly benefits to attract women physicians. Both American and Canadian medical associations have now drafted guidelines supporting the rights of physicians in training to negotiate special arrangements with their residencies in light of family commitments.

Another strategy for managing career and family demands in medicine is careful choice of particular practice specialties, in part to increase flexibility to balance career and family more successfully. For example, the majority of female residents in the US in 1990 were enrolled in internal medicine, pediatrics, family practice, psychiatry, and obstetrics/gynaecology. Several studies in Canada have demonstrated that women tend to choose general or family practice more often than a specialty practice (Sanmartin and Snidal, 1993; Williams et al., 1990; Woodward et al., 1990). The choice of a specialty depends on a variety of considerations that may be different for women and men, who are also typically differentially involved with family responsibilities.

Explanations for the growth in alternative work arrangements in law, medicine, and accounting focus on demographics and occupational characteristics. The most dramatic relevant demographic change is, of course, an increase in the percentage of women in these fields. In both the US and Canada the number of women physicians and lawyers increased fourfold from the early 1970s to the early 1990s (Donovan, 1990; Organ, 1993; Ryen 1989). In accounting, women have accounted for approximately half of all new hires in public accounting firms since the early 1990s (Coolidge and D'Angelo, 1994; Levy, Flynn, and Kellogg, 1998). As these women professionals have advanced in their careers and also started families, some have wanted more time with their children than the traditional full-time workload in their professions allowed. So they have negotiated a variety of alternative workload arrangements.

A related demographic explanation of the increase in alternative work options is the shift in family structure patterns, including a decline in the numbers of families with a husband working full-time in the labour force and a wife working full-time in the home and community. More and more families are dual career, or single parent single career, with no one parent devoted solely to the "family work." Recent US statistics show that 44 percent of all workers are female, and 65 percent of families have all available parents in the workforce (US Bureau of the Census, 1999). These new family structures are viewed as putting enormous pressure on those in high-prestige professions, like law, medicine, and accounting, because the long hours of work interfere with fulfilling family responsibilities (Bailyn, 1994). What has happened then is that in response to this time squeeze, some well-established, highly competent professionals have been able to negotiate reduced workloads which relieve them from the reality that "full time," translates into 50–60 hours per week or more in these fields.

A third explanation of the growth in reduced workloads in law, medicine, and accounting is that these occupations have some basic characteristics in common that make it easier for these arrangements to be negotiated and maintained. For example, lawyers, doctors, and accountants are all in the business of providing services, and individual professional productivity is measured and rewarded on the basis of client or patient load. This means that calculation of workload and appropriate remuneration is relatively straightforward. All three kinds of professionals also typically work in places other than their offices, whether travelling or working in alternate locations, in order to see clients, which makes the exact extent of their workload less visible. All three professions involve individuals working quite independently, yet at the same time routinely providing clients a comprehensive team-based coverage system, since each professional has multiple clients/patients at any given time and cannot be universally accessible to all. In addition, all three professions offer specialty options with different lifestyle implications, and all require advanced graduate-level training and certification. Law, medicine, and accounting are also high-status and highly remunerated professions. Furthermore, all three professions have in common a variety of contexts in which professionals can practice. For example, a lawyer can practice in a private corporation, a private law firm, a solo practice, or a government legal department. A physician can practice in a hospital, in a private group practice, in a public clinic, and so on.

A final explanation for this phenomenon of reduced-load work arrangements in these three professions has to do with the new challenges these fields are currently facing economically, as a variety of kinds of societal, governmental, and technological changes require significant adaptation for survival of individual firms or health care institutions. For example, individual firms and institutions in all three fields have been facing increased competition, and increasing costs to doing business have affected them all. Furthermore, computerized accounting programs have eliminated the need for certain kinds of services previously provided by accounting firms. In all three fields, there is an "unfreezing" or shake-up of the old structures because of changes in the kinds of demands for services and shifts in where and how certain services are delivered. These changes are requiring firms and practices to be innovative in designing more efficient means of accomplishing the work. In addition, individual firms and health care organizations have been under pressure to increase the percentage of women in the top ranks (for example, in senior partner positions in law or accounting, or in academic positions in medicine). The apparent existence of a "glass ceiling," given the recent dramatic influx of women in these fields, has led these professions to examine carefully potential barriers to women making it to the top. All of these trends within these occupations have perhaps made them fertile ground for the kind of experimentation with work arrangements which is apparently going on, at least at the margins if not more extensively.

The design of this study involved conducting a small number of semi-structured interviews with lawyers, doctors, and accountants working in a variety of kinds of reduced-load arrangements in a wide range of organizational contexts. Reduced load is defined as working less, and getting compensated for less, than whatever is considered full-time or a normal load by occupational or organizational norms. Respondents were asked questions about (a) the nature of their work, the scope of tasks and responsibilities, the load, etc. and how it differed from the norm (what was done by someone similar working full-time); (b) how they arrived at their current arrangement and how long they expected it to last; (c) how satisfactory the arrangements were from their own personal perspective, the organizational and/or client perspective, and the family perspective; (d) costs and benefits of working a reduced load; and (e) facilitating and hindering factors in their particular situation. The interviews lasted approximately one hour and were audio-taped and transcribed. The interview data were then content analyzed to identify recurrent themes within and across occupation.

Potential participants for the study were identified through professional contacts and informal networks of the co-authors. In addition, a few were suggested by other participants. The names of approximately 40–50 potential participants were generated to yield the total eventual sample of 24. Generating a pool of potential participants allowed for selectivity in order to increase the range of reduced-load arrangements sampled within each profession. The critical goal in constituting the sample was to achieve variety within each occupation. So in law, we wanted to include at least one or two individuals practicing in a private law firm at a partner level, one or two in a private corporation within a law department, and at least one person in government. In accounting, we sought to include some accountants in large public accounting firms, some in medium or small firms, and at least one self-employed. In medicine, we wanted to include at least one doctor employed by a hospital, one with an academic appointment, one practicing in a community health centre, and one in a private clinic setting. All potential participants were initially contacted by the first author by phone, or with an introductory letter followed by a phone call. The first author conducted all of the interviews face to face. All interviewees were promised confidentiality and a feedback report at the end of the study. Only one person contacted declined to participate – a male physician – for health reasons.

Tables 11.1 and 11.2 show relevant characteristics of the sample by occupation. Table 11.1 provides information on number of children and spouse occupation by

**Table 11.1**  Personal and family characteristics of sample

| | Lawyers | Physicians | Accountants |
|---|---|---|---|
| Gender | 8F 1M | 7F 1M | 7F |
| Age | X = 39 | X = 39 | X = 39 |
| No. of children | | | |
| 4 | | 3 | |
| 3 | 4 | 3 | 1 |
| 2 | 4 | 2 | 5 |
| 1 | 1 | | |
| 0 | | | 1 |
| Spouse's occupation | | | |
| Same | 5 | 5 | 1 |
| Other profession | 3 | 1 | 5 |
| Other | 1 | 2 | 1 |

respondent occupation. Seven respondents were located in Toronto, 6 in Ottawa, and 11 in Montreal. The age range was 32–45, and the mean age in each of the three occupations was 39. The number of years participants had been working reduced load ranged from a few weeks to 17 years, with the lawyers having had the most experience with a mean of 7 years experience, doctors next with a mean of 5 years experience, and accountants being relatively new at it with a mean of 4 years experience. All of those working for law firms, accounting firms, the government, hospitals or community health organizations had negotiated their arrangements through formal alternative work arrangement policies of their employers.

Table 11.2 shows the type of employer, and subspecialties where relevant, of the lawyers, doctors and accountants. Those interviewed were working in a wide range of kinds and "degree" of reduced load. Some were self-employed, or working on a contract basis, and others were working for a single employer. Some worked 20 hours or less per week; others worked around 40 hours, or even more, which was still significantly less than the typical number of hours worked on full-time status. Participants tended to describe their loads as some fraction of what a full load was in their line of work, for example 0.5, 0.6, 0.7, or 0.8. However, some simply gave an estimate of how many hours or days they worked on average per week. Some explained that their total number of hours worked included "non-billable" hours, for example involvement in community organizations, which they considered client development, and they were paid for that time. Others were paid on the basis of billable hours only. There was one participant who was technically working "full time," and was paid as such, but did not put in the normally expected amount of work evenings and weekends. She assumed that her annual bonus was "adjusted" accordingly each year.

The descriptive findings from the study are presented below under four main topics: initiation of reduced load, logistics of reduced load, outcomes of reduced load, and facilitating and hindering factors in achieving a successful reduced-load work arrangement. Under each topic, additional sub-topics are identified on the basis of the literature reviewed and the interviews. Consistent findings across the three occupations are highlighted below. Where there are observed differences across occupations, these are noted.

**Table 11.2**  Employment-related characteristics of sample

### (a) Lawyers

| | Employer/Specialty | | | | | |
|---|---|---|---|---|---|---|
| | Law Firm | | | | | |
| | Litigation | Tax | Corporate | Corporation | Government | Self-employed |
| Amount of reduced load | | | | | | |
| 0.8 | 2 | | | 1 | 1 | 1 |
| 0.7–0.75 | | | | 1 | | |
| 0.6 | | 1 | | 1 | | |
| ≤0.5 | | | 1 | | | |

### (b) Physicians

| | Employer/Specialty | | | | | | |
|---|---|---|---|---|---|---|---|
| | Hospital | | | | Community Health | Private Practice | Combination |
| | Internal Medical | Oncology | Pathology | Pediatrics | Family | Family | Family |
| Amount of reduced load | | | | | | | |
| 0.8 | 1 | 1 | 1 | | | | 2 |
| 0.7–0.75 | | | | | 1 | | |
| ≤0.5 | | | | 1 | | 1 | |

### (c) Accountants

| | Employer | | |
|---|---|---|---|
| | Accounting Firm | Corporation | Self-employed |
| Amount of reduced load | | | |
| 0.9 | 1 | | |
| 0.8 | 1 | 1 | |
| 0.6 | 3 | | |
| ≤0.5 | | | 1 |

### ■ Initiation of reduced load arrangements ■

There was a remarkable amount of variation in how participants described arriving at their reduced workload arrangements. That variation will be described along several dimensions: precipitating factors; timing in career; timing in family; formal versus informal; leaving versus staying in previous position.

### Precipitating factors

The most common reason participants gave for going to a reduced load was the fact that there was just too much to do to try to maintain a very high level of career involvement while also having the kind of family life they wanted (with a significant level of involvement with children). In a variety of terms they also talked about experiencing high levels of stress in trying to do a good job at the office and at home.

> I began to have a lot of headaches, and I had never had them in my whole life. I tried cutting out certain foods, doing different things. I started going to the gym and trying to take care of myself. But the fact was I was only sleeping four or five hours a night, because I would spend a few hours in the evening with the kids and then be back at my desk by 10:00 at night for a few more hours. I started to find that I'd fall asleep on top of my work at the table.
>
> I guess I had it in my mind that if I was really, really unhappy, I would ask them to consider letting me work part time. And then I found out I was really, really unhappy. I think what made me unhappy was I felt I was failing. I felt I was failing in terms of living up to what was expected of me in the office. I was failing in terms of what I expected of myself, in terms of being with my child. You know, I wanted to spend more time with my child, but it was even – it wasn't even just wanting to spend more time with my child, it was feeling like I was failing both ways, and it didn't do anything for my self-esteem. I just couldn't figure out how to give it up (work), *or* give up my child, which is what I thought I was faced with.
>
> It was the hours. I rushed my guts out to work in the morning, and no matter what time I left, I rushed my guts out to get home. And I was always home too late. I was always at the office too early. And I was at the office too late. I said, "How long can you do this for, how long can you pretend that this thing works?"
>
> Before children I worked routinely till 7:00 or 8:00 p.m. at the office and at least one day on the weekend. After children, I didn't want to put those hours in. Yet I didn't want live-in help. I wanted to be with my children. And later when they went to school, I wanted to be there at 4:00 when they got off the bus. They'd get off the bus and there was so much to talk about . . . I also didn't want somebody else being with my children, having that much influence over my children.
>
> I had this horrible burnout. I was just in terrible shape, so I decided to restructure my life. I knew I had to stop being the mother of the universe and stop pretending I could work like a man, like all those guys in the department who have wives at home.

In the case of the lawyers and accountants two or three or more of those interviewed moved toward reduced load because they felt torn and stretched thin by their responsibilities and commitments in the two arenas, career and family. However, less than half of the physicians fell into this category. They were more likely to anticipate the work overload problem that would arise once children entered the picture. So they tended to negotiate reduced load, or choose to work in practice contexts where they could set their own hours, *before* returning from their first maternity leave.

A second precipitating factor theme among those interviewed was physical health problems on the part of individual participants or family members, for example repeated miscarriages, aging or ailing parents, or children with chronic health conditions. However, only six individuals mentioned such factors.

## Timing in career

The majority of those interviewed began working reduced load quite early in their careers, generally after working full time only three to seven years after finishing their graduate-level degrees. They typically had not yet come up for partnership, if they were in law or accounting firms. If they were physicians, they typically already had children by the time they finished their residencies, and set out to establish a reasonable work-load right from the start. About one-third of the sample initiated the reduced load at a point in time when they were well established in their careers, for example had already been made partner or had obtained an academic appointment as part of being hired by a university hospital. All of the lawyers interviewed began working reduced load early in their careers, and most of the accountants interviewed began after they were well established. The physicians were half and half.

## Timing in family

Approximately half of those interviewed in all three professions began working reduced load immediately following the birth of their first child. Several others returned to work full time for less than a year after their first child, before arranging to work less. An additional quarter of the sample began working reduced load following the birth of their second child or within a year or two after the second child.

## Formal versus informal

In approximately half the cases, the reduced-load work arrangements were formally acknowledged and legitimized through written organizational policies. There was an existing organizational framework for negotiating an alternative work schedule, and the organizations played an active role in determining how the reduced workload would be accomplished. In the other half of the cases, individuals arranged their reduced workloads more informally, for example by finding a corporation looking for a part-time chief counsel, or by working on a contract basis.

## Leaving versus staying

Half of all those interviewed found they had to leave the organization or practice context where they had been working full time in order to achieve a reduced-load work arrangement. The other half were able to stay with the same organization, and four actually came up for partner in their firms while on reduced load, and were successful in becoming partners.

## ■ Logistics of reduced load ■

As Table 11.2 indicates, there was a wide range of kinds of reduced load arrangements among those interviewed, in terms of the extent of the load and how it was reduced; the work schedule itself and degree of flexibility in the schedule; financial compensation and benefits; and the length of time reduced load was expected to continue. The variation is described below. However, it should be noted that for most of those who had worked reduced load five years or more (close to half the sample), they had experienced several different reduced-load work arrangements – with different employers, with different percentages of full time, with different kinds of contracts. The summary covers only the kinds of arrangements respondents had at the time of the interview.

## Extent of load and how accomplished

By far the most common degree of load reduction involved working 80 percent, or four-fifths, the equivalent of four days rather than five, which was reported by 12 out of 24 participants. Most of these respondents specifically negotiated to be employed on a 0.8 basis, but two doctors and one lawyer who were self-employed described practices consisting of a variety of activities and schedules which ultimately were designed to free up (from work) the equivalent of one day a week. The strategies typically used to reduce the amount of work were: (1) taking on fewer clients or reducing the number of patient contact hours; and (2) being selective about the kinds of clients or cases accepted. However, half of those working 0.8 arranged such a load by leaving one employer and starting with another or becoming totally self-employed. Most of those working 80 percent commented ironically that they probably work 40 hours a week, but that they don't mind because a normal load means 50–60 hours a week.

The next most common amount of work reduction was 60–75 percent, reported by six participants. All of these individuals had very specific employment contracts, with organizations laying out the percentage of work expected, and none of them had to change employers in order to negotiate their arrangements. Their workloads were reduced by the organizations reallocating tasks and responsibilities and reducing client or patient load. Three individuals worked what they considered to be less than a half load (15–20 hours a week) and were in total control of how much they worked. One individual originally did not define her workload as reduced, and in fact she is on full salary and works approximately ten hours a day, plus a half-day on Saturdays three months a year. However, as a partner in her firm, she does not keep the same hours as other partners, that is, working till 7 or 8 p.m. during the week, as well as working Saturdays throughout the year. So in her own mind she works a reduced load.

## Work schedule and flexibility

The most common allocation of the reduced load over time involved working fewer days or half-days per week to correspond to the degree of reduction. So those working 3/5 or 4/5 worked three days instead of five, or four days out of five. However, there were two lawyers and two accountants working 4/5 who spread their reduced load over the five-day week and ended their working days early in order to be at home for after-school time with children. For most of those working 3/5 or more, there was a great deal of flexibility in their schedules. That is, there was an implicit, and in some cases an explicit, understanding that, as professionals, they would not stick rigidly to their reduced-load schedules, but adjust their work time to accommodate client demands or colleague requests wherever possible. However, it was also understood that when accommodations were made to work more than usual in a given week or over a longer period, compensatory time would be taken off later. In the case of a few lawyers and accountants, they also had the option to take compensatory pay rather than compensatory time off in exchange for working more than their normal reduced load. One accountant interviewed had recently requested to be shifted temporarily to full-time work due to her department workload, as she found she was working long hours for reduced-load pay. She had the flexibility to shift back and forth from full to reduced load, at will. The flexibility inherent in these reduced-load arrangements meant that most of those interviewed had full-time help for child care, even on the day or days they typically were not working.

The other common kind of scheduling of reduced workload arrangements among those interviewed involved contract- as opposed to employment-based relationships. The individual lawyer, accountant, or doctor was in a position of "selling" their services, either directly to clients or to intermediary service organizations, to do the amount of work they wanted to do, in whatever time-slots they decided on, as long as the clients or organizations agreed. So, for example, one respondent has an agreement with a private law firm, where she was at one time partner, to do approximately 500 billable hours a year, which amounts to about one-third of a full-time load in her specific area of practice. The scheduling of her work time is left completely to her and the clients she serves and has served over many years. A doctor rents space from an existing practice group, to do four half-days of clinics with patients per week. In some cases, professionals who arranged reduced load in this way contracted to do work in several contexts. For example, two doctors worked in clinics seeing patients for two or three half-days a week, and then also worked for a hospital one day a week, either teaching and supervising residents and interns, or seeing day hospital patients. These doctors were also involved in research and/or community service work as well, which was not directly remunerated but which they considered an integral part of their workload. There was a great deal of flexibility in these kinds of work schedules for the lawyers and accountants, who mostly worked out of offices in their homes. For the doctors, they had flexibility to determine their schedules in whatever way they preferred, and then to change them from time to time. But on a week-to-week basis they were not free to change the day or time of a clinic, because patients were scheduled.

## Financial compensation and benefits

For those employed by an organization on a reduced-load basis, the standard financial compensation and benefits arrangements involved a pro-rated salary and benefits. However, doctors who worked for hospitals only received pro-rated salaries, no benefits, as benefits are typically not provided even for full-time physicians. In law firms pro-rated salaries tended to be based on billable hours rather than hours worked; salaries of full-time lawyers in private firms are also commonly determined on the basis of billable hours. Accountants' pro-rated salaries were based more on hours worked rather than billable hours only. There were four lawyers and accountants who were "equity" partners in their firms, meaning they were part-owners of their firms. Three received a draw from the firm's profits based on partner performance criteria which were public, and they were assessed on a point system basis; the other partner also took a draw from the profits of her firm but had no idea how her share was computed, for the criteria were private and assessed qualitatively by the managing partners.

As far as bonuses are concerned, there was a wide variety of practices among those interviewed. Some got considered for bonuses on the basis of individual performance as well as firm performance, and they were evaluated as if they were full time, but the bonus they actually received was proportionately reduced according to their workload. Others were simply considered not eligible for bonuses for individual performance because of their reduced-load status. They only received the company performance share of bonuses.

Most physicians in the study did not receive benefits as part of their compensation for services rendered. The few that did had their benefits pro-rated on the same basis as their salary. This was also the most common practice among those working in law firms or in a government office. However, some accounting firms and one corporation paid full benefits for all their professionals working at least 0.6, except for vacation days which were pro-rated.

## Future plans

Of the 24 individuals interviewed, 20 stated that they do not expect or wish to return to work full time in the foreseeable future, for example not until their children are out of high school. However, there were different reasons for this. For some it had to do with the way they felt about their productivity at work and the place of work in their lives.

> Actually I don't think I ever want to be 100 percent again. Maybe when my kids are grown up I'll feel differently, but I doubt it. I don't really ever want to be, you know, sitting in the office at 6.30 at night thinking, "I've still got to get another billable hour here," when instead I could go home and have dinner and be with my kids..bility, I offer more. And that's the way I am. I don't see myself doing anything differently in the immediate or distant future. Even if my kids were all grown, why would I want to work that hard again?
>
> I can't imagine ever stopping doing this. Because I personally think I work better under this type of arrangement. I work more, knowing that I'm not obliged to work that much. The less you ask of me, perhaps, the more you get, to a certain extent, knowing I'm not locked in, knowing that I have that flexibility, I offer more. And that's the way I am. I don't see myself doing anything differently in the immediate or distant future. Even if my kids were all grown, why would I want to work that hard again?
>
> I have to ask myself whether I ever want to work the way I was before, what 100 percent means in my firm.

Others talked about wanting to stay at reduced load because of family demands.

They asked me, "When do you see yourself, or do you see yourself working full time?" And I said, "I really wouldn't want to make a commitment about that." And I'm glad I said that, because at the time I sort of thought, "Well, maybe in a couple of years from now when the kids are in school." But now the kids are in school, and I'm looking at it and saying, "Well, they need me home to do homework." I don't even know, maybe I'll switch the part-time arrangement so that I finish at 3:00 every day or something. Because I don't know how they're going to get through their afternoons. They're in French school, it's a private school, and I want to be there for them; I want to hear what happened at school. I already don't like it with——in kindergarten. I don't like getting home at 6:00 and we have an hour, and he's tired and he doesn't want to talk much, and he's in bed about 7:30 and he's tired. I don't know. I might switch the time around, but I can't do much, and I don't see that changing until the kids are certainly through elementary school.

For others, the gain of time was for themselves, their sanity, as well as for the children. And they couldn't imagine ever wanting to give up that extra day. Working full time meant never getting a break, because weekends were spent doing family "work" non-stop, even when spouses were pitching in on an equal or close-to-equal basis – on top of a 50–60 hour work week. The day "off" during the week represented a psychological respite.

I'll never go back to full if I can avoid it. It's just so relaxing to have that day, even though it's not necessarily a relaxing day. But eventually it would be nice to take an afternoon that I could do some things with the kids, once they are a bit older. And I don't think it's going to get any easier the older they get – you know there will be all of the after-school activities, etc.

I really feel very lucky to be able to have the option. And having that one day off a week, I just love Monday morning, thinking of everybody going to work. I can go back to bed if I want to read the newspaper, or sometimes I'll go skiing in the winter. I plan tennis in the summer. And I just – I really, really value that Monday off, and I wouldn't give it up.

Four would like to work less than they are doing currently, and four expect to increase their workload once their children are in school a full day, but not up to full time. They didn't see family demands decreasing that much for a long time. Only one person had definite plans to return to full time when her children all start a full day of school. Two had only very recently begun their reduced-load arrangements and were not able to project into the future.

## ■ Perceived outcomes of reduced load ■

All of those interviewed who had been on reduced load for three months or longer stated they were quite satisfied with how it was working out. On a scale of 1 to 7, with 7 being Very Satisfied and 1 being Very Unsatisfied, a rating of 5 was the lowest given, and the mean rating was 6.2. However, there were three participants who expressed significant ambivalence about reduced-load work arrangements in general. Themes across all participants' comments about the benefits and costs of reduced load are summarized below, from a personal, family, and organizational perspective.

## Personal/Career perspective

All of those interviewed identified both costs and benefits to working reduced load, but the benefits outweighed the costs in their minds. They were generally quite adamant that the trade-offs they were making were worth it to them. There were four predominant themes in their assessment of benefits to them personally. The most common theme was a feeling of great personal fulfillment and satisfaction in being able to have a meaningful and successful career while also maintaining significant involvement in family life and feeling effective in both roles. The second most common theme was that working reduced load gave them more time to play with their kids, or be with their kids.

> I had a strong sense that I just wanted to play with the kids or be with the kids, or do something with them, and that's what I wanted the time for. It's actually fairly selfish, really. They are only little for such a short time, and if you are not there then, you know, you don't get to do it over again.

The third most common theme was gaining time for themselves, whether it was used for sleeping in and reading in bed one morning a week, or doing aerobics, or doing errands usually saved for the weekend. There was great variation in what participants did with the time gained from working reduced load, but what was common to all was the subjective experience of having more time and a sense of greater freedom and control over their time. Several talked about feeling relaxed on their day off, even if what they were actually doing wasn't particularly relaxing, for example doing grocery shopping and picking kids up from school.

The final recurring theme in reflections on the positive aspects of reduced-load work arrangements was less stress, or time to "decompress." Many of these professionals felt that a great deal of pressure was removed, that they could breathe again and lead a less hectic life.

> If I was working on a full-time, partnership track basis, I would be staying here until 10 at night and working weekends. I would have a much more stressful practice, not necessarily because of the files themselves, but having to worry about getting to work on the right files and working for the right people.

On the cost side, there were three recurring themes: difficulty in containing their workload, financial loss, and negative effects of reduced load on their career status. The most common theme in comments on costs of reduced load was the incessant pressure to work longer than they wanted to, and their continuous struggle to "contain" the work load. Although many discussed reduced stress as a benefit of reduced load, others complained of the stress they experienced in trying to squeeze their work into a limited amount of time in the office, or to contain the work they had to do to conform to their reduced load arrangement. Some talked about needing to make adjustments in their own high expectations of themselves in order to make reduced-load arrangements feasible.

> It took me about eight months to get over the Type A personality and wanting to get on the best files and the whole bit. Once I got over that, and just realized that this was actu-

ally very liberating because I could practice law for the sake of just practicing law as opposed to impressing somebody else, I enjoyed my work a lot more.

I had to come to terms with that really fast. You know, either you choose the career track or you choose the mommy track, and the people who could go on both tracks at the same time are few and far between. And either they have exceptional efficiency skills or incredible energy, or . . . But if you expect that from yourself, then you'll always be frustrated. So sure there are times when I look and I say, "So and so has published this paper and look what I'm doing, fiddling around." But there is no question in my mind that I really want my kids to be sane and whole. So if I have accomplished that, then the rest will just wait for a bit, that's all. That's my set of priorities.

I've always exceeded in school and succeeded in what I'm doing, so I also want to do that. And I have very high demands on myself. When I graduated, I graduated first in my program. And when I went to the school of accountancy, I came in the top 10 percent, also when I wrote my UFE. In the firm I've always been rated in the top of my tiers. So I have these demands, and I see I have this potential, but yet I want to do this, so I try to do it all, and you're not really happy.

Others approached the challenge of containing the workload by working in a more concentrated way, and becoming more efficient and better organized, and doing more delegation to lighten the load. But some found this quite stressful.

Well, I guess the stress level is high, because I find I'm managing my life at the firm and I'm managing life at home, too. And that's stressful. I find that I'm always speeding to get home on time. I find that stressful. I find not being able to sort of relax during my workday stressful; always go,go,go,go. So that's definitely a con. Trying to balance it all. Because even if, you know, I have a great nanny, even though I'm not doing the labour-intensive stuff, I'm doing the management of it all. And it's the delegation and the management. I wish someone would just take that over from me. You know, being at the kids' teacher meetings, being at the Christmas concert, you know, the typical stuff that every full-time woman has to deal with. Trying to fit it all into a reduced work day, that's what I find hard.

The second most frequently mentioned disadvantage of reduced-load work was the financial sacrifice, although all participants expressed the opinion that the gain was well worth the financial loss. One equity partner in a law firm put it this way:

The fact is that people make a lot of money in law firms, and taxation takes so much it almost isn't worth it for me to work extra. I sort of alluded to it earlier, but if I went from working 60 percent to 80 percent, I would earn perhaps another $40,000 a year. It sounds like a lot of money, but more than $20,000 would go to taxes. And to make it work I really would need extra help at home, and I'd be paying probably another $1,000 a month to somebody to be at home. Now it would reduce my work at home. But still, in terms of money, I would end up maybe $8,000 ahead. And it just isn't worth it.

A partner in an accounting firm said:

It cost me a lot, monetary wise. And I believe it was money well spent. I was willing, because in our business we are well compensated, very well compensated. And so to take a little less to have so much more in my life meant a lot to me.

Many of those working 4/5 pointed out that because they were in a high tax bracket, the 1/5 decrease in salary was barely perceptible after taxes. However, the loss was more significant for those who were partners and had their shares or units, or increase in units, affected by working reduced load.

> Normally you progress. Say you start off as a partner with 100 units. Then after two or three years, you're offered another 25 units, which you buy. You buy these units and then you share more in the profits, and so on. I wasn't offered any additional units over the years I was working reduced load.

The final recurring theme in participants' reflections on the costs of working reduced load was the negative impact these arrangements had had on their career status. Slightly less than half of those interviewed mentioned this aspect of reduced load, and they talked about two kinds of things: others' treatment or perception of them professionally; and their own dissatisfaction with their professional development. Respondents mentioning this "downside" of reduced load did not talk about negative effects on their actual career progress. Rather, they felt judged harshly by their peers or unable to meet their own expectations of themselves by not following the traditional male model of working long, gruelling hours.

> They know what I am about, but it is still tremendously embarrassing to leave this office at 6:00 p.m. at night. Extremely embarrassing. In front of staff and in front of partners. I don't know why, but I don't feel good about it.

> If you want to be seen as an excellent doctor, you have to be working long hours. That's the way it's always been.

> There is a stigma against someone who is working part-time in medicine. They're less academic, or maybe they're less keen, or maybe they know less. I felt that right from the beginning . . . And for those of us who are part-time teachers, we have to be loud about what we do, because it's easy to be marginalized when you're part time.

Such respondents resented being treated as second-class citizens at times because of their choices and priorities. For example, one told a story of being given an obviously inferior office and furniture when she and several other partners were relocated to a new building.

Those who mentioned dissatisfaction with their career status from a more personal perspective talked about comparing their careers with their cohorts from school; for example:

> Well, sometimes I see colleagues of mine from school who didn't do nearly as well as I did – I was at the top of my class – and see them ahead of me in life, so to speak, by certain standards, and I have these pangs where I feel, "Why not me?" But then I remember why not me, and I'm happy with my choice.

A few participants also felt their reduced-load arrangements had had a negative impact on their professional development in their careers. One physician who had been working 20 hours a week or less for several years talked about gaining experience and wisdom a bit more slowly, and thus developing professionally more slowly. This seemed to be an especially salient issue for physicians, who are more likely to be self-employed and therefore must take care of their own professional development. But accountants and lawyers also talked about what they miss from not being able to work on the prestigious, highly demanding files, because of their reduced-load arrangements.

While the theme of loss of status in career was clearly an important one, it should be noted that participants did not talk about reduced load as a barrier to objective career success. In fact, several participants explicitly mentioned that they felt reduced load had *not* had a negative effect on their career achievements so far.

## Family perspective

There were three predominant themes in participants' discussion of the benefits of reduced-load work arrangements from a family perspective. The most frequently occurring theme was that children benefit from parents' greater presence at home and a less hectic pace in the day-to-day, week-to-week schedule of family activities. The kinds of specific things these professionals believe their children gain from greater parental involvement at home include: help with homework, music practice, or problems brought home from school; greater security and independence from experiencing the behavioural commitment of the parent on reduced load – by picking children up from school certain days, etc.; more supervision and discipline, as well as more play time with a parent; more parental involvement in children's schools; more attention when sick; higher-quality time with children evenings and weekends because not so exhausted and "sapped" of energy.

> I feel that what happens to a kid growing up in a family is very important – and somehow I feel I have an important role or say in that experience. I don't see myself as some kind of breadwinner or the person who looks after the financing and the pragmatic issues, whereas the woman looks after the caring of the children issue.
> When I was working full time and we would take the kids on holiday, they wouldn't leave me for a moment, including going to the bathroom. If I tried to close the door, they'd bang on it. And my older daughter was beginning to blink a lot, and sort of twitch and I didn't know why until I was with her for two or three weeks straight, and it began to go away. I started recognizing that they needed more time.
> So I think you have to have that certain amount of time where you can do your normal parenting role of supervision and fun, and a mix of that. And if you can't, then it's hard. And I don't see, if I was working full time, how I could do that. Because I know that when I'm going to come home from work and I'm tired, I know the days that I work, I come home and I really just would like to put them into bed. So you have a shorter fuse and you don't have the energy. So if you're only parenting at those times, when you're in that state of mind, then it's not optimal. I can think of one family I know in particular where the children are particularly badly behaved and rude because the parents are too tired when they come home from work to do disciplining. It's not that they don't love the children, but it's just too much hassle. They want quality time with their kids and don't want to be "on their

case." But those are going to be unhappy children because they won't function well in the world.

I think it's a really important time when kids come home from school, they want to tell you about their day, whereas an hour later they have forgotten about it. And I sometimes think about the children of a colleague, whom I pick up from school with mine three days a week and their nanny picks them up the other two days, and I don't think she realizes what she's missing, because I know when I worked full time, you're just so focused on getting everything accomplished, you don't even really see those things. But I feel sorry for her that she's not having the opportunity of being with her children at that time.

Once my daughter called me at the office to ask when I'd be home because she needed help with her homework. And I told her to ask the baby sitter, but she said the baby sitter couldn't help her with her Hebrew and French. So although I had planned to work late, I decided to go home and spend a couple of hours and then return to the office after they were asleep. But I realized I couldn't do that always, and that I also couldn't tell her that her homework was less important than my work, because it wasn't. Her homework, the day she got it, was as important or more important to her and to me.

The second most common theme in benefits of reduced load from a family perspective was more time for whole-family leisure activities on the weekend, because there weren't as many chores and obligatory activities accumulated from a week of full-time, flat-out work at the office. Respondents talked about being able to enjoy the family more and give their best to children, *because* they had an enjoyable, challenging career, but not one which was so demanding that it sapped all of their time and energy. Of those who talked about this advantage of reduced load, most routinely did some chores and errands during their day(s) off from their professional work. While most of them explained that they didn't mind their time off being filled up in this way, and in fact felt it was their own choice (that is, they had the freedom on any particular day not to do the errands), the fact of the matter was that they gained pleasurable weekend time with the family by doing more "family work" during the week.

The final recurring theme in positive family outcomes of reduced workload was greater marital harmony. Although in only one case was the reduced load initiated because of a spouse's request or suggestion (in this case a wife suggesting that both she and her husband work a reduced load), in several cases spouses were extremely supportive of the reduced load arrangement and felt that it improved the marital relationship. There was more time for the couple to communicate, spend a little leisure time together, and not always be negotiating about coverage of family responsibilities.

Very few participants identified disadvantages of reduced-load work arrangements from a family perspective. But two themes emerged in at least five cases. Women professionals complained that their working reduced load had translated into their having an increased family workload, and had in fact resulted in reinforcing a traditional division of labour in the family where the woman does significantly more than the man. Second, there were some interviewed who still felt that life was quite stressful, and that they were still quite frazzled in their family life, because they were not finding time at home to get to that journal article they needed to read, or because their spouse expected the reduction in workload to be greater than it turned out to be.

## Employer/Client perspective

There were four main themes in participants' discussion of benefits of reduced load work arrangements from the employer or client perspective. The most common comment referred to greater productivity and efficiency because of the incentive to be able to reallocate their time to family. In fact, some of those working 4/5 suggested that most of the time they were really doing 100 percent in 80 percent of the time and for 80 percent of the money; so in fact, the company gets more for less. Although some resentment was expressed about this, respondents generally felt it was worth it to them to have the extra time, and that the financial loss was minimal. In accounting and law firms the creation of a non-partner track for professionals interested in working less had simply provided a structure for these kinds of arrangements. These firms believed they were gaining increased partner leverage and long-term commitment from highly skilled professionals with minimum investment. Another aspect of the increased productivity mentioned was greater creativity, which many felt was a direct result of not being pressed and not having to work so long and hard.

> Being able to be away from the office three days a week, even though on Fridays I might be contacted by phone, I just feel that I have a lot more energy toward my work because I'm not feeling suffocated and locked in. And sometimes I feel that people that work five days a week, by about the last day, I'm not sure that they have the energy any more, and they're not necessarily bringing the interest and creativity to solving the problems at hand.

Another recurring theme which emerged across all three groups was that organizations which have formal or informal policies and practices which allow reduced-load arrangements have an advantage in attracting and retaining the top talent these days. This is because there are few young lawyers, doctors, and accountants with the kind of traditional family structure in place to allow them to give their all to career.

The remaining two common themes emerged among the lawyers and accountants, but not the physicians. First, the lawyers and accountants were unanimous in asserting that client service had not suffered, and that in fact clients were highly satisfied. Since most of those working reduced load were not rigid about their work schedules, they returned calls or took calls even on their days off, if necessary. If anything, they were more vigilant about responding in a timely manner because of their alternative work arrangement. Some participants pointed out that in fact because of their reduced loads, they were divided less among multiple clients. Finally, lawyers and accountants were extremely grateful to their firms for the opportunity to work reduced load, and indicated they felt quite loyal and committed to the firms that had found a way to accommodate them. They believed that their firms had "gone the extra mile" for them, and they were willing to do the same for their firms.

On the cost side there were only two predominant themes, and they were more occupation specific, as with the benefits above, because of the differences in kinds of typical employment for lawyers and accountants as opposed to physicians. From the perspective of lawyers and accountants, the main drawback for firms of having reduced-load professionals, was that if the individual was a partner, reduced load represented fewer billable hours and therefore less profit to be shared among the partners. Reduced-load partners agreed that they did less socializing and had a lower client-generating capacity than those working full load. If the individuals on reduced load were not partners, then the cost to firms was the "full-time" overhead of professionals which had to still be covered with fewer billable hours. Theoretically, the administrative overhead of more individual professionals working reduced load and producing an equivalent amount of billable hours translated into higher costs to the firm, unless there is very efficient usage of office space, equipment, secretarial support and so on.

The main theme in costs to employers or patients from a physicians' perspective was that reduced-load work arrangements increased the importance of having closely coupled coverage systems for patient care. Several physicians mentioned that their spending fewer hours in clinics resulted in a greater likelihood that patients would wait longer to get appointments, or that patients might "slip between the cracks" because of holes in the coverage system. Of course, physicians have to have coverage systems because of the necessity of 24 hours a day, seven days a week services being available. But when there are fewer doctors involved with a given set of patients, there are generally fewer errors and greater reliability. More physicians working less translates into more physicians involved in any one team covering a service or set of patients.

## ■ Facilitating and hindering factors ■

In examining respondents' comments about facilitating and hindering factors related to reduced-load work arrangements, there was a very wide range of factors mentioned, but not a great deal of convergence. However, the comments fell into three categories: occupational, organizational or job related, and personal or family factors.

## Occupational factors

Factors related to the particular occupations being studied were most frequently mentioned. For example, the fact that law, medicine, and accounting are prestigious, highly remunerated professions was viewed as highly facilitative of reduced-load arrangements, because even if working on a reduced-load basis, these professionals still earn a respectable salary. Furthermore, because these professions are high status, respondents believed people were less likely to denigrate individuals working less than full time. Another characteristic of these professions which respondents viewed as conducive to alternative work arrangements was the fact that they include a range of subspecialties, and/or practice contexts, which allow individuals to choose kinds of work conducive to their personal life situations or commitments. So for example in medicine, specialties in family medicine, pediatrics, psychiatry, dermatology were seen as more "family friendly" than others. Also, since physicians are often self-employed, they can design highly individualized schedules to suit their particular penchant for combinations of clinical practice, teaching, and research. There is high variability in medicine in where and how much any given physician works at any given point in time. In law, working for the government or for a private corporation was viewed as more compatible with an enjoyable family life than working for a private law firm.

## Organizational/Job factors

Of those facilitating factors respondents identified related to their employer or their specific job, the most frequently occurring one was support from their boss, or other senior level partners or managers. There were many examples given of different kinds of support which at the basic level just involved agreeing to the reduced-load arrangement and making it possible by taking the necessary action. However, many talked of support which went beyond this basic level.

> One of the adjustments which people had to make in our group was realizing I was no longer there on Fridays and that they shouldn't schedule meetings on that day. The way my partner helped phase it in was, people would try to schedule meetings on Friday, and she would turn to them and say, "Well, let's do it on Sunday." And they'd go, "I'm not going to be at a meeting then." And then she'd say, "Well, Mary's coming in on Friday to do this, and that's her weekend; I expect you to come in too . . ." And then people sort of got the idea. I'd say that's partner support.

Another respondent said:

> My boss has been 150 percent in making sure I don't just get routine work, but quality work that's leading me in my career just like anyone else that's working full time . . . And I think it is a question of establishing trust and confidence so that everybody knows that you're working and working well and doing your best at a reduced level. For me that's even meant getting a special achievement award for a project I did while on reduced load.

Other themes in facilitating factors related to the organization or a specific job included: having control over their work, whether the amount of it, or the scheduling of it, etc.; having the opportunity to design their own job or workload at the time of starting the reduced load, so that it could be shaped to fit the circumstances; and having experience, a high level of competence, or a high level of seniority in the organizational context. Other less frequently mentioned factors were: the existence of specific work and family policies and practices in the firms or institutions; and concrete organizational resources and supports which minimized the impact of reduced-load work, for example computer and fax capability in the home.

## Personal/Family factors

Finally, at a personal and family level, there were three facilitating factor themes: exceptional child care support at home; spouses who were either highly involved or very minimally involved in the day-to-day care of children; and clear values and beliefs about the importance of family and fulfillment of personal and family life roles. Over half of those interviewed mentioned that they could not be successful with their reduced loads without the support of a full-time babysitter or nanny, because they needed to be flexible to respond under unusual circumstances to client needs, even on one of their days off.

Spouses also came up quite frequently in discussions of what made reduced-load work arrangements feasible. About half of the time respondents talked about the critical spouse collaboration necessary to sustain the drop off and pick up arrangements with children, and to maintain their capacity to work more when necessary in response to the demands in their offices. However, the other half of the time, spouses' inability to pitch in and participate in family-related errands and chores was mentioned as a factor which made the reduced-load work arrangement an absolute necessity. In some cases, these spouses' low level of involvement in the "family" work was defended as a function of their occupation (for example, high level of out-of-town travel required), and in other cases there was resentment expressed. However, even in the few cases where there were egalitarian marriages, the heavy involvement of the spouse in the family chores and errands did not mitigate the respondents' felt need to work less in their careers.

Finally, respondents suggested that their own personal values, for example wanting to have three or four children, and their acceptance of likely limitations placed on their career potential by their choice of reduced workload, were certainly strong factors contributing to the success of these arrangements. Some commented that they knew they had very high expectations of themselves in their parental role, and that they had been told they had a stronger need than most to be with their families. Others talked about the high level of satisfaction they got from their personal or family lives. They explained that they simply have a higher level of interest in and commitment to children and family compared to their careers.

### ■ Factors hindering reduced-load working ■

There were few recurring themes in factors mentioned as hindering reduced-load work arrangements. However, one that was mentioned was that in spite of the dramatic increase in women in these three professions, the power structure is still predominantly male, and those men tend to have wives not working outside the home. Thus, these men continue to expect of colleagues the kind of long, gruelling hours which are possible in the context of family life only when there is a traditional division of labour with a wife in charge of family and home. Those working on a reduced-load basis feel stigmatized and marginalized in that kind of work culture. A second recurring theme was that, for partners in law or accounting firms, allowing reduced load arrangements translates into lower billables for the firm, which affects the pool of profits out of which everyone is compensated. This ineffable fact limits the attractiveness of making reduced-load arrangements widely available. Finally, several respondents commented that the flexibility in their reduced-load arrangements, in order to be responsive to clients, can also be a liability, because it is hard to draw boundaries and easy to overwork, especially when one is a partner and knows that extra hours not worked affect the partnership, not just the individual.

# ■ Findings of the study ■

The findings from this pilot study investigating the extent and outcomes of reduced-load work arrangements in law, medicine, and accounting must be interpreted with great caution given the small size of the "convenience" sample used. However, a few tentative, general conclusions can be drawn based on trends in the literature combined with recurrent themes in the data. Second, findings concerning occupational similarities and differences relevant to reduced-load work arrangements suggest some explanations for the growth of this phenomenon in these professions and predict its further spread to other fields. Finally, some of the findings are linked to recent research results from a subsequent study of reduced workload among professionals and managers in private corporations.

In these professions there is a wide array of experimentation going on in reduced workload arrangements, not only among women and not only in practice contexts typically assumed to be more "family friendly," for example government jobs, or family medicine, or private solo practice, or non-partnership track jobs. The literature search uncovered clear evidence of the growth of "part-time" work in the three professions, and the principal investigator found it relatively easy to locate potential participants for the study. Furthermore, there was a great deal of variety in amount and logistics of reduced load, the negotiations surrounding its initiation, and the existence of formal policies and programs supporting this kind of alternative work arrangement. The various kinds of arrangements observed can be interpreted as representing different kinds of challenges to the status quo. Study participants were grouped according to the degree of reduced load being worked, and the groups were labelled as follows: Redefining Full Time, Challenging Professional Norms, and Part-time Professionals.

## Redefining Full Time

Those who worked 80 percent or more of a normal load represent a group experimenting with a minimal degree of reduced load. They typically worked between 35 and 45 hours a week, instead of 50 to 60 on full load, and might be viewed as simply attempting to redefine "full-time." Thirteen of the 24 participants were classified into this group – five of nine lawyers, five of eight doctors, and three of seven accountants. The two men were in this group. Two of the four lawyers and accountants who were partners were in this group, as were two of the three physicians with academic appointments. These professionals expressed the view that they were as productive, if not more so, than some colleagues who work full time. Lawyers, doctors, and accountants who fit this pattern reported a high level of integration in their profession or institution. The financial implications of this amount of workload reduction were minimal, because of high tax brackets. So these professionals can be viewed as simply adjusting performance and reward expectations around the margins in order to make combining career and family more manageable. However, they felt they still performed at a very high level, but simply carried a lighter load. Some mentioned they sometimes question: "Why not get paid for full time if we are really working 40 hours?", but they also reasoned that their reduced load legitimized their working less and made things appear equitable. If the norms in a profession or in a firm are to work 50 to 60 hours per week, 40 is not acceptable even if it is technically full time.

It is interesting that these professionals found a real difference between working 35 to 45 versus 50 to 60 hours a week, in light of a recent longitudinal study of children in dual-career families. Menaghan and Parcel (1993) reported a significantly higher rate of emotional and school problems among children whose parents worked more than 45 hours a week, compared to those working 45 hours a week or less.

This minimal type of workload reduction may have the fewest negative implications for organizations, and in fact may represent a bargain, in that they pay these individuals, who tend to be high performers, 80 percent for what is essentially full time work. From an individual perspective, the danger of this kind of reduced-load arrangement is that it may not provide enough of a respite, or make enough of a tangible difference in freeing up time from work to reallocate to family. There is also a fine line between simply working a compressed work schedule (doing the same amount of work in fewer days) and a truly reduced workload. Those working 80 percent or more found organizational expectations still very high and experienced pressure to reassume a full load. Only those very rigorous and persistent in limiting their load, with clear organizational support, seemed able to sustain this minimal work load reduction and thrive in it.

## Challenging Professional Norms

A more significant degree of reduced load was found among those who worked at least half, but less than 4/5, of a full load, most commonly 3/5 or 2/3. This group included three lawyers, two doctors, and three accountants. Two were partners in their firms, and one of the doctors had an academic appointment. They were serious professionals who believed they were no less valuable and no less important contributors because of their wish to work less. They were highly flexible in their actual scheduling of work and remained closely in touch with their colleagues, clients, patients, even on their days or times off. Their reduced-load arrangements were more visible to all because they worked significantly less. They were more likely than those classified as Redefining Full-time to state that they had made some conscious career trade-offs in pursuing alternative work arrangements. This pattern of reduced load represents a more significant challenge to the status quo because it is more visible and requires more organizational accommodation. Those who work in this way are not just making adjustments at the margins, for example, working 40 instead of 50 hours. They are working around 30 hours and questioning established norms that presume number of hours worked is a good measure of motivation, commitment, and competence. Study participants in this category were clearly still in the mainstream of their professions, performing at a high level, and maintaining the respect of clients and colleagues.

## Part-time Professionals

A third pattern of reduced load identified in the study was found among participants who worked around half, or less, of what is considered a full load, and were viewed as experimenting with a maximum degree of workload reduction. There were only three participants classified in this pattern, one from each profession. They were all self-employed or worked strictly on a contract basis. These professionals were more rigid about protecting their family life from their career commitments. They also tended to compartmentalize career and family, with clearer boundaries between the two. They liked operating with a great deal of control over their work schedules and tried to minimize intrusions of work into family time or family into work time. These individuals had experimented with different alternative work arrangements, and they were quite clear about just how much and on what basis they wanted to pursue their careers. They also seemed to be very good at what they did, so indeed there was a demand for their services on their terms. However, their salaries were unlikely to contribute significantly to the family income once child care costs for the time they were working were covered. They were working for their own professional fulfillment or their desire to make a contribution. Those professionals working in this way tended to be paid on an hourly or daily basis, more like traditional part-time work, and as contractors rather than employees. Although there has been resistance to calling reduced-load work among professionals "part-time," because the term has been used for so long to refer to those working around 20 hours a week in low-paying, unskilled jobs, the label seems to fit for this subgroup of those interviewed. They were individuals who felt highly fulfilled in their family roles, or who had strong personal interests or hobbies which they enjoyed pursuing. Their professional careers were certainly important to their sense of identity and self-esteem, and they did not want to give them up. However, family was clearly the priority at this stage in their lives.

The fact that more than half of the study participants were working 4/5 or more, by choice, suggests that the cost–benefit analysis for this degree of reduced-load works out more favorably for both the individual and the organization or client. However, participants in the other patterns expressed an equally high mean level of satisfaction with their arrangements, and the three participants who expressed some ambivalence about their arrangements were all in the Redefining Full-time category. Their ambivalence had to do with difficulties in containing the load and being neither full time or part time. Furthermore, those classified as Challenging Professional Norms included professionals who were clearly as successful and ambitious as those in the Redefining Full time category.

One of the surprising findings across the entire sample was that very few saw their reduced-load arrangement as a temporary accommodation, and in fact most expected to continue indefinitely. Furthermore, younger women were more likely to initiate arrangements earlier in their careers, and were more confident in their "right" to do so. They expressed more of a sense of entitlement and the sentiment that their professions and employers simply must adapt. Another interesting finding was that the degree of reduced load, as measured by the percentage of full time worked, was not related to level of career success achieved as measured by salary or status of position. In career research it is generally assumed that the number of hours worked is a valid indicator of career ambition and commitment, and certainly a good predictor of career success. The findings here raise questions about the validity of these kinds of assumptions. Furthermore, only one participant described her reduced load as requiring trade-offs, as in Felice Schwartz's "mommy track" (Schwartz, 1989). Most spoke about their different ways of working as legitimate alternatives not necessarily affecting their long-term career achievements. The physicians in particular did not use the traditional male career path as their primary referent point. They viewed themselves as breaking new ground unceremoniously, by simply forging new sorts of work structures and contracts.

## Occupational effects: similarities and differences

The review of literature and analysis of the interview data point to a number of similarities and differences in the three professions which may help to explain and predict the emerging manifestations of alternative work arrangements among professionals in general. Some of the similarities have already been mentioned above, for example the dramatic increase in the percentages of women in the three fields, as well as the accompanying emergence of strong women's caucuses within professional associations and the pressure to increase the representation of women at the top levels of these professions. The interviews confirmed that in fact women who initiate reduced-load arrangements often do so after they have heard of or talked with other women in their fields who have had successful experiences with such arrangements. It is well known in the accounting profession that one of the prime motivating factors in new policies allowing reduced-load arrangements is the necessity of decreasing the high turnover rate of experienced, seasoned women just as they are ready to enter the partnership level. Several accountants in the study remarked that most of the female partners in their firms are still women who "made it" by following the male model. They either do not have children, entered the profession after their children were grown, or are single or divorced. The lack of female role models with families in the top tiers of the profession was mentioned by several respondents as discouraging experimentation with reduced-load arrangements.

The high status and high level of remuneration in these occupations makes them a natural for experimentation. Professionals in these fields are paid so well they can afford to make slightly less without feeling the pinch. The common prolonged training period and rigorous licensure procedures means that these professionals jump a lot of the requisite hoops to prove themselves and arrive at a fairly high level quite early on in their careers. This may explain why so many were not waiting to have children. Entry requirements to the profession are held so high that simply gaining entry constitutes clearing the major hurdle. Although attaining partnership is the other common career marker, at least in law and accounting, failure to attain partnership doesn't disqualify an individual from practising his or her profession.

The nature of the work in these professions being client based, and the fact that these professionals work as independent contributors, not responsible for a group of subordinates, also seems to make reduced load easier to arrange. Although within any one file the work might be multifaceted, these professionals focus on getting work done for a limited set of clients, and the focus is on individual bottom-line performance, billable hours. The wide use of billable hours as a measure of workload also provides a universal standard from which to gauge just how much someone should be doing on a reduced load, in comparison to others in the firm. The work is also such that these professionals are not always or even usually at their desks. They may be working in a client's office, or travelling, or in court, or in a hospital, and so on. This contributes toward the reduced load being invisible.

Finally, the widespread change and reorganization going on in these three fields as a result of increasing competition, increased operations/production costs, flat growth rates, and consolidation leaves them ripe for innovation in the ways they organize and deliver services.

These occupational similarities identified suggest that we will see more reduced-load work arrangements in fields where women are increasing their representation dramatically, and in sectors with a predominantly female workforce. The experimentation in these fields also suggests that reduced load will be more successful when jobs: are not too multifaceted; have clear boundaries, and it is easy to hold individuals accountable for a specific amount of work; and are constituted so that the nature of the work is independent. Furthermore, it may well be that a high degree of change in a given sector of the economy, for example accounting or health care, creates fertile ground for negotiation of alternative work arrangements because there is greater openness to innovation, and because competition for the best and the brightest is fierce.

While the similarities of the three professions have gotten the most attention in this paper, there are some obvious and not so obvious differences. These differences may partially account for different recurring themes in the interview data already pointed out. For example, differences in timing of reduced-load arrangements may be linked to different initiation and socializing practices in the three professions. Medicine has the longest period of training (six to eight years) and postponement of full initiation into the occupation. This means that when women physicians postpone having children (and possibly working reduced load) until after training and establishing themselves in a practice, they are likely to be mid to late thirties when they start a family. Lawyers' training and certification typically lasts three to four years, but the rigorous path to partnership is usually another six to eight years. However, for accountants the postgraduate training is only a year, and partnership can be attained in four to six years. So it is not surprising that the accountants were more likely to be further along in their careers when they negotiated reduced load.

In the logistics of reduced load, physicians in the study took the most radical stance in proposing and instituting alternative work arrangements. They designed and demanded what they wanted and worried less about consequences. Because they function more as independent contractors, they are subject to less peer pressure about the way they work. Furthermore, physicians are usually self-employed, and when they work for a hospital, they are paid only for a certain number of hours and do not receive additional benefits. So negotiations are simpler, and there is not a hierarchy of levels in the profession (for example, associate to partner). Furthermore, patients always require, at least theoretically, a 24-hour coverage system, which means some kind of team-based practice or coverage system is standard. Lawyers and accountants also work in teams on big accounts, but are not as accustomed to sharing the load. Also, in law and accounting there is great value attached to strong client relationships, which are presumed to lead to repeat business as well as new business through referrals. Most established physicians have more patients than they can handle, and in fact they often "close" their practices for periods of time. So in law and accounting there are clear rewards to maintaining strong, close, client relationships; not so in medicine.

The meaning of "face" time is also different in the three professions. In medicine, the less you are seen, the more busy you are assumed to be, and the more in demand. The best doctors are often said to spend very little time with each patient. Being present or highly visible gets a physician nowhere. In law and accounting, especially at the partner level, "face" time is considered a measure of commitment and loyalty to the firm, whether you're actually producing more billable hours in that time or not. So junior lawyers are expected to come in early and stay late to prove their commitment and loyalty. A difference between lawyers and accountants is that accountants spend more time out of their offices and in clients' offices, so that face time is a less valid measure of loyalty.

## ■ Links with subsequent study of corporate professionals and managers ■

A subsequent study of 86 professionals and managers working reduced load in 42 different companies in the US and Canada found similar patterns in terms of the outcomes of this kind of alternative work arrangement. This research was undertaken by the first author along with several collaborators (Lee, M. D. and MacDermid, et al., 1998). A case study approach was used, which involved interviewing multiple stakeholders in each reduced workload arrangement (for example, boss, co-worker, spouse, human resource representative), in addition to the target professional or manager working on a reduced-load basis. Several articles on different aspects of this study have recently been published (Buck, Lee, MacDermid, and Smith, 2000; Lee, MacDermid and Buck, 2000).

This study found a remarkable level of success of the reduced-load arrangements, according to both objective and subjective indicators. For example, the managers and professionals studied were working an average of 18 hours less each week than they had worked when full time. Their work arrangements had stood the test of time, having been in place an average of 4.2 years. Only 10 percent planned to return to full-time work within the next three years, and one-third of the sample had been promoted while on reduced load. Furthermore, 70 percent of the bosses of these individuals were rated by the interviewers as highly supportive of the reduced-load arrangement. This is especially impressive considering that only 40 percent were the senior managers who originally negotiated with the target managers or professionals to establish the work arrangement.

As for the subjective indicators of success, this study found that most of the managers (96 percent) and professionals (83 percent) reported being happier and more satisfied with the balance between home and work. In most cases they also reported positive results for their general well-being. They felt less stressed, less worn out, and more relaxed. Not surprisingly, most respondents also described positive effects on their children and their relationships with them 90 percent of managers, 81 percent of professionals. As with the study of lawyers, doctors, and accountants, they often mentioned being pleased with having more time with children, greater involvement with their schools, and being able to create a more stable, predictable and calm home environment.

As for career effects, two-thirds of the managers and professionals liked their jobs and felt that they were doing interesting, challenging work. Most respondents (96 percent of the managers and 69 percent of the professionals) also reported neutral or positive implications for their work performance. They reported being more efficient, creative, and focused. Most respondents also were satisfied with the likely career implications of their reduced-load work arrangement. They felt good about being able to place high priority on the quality of their family lives and still have a career. Some respondents anticipated no impact on their career progress, while others felt that their rate of promotion would slow, or that they could move laterally until they returned to full time, when they would resume upward progress.

## Conclusion

Future research on reduced-load work arrangements should be aimed at determining a more precise estimate of the extent of reduced-load work arrangements among specific professions, and within specific industries. With a larger sample of professionals on reduced load, one could compare more successful and less successful arrangements on a number of dimensions to determine what the critical variables are. Finally, further investigation or documentation of these grass-root experiments with alternative work arrangements could surface new ways of thinking about competency, performance, and career success, when these concepts are disentangled from work hours. There is no doubt that some of the kinds of reduced-load work arrangements observed in this study represent a real challenge to the status quo of what having a professional career means in these fields. We also need longitudinal studies which track the evolution of these arrangements in the context of ongoing changes in organization and family circumstances over time. Further research on reduced workload among professionals will increase our understanding of it, make more individuals and organizations aware of the viability of this alternative work arrangement, and expand our horizons about possibilities in the organization, structure, and meaning of work in organizations as well as in the family.

### REFERENCES

Adams, S. (1995): Part-time Work: Models That Work. *Women in Management Review*, 10, 7, 21–30.

ABA (American Bar Association) (1990): Commission on Women in the Profession. *Lawyers and Balanced Lives: A Guide to Drafting and Implementing Workplace Policies for Lawyers.*

Arthur, M. B. and Rousseau, D. M. (1996): *Boundaryless Careers: Work, Mobility and Learning in the New Organizational Era*. New York: Oxford University Press.

Baildam, E. M., Ewing, C. I., Jones, R., and Cummins, M. (1991): Job Sharing. *Archives of Disease in Childhood*, 66, 3, 282–3.

Bailyn, L. (1994): *Breaking the Mold*. New York: Free Press.

Bateson, M. C. (1989): *Composing a Life*. New York: Atlantic Monthly Press.

Blossfeld, H.-P. and Hakim, C. (1997): *Between equalization and marginalization: Women working part-time in Europe and the United States of America*. Oxford, UK: Oxford University Press.

Bond, J. J., Galinsky, E., and Swanberg, J. E. (1998): *The 1997 national study of the changing workforce*. New York: Families and Work Institute.

Brett, J. M. and Stroh, L. K. (1994): Turnover of Female Managers. In M. J. Davidson and R. J. Burke (eds), *Women in Management*, 55–64. London: Paul Chapman Publishing Ltd.

Buck, M. L., Lee, M. D., MacDermid, S. M., and Smith, S. (2000): Reduced load work and the experience of time among professionals and managers: Implications for personal and organizational life. In C. L. Cooper and D. Rousseau (eds), *Trends in Organizational Behavior*, 7, 13–36. New York: John Wiley.

CBA (Canadian Bar Association) (1993): Task Force on Gender Equality in the Legal Profession. *Touchstones for Change: Equality, Diversity and Accountability*. Ottawa, Ontario.

*Canadian Family Physician* (1986): Work Schedules of Family Physicians. March.

Catalyst (1997): *A new approach to flexibility: Managing the work/time equation*. New York: Catalyst.

Cejka, S. (1994): What Do Women Want? Practices Must Meet the New and Emerging Needs of Female Physicians. *Medical Group Management Journal*, 41, 2, 42–3, 46–9, 78.

Coolidge, L. and D'Angelo, D. (1994): Family Issues to Shape the Profession's Future. *The CPA Journal*, May, 16–21.

Donovan, K. (1990): Women Associates' Advancement to Partner Status in Private Law Firms. *Georgetown Journal of Legal Ethics*, 4, 135–52.

Epstein, C. F., Seron, C., Oglensky, B., and Saute, R. (1999): *The part-time paradox*. New York: Routledge.

Frank, T. (1994): *Canada's Best Employers for Women*. Toronto: Frank Communications.

Gallos, J. V. (1989): Exploring Women's Development. In M. B. Arthur, D. T. Hall, and B. S. Lawrence (eds), *Handbook of Career Theory*. New York: Cambridge University Press.

Hagan, J. and Kay, F. (1993): *Gender in Practice: A Study of Lawyers' Lives*. Unpublished manuscript.

Hooks, K. (1990): Let's Give Alternative Work Schedules a Chance. *Journal of Accountancy*, July, 170, 81–6.

Hooks, K. and Cheramy, S. J. (1994): Facts and Myths about Women CPAs. *Journal of Accountancy*, October, 79–86.

Kalands, K. (1993): The Part-Time Partner Debate. *Journal of Accountancy*, May, 74–5.

Kuechler, L. and Buszha, S. (1994): Part-time Employment Opportunities in the Field of Public Accountancy. *The CPA Journal*, May, 67–9.

Lee, M. D. (1993): Women's Involvement in Professional Careers and Family Life: Theme and Variations. *Business and the Contemporary World*, 5, 3, 106–27.

Lee, M. D. (1994): Variations in Career and Family Involvement Over Time: Truth and Consequences. In M. J. Davidson and R. J. Burke (eds), *Women in Management*, London: Paul Chapman Publishing Ltd.

Lee, M. D. and MacDermid, S. M., et al (1998): *Improvising New Careers: Accommodation, Elaboration, and Transformation*. West Lafayette, In: The Center for Families at Purdue University.

Lee, M. D., MacDermid, S. M., and Buck, M. L. (2000): Organizational paradigms of reduced load work: Accommodation, elaboration, transformation. *Academy of Management Journal*, 43, 6, 1211–26.

Levy, E. S., Flynn, P. M., and Kellogg, D. M. (1998): Customized work arrangements in the accounting profession: An uncertain future. Executive Summary of Final Report to the Alfred P. Sloan Foundation. New York.

Meiksins, P. and Whalley, P. (1995): Technical Working and Reduced Work: Limits and Possibilities. Paper presented at the Annual Meeting of the American Sociological Association, Washington, DC.

Menaghan, E. and Parcel, T. (1993): *Parents' Jobs and Children's Lives*. Hawthorne, New York: de Gruyter.

Mingle, C. (1994): The Shape of Firms to Come. *Journal of Accountancy*, July, 39–46.

Moen, P. (1999): *The Cornell couples and careers study*. Ithaca, NY: Cornell University.

NALP (National Association for Law Placement) (1994): *Report on Part-time Lawyering*. Washington, DC.

Organ, C. (1993): Toward a More Complete Society. *Archive of Surgery*, 128, 617.

Parks, J. M. and Kidder, D. L. (1994): Till Death Do Us Part . . . Changing Work Relationships in the 1990s. In C. L. Cooper and D. M. Rousseau (eds), *Trends in Organizational Behavior*, New York: John Wiley.

Robinson, J. K. (1993): The Status of Women in Dermatology. *Cutis*, 52, 6, 363–6.

Ryen, E. (1989): The Output of Canadian Medical Schools in 1989. *Forum*, 22, 7–9.

Sanmartin, C. A. and Snidal, L. (1993): Profile of Canadian Physicians: Results of the 1990 Physician Resource Questionnaire. *Canadian Medical Association Journal*, 149, 7, 977–84.

Schwartz, F. (1989): Management Women and the New Facts of Life. *Harvard Business Review*, January/February.

Sekaran, U. (1986): *Dual-Career Families*. San Francisco: Jossey-Bass.

Seron, C. and Ferris, K. (1995): Negotiating Professionalism: The Gendered Social Capital of Flexible Time. *Work and Occupations*, 22, 1, February, 22–47.

Stewart, E. B., Belcourt, M., Sherman, A., Bohlander, G., and Snell, S. (2000): *Essentials of managing human resources*. Toronto: Nelson Thomson Learning.

US Bureau of the Census (1999): Statistical Abstract of the United States, 119th ed. Washington DC: Government Printing Office.

Williams, P., Dominique-Pierre, K., Vayda et al. (1990): Women in Medicine: Practice Patterns and Attitudes. *Canadian Medical Association Journal*, 143, 194–201.

Woodward, C. A., Cohen, M. L., and Ferrier, B. M. (1990): Career Interruptions and Hours Practiced: Comparisons Between Young Men and Women Physicians. *Canadian Journal of Public Health*, 81, 16–20.

# 12

# DEVELOPING TOMORROW'S WOMEN BUSINESS LEADERS

*Susan Vinnicombe and Val Singh*

For the last half-century, MBA degrees have been the prized qualification for high flyers in a business world where almost all leaders were male. Traditional MBA courses have, however, generally been designed for and by men, based on male work experiences and male needs. Women's development needs are different to those of men, and women managers' needs are not adequately met in traditional MBA and executive development programs, where women usually constitute a minority of delegates and, indeed, tutors.

Using a psychoanalytic lens, we explore underlying differences in the child development and work–life experiences of males and females which need to be taken into account in designing women's leadership development programs. In taking this "gender in management" perspective, we are considering the different needs of women which are not met in current MBA programs. We argue that management is relational, and that as men and women are socialized differently and take on different work–life roles, then they manage differently. This approach also recognizes the gendered organizational relations and structures within which women managers live, learn, and work (Calás and Smircich, 1996; Hughes, 2000).

After consideration of the design of women's development programs, we report on a case study of a women-only executive development program established as an MBA elective in a leading British business school. This program takes account of female developmental differences in a more facilitative and productive environment than the traditional MBA, one in which women can learn to be more effective managers. Evidence of their learning is provided from the written assignments completed by women MBA students, reflecting on other women's leadership experiences in order to understand their own development. The chapter concludes by suggesting complementary women-only management development programs for the new millennium until more gender-balanced intakes of MBA students are achieved.

## ■ Reviewing current MBA programs ■

Catalyst (2000), a leading US non-profit organization working to advance women in business, reported research into top US MBA programs showing that women have comprised around 30 percent of MBA students for the past twenty years. The UK Association of MBAs (AMBA, 1997) estimated that the proportion of women MBAs had plateaued at around 25 percent, considerably lower than the US figure. Potential women MBAs, according to Sinclair (1995), seem to be rejecting the male model of management education.

Catalyst's main findings were that 95 percent of all graduates were highly satisfied with the experience and the value of the MBA. However, women were more likely to view their experience as problematic (in terms of aggression and competitiveness). Women often did not relate to the teaching because of lack of sensitivity to issues of gender, race, and diversity. According to more than half the women, there was a lack of females in leading roles in management case studies, and 40 percent felt there were too few female faculty. One student explained: "Case study groups are typically male-dominated. It was often difficult to get them to pay attention to a female perspective. The women often had the same or better answers but had a much more difficult time being heard" (Catalyst, 2000, p. 13). When MBAs were asked what should be done to attract more women to do MBAs, one-third of the males said "do nothing," compared to only one-sixth of the females, reflecting Tanton's (1994) comments on majority group members not thinking about minority members' experiences.

Sinclair's (1995, 1997) explanation of this phenomenon was that the MBA was constructed on gendered understandings of managerial identity. She described management education as based on a "masculinised set of practices" which reinforce male dominance, despite the rhetoric of gender-neutral measurement of competencies and capabilities. Sinclair examined women's experiences of UK, US and Australian management schools, finding that women often preferred to learn and be taught in ways which depart from traditional MBA approaches. The 16 women MBAs interviewed in her study identified four sources of tension. These were centralization of authority and power in the classroom; defences against admissions of uncertainty and ignorance; learning by looking outwards at "benchmarks" and "best practices" rather than inwards in terms of connecting with personal experiences; and emphasis on knowing by mastering analytical techniques rather than knowing through intuitive and emotional connections. According to Sinclair, "The MBA culture enacts and reproduces a narrow set of values which fail to connect with the diversity of managerial experiences and aspirations of many women and some men enrolled in the MBA." Women do successfully complete their MBAs: "Although they report a sense of achievement in having 'survived' it, and there is value in the rehearsal of the culture of most large corporations which they will encounter, the overall sense is of learning accomplished in the margins, rather than in the main stream of the curricula" (Sinclair, 1997, p. 325).

## ■ Gendered working life experiences ■

Women's experience of management is often significantly different from men's because of the particular roles they fill both at work and within life in general, yet these differences are not reflected in the nature of the management development process in traditional programs. Women's position in the workplace is different from that of men. Labour market trends show that women constitute 44 percent of the UK workforce, yet occupy only 32 percent of managerial and administrative positions (Thair and Risdon, 1999). The higher the level in management, the more glaring is the gender gap. Our study of women directors of top UK boards shows that around 6 percent of all top directors are female, but only 2 percent of executive directorships are held by women, and only 58 percent of top companies have any female representation on their boards of directors, down from 64 percent in 1999 (Singh, Vinnicombe, and Johnson, in press). Just as their entry into management has not assured British women access to top jobs, so it has not guaranteed them equal pay. According to the Institute of Management, UK male managers earn £36,000 and female managers £33,000 on average (Hilpern, 2000). On the positive side, the pay inequalities between men and women are generally shrinking and, overall, women now earn 80 percent of gross male earnings compared to only 62 percent 25 years ago (Johnston, 2000). Nevertheless, there is a new growing gender polarization in the economy between part-timers and full-timers. In the UK 27 percent of women managers are part time, compared to only 4 percent of male managers (EOC, 1997). Pay inequality for women managers comes in two forms. Part-time women managers are frequently restricted to lower grades (and salary scales) and often their official work hours do not reflect the long hours which they invest in their jobs.

The nature of women's career paths often blocks their progress up the organization. At junior and middle levels, women are often in staff functions, such as personnel or training, rather than in operational or commercial functions. Once women perform well in these support roles, it is often difficult for them to negotiate moves into other functions. These functional barriers at work are described as "glass walls" by McRae (1996). This trend is exacerbated by the exclusion of many women managers from informal networking with important, senior managers who might facilitate such transfers (Ibarra, 1997). Such networking is difficult for female managers since the networks are almost exclusively male. The male culture of politicking also often does not appeal to women's sense of authenticity (Mainiero, 1994).

Long working hours make it very stressful for women to combine careers and family responsibilities. Surveys continually show that women take the major share of activities related to child rearing and running a household. In the UK, 73 percent of women still do "nearly all the housework" and men with working partners have an average of six hours more spare time at weekends than their partners (Cooper and Lewis, 1993). Not surprisingly, many women see a conflict between family and career and hence decide not to have children or to work part time. Few women managers in "token" positions (that is, senior posts where less than 15 percent of positions are held by females (Kanter, 1977)) have families at home, according to Simpson (1997), in contrast to male managers. In a recent survey of male and female managers and long working hours, Simpson (1998) discusses how women are doubly disadvantaged. They may be unable or unwilling to put in the long hours so they are not seen as fully committed. In addition, their exclusion from late informal meetings means they do not have the same access as male managers to information. It is often difficult for women, particularly token women managers, to challenge the issue of long hours because of their vulnerable position (Simpson, 1998).

These different male and female experiences of being a manager come together in terms of personal definitions of career success. The traditional model of career success in organizations has emphasized the external criteria of hierarchical position and pay. Yet there is strong evidence from women that they do not define their own career success primarily in terms of these criteria. Sturges (1999) investigated how male and female managers saw their own career success, finding four types of managers. *Climbers* see career success chiefly in terms of the level of organizational seniority and pay achieved, are status conscious and competitive, but often want to combine material success with enjoyment at work. *Experts* define career success as being good at what they do and getting personal recognition for this accomplishment, are not goal oriented, and value the content of a job more than its status. *Influencers* associate career success with the degree of organizational influence achieved and may seek hierarchical advancement to gain greater influence, but do not value status per se. Finally, *Self-realizers* define success in terms of achievement at a very personal level, usually involving personal challenge and self-development, and seeing ability to balance work and personal life as an integral part of career success. Of the 36 managers interviewed, women were more likely to be Experts and Self-realizers and less likely to be Climbers. Men were more likely to be Climbers and Influencers than Experts and Self-realizers. This suggests that external criteria for career success such as pay and hierarchical position are far more central to men's conceptions of career success. Women define their own career success much more in terms of internal criteria such as accomplishment, achievement, and "intangible" criteria such as influence, personal recognition, and respect. These differences have implications for how women act as managers, and how their development needs differ from those of male managers.

## ■ The psychology of gendered development ■

Psychologists who write about gender are not surprised by these differences in career success. Women and men arrive in organizations with a differently constructed sense of self as a result of gendered upbringing. Moreover, it is apparent that the attitudes developed in men are more likely to be rewarded at work since many organizations are male dominated. If, as many writers have suggested (for example, Asplund, 1988), organizational practices build on the individual's sense of identity, then these are more likely to create tensions for women as they struggle to establish themselves as managers. Chodorow (1978) suggests that it is the social system of mothering that creates different patterns of behavior between boys and girls. She shows how women, as mothers, produce daughters with mothering capacities and the desire to mother. Boys are cared for by a primary care giver of the other gender. As boys develop a sense of identity, it is as separate from and other than the mother. Girls, in contrast, cared for by a same-gender care giver, separate later, and grow up to value closeness to others and to experience care and dependence as less anxiety-inducing than do boys. Girls, however, are more likely to be anxious in situations where independence is called for. In such a way, men are prepared for a more distant family role, and to engage in the impersonal world of work and public life. Chodorow (1978) argues that, to the extent that females and males experience different interpersonal environments as they grow up, feminine and masculine personality will develop differently and be preoccupied with different issues. The structure of the family and family practices creates certain differential relational needs and capacities in men and women that reflect themselves in the roles enacted in adulthood, including the managerial role. Undoubtedly, there is a spectrum of behavior within both sexes. There are some men who are far more nurturant that some women, and women who are more distant than some men. Some girls identify with their fathers and not all boys develop independence. But on the whole, there is a continuum in which some behaviour is more typical of one gender than of the other.

Evidence supporting this account is provided by a number of studies that show differences in the way people perceive and present themselves in the world. Among them are the work of psychologists such as Gilligan (1982), who identified differences in girls' moral approach to the world; Belenky, Clinchy, Goldberger, and Tarule (1986), who studied women's ways of knowing; and Levinson (1978, 1996) who charted the differences between the ways men and women develop their adult lives. Gilligan extended the psychoanalytic work of Chodorow to demonstrate how, by showing life as a web of relationships and stressing continuity, women portray autonomy rather than attachment as illusory and even risky. In her work based on studies encompassing all age groups, Gilligan (1982) explored concepts of self and morality, and experiences of conflict and choice. She discovered that:

> From the different dynamics of separation and attachment in their gender identity formation through the divergence of identity and intimacy that marks their experience in the adolescent years, male and female voices typically speak of the importance of different truths, the former of the role of separation as it defines and empowers the self, the latter of the ongoing process of attachment that creates and sustains the human community. (p. 156)

Thus, building on their early psychological development, girls "enact" their desire for connectedness, creating close relationships. This behaviour has an impact on occupational choice, concentrating women in caring roles in the workforce. Women's behaviour at work is likely to be influenced by such preferences, and this can reinforce women's later subordinate position in the workforce as they disdain male habits such as self-promotion and networking, and choose to work in sectors such as social work or health care with traditionally low pay. However, there is criticism of Gilligan's approach (Elam, 1994, p. 116), some taking issue with the attribution of the ethics of care to all women as a universal and natural phenomenon rather than taking into account the normative context in which women's caring exists.

Building on a theory of women's connectedness, Belenky et al. (1986) listened to the voices of women and showed how that sense, first identified in the infant by Chodorow, deepens with maturity. They saw causal factors later in the life cycle, notably motherhood, as reinforcing the sense of connectedness. According to Belenky et al., males tend to have linear careers, starting with a stage of dualism where they see everything as right or wrong. They move to multiplicity, where they recognize that others may have knowledge, and that their own knowledge and moral judgment is just as valid. Men then start to use analytical tools for evaluation, and eventually recognize that knowledge is constructed. At the same time, their moral judgment moves from right or wrong to an understanding of morality in relative contexts. In the male learning model, the males move through application of rules and logic to understanding the social construction of knowledge. The teacher in this model is like a banker of knowledge, giving facts and analytical tools which help the student to learn and apply to other situations.

In contrast, women tend not to have linear careers so typical of males, but pass through several stages and can be in any particular stage at any time (see also Gallos, 1989). Initially, in the stage of silence, women accept knowledge and their sense of morality from men, especially their father. Gradually they recognize that they are learning from that external authority, and are in a state of "received knowledge." Women then move to a stage of subjective knowledge where they start to use themselves as an inner authority and guide to learning about themselves. The fourth stage is procedural knowledge, where the woman starts to evaluate how she is learning, either by separate knowing (applying rules and processes), or connected knowing where she is able to put herself into the other person's experience in her own mind. The fifth stage is integrated knowing, through the intellect and emotion, integrating the context, tolerating ambiguity, and strengthening the self. Many women do not ever reach the fifth stage, and many will move backwards and forwards between the different stages at various times in their lives. The teacher in the female model of knowing is like a midwife, helping the woman to reflect on her knowing, and enabling her to bring forth understanding from her own experiences, through which her own analytical tools can be developed and applied to other situations.

Levinson (1978) evolved a phased approach to career development, defining a series of age-related achievements and transitions, in contrast to the staged approach of Belenky et al. (1986). Levinson's detailed, biographical studies of women and men demonstrate that gender is an essential influence in shaping their lives. His central concept is "gender splitting." This term refers not simply to gender differences but to a rigid division between male and female, masculine and feminine, in human life. Gender splitting has been pervasive in virtually every society, although there are wide variations in its patterning. Levinson (1996) says:

> To a much greater degree that is usually recognised, women and men have lived in different social worlds and have differed remarkably in their social roles, identities and psychological attributes. The splitting operates at many levels: culture, social institutions, everyday social life, the individual psyche. It creates antithetical divisions between women and men, between social worlds, between the masculine and feminine within the self. It also creates inequalities that limit the adult development of women as well as men.

These gender differences lead us to consider how best to design management training appropriate to women, alongside their core MBA courses.

## ■ The design of women-only management development programs ■

One response to the different developmental paths of men and women is to consider women-only development. For a comprehensive historical overview of such provision, see Gray (1994). She tracks women-only management training (WOMT) history from the 1960s, where the second wave of the women's movement led middle-class women seeking liberation to return to work, demanding the right to training. In the 1970s, equality legislation was enacted, and women's training focused on achieving equality with men at work. This shifted in the 1980s toward special treatment of women because of their psychological development differences. In the 1990s, the rhetoric was diversity management, where difference was defined in relation to white males, and difference had to be controlled and homogenized, followed by a move to value difference and enjoy the benefits of heterogeneity in management teams. Gray notes that "the boom in MBA programs in the USA and Britain in the 1980s took place without any attention being paid to the particular needs of women managers" (p. 221).

In the early years there was a trend in women in management research which identified various sex differences in the personal characteristics of managers. Following that lead, WOMT courses tended, in the 1970s, to focus on identifying and remedying perceived deficiencies such as lack of ambition and assertiveness, thereby adding support to the view that women were less able than men to be managers. In the 1980s WOMT programs started to respect and build upon the very differences between female and male managers which have been nurtured from early childhood. Essentially these programs provide women with the opportunity of reflecting and reinterpreting their managerial experiences exclusively with other women. Tanton's (1992) research on the "authenticity" of women managers is relevant in making a case for WOMT. When women managers are in the minority, they can often disregard their differences, values, and preferences in order to make themselves like their male peers. Tanton calls this an abrogation of their female self. On WOMT programs, women can contribute openly, their femininity can be freely expressed, and they can demonstrate authenticity to their values.

A key issue arising in women's management programs is women's interaction with organizational politics and personal influence (Mainiero, 1994). For many women managers, the focus at work is task accomplishment; they value challenge, high standards, expertise, and attention to detail. This fits with women managers' definitions of career success. They do not see the relevance of politics. They feel that if they are good at their jobs, others should notice and promote them. They should not have to make themselves visible, promote themselves, or network with senior managers to build sponsorship. Helping women managers to develop positive attitudes toward politics is one of the greatest challenges in these programs. The advancement of women into senior levels of management in present-day organizations is contingent on women understanding how politics operate in their own organizations and being willing to engage in the process. Post-structuralist feminists such as Fletcher (1998) would challenge the gendered structures which have led to such a culture, because other more collective and relational models of organization could be achieved valuing empathy, mutuality, reciprocity, and sensitivity to emotional contexts, allowing both men and women to flourish. However, our immediate concern is with developing women in present-day structures and enabling them to advance.

Research to support the idea of differences in the working styles of male and female managers is difficult to locate. The inappropriateness of the profiles used commonly in the leadership area to illuminate sex differences does not help this situation. However, research by Vinnicombe (1987) using the Myers Briggs Type Indicator (MBTI), based on Jung's personality types, has yielded some significant and interesting findings about the differences between male and female working styles. The most significant difference between male and female managers is along the sensing/intuition dimension. Sensing people tend to prefer practical problems, systems and methods; are patient with routine details; and search for standard problem-solving approaches. Intuitive people enjoy ambiguous problems, get bored with routine problems, frequently ignore the facts and search for creative approaches. Women managers tend to be much more intuitive. In the Vinnicombe (1987) study, 70 percent of male managers were sensing, whereas 40 to 60 percent of the women were intuitive. Interestingly, no stereotypical profile emerges for female managers. The implications for women in MBA classes is that while most of the males have similar MBTI types, some women may find few colleagues with similar characteristics. While women managers tend to be more intuitive than male managers, women managers are characteristically quite diverse in their working styles. This is a positive finding since organizations require many different qualities to be effective.

Until recently, many girls were traditionally not socialized to make a strong investment of self in future occupation or career. Hence, women who grew up within such an environment often have difficulty in identifying with, and articulating, a clear career strategy. This is a great block to career progress, as women managers often give the impression of not taking their careers seriously. In women-only programs, women managers can help one another to see the themes in their careers, using a structured career exercise such as Schein's Career Anchors (Schein, 1990). The latter is particularly relevant to women because it defines the individual's self-image (abilities and talents; motives and drivers; and attitudes and values) through analysing all her varied work experiences. In so doing, the exercise helps women to integrate what many women see merely as a series of jobs, and to see future possible career choices. Schein's exercise is additionally helpful to women managers, for not only does it pull together an understanding of women's past jobs and motivations but it also empowers women by showing them how they have influenced the shape of their careers to date. The importance of balancing career and family is often central to women, and the career anchors exercise facilitates an understanding of this dynamic.

The nature of women's stressors (the reasons behind their stress and women's responses to stress) is often different from those of men. Traditionally, women have been socialized not to be aggressive or competitive, but to nurture. Like Sturges (1999), Braiker (1987) identified that success means something different to women and men. While men tend to define success in terms of quantifiable measures of achievement – money, status, material possessions – women tend to define success in terms of how well life is going in an emotional or interpersonal sense. While many men's success is primarily geared to achievement in the workplace, women's success is defined in terms of meeting a relentless stream of demands (often conflicting) from everyone around her at work and at home. Braiker (1987) labels this stress syndrome the "Type E".

Type E women often assume unrealistic and excessive burdens. They want to keep everyone's approval – that is part of how they know that they're succeeding and they cope with the demands by trying to do it all, often at a substantial cost to their emotional and physical well-being.

Because women do not express anger or aggression as easily as men, they may not even recognize their feelings as being anger. The anger may be disguised as resentment, depression, or moodiness. Since most women's experiences of stress do not coincide with most men's experiences of stress, it is valuable to provide women with their own forum to discuss what stresses them, the consequences of their stresses, and how they handle stress. Women-only training is such a forum.

Ruderman (2000) suggests five goals for women's development which sum up much of the discussion above. These are seeking and achieving authenticity; feeling whole; living agentically; making connections; and gaining self-clarity. We believe that women-only programs, by virtue of their design and exclusion of males, have a better chance of achieving these goals for the women participants than do mainstream MBA programs.

## ■ The argument against women-only programs ■

A radical feminist argument against WOMT programs is that they often adopt a liberal feminist approach focused on rectifying women's deficiencies from the male model, thereby contributing to the continued subordination of women who do not fit the organizational mold. Poststructuralist feminists would criticize WOMT because it celebrates women's differences without giving sufficient attention to the underlying power structures and processes which hold them back. WOMT, in focusing on the special nature and development processes of women, may not see it as important to deconstruct the texts on which male authority has been legitimized (Elam, 1994; Calás and Smircich, 1995).

Some authors are in favour of WOMT courses being open to men as well as women (McKinney and Moore, 1985), on the grounds that mixed groups reflect the real organizational environment and that men should also be aware of the problems and possible solutions for their female colleagues. Even though women might be more comfortable in female groups, they would also be able to gain a male perspective on the issues, and breakout groups could be single sex where appropriate. However, we feel that the case for WOMT for women who have been managers for some time is very strong, as a complement, not a substitute, for mainstream management training, as the following section will demonstrate.

## ■ Women-only programs in action ■

It may be helpful to review these issues through a case study in a leading British business school. Women-only electives were started on the MBA programs at Cranfield School of Management in the 1980s, and are an accredited part of the MBA. All students do a core program for half of the course, followed by a selection of electives in the second half, of which the women in management elective is one. Not all women take the elective, some not wishing to identify themselves as needing this particular option, some are not interested, and some find themselves unable to attend because of clashes with other desired options. The average age of MBA students, who all have at least three years management experience, is usually about 31 for full-timers and 34 for part-timers, and women constitute 20 percent of full-time and 31 percent of part-time MBAs. The women in management elective primarily addresses the social-psychological issues facing women managers at work. Participants typically work with the following kinds of objectives. To:

- clarify their attitudes and feelings about themselves in relation to their work roles and personal roles (for example, colleague, boss, wife, mother, daughter)
- review their experiences of managerial life: the specific issues they face as women
- examine their management styles, in order to promote their personal strengths at work
- study the concepts of power and politics and enable themselves to apply these concepts effectively
- help themselves to become more proactive in managing their careers
- satisfy these goals in a safe environment in which they can test their own experiences against the experiences of other women.

Throughout the elective, the emphasis is on helping women managers to help themselves become more effective. Introducing participants to the concepts of role models, networking, and mentoring are invaluable here. Perhaps most important of all is the support and friendship which participants are able to give to one another. This all takes place in a particular learning environment which differs considerably from that of the mainstream MBA. Feedback from the MBA women's electives continually rate them as excellent across all the school's electives, (approximately 50 are offered) and across a number of indicators such as satisfaction, learning, and usefulness. Table 12.1 summarizes key points of difference between the traditional MBA and the women in management elective.

## Reflecting through the assessment process

As table 12.1 indicates, assessment of learning does not have to be the one-off replication of facts and use of managerial models. A more valuable kind of assignment is

**Table 12.1**  A comparison of the learning environments of the traditional MBA program and the Women in Management elective

| Focus: | Traditional MBA program focus on activities | Women's development program focus on process |
|---|---|---|
| Objective | Giving students knowledge | Helping participants with their issues |
| Culture | Fast, competitive, impersonal, guarded | Slow, deep, open, intimate |
| Media | Case studies, videos, techniques, models | Own experience |
| Teaching style | Lecturing, based on assumption that lecturer has the knowledge and the "right" answers | Leading discussion based on assumption that the tutor has relevant experience to offer |
| Assessment of learning | Replication of "knowledge" and ability to analyse managerial situations using particular models | Reflection and insightful self-analysis to evoke understanding of models |
| Learning path | From the general to the particular | From the particular to the general |

one which stays with the student for a long time, shaping their sense of themselves through reflection. An important part of the Cranfield MBA course elective for women is the undertaking of a small project in lieu of formal examination. Last year students were asked to interview a senior woman of their choice about her life and career and, in writing up the project, to reflect on their own situation, taking into account what they had learned during the course. The interviews provided a mirror for the MBA students.

> It absolutely amazes me that she is so focused in her career without a mentor. She seems to know exactly where she is going. I on the other hand discuss my working life and career with my father and yet, I don't know what the next position or ultimate destination in life will be . . . It rather explains that I really admire what she has achieved.
>     Personally I found talking to her very interesting and felt that I shared many of her views. I felt that she was someone I could aspire to and consider a role model for success.

Another female student commented on the problems which her interviewee brought up about the difficulties of studying part time when her partner was not keen on her spending so much time studying.

> I can empathize with her. I found studying for my accountancy exams incredibly difficult and eventually gave up. It was impossible to find time to sit down and study properly and there was a continual simmering resentment from my ex-partner.

The student, like her interviewee, decided that she needed to be independent.

Another issue of concern to women managers is the decision whether or not to have children. Reflecting on her interviewee's comment that a colleague wanted to work for six months in the winter and take time off to be at home in summer with her children, through a flexible contract, the student asks: "Is this vision of women being able to have a family and a challenging job part-time a reality?" The student then put this vision into context using Levinson's (1996) career model, thereby embedding her reflection into more academic learning. The Levinson model struck a chord in several students when reviewing their careers in the context of their interviews with successful women.

> When we looked at Levinson's article on "The seasons of a woman's life," it talked about fear of success and fear of the consequences of success. What I don't really know at the moment is how much my push for balance is fear of success and how much is sound, realistic decision making.

Paradoxically, the subjective reflection on another person's career and life story enables women to review their own experience more objectively and then bring to the surface an in-depth view of themselves in their personal context.

> I admired her focus and success. She is also a fighter and really believes in herself. Despite the resistance she had to overcome, she kept hanging in there. It is fair to say that I am a fighter too, and have had my share of success. Where we differ is that I am too often doubting myself, and hopefully one day I will be as confident and focused as she is.

Real life experience shows me that I am more than capable of dealing with challenges, and tend to shine when under pressure, but my natural tendency is to stick within my comfort zone and utilize my existing skills and experiences as much as possible.

The process is usually very affirming, thereby building self-esteem and confidence – qualities often lacking in women managers. One of the MBA students, an engineer in her early thirties, said:

I have just chosen to leave my job and take a short break before looking for a new direction in my career. Over the last year I have become more relaxed but also more confident about my career. This can in the main be attributed to the MBA and courses such as Women in Management which have helped me gain a better understanding of how I work and how that fits in with others around me. I plan to take more time and effort choosing the right place in which to work, and I no longer feel that I have to accept the challenge of proving that I can do just as well as the men in an environment that maybe just isn't right for me.

She had taken control of her career and her life, she was confident, ambitious, with an enhanced sense of her own identity, and an understanding of her personal needs. This psychosocial methodology of eliciting life histories and reflecting on one's own situation has been used to great effect as a developmental tool in the Cranfield women in management elective.

## Meeting women managers' particular developmental needs

A consistent theme running through studies of women managers is the lack of confidence they show in themselves. They tend to rate themselves lower than male colleagues, and they have difficulty in accepting praise from others (Rudman, 1998). This lack of self-esteem among women can lead to the so-called "impostor syndrome" where women fear they will be found out or unmasked as unworthy of the success they have attained or the positions they have won (Harvey and Katz, 1983). The MBA and associated traditional management development programs often fail to affirm in women their fundamental belief in themselves.

Before the course, women often feel they are alone in experiencing the masculine-gendered work culture, and the reflective women-only sessions and assignments allow them to make the link between their own experience and gender relations, so that they no longer see themselves as the cause of the experience.

## Conclusion

This paper has shown that the development process for women is not the same as the development process for men, but a mirror image, and that therefore different developmental programs from the traditional MBA are required for women to have an equal chance to succeed. Men's development is usually linked to increasing autonomy and separation from others as a means of strengthening identity and empowering themselves. It is only much later in men's development that men are ready to explore intimacy and accept others as equally important to themselves. Likewise, it is only much later in women's development that women can tolerate separation and finally see themselves as equal to others. The learning environment of the MBA is particularly suited to the male model and pace of development, and that pedagogy has been privileged. Women's management programs allow female managers to develop through a learning model more suited to female ways of knowing and learning, providing support during their undertaking of the traditional MBA course.

We suggest that women-only development programs should be designed around individual women managers' deepening understanding and strengthening of themselves in relation to other women managers and women tutors. This links back to the psychological theories of women's development discussed earlier in this chapter which highlight the importance of attachments and relationships in determining how women see themselves, their careers, their lives, and their continuing professional development. Eventually, we hope that the kind of development proposed would be available to both men and women, encompassed within new forms of MBA courses which take heed of a diversity of needs and learning styles, reflecting an inclusive rather than exclusive approach. But in the meantime, we propose that women-only management development courses can make a significant complementary contribution to traditional MBA courses and other executive development. Surely as we begin this new millennium, it is time to acknowledge that women's management development is different from that of men. This needs to be reflected in the design of complementary management development programs specifically for women, so that their progress in the new century can better reflect their talents and potential contribution to management practice.

## REFERENCES

AMBA (Association of MBAs) (1997): *MBA salary and career review*. London: Association of MBAs.

Asplund, G. (1988): *Women managers: Changing organizational cultures*. London: Wiley.

Belenky, M., Clinchy, B., Goldberger, N., and Tarule, J. (1986): *Women's ways of knowing*. New York: Basic Books.

Braiker, H. (1987): *The E type woman*. New York: Naldutton Press.

Calás, M. B. and Smircich, L. (1995): From 'The woman's' point of view: Feminist approaches to organization studies. In S. R. Clegg, C. Hardy, and W. Nord (eds), *Handbook of Organization Studies*, London: Sage.

Catalyst (2000): *Women and the MBA: Gateway to opportunity*. Ann Arbor: University of Michigan.

Chodorow, N. (1978): *The reproduction of mothering*. Berkeley: University of California Press.

Cooper C. and Lewis, S. (1993): *The workplace revolution: Managing today's dual career families*. London: Kogan Page.

Elam, D. (1994): *Feminism and deconstruction*. London: Routledge.

EOC (Equal Opportunities Commission) (1997): *Briefings on women and men in Britain: Management and the professions*. Manchester: Equal Opportunities Commission.

Fletcher, J. (1998): Relational practice: A feminist reconstruction of work. *Journal of Management Inquiry*, 7, 2, 163–86.

Gallos, J. (1989): Exploring women's development: Implications for career theory, practice and research. In M. B. Arthur, D. T. Hall, and B. S. Lawrence (eds), *Handbook of career theory*, Cambridge: Cambridge University Press.

Gilligan, C. (1982): *In a different voice: Psychological theory and women's development*. Cambridge: Harvard University Press.

Gray, B. (1994): Women-only management training – A past and present. In M. Tanton (ed.), *Women in management: A developing presence*, London: Routledge.

Harvey J. C. and Katz, C. (1983): *If I'm so successful, why do I feel like a fake?: The impostor phenomenon.* New York: St. Martins Press.

Hilpern, K. (2000): Graduates: Why men still earn more than women. *The Independent,* November 9, Education Section, p. 1.

Hughes, C. (2000): Painting new (feminist) pictures of human resource development (and) identifying research issues for political change. *Management Learning,* 31, 1, 51–65.

Ibarra, H. (1997): Homophily and differential returns: Sex differences in network structure and access in an advertising firm. *Administrative Science Quarterly,* 32, 422–47.

Johnston, P. (2000): Work inequality questioned as women catch up. *The Daily Telegraph,* November 27, p. 8.

Kanter, R. M. (1977): *Men and women of the corporation.* New York: Basic Books.

Levinson, D. (1978): *The seasons of a man's life.* New York: Knopf.

Levinson, D. (1996): *The seasons of a woman's life.* New York: Knopf.

Mainiero, L. (1994): Getting anointed for advancement: The case of executive women. *Academy of Management Executive,* 8, 2, 53–67.

McKinney, D. and Moore, L. L. (1985): Teaching undergraduate women in management courses: Resources for Teachers and Trainers. In V. J. Ramsey (ed.), *Preparing Professional Women for the Future,* Michigan Business Papers No. 67, University of Michigan.

McRae, S. (1996): *Women at the top: Progress after five years: A follow-up report to the Hansard Society Commission on Women at the Top.* London: Hansard Society.

Ruderman, M. (2000): *Developing women leaders: A strategy for success.* Paper presented at the International Women in Leadership Summit, October, Brussels.

Rudman, L. A. (1998): Self-promotion as a risk factor for women: The costs and benefits of counterstereotypical impression management. *Journal of Personality and Social Psychology,* 74, 629–45.

Schein, E. H. (1990): *Career anchors – Discovering your real values.* California: Pfeiffer & Company.

Simpson, R. (1997): Have times changed? Career barriers and the token woman manager. *British Journal of Management,* 8 (Special Issue), S121–S130.

Simpson, R. (1998): Presenteeism, power and organizational change: Long hours as a career barrier and the impact on the working lives of women managers. *British Journal of Management,* 9 (Special Issue), S37–S50.

Sinclair, A. (1995): Sex and the MBA. *Organization,* 2, 2, 295–317.

Sinclair, A. (1997): The MBA through women's eyes: Learning and pedagogy in management education. *Management Learning,* 28, 3, 313–30.

Singh, V., Vinnicombe, S., and Johnson, P. (in press): Women directors on top UK boards. *Corporate Governance: An International Review,* 9, 3, 206–16.

Sturges, J. (1999): What it means to succeed: Personal conceptions of career success held by male and female managers at different ages. *British Journal of Management,* 10, 239–52.

Tanton, M. (1992): Developing authenticity in management development programs. *Women in Management Review,* 7, 4, 20–7.

Tanton, M. (1994): Developing women's presence. In M. Tanton (ed.), *Women in management: A developing presence,* London: Routledge.

Thair, T. and Risdon, A. (1999): Women in the labour market: Results from the Spring 1998 Labour Force Survey. *Labour Market Trends,* March.

Vinnicombe, S. (1987): What exactly are the differences in male and female working styles? *Women in Management Review,* 3, 1, 13–21.

# 13

# FLEXIBLE WORK ARRANGEMENTS: A SUCCESSFUL STRATEGY FOR THE ADVANCEMENT OF WOMEN AT THE ROYAL BANK FINANCIAL GROUP

*Nora L. Spinks and Norma Tombari*

The financial services industry has experienced tremendous and rapid change over the past decade. The revolution of the industry has been profound. The changes have resulted in fundamental restructuring, realigning, and repositioning of the entire industry with more changes expected. These include:

- globalization and the changes in the Bank Act permitting greater foreign penetration of the Canadian and financial services market. The global marketplace is undergoing extensive changes
- by the introduction of financial services many operations including department stores, automakers, and grocery chains
- with the emergence of the knowledge and technological era, organizations are faced with a shrinking labor pool, an aging workforce, increasing competition, and expanding workloads, increasing mobility within industries, across sectors, and around the world

One of Canada's largest employers, Royal Bank Financial Group (RBFG) has over 56,000 people employed worldwide in over 1,400 service delivery units. RBFG's goal is to provide outstanding customer service to its 10 million customers in each of its key business areas: Personal and Commercial Banking, Wealth Management, Insurance, Corporate and Investment Banking and eBusiness. In response to marketplace forces,

## Box 13.1   Canadian Women In the Workforce

- Women are more likely to work part-time than men, and mothers in particular are more likely to do so. Of mothers with pre-school children, 40 percent worked part-time according to the 1996 Census (p. 146)
- Of mothers with children over age 6 30 percent participated in the paid labor force in 1996 (p. 86)
- 68 percent Of households having both partners in the labor force, (p. 89)
- Between 1976 and 1998 the percentage of mothers with children under three holding jobs more than doubled from 26 percent to 59 percent (p. 146)

RBFG has revolutionized everything, from products to customer interface, organizational infrastructure to management innovation, and local branch banking to a extensive array of global financial services and alternate delivery channels.

RBFG recognizes that the business performance is driven by their people performance. Their performance depends on coaching, mentoring, recognition, and rewards, and learning and development opportunities. These values are reflected in the workplace practices such as flexible work arrangements, commitment to people development, performance-based reward and recognition, and belief in the value of diversity.

## Box 13.2   Excerpts from the RBFG Work/Family/Life Policy Statement

RBFG recognizes the need for a pro-active posture and program to provide employees with an opportunity fir a flexible balance between work, family and personal obligations over a lifetime.

RBFG is open to flexible work options where it is in the interest of clients, the individual and the group.

RBFG will continue professional development and career opportunities to those employees who choose to pursue flexible work options.

©1992

To attract, retain, and motivate employees, and to meet customer demands and stakeholder expectations, RBFG has invested in workplace flexibility, the measurement of the impact of flexible work arrangements, support, development, and advancement of women, and the development of management tools, training, and accountability to meet these objectives. The impact on its predominantly female population has been positive.

- Seventy-five percent of the workforce are women
- Women are fully represented at all levels of Royal Bank. Significant progress has been made in the representation of women in executive positions, growing from 8 percent in 1992 to 27.8 percent in 2000.

---

## Box 13.3   RBFG Employees

- have high commitment to RBFG
- have high level of work involvement
- experience high levels of flexibility to meet personal demands
- feel a strong sense of support from their managers
- consider their jobs to be important to RBFG's success
- feel their jobs require high levels of skill and experience
- feel they are regularly able to deliver work of high quality on time

(Duxbury and Higgins, 1998)

---

### ■   Flexibility at RBFG   ■

Flexible work arrangements (FWAs) were first introduced at RBFG in 1990, as part of the Work/Family/Life Initiative, now called Work/Life. Since then, the initiative and related research efforts have expanded.

- In March 1996, RBFG eliminated the different designations between part-time, casual and full-time employees, making more employees eligible for full range of benefits: health, dental, pension, etc. Employees are now on either continuous[1] or intermittent work arrangements. Before RBFG reclassified its work categories 27 percent of the workforce were classified as part time.
- Approximately 30 percent of RBFG employees participate in an FWA.
- Work arrangements are determined by individual employees with their immediate manager. Individual employees initiate FWAs by making a proposal to their manager. Proposals must include a well-developed business case for the arrangement.
- Managers are responsible for providing support and guidance in developing the arrangements.
- Currently, approximately 1,000 employees job share.

Workplace flexibility, in its truest form incorporates both formal and informal (*ad hoc*/temporary) flex options. This principle has shaped the formation of RBFG flexibility policies and practices.

Changing attitudes and behaviours, altering work styles and transforming work environments is very challenging. Introducing workplace flexibility within a business case, positioning it within the organization priorities and communicating it as a management resource and support has been important from the beginning.

# ■ Strategically improving workplace flexibility ■

Research in recent years continues to emphasize the growing interest and need for non-traditional work hours within the workplace.

- In 1995, the Centre for International Statistics of the Canadian Council on Social Development Survey of Work Arrangements found that 25 percent of Canadian workers have access to flextime.
- According to Angus Reid (1997), commissioned by the Royal Bank, 77 percent of survey respondents consider flexibility as the most critical requirement for Canadian workers.
- In the Ipsos-Reid/Royal Bank Campus Online Internet Survey (2000) of 3,000 university students across Canada, 57 percent of respondents indicated flexible hours and sabbaticals were key considerations when assessing workplace benefits being offered by prospective employers.
- According to AON Consulting, management's recognition of the importance of personal and family life was the most significant factor affecting employee commitment (AON, 1998). The understanding of these drivers of employee commitment forms the foundation of the HR strategy including, but not limited to, workplace flexibility and work–life initiatives at RBFG (RBFG, 1997).

# ■ Results of the RBFG FWA impact assessment ■

In order to accurately assess the impact FWAs were having both on the business and employees, RBFG conducted two extensive internal surveys in both 1994 and 1997. Both surveys confirmed the benefits, with the 1997 survey revealing a stronger level of management support.

---

## Box 13.4  Summary of Benefits of Flexible Work Arrangements

- Attract and retain talent
- Support work–life balance and diversity
- Improve business performance
- Enhance customer service
- Reduce expenses
- Reduce stress and absenteeism
- Leverage enabling technologies
- Position company as a desirable employer.

---

Employees, using an FWA (users), their managers, and coworkers (non-users) participated in the study. The majority of participants felt that FWAs were extremely important. Employees tended to be more conservative and more passionate about the arrangements and the impacts on work performance than their managers.

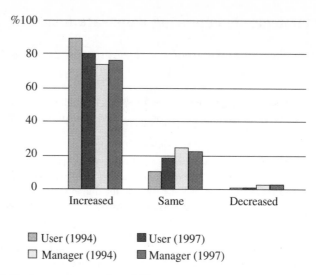

**Figure 13.1**  Ability to manage work and life

The results confirmed many theories and dispelled many myths. The findings indicate that FWAs have no negative impact on organizational efficiency, employee commitment, customer satisfaction, or the ability to meet deadlines. FWAs clearly help individuals manage their work and personal commitments. Although FWAs were originally developed as part of the work–family strategy, less than half of the FWA participants stated family responsibilities as the reason for the FWA. Fifty-two percent cited phased retirement, continuing education, community involvement, and personal interests as the reason for opting for an FWA.

FWAs help employees manage their work and life responsibilities (see figure 13.1).

- 81 percent of users reported they had become more effective in managing work, family and life, and 18 percent reported they remained equally effective since the implementation of FWAs.
- 76 percent of managers perceived their employees' ability to manage work, family, and life had become more effective as a result of FWAs, while 22 percent indicated it had stayed the same (figure 13.1).

As a retention tool, FWAs have been very effective: 36 percent of users said they would leave if FWAs were not available.

Popularity of workplace flexibility continues to rise. Participation rates are steadily increasing. A growing number of managers are recommending FWAs. Most participants in FWAs had more than ten years experience with RBFG. At the time of the survey, 45 percent said FWAs had been present in their work units for two or more years.

Work performance measures rating also saw increases: 99 percent of mangers indicated that job performance of employees on FWAs remained the same or increased.

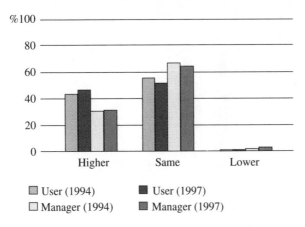

**Figure 13.2** Commitment

Employees (users and non-users) and managers concur that performance indicators – ability to meet deadlines, efficiency, and productivity – either increased or remained the same. Ability to meet deadlines was up: 19 percent users said it increased, 69 percent said it stayed the same. Of RBFG employees on a flexible work arrangement, 47 percent said they were more committed to the organization, while 52 percent said their commitment remained the same since starting their FWA. Most managers reported employee commitment was higher (32 percent) or the same (65 percent). See figure 13.2.

Employees using FWAs experience fewer unplanned absences from work. Sixty-three percent of users said they were absent less often, while 36 percent were absent the same amount of time.

Ninety-seven percent of managers and 92 percent of non-users believed customers and clients received the same or higher quality of service from users of FWAs. Virtually all users concurred. These results paralleled those related to employee satisfaction (94 percent of users were extremely satisfied and 4 percent somewhat satisfied).

Once on an FWA, employees do not necessarily have FWAs forever. Of survey participants that were non-users of FWAs at the time, 21 percent had previous experience with FWAs.

Employee health and well-being also is impacted by workplace flexibility: 70 percent reported lower stress, and 65 percent had more energy.

Nearly all users (85 percent), non-users (60 percent) and managers (63 percent) would recommend FWAs highly or with some reservations (users 14 percent, non-users 37 percent) (see figure 13.3).

## ■ Flexibility and the advancement of women ■

Participants in RBFG's FWA Impact Assessment felt that FWAs did not have a negative impact on their opportunity for advancement (figure 13.4).

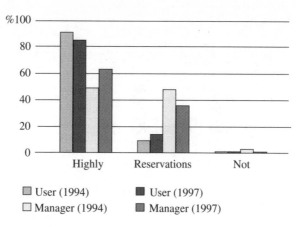

**Figure 13.3**   Recommending FWAs

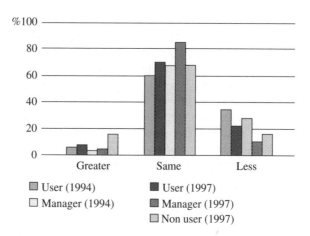

**Figure 13.4**   Perceived opportunities for advancement

Seventy-eight percent of users reported that opportunities for advancement were the same or better than before – an 18 percent increase from the 1994 survey. Ninety percent of managers indicated that opportunities for advancement were the same or better – a 25 percent increase from 1994 figures, and 84 percent of non-users stated that opportunities for advancement were the same or better than before FWA.

Similarly, Catalyst, a US-based research firm, found that 53.3 percent of women on a flex arrangement received a promotion while working flex (Catalyst, 1993, p. 39). Employees initiated discussion for the promotion, and discussed with the manager their career goals, the kind of experiences they wanted, and their plans for advancement.

Lee and McDermit found that 35 percent of individuals, in their study that employees who were on reduced workload or customized work arrangement had received promotions while participating in the flexible arrangement. Two-thirds believed their career progress had not stopped and their bosses agreed, and most believed that

## BOX 13.5 WORKPLACE FLEXIBILITY AT RBFG: EMPLOYEE COMMENTS

- *Flextime has enhanced our relationship with our high value clients.*
- *Reliability is increased as we arrange coverage for each other (job shares).*
- *I'm more relaxed.*
- *There's less leave due to illness because of the reduced stress.*
- *The FWA has allowed me to continue my education.*
- *My commitment to RB has always been strong but now it has increased.*
- *My FWA has enable me to stay with the company which I otherwise would not have been able to do due to family responsibilities.*
- *With coaching and sales so important, people in the branch have told us it's a real bonus to get input from two managers personal banking.*

(Impact Assessment on Flexible Work Arrangements, 1997)

although they had made some career tradeoffs they were comfortable with their choices.

### ■ Closing the gender gap at RBFG ■

In 1994, RBFG embarked on an initiative to explore the impact of gender issues. The research included data collection through Canadian field conferences to surface issues and generate recommendations. The follow-up to the field conferences entailed Thirty-day Teams charged with planning and implementing actions appropriate in their field or province. During a national conference held in August 1994, the following issues were identified:

## BOX 13.6 THE GENDER GAP

Defined as the disparity that may arise between:

- the status of men and the status of women in the bank
- the bank's policies and the bank's practices regarding workplace equity
- myths and realities of workplace equality
- the ways things are and the way things could be.

(Royal Bank, *Closing The Gender Gap: What We Can Do*, 1995)

- women in senior management
- development process for high potential women
- lack of understanding of the impact of gender
- mobility

- career counseling
- mentoring
- work and family support
- accountability and recognition
- pay disparity
- barriers to training
- senior management communication
- overall communication.

The Gender Gap Action Council was then formed to research, prepare, and finalize the implementation of national recommendations. This systems change process continued to engage employees at the grassroots level. The results of the Action Council's review included five objectives and 25 actions that were presented to Group Office in 1995. Actions were reviewed by the Diversity Business Council and integrated into a three-year Leveraging Diversity Process (1996–99).

The Closing the Gender Gap objectives were:

- providing an environment where employees can manage their work, family and life needs
- becoming an organization others wish to emulate with regard to gender equity
- eliminating gender-related biases and assumptions so that systems, policies, and practices are equitable and fair
- achieving a more equitable representation of men and women in all positions
- attracting and retaining both men and women who best meet the banks business requirements.

A booklet focused on highlighting the different ways men and women perceive the world, communicate, think, act, and make decisions was written and widely distributed. It provides guidelines for individuals to increase their understanding of traditional differences between men's and women's cultures and perceptions, and how we can effectively leverage those differences.

---

## BOX 13.7  CLOSING THE GENDER GAP: WHAT WE CAN DO

1  Effect real change regarding gender issues (e.g. support work–life policies through actions).
2  Gain added value from differences (e.g. strive to include and solicit the views of both men and women).
3  Foster dialogue to close the gender gap (e.g. mentor both men and women formally and informally).

---

The 14 member cross-functional Business Diversity Council reviewed all 25 action items in 1997; some had been realized, others were no longer required, and others moved forward and integrated into the Leveraging Diversity Strategy which represents a long-term, ongoing systems change process for culture and environment.

## ■ Men and women working as partners ■

In 1996, Carleton's University's Centre for Research and Education on Women and Work (CREWW), under the direction of Linda Duxbury, undertook a study on human resources and gender issues in the Canadian workplace, sponsored by Royal Bank. The purpose of the study was to determine what Canadian organizations were doing, and what needed to be done to make it easier for men and women to work together as partners within the workplace.

The five key categories of questions focudes on the following:

1  What have Canadian organizations done to create an environment that allows them to use a diverse workforce more effectively?
2  What issues still need to be addressed?
3  In what order should Canadian organizations address these issues?
4  Do men and women share similar perceptions with respect to these issues?
5  Do human resource professionals, executives with frontline responsibilities, and academics who conduct research in these areas share similar perceptions?

Academics, HR professionals, and executives were interviewed. The five issues identified by the study were:

1  recognition of diversity as a business issue
2  measurement and accountability
3  balance between work, family, and life
4  understanding gender differences
5  inequities in the workplace.

From the interviews, researchers Linda Duxbury and her team found that best-practice organizations had the following:

- firm-wide, objective, competency-based performance measures to ensure equity with respect to promotion and opportunities for advancement
- managers held accountable for progress; incentives tied to diversity
- data collections and monitoring processes allowing organizations to monitor hiring, promotions, and retention issues
- policies in place on FWAs and employees encouraged to propose FWAs
- support service and programs, including employee assistance programs to help employees deal with work/non-work issues
- diversity training for employees at all levels, and diversity training for managers on relationship building and people skills; and cross-training for employees
- equity goals established and women found at all levels
- women working in positions that were traditionally male dominated
- formal policies prohibiting workplace harassment and discrimination
- formal or informal mentoring programs
- training for managers on how to assess employees performance objectively.

The interviews also revealed that barriers to leveraging men and women working effectively together still exist.

- The organization failed to link diversity issues and initiatives to the business bottom line.
- Managers equated face time with productivity and success.
- Mangers were not held accountable for implementation of policies related to gender, diversity.
- Concepts of work and career needed to be redefined.
- Organizations generally treated everyone the same rather than recognizing individuals differences.
- Uncertainly and structural changes made it difficult for employees to use support programs.
- Women management style was under-appreciated.
- There was lack of understanding regarding the differences between how men and women communicate.
- There is still a backlash against working mothers.
- Women' success was attributed to legislation and not ability.
- Women lacked mentors/support networks.
- Gender bias existed with respect to hires, promotion, and pay.
- Managers did not have access to FWAs.
- Women were underrepresented at the top.

Another finding from this work was the identification of the balance between work and family as the top priority issue that should be addressed by Canadian business. In addition, the results indicated that men and women did not always share similar perceptions: men were more likely to feel organizations had made significant progress while women were more likely to identify issues that had yet to be resolved.

These results were incorporated into action plans implemented over the following few years.

## ■ Extending RBFG's commitment to the advancement of women ■

### Products and services aimed at women

Not only is RBFG interested in and actively facilitating the advancement of women within the firm, their commitment is extended into a variety of products, resources, and supports for their clients and customers. RBFG actively promotes the advancement of entrepreneurial women, including:

- access to affordable business banking services (lines of credit, visa merchant services, loans)
- seminars and training resources on marketing, exporting, finance, credit; networks with other women business owners and connections with international organizations that support and promote women business owners and formal mentoring programs
- Videos Beyond Borders (17-minute video on women's experience with international trade) and Making it Happen (half-hour documentary on how many entrepreneurs are turning their dreams into successful businesses)
- access to advisors and experts in marketing, law, accounting, finance, and technology, free and private for RBFG clients

> ## Box 13.8 Career Implications of FWAs Based on Organizational Development
>
> The impact of FWAs on women's advancement varies, based on the organization's position along the Work–Life Continuum (Spinks, 1998). In the first stage of development, the Inactive Stage, flexible work arrangements are not an option and women have little or no access to flexibility if they are interested in pursuing a career.
>
> For organizations that are in the ReActive Stage, a women working a flexible arrangement will find their career marginalized, temporarily or permanently stopped. There will be pressure to return to a traditional arrangement. There will be little or no investment in professional development and no removal of barriers to participation in development opportunities.
>
> In the Active Stage, a women working a flexible arrangement will find her career slows or is temporarily on hold. Career progression is limited, but the investment in development continues, participation in developmental opportunities is facilitated, and career plans are consciously adjusted.
>
> In the ProActive Stage, a women working a flexible arrangement will find her career continues to progress, she is considered for promotions, her contributions are recognized and valued, she is given assignments, developmental opportunities, and advancement irrespective of her work arrangement. She is considered for her overall contribution to the firm, not based on hours on the job or work arrangement.

- communication about conferences and events of interest to women in business
- sponsorship of community-based awards programs honouring the contributions of women and their successes
- establishment the Women Entrepreneur Advisory Council of leading female entrepreneurs and consultants providing strategic advice to RBFG on the needs of women in business.

### ■ External leadership ■

Not only has RBFG demonstrated its commitment to women's professional and economic advancement within the organization and in the community, they also provide leadership in the promotion of workplace flexibility within the business community through a variety of initiatives, including the distribution of their corporate communication materials to employers and researchers across the country and around the world (brochures and information kits via *www.royalbank.com*) and through active involvement in the following external activities:

- Conference Board of Canada's Council on Workforce Solutions
- Government of Saskatchewan Task Force on Work and Family

- Families & Work Institute: Corporate Leadership Circle
- Canadian Business Collaboration and Collaboration on Work-Life consortiums
- The Learning Partnership (Toronto)
- National Take Your Kids to Work (over 500 children participating in 1998)
- YWCA Board of Directors (RBFG representative since 1998)
- Vanier Institute of the Family – former board member.

---

## Box 13.9  RBFG FWA Guiding Principles

- FWA is a PARTNERSHIP between the employee and manager.
- Clear and timely COMMUNICATION is essential for a FWA.
- A successful FWA is FOCUSED ON RESULTS.
- A FWA needs FLEXIBILITY (Company and employee needs may change).
- A FWA is an OPPORTUNITY – not an entitlement.
- Not all employees are SUITABLE candidates nor do all positions lend themselves to every FWA.
- A well managed FWA can keep your career RIGHT ON TRACK.
- PILOTS and TRIAL PERIODS are good ways to learn.
- A FWA is APPROVED by the manager and documented in an AGREEMENT.

(RBFG FWA Handbook)

---

## ■  Flexible or alternative work arrangements  ■

Flexible or alternative work arrangements[2] are variations to a typical work pattern of eight-hour days, Monday to Friday, for 12 months of the year, less holidays. Flexible work arrangements (FWAs) involve altering time – hours, days or weeks – of work. It may include altered job design, part-time working and, job sharing. It may include altering career breaks or regular short-term absences from work such as a personal leave or sabbatical. Or it may include a combination of all three, FWAs, work design and strategic career breaks.

Managing and coordinating meetings and training events can be challenging, particularly if several employees are on flexible work arrangements or on variable, compressed, or extended workweeks. Managers need to apply a variety of communication strategies and supervision techniques, and effectively and realistically manage workloads.

### Flextime

Flextime involves arranging variable daily start and end times. Employees working full or part time arrange to start and end each workday at predetermined times. Organizations usually set limits within which the hours must be worked. For example, the organization establishes core hours of 10:00 a.m. to 4:00 p.m. during which meetings are scheduled and everyone is expected to be on the job. Employees negotiate start and end time before of after core hours. Flextime does *not* mean come and go as you please. Flextime hours are usually set in advance. It may allow for extended midday breaks, usually from 11:30 a.m. to 1:30 p.m. during which employees are expected to take a lunch break. Employees with extended breaks make up the hours before or after the break so each employee works 7.5 or 8 hours per day.

An example or how this works would be as shown below.

| Variable start times | 7:00 a.m.–10:00 a.m. |
|---|---|
| Core a.m. hours | 10:00 a.m.–11:30 a.m. |
| Lunch breaks | 11:30 a.m.–1:30 a.m. |
| Core p.m. hours | 1:30 p.m.–4:00 p.m. |
| Variable end times | 4:00 p.m.–7:00 p.m. |

Employee 1    7:00 a.m.–4:00 p.m. and takes a 1-hour midday break
Employee 2    7:30 a.m.–5:30 p.m. and takes a 2-hour midday break
Employee 3    8:30 a.m.–6:00 p.m. and takes a 90-minute midday break

- Flextime helps women take control of their day, plan the activities, fulfill their family or household-management responsibilities, and/or find time for themselves.
- Flexibility reduces stress, reduces guilt, and increases employee satisfaction.
- Flexibility provides women with the opportunity to remain attached to the labor force and to demonstrate their capabilities, competencies, and potential.
- For employees with long or unpredictable commutes the option of starting before or after rush hour can be very appealing to individuals and reduces demand on public transportation systems, traffic congestion, and commuter-related air pollution.
- Flextime can be an effective management tool for employees who are very productive early in the day (morning people) or for employees who are not fully awake until after 10:00 a.m. (not morning people).
- Mangers often work longer hours if their employees work flextime. They often feel they must be on the job when their employees are working. Mangers have to learn to trust and respect their employees, they have to set realistic and measurable performance objectives, and ensure the employees have access to the resources they require to get on with the job done.
- Managers need to model appropriate work habits, that is, demonstrate working smart, not long, hours; reward contributions, not presence; practice time management and stress management, and demonstrate continuous learning and self-care.

## Modified workweeks

Modified work weeks are compressed work weeks (working full time in less than five days – more than average hours per day) and variable work weeks (working long days some weeks to take time off in the future; five days one week, four days the next).

## Compressed workweek/month

A compressed workweek consists of full-time hours in less than five days, for example, 37.5 hours per week worked in four or four and a half days. Each day is longer than a typical full-time day. Managers need to pay particular attention to their local employment legislation. It is easy to violate the law when approving or allowing compressed. Before setting up an arrangement involving flexible weeks managers must check the regulations and restrictions.

Like with all other flexible options, workload management is very important with compressed workweeks. Overachievers or well-intentioned employees can accumulate excessive overtime. For example, an employee arranges to work "9 days in 10", that is, 75 hours in eight days at eight and a half hours per day, and one day at seven hours per day with every other Friday as a non-work[3] day. During a particularly busy time employees often find it difficult to stay away or are asked to work on their non-working day because it is a workday for everyone else.

Managers need to monitor employee fatigue. Employees with very full and busy lives who work compressed workweeks can often become fatigued, make mistakes, get sick, get injured, and lose their ability to handle stressful situations and resolve conflicts. Managers should carefully consider job responsibilities and the physical and mental demands of a job before approving an alternative workweek.

---

## BOX 13.10   COMPRESSED WORK WEEK AT RBFG

CWW options has been applied in branches opened six days per week as well as operation centers across Canada involved in high-volume processing and tight deadlines.

---

## Job redesign: job sharing

Job sharing involves at least two people sharing one job. They share the responsibility, accountability, compensation, and benefits, and the vacation of one job. Although most job sharers work part time, some job-share team members may work in two job-share teams, equalling full time employment.

Successful job sharers have excellent communication, organization, and interpersonal skills. Job sharers are both great team players and able to work independently.

Front-line employees, managers, and executives have successfully shared jobs. Successful job-sharer teams tend to have compatible or complementary strengths, and usually have similar work experiences, work styles, and career goals. Some employers are linking job-sharing strategies with mentoring and/or training or career development strategies by linking two employees in job share teams.

The job-share split may be 50–50 split. Each employee works half time and the compensation is split equally. Employees may work 2.5 days/week or alternate two days–three days every other week, or work one week on, one week off. The job-share split may also be a 60–40 or an 80–20 split. Many successful job-share teams recommend some time overlap, for example a half–day per week when each team member is present on the job at the same time. This time is used for planning, supervision, and problem solving.

Managing a job-share team requires excellent communication skills. The common mistake is to treat the job-share partners as two part-time employees. By doing so the manager/supervisor takes responsibility for the team's communication and repeats instructions. Job-share partners should be responsible for ensuring each member of the team is kept informed about the organization, the jobs, the clients/customers, etc.

Organizations with successful job-share arrangements report a reduction in supervisory workload over time. Once a strong level of trust is established, support for the job-share partnership is demonstrated, skills and competencies are developed, and evaluations and monitoring strategies are implemented, managers report a reduction in workload and frustration levels.

---

## Box 13.11  Job Sharing at RBFG

Approximately 1,000 employees participate in job-sharing arrangements at RBFG. Most are women with dependent care responsibilities. Schedules vary from adopting a two-day/three-day time frame to one week on/one week off. These arrangements have been highly successful from all perspectives – employees, managers, and clients. Employees are able to work as a team to solve work issues while enjoying a more balanced lifestyle. Managers have noted an increase in productivity, enthusiasm, and commitment from their teams. Several job sharers have been promoted as a team – something which was originally deemed improbable – while others have either returned to full-time work or have remained on long-term reduced work arrangements. Clients have noted continued excellence in customer service and are quite delighted to have two knowledgeable professionals dealing with them.

---

## Reduced hours

Employees working on a reduced hours basis work less than $37^1/_2$ hours per week, have the same privileges, benefits, and opportunities as employees working full time, and receive pro-rated compensation, benefits, and vacation. Full time is determined is typically $37^1/_2$ hours per week. Employees on a reduced hours arrangement may work shorter days, five days a week, or regular hours for less than five days.

Employees on reduced hours may be thought to be less committed to the organization and less interested in career advancement. This can be a serious impediment for women who are the majority of permanent part-time workers. Learning to treat all employees equally is often a challenge for managers. Dispelling myths, and focusing on contributions and potential, not hours worked or "face time" (time physically at work), as an indicator of value to an organization is critical for the success of any flexible work arrangement.

---

## Box 13.12   Reduced Hours at RBFG

Approximately 20 percent of Royal Bank's workforce works some form of reduced hours on a continuous basis. Employees on continuous work arrangements are entitled to full benefits and access to incentive and performance-based programs. Positions vary from customer service representatives, personal bankers, to account managers and functional staff. Women hold the majority of these positions. (October 2000)

---

### Flexiplace (remote location work/community telework/virtual work site/satellite office[4])

Remote location is a location that is not the regular or traditional work site (e.g. client's home or office) where employees go to perform some or all of their work responsibilities on a regular basis. A virtual work site is the "any place/anywhere work location". An employee working virtually tends to be mobile and accessible via cell phones, pagers, email, and vmail.[5] Such employees often visit multiple sites in one day or perform their job functions in many sites during the week or month. Virtual work sites are supportive to employees who have client/customer responsibilities or work on site-specific projects. Virtual work can be extremely beneficial for employees who are required to travel extensively.

Remote location or a community telework centre can be effective work arrangements for people with challenging commuting patterns (long distances, severe or unpredictable weather, geographic barriers, and/or insufficient or inadequate public transportation systems).

Remote or virtual employees need to receive full management support, trust, and respect, to be effective. They need to have the appropriate resources, for example equipment (cell phones, beepers, portable computers, printers, etc.) and supplies (stationary, office supplies).

A supportive and effective manager develops strategies to include remote and virtual employees in organizational social (birthday celebrations, sports pools, retirements, etc.) and work-related events (meetings, awards ceremonies, training events). Remote and virtual employees need to feel part of a team. They need to see the contribution they are making to the organization and they need public as well as private recognition for their efforts.

# Working from home/telework/telecommute and work-at-home

***Telework/work from home.*** An employee who works full time or part time from their home on a regular and consistent basis and is connected to the regular work site via computer is a teleworking. A telework arrangement involves the establishment of a work site in the employee's home. RBFG provides the equipment and supplies used by teleworker or the employee is compensated for using their own resources to perform their work responsibilities.

Teleworkers may work full or part time from home, and may have a regular time at the regular work site on a weekly or monthly basis. They have access to a designated shared workspace, common space, or hoteling[6] at the regular work site.

***Work-at-home.*** Work-at-home is occasional or short-term temporary work performed at the employee's home.

Self-managed, independent, well-organized and self-motivated employees are typical teleworkers. Teleworkers tend to perform most of their job responsibilities with the aid of technology (phone, fax, and/or computer). Researchers, managers, writers, customer service representatives, and clerks, are examples of teleworkers.

Often managers, supervisors, or professionals work at home on occasion to complete a task, read, train, write reports, etc. Employees who have temporary or short-term family or personal responsibilities may also work at home, for example self or family member recovering from illness or injury, or waiting for service/repair or home delivery.

Managers supporting and supervising teleworkers have several challenges. First, they have to endorse the option. Second, they need to plan and carefully prepare for the experience (do their homework, talk with other telework managers, regularly evaluate and assess the arrangements, develop communication and accountability strategies). And third, they need be respectful of the employee and their personal workspace. Managers have to be careful not to neglect the teleworker and fall into the "out of sight – out of mind" trap. They need to find ways to assess and evaluate success, and to clearly communicate performance expectations. They must budget and plan for the equipment and supplies required for the telework locations. They need to understand their responsibilities and liabilities regarding insurance, health and safety, security, and confidentiality.

In the absence of a formal organizational policy they, managers must to be aware of any precedence set by other managers. In a unionized setting a manager needs be fully aware of the implications regarding the collective agreement. Workload management and preventing the tendency to overwork are primary challenges for supervisors and managers of teleworking employees. Managers need to help employees set their hours and manage their time and job responsibilities.

## ■   RBFG in good company   ■

At Deloitte and Touche, it is acceptable to have a flexible arrangement. There are no repercussions. Nor are FWAs restricted to women, as 15 percent of participants are men – something that was not expected (*www.deloitte.ca*).

---

### Box 13.13   Flexiplace at RBFG

Individual flexiplace or work-at-home arrangements vary from the formal one/two/three set days per week to the *ad hoc* work from home to accommodate personal needs or work priorities. Some departments such as the Vancouver audit department work entirely from home and client offices, while others such as the Royal Learning Network (training arm) make regular, weekly use of flexiplace. Equipment support can vary depending on circumstances and can range from the use of a laptop, to additional phone line or fax lines.

---

According to company surveys, 76 percent of the recruits who accepted offers with the firm in 1999 did so because of its work–life balance policies, while 95 percent of respondents consistently say they would have left had it not been for flexible work arrangements. Watson Wyatt Worldwide's Human Capital Index analyzed and measured human resource practices at 400 public companies in Canada and the US. The companies that scored high (75 out of 100) on the index by encouraging trust, teamwork and cooperation, flexible work arrangements, high employee satisfaction, and less formal authority structures (figure 13.5) saw average shareholder returns of 103 percent over five years. That was twice the 53 percent gain recorded by companies with a low index rating (less than 25).

---

### Box 13.14   Advancement and Retention of Talented People (ART)

Making Deloitte & Touche a place where talented men and women want to contribute their best because the firm supports them in doing so is what ART is all about. ART will secure our long-term competitive advantage by creating an environment that attracts, retains, and promotes the talented people that our clients and our business demand.

---

## Conclusions

The level of support in the work environment impacts many aspects of the corporation such as productivity, retention, absenteeism, and organizational effectiveness. Measuring and communicating the impact of workplace flexibility and tracking the advancement of women against significant business indicators remains a priority today. By making the connections to these business indicators and corporate objectives RBFG continues to increase understanding and awareness of the initiatives, and encourages and endorses workplace flexibility within the organization and within the community.

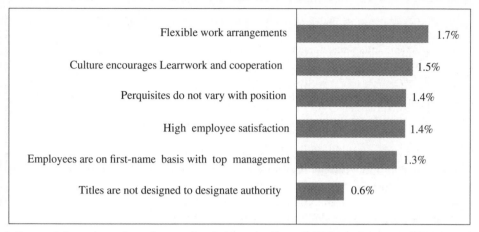

Expected change in market value associated with a significant (1 SD) improvement in HCI practice

**Figure 13.5** Links between collegial, flexible workplace, and value creation
*Source*: Human Capital Index: Linking Human Capital and Shareholder Value, Watson Wyatt

## BOX 13.15 FLEXIBLE WORKPLACE TOOLS AT RBFG

Employee resources and manager tools at RBFG include:

- detailed handbooks on establishing and managing FWAs (reduced hours, job sharing, flextime, modified/compressed work weeks, flexiplace, phased retirement)
- an employee-managed job share registry to facilitate location of suitable job share partners
- a FaxBack Info Line that includes a manager's network and success stories
- an intranet info site
- diversity training available through RBFG's multimedia Personal Learning Network

## BOX 13.16 HR STRATEGIC PLANNING AT RBFG

**Succession Planning** – ensuring continual development of a pool of fully qualified top talent to systematically satisfy the succession needs throughout the corporation. The prime components of this process include:

- identification of our highest potential employees – senior managers, the feeder population for executive ranks, and executive
- assessment and management of the talent pool at the senior management and executive levels
- identification of specific and systemic developmental opportunities and ensuring, through close working partnership with our leadership development group, the availability and provision of the necessary learning interventions to meet these opportunities.

**Diversity** – RBFG recognizes that Leveraging Diversity helps us to meet our corporate vision and strategic priorities. Diversity in RBFG is the primary and secondary dimensions that add up to who we are as individuals and distinguish us as an organization. It encompasses our employees, our customers, our communities, our organizational functions, structures, and processes. RBFG is dedicated to leveraging diversity to make a better place for all employees, to build an environment recognized for full inclusion, to gain a competitive advantage, and to ensure continued recognition as a world class best practices organization.

Diversity in RBFG encompasses and describes the process that began in Royal Bank two decades ago, including Employment Equity. Employment Equity continues to be a business priority at RBFG as a function of Leveraging Diversity.

**Skills and Competencies** – Our objective is to increase employee capability and commitment by emphasizing specific behavioural and technical competencies and skills which contribute most to the success of the individual and organization. Competencies set a foundation piece against which other HR disciplines build: IE recruitment, planning, performance management, etc.

Specifically, the target is for all employees to know and understand specific competencies to which they can target their learning and development. To provide assessment ability to the employee to determine gaps. To organizationally have tools to measure the level of success of various competency components.

**Training and Development** – RBFG has a proud history of commitment to the stimulation and development of people. The quality, diversity and scope of learning interventions are impressive and the level of investment significant (in excess of $100 million in 1997). Building on that solid foundation, RBFG has entered an era of providing more and different learning support to employees under a new banner for training and people development – **Royal Learning Network**. We are a recognized leader in training and through our Personal Learning network, a multi-media self-study platform we provide access to learning right in the workplace.

**Flexible Work Environment** – RBFG provides an environment which supports employees in their management of the conflicting demands of their lives. The reality of work/family/life demands dictate how we develop and deliver training/learning.

Human Resource Policies & Practices 2000–2001
*www.royalbank.com*

## NOTES

1   Continuous salaried: the term used for employees who work regularly scheduled hours, on an ongoing basis, whether a full 75 hours per pay period or less than 75 hours; eligible to participate in benefits.
2   Alternative Work Arrangements, or AWAs, was the original term used to describe the changes in working patterns since they were an alternative to the traditional. Now that "traditional" is harder to define most organizations are opting for the broader "flexible" work arrangements.
3   The day(s) or time(s) that the compressed workweek employee is not working as a non-work day instead of a day off or flexday. A day off or flexday, for most people, implies a vacation day or time in lieu, which are usually taken at a "mutually convenient time." It is therefore easy to ask people to work the time even if you fully intend to offer an alternative day off sometime in the future. Employers should think of a non-work day as like a Saturday – would you ask an employee to come to work on a Saturday if your typical workweek was Monday to Friday? If not, then don't ask an employee to be on the job on a non-work day.
4   Satellite office is a location maintained by the organization for use by employees on a regular or semi-regular basis. It usually contains all the support services associated with an office (copiers, supplies, work stations, meeting rooms, shredders, etc.) for use by virtual workers or teleworkers.
5   Vmail is voice mail or telephone messaging systems.
6   Hoteling is a form of shared common space that is managed at the regular site by a coordinator or hotel manager. The employee calls ahead to reserve personal and group-work space similar to the way one reserves a hotel room when traveling. Some organization offer a "work-site concierge" to help employees make copies, prepare for meetings, arrange for refreshments to be delivered to a meeting room, etc.

## REFERENCES

Angus Reid and Royal Bank (1997): *Workplace 2000 Being Bold is Back*. Toronto: Royal Bank Financial Group.

Angus Reid, Royal Bank, and d~Code (1997): Workplace 2000 Building Bridges: New Perspectives on the Nexus Generation. Toronto: Royal Bank Financial Group.

AON Consulting (1998): *America @ Work: An Overview of Employee Commitment in America*. On line, *http://www.aon.com*

Banducci, B., O'Mara, J., and Wildfogel, J. (1995): *Closing the Gender Gap – What We Can Do*. Toronto: Royal Bank of Canada.

Canadian Work & Family Services and Royal Bank (1994): *Impact Assessment of Flexible Work Arrangements*. Toronto: Royal Bank Financial Group.

Catalyst (1993): *Flexible Work Arrangements II: Succeeding with Part Time Options*. New York: Catalyst.

Duxbury, L. (1996): *Men and Women Working as Partners: A Reality Check of Canadian Organizations*. Centre for Research and Education on Women and Work, Carleton University School of Business and Royal Bank of Canada, Ottawa.

Duxbury, L. and Higgins, C. (1998): *Employee Wellness at RBFG: January 1998 Executive Summary*. Toronto: Royal Bank Financial Group.

Ipsos-Reid and Royal Bank Campus Online Survey (2000): *Attracting Employees – Keeping Employees*. Toronto: Royal Bank Financial Group.

Lee, M. D. (1999): Flexibility Through Customized Work Arrangements. Presentation at the Work & Family Conference, The Conference Board and Families and Work Institute, New York.

Royal Bank Financial Group (RBFG) (1998): *Flexible Work Arrangements Impact Assessment: A Special Report*. From Royal Bank Financial Group, Survey Highlights, Toronto. Online at *http://www.royalbank.com/careers/workressurv/flexible_work.html*

Simonsen, B. (2001): *Deloitte & Touche ART: The Attraction and Retention of Talented People*. Presentation to Executive Work–Life Roundtable, Work–Life Harmony Enterprises, Toronto.

Spinks, N. (1998): *The Manager's Work–Family Tool Kit*. Vanier Institute of the Family, Ottawa.

Watson, W. (1999): Human Capital Index: Linking Human Capital and Shareholder Value. Online Available at
*http://www.watsonwyatt.com/homepage/us/new/Human_Capital_Index/index.htm*
White, L. and O'Mara, J. (1995): Closing the Gender Gap: The Royal Bank Experience. *The Diversity Factor*, Fall, 4, 1, Royal Bank Financial Group, Toronto.

# NEW DIRECTIONS

# 14

# BOUNDARYLESS TRANSITIONS: GLOBAL ENTREPRENEURIAL WOMEN CHALLENGE CAREER CONCEPTS

*Dorothy Perrin Moore*

The rising numbers of female entrepreneurs worldwide clearly suggest that business ownership has emerged as an important career alternative for women. Moreover, the patterns women are following in the establishment of their businesses suggest they are pursuing careers without boundaries.

## ■ Working women ■

The recent rise in female entrepreneurship has been preceded by more than three decades of increased female participation in the labor force. By 1997, labor force participation rates had soared to all-time highs for both white (59.9 percent) and black women (64.0 percent) age 20 and over. By 1995, women held nearly half of all managerial and executive positions (48.1 percent) and accounted for more than one-half (52.8 percent) of the people employed in professional occupations. In the fields of business and marketing, they were earning more than two-thirds (69 percent) of all associate degrees awarded and nearly half (48 percent) of the bachelor's degrees. Projections from current population surveys (Bureau of Labor Statistics, 1998–1999) are that by the year 2008 women and people of color will make up 70 percent of the new entrants in the labor force.[1]

The increase in the number of female entrepreneurs has accelerated in recent years. In the United States, over the past 12 years, the number of women-owned businesses has doubled to more than 9.1 million and now constitutes 38 percent of all firms in the US. These financially sound and stable businesses show success rates equivalent to men's and generate $3.6 trillion in sales yearly (National Foundation for Women Business Owners, 2000). Like their men-owned counterparts, the largest numbers of women-owned firms, more than one-third of the total, are in the economy's service sector. But the greatest recent growth has taken place in the fields of construction, wholesale trade, and other areas previously dominated by males.[2] One in eight of these US women-owned businesses (13 percent) are owned by a woman of color. The US Small Business Administration forecasts that female entrepreneurs will head half of all US businesses by 2002 with businesses headed by Afro-American women the fastest-growing minority sector.

The movement of women into the labor force changed American family life. Between 1950 and 1996 the number of the so-called "traditional families" – husband at work and the wife at home – shrank dramatically as the number of dual-worker families doubled and the number of families headed by female single parents increased fourfold. In 1999 dual-earner marriages constituted 40.5 percent of families. While more than half of the members of dual-career families (58 percent of women and 53 percent of men) say the "lack of time" is their biggest marriage challenge, both sexes report a working spouse has a positive impact on their own careers and both love the freedom the two-earner arrangement gives them in their jobs. It is the lifestyle and opportunities, not money, that attracts these couples; even if financial needs were removed, the majority would continue to pursue careers working outside the home (Catalyst, 2000; Bureau of Labor Statistics).

Already an important segment in the American economy, women-owned businesses have also become a global force. In the United Kingdom, female entrepreneurs founded almost one-third of all the new businesses started in 1997, a figure that does not include the many micro or "lifestyle" businesses run by women (Gracie, 1998, p. 6). Canadian women, who in recent years have been opening firms at rates equivalent to men, today own or operate 30 percent of all businesses and provide 1.7 million jobs (Kulmala, 1999). Across Europe, according to the Fourth Annual Report of The European Observatory for Small and Medium-Sized Enterprises (SMEs), women now account for 30 percent of the new enterprises or business registrations (EIM, 1998). In Australia, Canada, and Germany, the percentages of women-owned businesses approach US figures (Moore, 1999). In Poland's recently established enterprise culture, women are opening and operating businesses from motivational and personal characteristics similar to both their Polish male counterparts and those of Western capitalist entrepreneurs (Zapalska, 1997). In Hungary, women head two out of every five enterprises (41.1 percent) that have been established since 1990, an increase of 29.3 percent compared to the previous decade (Gere, 1999). Asian women are starting businesses for the same reasons found in the West: autonomy, flexibility, money, and profits (Deng, Hassan, and Jivan, 1995; Maysami and Goby, 1999). Elsewhere, the increase in female entrepreneurship appears to be driven by more pressing conditions. In Russia's collapsed economy, and under adverse conditions, millions of women have chosen micro-entrepreneurship as their way of economic survival (Izyumov and Razumnova, 2000). In Turkey, despite unfavorable elements in the country's social structure, women entrepreneurs are beginning to appear in increasing numbers (Hisrich and Ozturk, 1999). Worldwide, women-owned firms comprise between one-quarter and one-third of all businesses. The rapid expansion of gender-neutral business structures that has followed naturally in the wake of the spread of democratic institutions and the undeniable success of market-driven economic systems worldwide amounts to a major cultural revolution.

## ■ Careers and the entrepreneurial route ■

The study of the careers of women who seek both managerial-corporate and entrepreneurial challenges, the boundaryless careers, begins with the work of Edgar Schein. In the mid 1970s, Schein proposed that, for most people, careers were constructed from a self-perception of their own talents and abilities, basic values, and a growing understanding of their motives and needs as these evolved through life. As a person gained occupational and life experience, said Schein, the evolving self-perception functioned both as a career guide and a stabilizing force, an anchor of values and motives that a person would not abandon when forced to make an important choice. The early research Schein conducted indicated that most people's career anchors revolved around the five basic categories: autonomy/independence; security/stability; technical-functional competence; general managerial competence, and entrepreneurial creativity. Schein's studies in the 1980s led him to add three additional categories: service or dedication to a cause; pure challenge; and lifestyle (Schein, 1978, 1990, 1993, 1996, pp. 80–1).

While Schein's original model explicitly allowed for a gender-blind study of entrepreneurship subsumed under the larger field of career studies, most research conducted on entrepreneurs and business start-ups did not initially head in this direction. Until the mid 1980s, studies of entrepreneurs either tended to imply that large numbers of women were not likely to start new businesses or to assume that those who did acted no differently from men (Moore, 1990; Moore, Buttner, and Rosen, 1992; Moore, 1999; Marlow and Strange, 1994). Studies of entrepreneurship also tended to aggregate people in the workforce into the distinct categories of employment in someone else's business or operating their own. Having separated entrepreneurs as a group, research into their characteristics, with many studies incorporating Schein's career anchors, tended to compare and contrast the self-employed and organizational types as discrete entities.

Observing the state of career research at the end of the decade, Kanter (1989) noted that observers seemed to conclude that careers could be fitted into one of four categories. There were, she said, organizational or bureaucratic careers with advancement through a formally defined hierarchy; intrapreneurial careers describing those who were able to add something of value to an organization; professional careers where people had portable talents or skills; and entrepreneurship. With the distinction between being an employee and an entrepreneur appearing to be clear, it was a short step for many researchers to conclude that the behavior and values of the self-employed and the organizational employee differed fundamentally (Gartner, Bird, and Starr, 1992).

The rapid changes in the US economy in the past two decades, particularly the corporate restructuring and introduction of knowledge technologies that flattened organizations, not only put an end to old notions of lifetime organizational employment, they also undermined some certainties in career research. Because the changing job contract shifted the burden of career planning to the individual, one now had to focus on portable skills and knowledge, meaningful work, on-the-job learning, and contacts (Sullivan, Carden, and Martin, 1998; Sullivan, 1999; Bird, 1994). Researchers began to take the new phenomena into account. Dyer (1994) identified missing elements in research in the fields of careers and entrepreneurship and proposed a model to bridge the boundary. Katz (1994) noted that while the concept of entrepreneurship had always been included within Schein's career framework, career theorists for the most part had not reported on entrepreneurs, and had adapted Schein's model to refocus on people and the processes of entrepreneurship. To do this, Katz adopted "three major cone variables, hierarchy, function, and centrality to fit with career-relevant findings from entrepreneurship research." To increase the applicability of Schein's model he added employment duration, job multiplicity, and self-emergence. Katz then used Schein's two career anchors uniquely applicable to the self-employed, "Autonomy /Independence (the desire for freedom from the rules and control of others) and Entrepreneurship (originally called creativity)", to construct a model to analyze the careers of the self-employed and better explain their career development (pp. 24–5).

Katz's (1994) suggestion struck down the artificial barriers between entrepreneurship and other career paths previously imposed by career theorists, and was followed by Schein's (1996) revisitation of his concept of career anchors. Observing that the numerous changes in the work environment were causing people to view their best interests as being independent of any particular organization or job, and that people were redefining the whole concept of work as the boundaries between jobs, organizations, and family life became more fluid and ambiguous, Schein pointed out that, while people still valued management positions and opportunities to climb the corporate ladder, they now questioned the relationship of these factors to maintaining their own technical and functional competence. Career development in the new age, Schein suggested, depended not only on one's own interests but also on the massive changes in organizational and political environments in the large firms. The combination of new organizational uncertainties and new technology also worked to encourage creativity and entrepreneurship as a career path. The changes in the relative importance of one's career anchors, Schein concluded, were now as much environmental as were anchors within the person (pp. 82–5). Feldman and Bolino (2000) used Schein's concept of career anchors to examine how goals, interests, and values were used in differential patterns to not only attract people to entrepreneurship but also to maintain the attraction. While their findings supported the usefulness of career anchors in examining self-employment, the authors also discovered great variance in the motivation to pursue and remain self employed as an entrepreneurial career, especially because "self-employment is often attended by surprises and ambivalence about the chosen career path" (pp. 53–4).

In addition to the work of researchers in the field of careers, a number of prominent gender and diversity researchers began to point out that the older models also did not account for the career patterns of women which, they said, were distinctly different from those of men. Bailyn (1993) and Schein (1996) noted that both work and non-work influences guide career development. Powell and Mainiero (1992) found that this was especially true for women. Caputo and Dolinsky (1998) pointed to a number of cultural changes influencing the role of financial and human capital in women's choice to pursue self-employment. In their River of Time Career Model, Powell and Mainiero (1992, p. 219) suggested that women had on the one hand concerns for career and personal achievements, which the authors called "concern for career," and on the other hand concerns about family and personal relationships outside of work, which they called "concern for relationships" or "concern for others." Powell and Mainiero concluded that women are likely at all times to be concerned both with career and with others, "but they place different degrees of emphasis on career versus others in their actions and decisions at different times." In a study of women business owners, Brush (1992) proposed an Integrated Perspective Model that focused on the power that relationships exert on choices made by women business owners. Defining female careers as being centered in a network of relationships that include family, community, and business, she suggested that "women view their businesses as a cooperative network of relationships rather than a separate economic entity, and when a woman starts or acquires a business the set of business relationships are then 'integrated' into her life (p. 16).

## ■ The boundaryless option ■

Implicitly assuming that entrepreneurship could be viewed as a progressive step or a window of opportunity in career development as proposed by Harvey and Evans (1995) rather than a separate construct, Moore and Buttner (1997) studied the characteristics of female entrepreneurs who had considerable exposure to corporate life before striking out on their own, and concluded that organizational experience and success was an important prerequisite to a successful entrepreneurial venture. With the connections between working for others and working for oneself so clearly apparent, from a field study Moore (2000) went on to note that as many women entrepreneurs had not only moved readily from one organizational position to another and into entrepreneurship but also moved back to organizational life again. This suggested that the distinctions between entrepreneurship and organization life, between being self-employed and other employed, were perhaps less important than an understanding of how both paths related to each other in career development (Moore, 2000, pp. viii, 3–4).

## ■ State of current research: what we know and what we don't ■

Today there is considerable interest in the field of female business owners. Studies have recently been commissioned by think-tanks such as the Research Institute for Small and Emerging Business; comprehensive investigations have been done by the Small

Business Administration and various foundations specifically interested in promoting women, such as Catalyst; and the National Foundation for Women Business Owners have produced numerous papers on a variety of topics. Curiously, this interest in the increasing number of women-owned businesses has not transferred to numerous publications in the professional academic literature. Given the rapid growth of women-owned businesses, one might reasonably expect an outpouring of new findings in the major research outlets. But as surveys of the published literature conducted in 1992 and 1999 show, this has not occurred. In fact, Moore's (1999) study, an examination of data from 70 journal articles plus proceedings papers and books that appeared between 1992 and 1999, revealed an enormous void in the professional literature as defined as the major journals in the field by Katz (1997). The vacuum suggests at the very least the academic world has not caught up with the visible changes in the environment.

The absence of a large number of studies leaves scholars interested in female entrepreneurs facing some research difficulties. Many data sets use college student respondents. In developing a career construct, this poses an immediate problem, as Schein (1996) has pointed out. Other data sets are collections done in classes by students who track down entrepreneurs and ask them to complete questionnaires. Measurement techniques have been imported from diverse fields. Uneven sample sizes and data that were not collected by any systematic method can be found in the research. The majority of the early field studies used questionnaire and interview formats that relied on instruments developed in other disciplines, particularly psychology, with its focus on personal characteristics. Other research problems include a lack of focus due to differing frames of reference, and even disagreement on the definitions of entrepreneurship and the firm (Moore, 1999). The result is that we know much less than we should from the existing literature.

## ■ Career characteristics of women entrepreneurs ■

Prior to the 1960s, when occupational and other barriers to female advancement began to break down, and the 1970s, when enough women entrepreneurs came on the scene for researchers to notice, the infrequent studies of women going into business for themselves described what might be called a traditional female entrepreneur. Lacking any background in finance, marketing, and business experience, she faced major problems in obtaining capital. The businesses she started consequently tended to be low income, low equity, small, and slow growing. Beginning in the 1970s, a new breed of women entrepreneurs came on the scene. About half of the businesses they founded were headed by women who had no thought of entrepreneurship when they first embarked on a business career. Later, exiting organizational life, they brought to their firms considerable education, training, and business experience, all kinds of professional expertise, technical and planning skills, network contacts, and an average of ten to twelve years of wisdom, insight, and judgment (Moore, 2000, pp. x–xi). More than half of these women heading their own businesses had come out of the service-producing sector of the economy, almost one-third of them from the retail trade and one-sixth from manufacturing (Catalyst, 1998, p. 10). They were typically better educated than their male counterparts (Brush and Hisrich, 2000; Maysami and Goby, 1999; *Zapalska*, 1997), and had professional management experience (Moore, 2000; Catalyst, 1998; Moore and Buttner, 1997, p. 56). As active and successful as men in building networks (Aldrich, Elam, and Reece, 1997), their business success appeared to be closely tied to their social skills (Baron and Markman, 2000).

Abroad, female entrepreneurs exhibit many similar characteristics. In Hungary, female entrepreneurs report a higher level of educational achievement than the average woman worker (Gere, 1999). A study of Polish female business owners revealed they demonstrated better communication and human resource management skills than male entrepreneurs (Zapalska, 1997). Among Israeli women business owners, profitability is highly correlated with previous business experience and networking (Lerner, Brush, and Hisrich, 1997). In Singapore, where nearly one-third (30 percent) of successful women business owners reported no previous work experience (Teo, 1996), business success appears related to their skill in overcoming social obstacles during the start-up phase of their business (Maysami and Goby, 1999).

## ■ Business operations and gender differences ■

Studies of the careers of women entrepreneurs have focused on the presence or absence of female–male differences in the areas of leadership and management, networking, and negotiating styles.

## Leadership and management

Researchers have found considerable support for ideas that women behave more democratically, and men more autocratically, in leadership situations, use interactive skills more frequently than men, place greater emphasis on maintaining effective working relationships at work, and not only value cooperation and being responsible to others but also are interested in achieving outcomes that address the concerns of all parties involved (Moore, 2000, p. 103). Studies also show that women are more likely to view power as related to the time and place it is employed, and the people involved, rather than a structured process where subordinates carry out decisions handed down from above. Some studies of culture argue that a "female" style emerges from a socialization process that teaches women one set of values about gaining and using power and men another (Moore, 2000, p. 104). Workplace observations have also reinforced ideas that gender and culture together program women and men to behave differently at work.

The problem with concluding that men and women are genetically or culturally programmed to manage differently is that it requires us to ignore a considerable body of other evidence. No research study has found any differences between men and women in verbal, math, or spatial abilities, moral character, or several other dimensions. No research study has found any gender-related differences among those who seek power, exercise power, get anxious about exercising power, or the style of leadership they exercise when in power. In fact, when women attain the leader's role, they tend to behave exactly the same way men do (Kelly, 1991, pp. 99–103; Watson, 1994). What causes leadership styles to vary, as a review of the literature on how people negotiate tells us, is the situation in which people find themselves. People in powerful positions are more comfortable, competitive, and successful (Watson, 1994).

An insight into women's management practices has been suggested by comparative studies of the transactional (old-style) leader who focuses on short-term goals and stability and offers rewards for performance, and the transformational (new-style) leader who articulates a vision of the firm that can be shared by peers and subordinates, empowers and encourages subordinates, models effective behavior, shows respect for individual differences among subordinates, and prefers effectiveness over efficiency. Female leaders more than males tend to utilize transformational behaviors (Bass, 1985, 1990; Bass, Avolio, and Atwater, 1996; Moore and Buttner, 1997, p. 100). Brush and Bird (1996) explained the highest amount of gender variance by defining two new terms. Women, they said, practiced "innovative realism," defined as flexibility, innovation, action-oriented, integrated, changing and inspirational rather than placing emphasis on long-range formalized and strategic planning.

## Gender, power, and negotiation

Numerous studies have attempted to differentiate male and female styles of negotiation. Few have found anything even remotely relating negotiating success to gender differences. The biggest difference, some research suggests, is that women tend to employ management styles that emphasize a relationship with the other party rather than the issue at hand, with possible effects in negotiations. The one negotiation study that showed that women tended to be more cooperative, however, linked this to the fact that they generally had less power in organizational negotiation settings. Gender may also have some indirect effects. Managerial women, for example, report feeling less confidant about themselves as negotiators, despite the fact they are as effective as men. There is also the possibility that a male negotiating with a woman who has a low-key or cooperative management style assumes she is less capable and thus easier to manipulate because she is not overtly aggressive (Watson, 1994; Moore and Buttner, 1997, pp. 106–14).

## Networking approaches

Male managers and professionals have always operated successfully in organizational networks. As the number of women in organizations increased, they constructed ties for the same reasons men do: effective networking is a requirement for organizational success, and relationships are vital to a business career. Women business owners have become as active and successful as men in building networks to obtain assistance (Aldrich, Elam, and Reece, 1997). Their business success appears to be highly tied into their networking and social skills (Baron and Markman, 2000). These characteristics appear transnational. A study of Polish female business owners revealed they demonstrated better communication and human resource management skills than male entrepreneurs (Zapalska, 1997). Among Israeli women business owners, profitability is highly correlated with previous business experience and networking (Lerner, Brush, and Hisrich, 1997). In Singapore, where nearly one-third (30 percent) of successful business owners reported no previous work experience (Teo, 1996), business success appears related to their skill in overcoming social obstacles during the start-up phase of their business (Maysami and Goby, 1999).

Studies show that men and women in organizations do not inhabit the same networks primarily because organizations seldom provide identical cultures and opportunities for men and for women. As a rule, women have to adapt to male-dominated, gendered institutions. The result is that while a woman's organizational networks can be very similar to those of men in terms of activity and contacts, she forms them differently and they may vary greatly from the networks created by her male colleagues. This does not mean that men and women are necessarily predisposed to form and maintain separate networks, though it may sometimes seem that way. That they do is mainly because it is the positions individuals hold within organizations that confer status, determine who speaks to whom, who defers, and otherwise directs how contacts are carried on. It is the fact that fewer women than men occupy the high-level, high-profile positions that create separate gender effects (Baker, Aldrich, and Liou, 1997, p. 235; Cromie and Birley, 1992, p. 238; Moore, 1990, p. 734).

The findings on organizational networking suggest two things, one important for women pursuing organizational careers, the other for aspiring entrepreneurs. In the corporate world, men naturally make the informal organizational contacts that comprise a well-understood part of the status quo. Women have to learn the networking skills to enable them to tap into the informal organization. Women entrepreneurs need to understand that networking is continuous, a learned skill, and that the old organizational networks and the networking style practiced in a previous corporate environment may not transfer well to business ownership. Because the positive impact networks have on business start-ups is well established, constructing networks has to be a vital part of the female entrepreneurs business plan (Moore, 2000).

## ■ Why women start their businesses ■

Comparisons of male and female entrepreneurs suggest they open businesses for many of the same reasons: job freedom and flexibility, independence, personal development, and approval, along with making money. Historically, female entrepreneurs tended to come from the ranks of women who grew up self-reliant. Some female entrepreneurs are driven into businesses by familiar economic necessities such as making a living after a divorce, the two-income requirement for a desirable standard of family living, or company downsizing or other workplace reversals. Recently, more and more women are jumping from organizations. While discrimination and glass ceilings, walls, or concrete issues play a role in this, more often than not women leave organizations for the gender-neutral reason of seeking more opportunity (Moore and Buttner, 1997, pp. 14–18). The fact that women hold only slightly more than one-tenth of board seats at the 500 largest publicly traded US companies (11.2 percent), for example, may be just one of many driving forces which enhance the link to entrepreneurship as a viable career option (Catalyst, 1999).

Daily, Certo and Dalton (1999) noted that the increased frequency of female entrepreneurship is, in part, attributable to the glass ceiling which has denied leadership
roles to women at early stages in their careers. In tracking progress in the executive
suite and boardrooms over a ten-year period for Inc. Magazine 100 firms, they found
no progress in CEO or board positions. Lack of opportunities has had a special impact
on African-American women. The Catalyst (2000) report on women of color indicates
that problems are more than just a passing perception. Women of color represent 1.9
percent of board directors in the *Fortune* 1000. Of African-American women managers
40 percent have college degrees and yet earn less than white women managers. Cited
reasons for lack of advancement in management for women of color are related to the
lack of an influential mentor, informal networking opportunities, company role models,
and visibility assignments, all of which contribute to the fact, noted above, that this
group of women represent the fastest-growing sector of the minority business sector of
the US (Catalyst, 2000, pp. 1–4; US Department of Census, 1996). Other studies have
found gender differences in salary expectations and values, with women rating helping
others, doing work important to society, and regular hours more important than
making money, but this is not a consistent finding in the research (Cheskin Research,
2000, p. 3).

In the United States and abroad, for both men and women, the primary reasons for
self-employment appear to be the same. In Poland, they center on having control over
one's life, ending problems of dissatisfaction inherent in working for someone else, and
greater financial rewards (Zapalska, 1997). In Asia, two-thirds (66 percent) of female
entrepreneurs in one study were motivated primarily by the desire for autonomy and
the freedom and flexibility offered in running one's own business (Deng, Hassan, and
Jivan, 1995). Where differences in the areas of reasons and motivations for setting up
a business do exist, as in Turkey, the reasons can usually be attributed to the country's
social structure (Hisrich and Ozturk, 1999). In Russia, where unemployment among
women grew faster than that of men between 1992 and 1999, and women's incomes
dropped, absent the usual prerequisites of training and experience, millions of women
chose micro-entrepreneurship for the simple reason of economic survival (Izyumov
and Razumnova, 2000).

■ Start-up issues, start-up process ■

As noted by Katz (1990), for nascent entrepreneurs, the three hurdles involved in the
start-up process are aspiring, preparing, and entering (see also Carter, Gartner, and
Reynolds, 1996). While research on this phase of entrepreneurship is very limited, and
in the case of women entrepreneurs exceedingly so, most studies suggest one of two
partially contradictory findings. The first is that male and female business start-ups
exhibit more similarities than differences, and the second that women were more likely
to have been working part-time, come from households with lower incomes, have lower
expectations about loan acquisitions, and have a higher attrition rate than men.
Perhaps more important is a recent finding, from a study of Norwegian entrepreneurs,
that differences in the start-up process do not lead to different probabilities of succeeding in establishing businesses (Alsos and Ljunggren, 1998). Recent research also sug-

gests that, because the growth in new women-owned businesses is concentrated in the retail and service sectors that represent traditional areas of employment for women, these entrepreneurs exhibit expectations different from female entrepreneurs in non-traditional industries (Anna, Chandler, Jansen, and Mero, 2000). With regard to business financing, a study using 1993 data concludes that while women-owned businesses are significantly smaller and newer than those owned by men, are less likely to use external financing, and may pay higher rates when they do get loans, the lenders do not appear to discriminate on the basis of gender but instead, preferring larger firms and longevity, base loan rates on these factors. Overseas, somewhat similar conditions exist. Women entrepreneurs in Hungary, for instance, where only 6.5 percent received bank loans, tended to raise the capital for their businesses from savings and loans from family or friends (Gere, 1999).

# ■ Work and family ■

Research suggests that women and men share the same motivations that drive them in their business and entrepreneurial pursuits. But contrary to conventional wisdom, for both sexes making money is not the primary motivation. In Poland and the United States, as Zapalska (1997) has found, the primary reasons for self-employment are to have more control over one's life (Moore and Buttner, 1997). However, as the Women Entrepreneurs Study (Cheskin, 2000) points out, there are differences between the genders in expectations for balancing work and family, and other aspects of a working career (p. 3). Interesting research suggests that an important key for the woman entrepreneur is the level of balance in her work and family life. Among the situations making a difference are whether the entrepreneur is a working mother, a sole entrepreneur, or a single mother trying to make it on her own; the presence or absence of spousal support, membership in a dual career couple, or a copreneur venture in a husband and wife business; and whether or not the business is a family firm. Findings consistently confirm the importance of family support among women entrepreneurs. Entrepreneurial women in Canada, Singapore, the United Kingdom and the United States who enjoy family support in coping with the demands of running a business find it provides them with the freedom and flexibility to meet their combined business and home responsibilities (Maysami and Goby, 1999). Findings that women perceive a higher degree of social support during the business gestation process than men are reported by Ljunggren and Kolvereid (1996). Some successful women entrepreneurs handle the increased demands on their time by contracting duties to others. A recent study by the National Foundation of Women Business Owners found women entrepreneurs (47 percent) more than other working women (22 percent) were likely to hire people to help with household tasks or a yard service, and more likely (68 percent) to dine out with family one or more times a week (NFWBO, 2000). While there is little doubt that self-employed workers have greater independence and scheduling flexibility in their lives to meet family demands, at least one study suggests that this window of time is narrowed considerably by the heavy job insecurity and significant financial risks that accompany ownership of a competitive business (Douglas and Shepherd, 1997).

Work and family relationships have come in for considerable study. For all entrepreneurs, men as well as women, business ownership involves an interaction of work, family, and personal life, as opposed to just a work role (Schein, 1978). Some research suggests there is a special gender effect revolving around the disparities between men's and women's involvement in work and family roles, especially when there are children, particularly young children, in the family (Greenhaus and Parasuraman, 1999, p. 407). But the implications of this research cannot be stretched too far. Foley and Powell (1997) point out that most of what we know about work–family conflict applies to specific organizational roles rather than to business ownership. Marshack (1994) has noted that women and men take on more stereotypical and traditional sex roles in business ownership and in later work. Marshack (1998, 2000) has also identified three important and different family–business situations: the solo entrepreneur with a supportive spouse; a dual entrepreneurship where both partners are self-employed; and copreneurial ventures where both partners own and manage a joint business. Among copreneurs, she finds, women took on the more traditional and stereotypical roles. Recent research (Caputo and Dolinsky, 1998) into the role of financial and human capital in women's choice to pursue self-employment also suggests that while higher levels of the husbands' self-employment greatly increase the likelihood of the women being self-employed, it is the husbands' business knowledge and experience, and not his earnings, that make the difference (p. 8). As for entrepreneurship and career development, Powell and Mainiero (1992) concluded that, because a women's career development is guided by both work and non-work influences, it is the two together that explain a great deal about why women interrupt careers or change their career tracks.

## Summary: entrepreneurial careers, boundaries, and options

Edgar Schein's model of career development incorporated from the beginning elements of gender-blind study of entrepreneurship as one of many possible career paths (Schein, 1978, 1990, 1993, 1996). But during the 1970s and 1980s research in various fields tended to separate studies of people in organizations from the self-employed. Amid the great changes in the American economy taking place at the same time, Katz (1994) adapted Schein's model to incorporate career-relevant findings from entrepreneurship research. His work, and Schein's 1996 revisitation of his concept of career anchors, widened the utility of Schein's models in the study of entrepreneurs. Other research showed the usefulness of career anchors in examining self-employment and highlighted the variance in motivations among entrepreneurs. Pointing out that many of the career models did not accurately portray the careers of women, gender and diversity researchers advised the consideration of new typologies and pointed to the need to include a number of cultural and personal elements in models of self-employment. Studies relating prior organizational experience and success to entrepreneurship noted that for women organizational life and entrepreneurship were not compartmentalized and that many women moved fluidly between them.

Though hampered by research and methodological problems and an apparent reluctance of major journals to publish findings from studies of women, researchers have been able to construct a rough history of the changes in women's entrepreneurship over the past several decades, to fill in with descriptions of the career characteristics of female entrepreneurs, and to note important similarities and differences from male entrepreneurs in business operations and management styles, motivations and start-up experiences, and the reconciliation of work and family life.

The present state of research suggests the condition incorporated in the title of this chapter, boundaryless career. Numerous patterns and varieties of career progression have been observed among female entrepreneurs. Some had always intended to own their own businesses, some had always owned a business, others were delayed by events in their personal lives related to families and relationships, some discovered later in life that they had an entrepreneurial talent, some were copreneurs, and others were family business owners.

In my own work, I have identified three distinct career patterns. Some women are corporatepreneurs, managing their career within or across organizations and fields. Others are entrepreneurs, operating businesses of their own. Still others are boundarypreneurs who cross back and forth between business ownership and organizational life. How prepared these people were before ascribing to one career track development or the other, and the degree they identified their career anchors prior to setting out on a course of action, is uncertain. The original concepts of Schein's ideas of career anchors, modified by other research suggesting the importance of environmental factors in career development appear, to point the way to profitable courses of investigation.

## NOTES

1  Council of Economic Advisors (1998), table B-40; Lynch and Post (1996). What glass ceiling? *The Public Interest*, 124, 27–37. Web site: *htt://web7.searchbank.com/infotra* (6 pages, pp. 5–6 on website). Statistics also based on recent releases of information from the National Foundation for Women Business Owners, Catalyst, United States Department of Labor, and *The Chronicle of Higher Education*. The 2008 projection is from Catalystwomen.org (2000). The Glass Ceiling in 2000: Where are Women Now? *Labor Day Fact Sheet* (On-line). Available at: *http://catalystwomen.org/press/factslabor00.html* It is based on Bureau of Labor Statistics, Projections from Current Population Survey, 1988–1998.

2  National Foundation for Women Business Owners, NFWBO Research Summary, May 11, 1999, Facts of the Week, May 11, 1999, *Http//www.nfwbo.org*. As noted in the SBA Office of Advocacy, Economic Statistics and Research on Small Business, Women in Business, October, 1998. A report on statistical information about women-owned businesses prepared by the US Small Business Administration's Office of Advocacy, p. 4. The federal government collects and disseminates the most comprehensive federal statistics under a special program of the Census Bureau's Economic Censuses, the Census of Women-Owned Business (WOB). The most recent data available, released in 1997, are for 1992 and are the only federal data that cover all women-owned businesses. The data may be accessed at *http://www.sba.gov/ADVO/stats/wib.html*

## REFERENCES

Aldrich, H. E., Elam, A. B., and Reece, P. R. (1997): Strong ties, weak ties, and strangers: Do women business owners differ from men in their use of networking to obtain assistance? In S. Birley and I. C. MacMillan (eds), *Entreprenerurship in a Global Context*, Fourth Annual Global Conference on Entrepreneurial Research, INSEAD, France.

Alsos, G. A. and Ljunggren, E. (1998): Does the business start-up process differ by gender? A longitudinal study of nascent entrepreneurs. *Frontiers for Entrepreneurship Research, Babson Conference Proceedings* (online), available:
*http:www.babson.edu/entrep/fer/papers98/V/V_A/V_A_text.html*.

Anna, A. L., Chandler, G. N., Jansen, E., and Mero, N. P. (2000): Women business owners in traditional and non-traditional industries. *Journal of Business Venturing*, 15, 3, 279–303.

Arthur, M. B. and Rousseau, D. M. (1996): A career lexicon for the 21st century. In M. B. Arthur and D. M. Rousseau (eds), *The Boundaryless Career: A New Employment Principle for a New Organizational Era.* New York: Oxford University Press.

Bailyn, L. (1993): *Breaking the mold.* New York, NY: The Free Press.

Baker, T., Aldrich, H. E., and Liou, N. (1997): Invisible entrepreneurs: The neglect of women business owners by mass media and scholarly journals in the USA. *Entrepreneurship & Regional Development*, 9, 221–38, 235.

Baron, R. A. and Markman, G. D. (2000): Beyond social capital: How social skills can enhance entrepreneurs' success. *The Academy of Management Executive*, 14, 1, 106–16.

Bass, B. (1985): *Leadership and Performance Beyond Expectations.* New York: Free Press.

Bass, B. (1990): From transactional to transformational leadership: Learning to share the vision. *Organizational Dynamics*, 18, 19–31.

Bass, B., Avolio, B. J., and Atwater, L. E. (1996): The transformational and transactional leadership of men and women. *Applied Psychology: An International Review*, 45, 5–34.

Beggs, J. M., Doolittle, D., and Garsombke, D. (1994): Diversity in entrepreneurship: Integrating issues of sex, race, and class. In D. P. Moore (ed.), *Academy of Management best papers proceedings*, Abstract, p. 482, Madison, WI: Omnipress.

Bird, A. (1994): Careers as repositories of knowledge: A new perspective on boundaryless careers. *Journal of Organizational Behavior*, 15, 325–44.

Brush, C. G. (1992): Research on women business owners: Past trends, a new perspective and future directions. *Entrepreneurship Theory and Practice*, 16, 4, 5–31.

Brush, C. G. and Bird, B. J. (1996): Leadership vision of successful women entrepreneurs: Dimensions and Characteristics. In W. D. Bygrave, B. J. Bird, S. Birley, N. C. Churchill, M. G. Hay, R. H. Kelley, and W. E. Wetzel, Jr (eds), *Frontiers of Entrepreneurship Research*, summary, Babson Park, MA: Center for Entrepreneurial Studies, Babson College, On-line, available: *www.babson.edu/entrep/fer/papers96/summ96/brush.html*

Brush, C. G. and Hisrich, R. D. (2000): *Women-owned businesses: An exploratory study comparing factors affecting performance.* Research Institute for Small & Emerging Business, Inc. (RISEbusiness), On-line, available: *http:www.riseb.org*

Buttner, E. H. and Moore, D. P. (1997): Women's organizational exodus to entrepreneurship: Self-reported motivations and correlates with success. *Journal of Small Business Management*, 35, 1, 34–46.

Caputo, R. K. and Dolinsky, A. (1998): Women's choice to pursue self-employment: The role of financial and human capital of household members. *Journal of Small Business Management*, 36, 3, 8–17 (see p. 8).

Carter, N. M., Gartner, W. B., and Reynolds, P. D. (1996): Exploring start-up event sequences. *Journal of Business Venturing*, 11, 151–66.

Catalyst (1999): The 1999 Catalyst Census of Women Board Directors of the *Fortune* 1000. New York. On-line, available: *http:www.catalystwomen.org/press/factswbd99.html*

Catalyst (2000): The glass ceiling in 2000: Where are women now? Labor day fact sheet, On-line, available: *http://www.catalystwomen.org/press/factslabor00.html* pp. 1–4. (See also Women of Color in Corporate Management: A Statistical picture, pp. 1–2.)

Catalyst (1998): *Paths to entrepreneurship: New directions for women in business.* With the National Foundation for Women Business Owners (NFWBO) and the Committee of 200 Foundation, sponsored by Salomon Smith Barney, New York: Catalyst.

Cheskin Research (2000): *Women entrepreneurs study.* (On-line) With Santa Clara University Center for Innovation & Entrepreneurship (SCU-CIE), & Center for New Futures (CNF), available: *www.cheskin.com; www.scu.edu/entrepreneur/www.centerfornewfutures.com*

Coleman, S. (2000): Access to capital and terms of credit: A comparison of men- and women-owned small businesses. *Journal of Small Business Management*, 38, 3, 37–52.

Cromie, S. and Birley, S. (1992): Networking by female business owners in Northern Ireland. *Journal of Business Venturing*, 7, 3, 237–51.

Daily, C. M., Certo, T. S., and Dalton, D. R. (1999): Entrepreneurial ventures as an avenue to the top? Assessing the advancement of female CEOs and directors in the Inc. 100. *Journal of Developmental Entrepreneurship*, 4, 1, 19–32.

Davis, S. E. M. and Long, D. D. (1999): Women entrepreneurs: What do they need? *Business and Economic Review*, 45, 4, 25–6.

Deng, S., Hassan, L., and Jivan, S. (1995): Female entrepreneurs doing business in Asia: A special investigation. *Journal of Small Business and Enterprise*, 12, 60–80, as cited by Maysami, R. C. and Goby, V. P. (1999), Female business owners in Singapore and elsewhere: A review of studies, *Journal of Small Business Management*, 37, 2, 96–105.

Douglas, E. J. (1999): Entrepreneurship as a career choice: attitudes, entrepreneurial intentions, and utility maximization. *Frontiers for Entrepreneurship Research, Babson Conference Proceedings*, On-line, available: *http:www.babson.edu/entrep/fer/papers98/V/V_A/V_A_text.html*

Douglas, E. J. and Shepherd, D. A. (1997): Entrepreneurship as a utility-maximizing response. Working Paper No. 97–1, at J. L. Kellogg Graduate School of Management, Northwestern University.

Drucker, P. (1999): Managing oneself. *Harvard Business Review*, 77, 2, 64–74.

Dyer, W. G. Jr (1994): Toward a theory of entrepreneurial careers. *Entrepreneurship Theory and Practice*, 19, 2, 7–21.

EIM (1998): *Fourth annual report of the European observatory for SMEs – Women in SMEs*, On-line, available: *http://europa.eu.int/comm/dg23/craft/craft-women/craft-obswomen.html*

European Commission DG XXIII (1996): The European Observatory for SMEs. Fourth Annual Report. http//www.eim.nl/uk/eu02.html

Feldman, D. C. and Bolino, M. C. (2000): Career patterns of the self-employed: Career motivations and career outcomes. *Journal of Small Business Management*, 38, 3, 53–67.

Foley, S. and Powell, G. N. (1997): Reconceptualizing work–family conflict for business/marriage partners: A theoretical model. *Journal of Small Business Management*, 35, 4, 36–47.

Gartner, W. B., Bird, B. J., and Starr, J. A. (1992): Acting as if: Differentiating entrepreneurial from organizational behavior. *Entrepreneurship Theory and Practice*, 16, 3, 13–27.

Gere, I. (1999): Women entrepreneurs in Hungarian society today. In Z. Laczko and A. Soltesz (eds), *The status of women in the labour market in Hungary: Entrepreneurship as an alternative*. Institute for Labour Research SEED survey of women entrepreneurs, Foundation for Small Enterprise Economic Development (SEED) with support from the Center for International Private Enterprise and USAID, On-line, available:
*http:www.socialsectornet/casestudy/seed.htm.*

Gracie, S. (1998): In the company of women. *Management Today*, 66–70.

Greenhaus, J. H. and Parasuraman, S. (1999): Research on work, family, and gender – current status and future directions. In Gary N. Powell (ed.), *Handbook of gender in organizations*, Thousand Oaks, London, and New Delhi: Sage.

Hall, D. T. (1996): Protean careers of the 21st century. *Academy of Management Executive*, 10, 4, 8–16.

Harvey, M. and Evans, R. (1995): Strategic windows in the entrepreneurial process. *Journal of Business Venturing*, 10, 5, 331–408.

Hisrich, R. D., Koiranen, M., and Hyrsky, K. (1996): A comparison of men and women entrepreneurs: A cross-national exploratory study. In W. D. Bygrave, B. J. Bird, S. Birley, N. C. Churchill, M. G. Hay, R. H. Kelley, and W. E. Wetzel, Jr (eds), *Frontiers of Entrepreneurship Research* (Summary). Babson Park, MA: Center for Entrepreneurial Studies, Babson College, On-line, available: *www.babson.edu/entrep/fer/summ96/hisrich.html*

Hisrich, R. D. and Ozturk, S. A. (1999): Women Entrepreneurs in a developing economy. *Journal of Management Development*, 18, 2, 114.

Hokkanen, P., Lumme, A., and Autio, E. (1998): Gender-based non-differences in bank shopping and credit terms. *Frontiers of Entrepreneurship Research*, Babson College Proceedings, On-line, available: *http:www.babson.edu/entrep/fer/papers98/V/V_A/V_A_text.html*

Izyumov, A. and Razumnova, I. (2000): Women entrepreneurs in Russia: Learning to survive the market. *Journal of Developmental Entrepreneurship*, 5, 1, 1–19.

Jamal, M. (1997): Job stress, satisfaction, and mental health: An empirical examination of self-employed and non-self-employed Canadians. *Journal of Small Business Management*, 35, 4, 48–57.

Kanter, R. M. (1989): Careers and the wealth of nations: A macro-perspective on the structure and implications of career forms. In M. B. Arthur, D. T. Hall, and B. S. Lawrence, *Handbook of Career Theory*, Cambridge: Cambridge University Press.

Katz, J. A. (1990): Longitudinal analysis of self-employment follow-through. *Entrepreneurship & Regional Development*, 2, 15–25.

Katz, J. A. (1994): Modeling entrepreneurial career progressions: Concepts and considerations. *Entrepreneurship Theory and Practice*, 19, 2, 23–39.

Katz, J. A. (1997): Core publications in entrepreneurship and related fields: A guide to getting published. United States Association of Small Business and Entrepreneurship web listing, On-line, available: *http://www.usasbe.org/pubs/journalist.htm* (website maintained by Michael Meeks).

Kelly, R. M. (1991): *The Gendered Economy: Work, Careers, and Success*. Thousand Oaks, CA: Sage.

Kulmala, J. (1999): *First-ever Canada/US businesswomen's trade summit report*. Totally-U Image Communications, On-line, available: *http://www.kulmala2.canada.htm*

Lerner, M., Brush, C., and Hisrich, R. (1997): Israeli women entrepreneurs: An examination of factors affecting performance. *Journal of Business Venturing*, 12, 4, 315–39.

Lewis, K. M. (1999): African-American female adult development: The journey from employee to business owner. *Dissertation-Abstracts-International*: 60(4-B), University Microfilms No. AEH9928261.

Ljunggren, E. and Kolvereid, L. (1996): New business formation: Does gender make a difference? *Women in Management Review*, 11, 4, 3–12.

Lynch, M. and Post, K. (1996): What glass ceiling? *The Public Interest*, 124, 27–37, On-line, available: *http://web7.searchbank.com/infotra* pp. 5–6.

Marlow, S. and Strange, A. (1994): Female entrepreneurs – Success by whose standards? In M. Tanton (ed.), *Women in management: A developing presence*. International Thomson Business Press.

Marshack, K. J. (1994): Copreneurs and dual-career couples: Are they different? *Entrepreneurship: Theory and Practice*, 19, 1, 49–70.

Marshack, K. J. (1998): *Entrepreneurial couples – Making it work at work and at home*. Palo Alto, CA: Davies-Black Publishing.

Marshack, K. J. (2000): *How marriage and family life affect the business*. Symposium paper presented at the annual meeting of the Academy of Management, Toronto, Canada.

Maysami, R. C. and Goby, V. P. (1999): Female business owners in Singapore and elsewhere: A review of studies. *Journal of Small Business Management*, 37, 2, 96–105.

Moore, D. P. (1990): An examination of present research on the female entrepreneur – Suggested research strategies for the 1990s. *Journal of Business Ethics*, 9, 4/5, 275–81.

Moore, D. P. (1999): Women Entrepreneurs approaching a new millennium. In G. N. Powell (ed.), *Handbook of gender in organizations*, Thousand Oaks, London, and New Delhi: Sage.

Minniti, M. and Bygrave, W. (1999): The microfoundations of entrepreneurship. *Entrepreneurship Theory and Practice*, 23, 4, 41–52.

Moore, D. P. (2000): *Careerpreneurs – Lessons from leading women entrepreneurs on building a career without boundaries*. Pal Alto, CA: Davies-Black Publishing.

Moore, D. P. and Buttner, E. H. (1997): *Women entrepreneurs: Moving beyond the glass ceiling*. Thousand Oaks, CA: Sage.

Moore, D. P., Buttner, E. H., and Rosen, B. (1992): Stepping off the corporate track: The entrepreneurial alternative. In U. Sekaran and F. Leong (eds), *Womanpower: Managing in times of demographic turbulence*, Newbury Park, CA: Sage.

National Foundation for Women Business Owners (1999): *NFWBO research summary*. On-line, available: *http:www.NFWBO.org* (Facts of the week)

NFWBO (National Foundation for Women Business Owners) (2000): *NFWBO Key Facts*. On-line, available: *http:www.NFWBO.org*

Powell, G. N. and Mainiero, L. A. (1992): Cross currents in the river of time: Conceptualizing the complexities of women's careers. *Journal of Management*, 18, 215–37.

Powell, G. N. and Mainiero, L. A. (1993): Getting ahead in career and life. In G. N. Powell (ed.), *Women and Men in Management*, Newbury Park, CA: Sage.

Schein, E. H. (1978): Career dynamics: Matching individual and organizational needs. Reading, MA: Addison-Wesley.

Schein, E. H. (1990): *Career anchors: Discovering your real values*. (Revised edn 1993), San Diego, CA: Pfeiffer & Company.

Schein, E. H. (1996): Career anchors revisited: implications for career development in the 21st century. *The Academy of Management Executive*, 10, 4, 80–9.

Shane, S. and Venkataraman, S. (2000): The promise of entrepreneurship as a field of research. *Academy of Management Review*, 25, 1, 217–26.

Stewart, W. H., Jr, Watson, W. E., Carland, J. C., and Carland, J. W. (1999): A proclivity for entrepreneurship: A comparison of entrepreneurs, small business owners, and corporate managers. *Journal of Business Venturing*, 14, 2, 189–214.

Sullivan, S. E. (1999): The changing nature of careers: A review and research agenda. *Journal of Management*, 25, 3, 457–84.

Sullivan, S., Carden, W. A., and Martin, D. F. (1998): Careers in the next millennium: Directions for future research. *Human Resource Management Review*, 8, 2, 165–85.

Teo, S. K. (1996): Women Entrepreneurs of Singapore. In A. M. Low, W. L. Tan, and L. A. Meng (eds), *Singapore business development series. Entrepreneurs, entrepreneurship and enterprising culture*, Singapore Business Development Series, Singapore: Addison-Wesley Publishing Company.

US Small Business Administration (SBA's) Office of Advocacy (1998): *Economic statistics and research on small business: Women in business*. On-line, available: *http:www.sba.gov/ADVO/stats/wib.html*

Watson, C. (1994): Gender versus power as a predictor of negotiation behavior and Outcomes. *Negotiation Journal*, 117–27.

Zapalska, A. (1997): A profile of woman entrepreneurs and enterprises in Poland. *Journal of Small Business Management*, 35, 4, 76–82.

# 15

# TIME IN ORGANIZATIONS: CONSTRAINTS ON, AND POSSIBILITIES FOR, GENDER EQUITY IN THE WORKPLACE

## Lotte Bailyn

> Life holds one great but quite commonplace mystery. Though shared by each of us and known to all, it seldom rates a second thought. That mystery, which most of us take for granted and never think twice about, is time.
>
> Calendars and clocks exist to measure time, but that signifies little because we all know that an hour can seem an eternity or pass in a flash, according to how we spend it.
>
> Time is life itself, and life resides in the human heart.
>
> **From Momo by Michael Ende**

Momo, in Michael Ende's charming tale, lives in a world where people's lives are not held to the clock, and so they have time to talk and to reflect, and to do their work in a way that enhances them and their community. Until, that is, the time thieves, the men in gray, appear on the scene and convince the community that every second must be saved. They count up the seconds wasted and convince the people to put them into a time-saving bank. Pretty soon the community begins to change. No longer is there time to reflect, or to go to the fields and have Momo listen to one's worries and thus make them disappear, or to enjoy the open air, or to spend time with one's friends and family. Everyone is too busy saving seconds to put into the time-saving bank. Pretty soon the community looks like life as we know it and as it is experienced by women and men in today's corporate world. But our time thieves are not the men in grey; they are our own collective conception of time as an external, objective marker of competitive success in an ever faster-paced, global world.

---

I am grateful to Wanda Orlikowsi for insightful comments on a previous version of this paper.

In pre-industrial times, when home was a production-consumption unit, time had a cyclical, repetitive, task-oriented aspect to it. But with the movement of production outside the home and the gendered separation of men into economic production roles under industrial, clock time, and women into caring roles, time began to be seen as a problem. In the public, economic sphere – where men predominate – industrial time came to be seen as a commodity, to be bought and sold (Thompson, 1967; Giddens, 1987; Adam, 1990), while women's caring work in the private, domestic arena continued to follow the pre-industrial temporal pattern.

This gendered separation of spheres has pitted a "nurturing or responsibility rationality" against a "technical-economic" one (Davies, 1990), with the first embedded in a caring or process sense of time, the second in industrial clock time. In societies such as ours, where economic value dominates, the former becomes defined as feminine, cyclical, and undervalued. In contrast, the latter – masculine, linear, and economically productive – becomes the dominant temporal mode (ibid.). All of this, the separation of spheres and the commodification of time in the dominant economic arena, leads to a sense of scarcity of time and the kind of life that the gray men brought to Momo's community (Marks, 1977; Fabian, 1983). Though there are women who have always negotiated multiple times (for example, see Hall, 1983; Whipp, 1994; Glucksman, 1998; Jurczyk, 1998), the current dominant conception remains anchored in the economic, masculine sphere.

Jules Henry, an anthropologist, writes in his book *Pathways to Madness* (1965) of the close connection in the industrial world between time and people's emotional lives. He talks of two ways to transform "astronomical time into social time" – by empathy, as in well-functioning close relationships, or by fear, as in most hierarchical connections:

> Everyday affairs bind the time of all of us. A man's time is bound from the moment he opens his eyes in the morning until he quits for the day . . . None of that time – from getting up in the morning till quitting time – is his own, because he has sold it to the job. Sold time is bound and is governed by fear. Time not so bound, time that is not sold, is unbound and is therefore free for empathy and love. (Henry, 1965, p. 14)

The trouble, according to Henry, is that bound time or work ("sold time") controls fear, with the result that time that is not used productively creates anxiety. "When work binds anxiety, not to work frees it" (p. 15), which results in bound time dominating unbound, empathic time.

So, as women move in ever increasing numbers into the dominant world of paid employment (bound time), they face norms and practices that seem to conflict with the responsibilities and pleasures associated with an unbounded, more subjective sense of time (see Daly, 1996). Nor does this clock-based, objective way of organizing working time any longer fit all men, and it certainly doesn't fit women (Kanter, 1977; Hewitt, 1993). From it has emerged a pattern of work practices and work norms that create barriers to women's careers and difficulties for both men and women in integrating their work lives with their personal lives.

And so we are faced with the situation that work is organized around industrial time, even as the character of work changes to a post-industrial mode. We want employees to have a quicker, more flexible response to their tasks and to environmental changes;

we want them to coordinate their work in more interdependent, less hierarchical ways; we count on their commitment, their intrinsic involvement with work as a source of motivation. And yet, all of this is superimposed on a notion of time that fits the industrial age, which makes it difficult to reach these post-industrial goals.

## ■ Temporal norms in organizations ■

Organizational temporal norms are so ingrained, so taken for granted, that they seem immutable. One is hardly aware how they determine how one works, and how current work practices continuously recreate and reinforce them (Orlikowski and Yates, 1999). And so, in response to faster product development cycles, to globalization which breaks the cycle of day and night, to new technologies like the cell phone and the pager that allow for continuous accessibility, one finds work encroaching on all aspects of life. This clearly has an ill effect on employees' health, as well as on their families and communities. But it is assumed to be necessary in order to remain competitive. It is this connection that our work has challenged (Rapoport and Bailyn, et al., 1996; Bailyn, Fletcher, and Kolb, 1997; Perlow, 1997; Fletcher, 1999). When we look at how time is used and how cultural norms and assumptions that surround time affect work practices, we find that these same norms also have a negative effect on organizational effectiveness.

The basic underlying character of industrial time that neither fits current demographics and lifestyles, nor the needs of organizations in a knowledge-based, globally competitive world, is that it is based on the clock. Though most work is no longer controlled by punching a time clock, clock time – objective, abstracted from the situation – continues to guide work practice. For example, national labor law, which was enacted to deal with depression conditions, is geared entirely to the clock and actually constrains some innovative flexible time arrangements that would benefit both employees and their employers. And we know that companies prize punctuality and give demerits for lateness. It seems, at times, that it is more important to be present than to produce (Perin, 1991; Perlow, 1997). There are examples of people leaving their lights on and their coats over a chair to indicate presence even when they are not physically in their offices. Taking time off in the middle of the day is easier than leaving work early. The emphasis on "face time" is based on the clock, and is still seen as important for career success (Bailyn, 1993).

But it is not at all clear that this emphasis is effective for accomplishing organizational tasks. Task time is not the same as clock time. Tasks, as defined in a particular context, have their own rhythms and cycles within that situation. And the emphasis on clock time may prevent work from entraining to those cycles in a productive way (Ancona and Chong, 1996). Look at the reaction to compensatory time. There are still companies that pay overtime rather than providing time off after a particularly hard push to meet a deadline. And one middle manager complained bitterly that, after an exhausting trip, his company insisted he appear in the office, even though there was nothing particular to do. Similarly, salesmen are expected to check in at the beginning and end of the day, even when their appointments are far away. All of this adds to working hours and to pressure on employees without producing value for the organization. Thus, work practices anchored to clock time can be inefficient when viewed from the point of view of organizational tasks.

In our work in organizations we have actually found people, a minority to be sure, who do work differently. For example, a few program officers in one research foundation where travel to client countries is highly valued, managed to accomplish their work with much less travel than their peers. And a few engineers in a high-pressured product development group found ways to meet their deliverables as well as the needs of the overall project by more up-front planning, more thoughtful approaches to coordination, more concern about the project as a whole rather than only their individual parts, and thus were able to be productive without the same long hours of work put in by their peers. Two points are relevant about these examples. First, these constructive modifications in work practices were usually made by employees, often women with child care responsibilities, with time constraints, which shows that, when necessary, it is possible to adjust the way of working to "work smart, not long." But, second, these changes, though clearly effective, were invisible and not recognized as signs of competence (see Fletcher, 1999). The underlying norm of clock time as a referent point was too strong.

A number of temporal norms flow from clock time that, I believe, constrain the way we work as well as our personal lives. Three, in particular, seem to be critical:

1   a presumed linear relation between time put in and output
2   a tendency to throw time at problems
3   coordination by instant accessibility.

## Linear relation between time put in and output

Part of the effect of reckoning time by the clock is that it abstracts time from the tasks being accomplished. By this linear, objective logic, there is a clear and predictable relation between the amount of time one devotes to a task and the output expected from that work. Hence 12 hours of work will produce twice as much as six hours, and every additional hour will add a fixed amount to the product. From personal experience, of course, we know this not to be true. For many people a few hours in the morning are three times as productive as the same amount at night, and vice versa for others. Also, as we all know, fatigue sets in. The first hour at a task, or at least the first hour after any necessary start-up issues have been settled, is usually considerably more productive than the fifth, or tenth.

And yet, time and productivity continue to be framed in this linear relationship. This conception of time is based on a machine logic. Even though machines also show signs of fatigue, on the whole their output is regular and predictable; they do produce twice as much in 12 hours as in six. But when this logic is applied to human workers, especially to knowledge workers, it becomes clear that what is served is control, rather than production. Perin (1991) distinguishes between a panopticon discourse, a logic of authority and control, and a performance discourse, which shifts to a logic of work. The assumption that time put into work is linearly related to output is part of the logic of control.

A consequence of this logic is that time put into work becomes the primary indicator of good performance and success. One engineering manager, for example, explained that he knows who his good engineers are when "they don't know enough to go home." And in his division, people were in their cubicles at all hours of the day and night, even though, as some admitted, there was no real reason to be there. So time becomes a proxy for output, which happens particularly in those situations where individual output is difficult to measure, as for example in knowledge work.

There is evidence, moreover, that the linear relation between time and productivity does not apply even to very output-oriented work. For example, Bank of America was testing the value of offering part-time work to its check processors. The measure of performance was easy in this case: the number of checks processed. What they found was that the average output for full-time employees was 1,200 to 1,300 checks per hour, compared to 1,500 to 1,650 for part-time workers (quoted in Olmsted and Smith, 1994, p. 97). Others have also found the hourly productivity advantage of reduced hours work (see Cohen and Gadon, 1978; Ronen, 1984).

The presumed linear relationship between time and productivity, therefore, seems not only to add stress to employees' lives through its reinforcement of long hours, but may actually interfere with the efficiency of work. Take the example of a small computer company. When employees found their workday expanding, they declared they would no longer work past 5.00 pm. And, surprisingly, they discovered that they could do the same amount of work in this shortened day as they had previously done (described in Bailyn, 1993, p. 82). Obviously, using time as an indicator of high performance in this case would have meant rewarding inefficiency instead of productivity. This conclusion is confirmed by psychological experiments that show that when time is constrained, work that must be done can be fitted into whatever time is available (see Bluedorn and Denhardt, 1988, for a summary).

These examples point to the negative consequences of conceiving of time as linearly related to productivity. First, this norm leads to evaluation procedures that use the input measure of time as a proxy for output, which reinforces the tendency toward ever longer hours at work. And second, it provides no incentive for more effective work practices based on a reframing of long hours as a sign of inefficiency, rather than of productivity.

## Throwing time at problems

There was a time when companies threw people at problems. But since reengineering and "rightsizing" this solution is no longer used. Now, it is time that is thrown at problems. People pull all-nighters to finish a sales presentation; a slipping deadline in a project leads to evening and weekend work; a shorter time to market means longer hours for each individual working on the product. Problems are dealt with by people working harder and longer, and the organization is in a continuous crisis mode.

There are obvious difficulties with this picture. Such an approach precludes attention to the prevention of problems, to upfront planning designed to minimize the continuous sense of crisis, to the tendency to consider everything equally urgent and important. And the individualized incentive system in most high-pressure situations, where rewards are given to individuals who visibly solve problems, reinforces this tendency. Perlow (1997, 1999) gives a vivid example of the dynamics underlying this norm.

She studied a group of design engineers. Because they were working on a product with an unusually short time-to-market goal, they found themselves working longer and longer hours. Some engineers would come in during the night to finish individual assignments they could not get done during the regular working day. Why? Because they were constantly interrupted: by others asking for help, by nervous managers asking for frequent progress reports, by meetings called to deal with the problems that emerged. Everyone was aware of the stress they were under, but no one questioned the necessity of these long hours in order to meet the tight schedule. The belief that problems can be solved by throwing time at them prevented this group from rethinking their work patterns into what might have been a more effective mode.

The situation described by Perlow exhibits two temporal confusions. First is the confusion between pace and duration. The group implicitly assumed that in order to decrease the duration, that is, a shorter time to market, the pace must speed up. And, second, there was confusion between individual time and system time (Bailyn, 1993). There was an unrecognized, taken-for-granted assumption in this group that the only way to shorten system time was for the individuals involved to throw more time at the effort, that is, to work longer hours. Time was seen as an individual resource but problems were defined at the system level. There was no realization that individual work patterns and project developments each proceeded at different rates and with different pacing, and that there was a need to mesh these temporalities (Perlow, 1999).

## Coordination by instant availability

The belief in the importance of having people always around (in case they are needed) permeates the structure of work. Now, with the pressure of global contact as well as technologies like cell phones, e-mail, and pagers, work is beginning to move to a 24/7 pattern; again, an expansion of time – which has been called the "last frontier" (Melbin, 1978). But the assumption that one needs instant access in order to coordinate work feeds inefficiencies in the system. It allows the system to be entirely reactive, instead of emphasizing the value of preplanning and learning from reflection on past performance.

So, for example, a manager of a newly distributed team discovered, much to his surprise, that having to plan meetings in advance, which he had previously not had to do, actually enhanced the value of the meetings (Bailyn, 1988). The necessity to think about an agenda, instead of being able to bring people together on the spur of the moment, made the work of the group more rather than less effective. Similarly, in the engineering design group described by Perlow (1999) and mentioned above, changing the structure of the day to include periods of "quiet time" where no one was available to anyone else allowed the group to work more efficiently.

The tension about working from home is an interesting example of the power of this norm. Managers are reluctant to have their employees out of the office and are likely to insist that even when they are working from home they remain accessible during normal working hours. But this defeats some of the organizational and personal gains from this way of working which center on the control over time, and on building in the advantages that can be gained from asynchronous coordination. For example, people have individual cycles of productivity. In one study of systems workers it was found that one-quarter of them had their most productive periods of work outside the 9–5 period but, because they had to be in the office during this "normal" time, they could not take advantage of their personal productivity cycle. In contrast, an equivalent group working from home did have control over their time and were able to use it advantageously (Bailyn, 1994). Managers, of course, had to learn to manage in a different way, and discovered that coordinating work by clearly specifying goals, rather than monitoring continuously the conduct of the work, had clear advantages (Judkins, et al., 1985).

These examples show that continuous accessibility is not necessarily the most effective way to manage and coordinate work. But this norm is so basic, and so embedded in the notions of control based on clock time, that it is not easy to consider alternatives.

## Summary

Taken together, these temporal norms emerge from industrial time, a sense of time guided by the clock in an external, linear, objective way. They lead to long hours and an emphasis on presence, on the input rather than the output of work. They reinforce face time, crisis management, lack of planning, solving rather than preventing problems. They leave little time for reflection or for rethinking work practices, and thus these norms constrain innovative patterns of working. They also make it difficult to take advantage of differences in individual or task time cycles.

These norms also have clear consequences for society. They create stress and burnout for individual workers which translate into productivity loss and health costs. They also contribute to the crisis of care we are currently concerned with: the care of children, of elders, and of communities. And, finally, they reinforce gender inequities. Women are more likely to be care givers and hence more likely to have constrained hours. Even though, as mentioned above, they are often able to be productively innovative in the way they work, as long as such innovation is not recognized and valued, and as long as long hours are seen as an indicator of top performance, they are unlikely to win in the selection for top positions. These temporal norms, therefore, derail our attempts to achieve a gender-equitable workplace.

## ■ Alternatives to clock time ■

In contrast to industrial time, which dominates in the public economic sphere, we can look to the private sphere, to what some have called "natural" or "social" time (Nowotny, 1975). This is a conception of time that is subjective, rather than objective; geared to events, rather than to the clock; cyclical, rather than linear; and anchored in a logic of care. Some have called it "feminine" or "process" time (Davies, 1990; Jurczyk, 1998). It differs from industrial time by not being commodified or quantified, not seen as a resource to hand out, waste, control, or sell (Adam, 1990). It is Henry's (1965) unbounded time, responsive to and constitutive of the tasks and interactions one is currently involved with. It is integrally linked to activities, not abstracted from them (Adam, 1990). It conceives of time as more personal, more expansive, more responsive, more socially and situationally defined than "public time," which is "occupied, measured, and allotted by the powers that be" (Fabian, 1983, p. 144).

It is the difficulty of integrating this more personal sense of time with industrial production time that makes women's lives, and increasingly also men's, so difficult. And, since the economic sphere provides the dominant temporal mode, what we find today is that clock time is invading the private sphere. Overworked parents spend one hour of "quality time" with their children, which results in alternate periods of attention and neglect geared to the clock rather than the needs of the child. In other situations, as well, we see the commodification of care: doctors in Health Maintenance Organizations are guided by productivity goals, the number of patients per hour, independent of those patients' needs; paid care givers are controlled by the clock. In all of these cases, quality goes down. All life begins to be guided by a scarcity approach to time. Is there an alternative?

Stephen Marks, in a 1977 essay, laid out a different approach, an expansion approach to time, commitment, and energy. He locates scarcity in the gendered separation of spheres and in the socially defined imbalance of commitments. Hence overload results from an overcommitment to work, an overcommitment that is continually recreated and reinforced by ongoing work practices and patterns of recognition and reward. Such an imbalance leads to a sense of scarcity of time and energy in any other area of life. In contrast, Marks's thesis is that a balanced commitment structure would lead to a different understanding of time, one that would create rather than deplete one's energy. In other words, he claims that feelings of time scarcity and the consequent depletion of energy stem from an imbalance of commitments, not from an absolute lack of hours. An analogous argument has been made on the individual level by Barnett and Baruch (1985) and Barnett et al. (1992), who have shown that multiple roles for men and women are not a recipe for tension and conflict, but actually alleviate stress and enhance well-being.

So the question arises, what actions would be necessary to bridge these two domains? Instead of bringing clock time from the world of work into the home, as is currently happening, what could one do to bridge these domains in a more equitable way? To do so would require a more fluid, more responsive orientation to time, one that would flow with the needs of the moment, responding to a situation as it is evolving. It would be based on an enacted sense of time, which "suggests that time is experienced both objectively (when we use it to coordinate our action), and subjectively (when we create or change temporal parameters through our action)" (Orlikowski and Yates, 1999, p. 12). With such an orientation to time one would not substitute pace for duration, but that could be a gain, not a loss, since neither creative work nor caring work can be compressed into a fixed period of time. Such an approach raises the possibility of designing work to be responsive both to the defined work tasks and to the temporal needs of employees' private lives.

Let me give one example of how this might be done. It stems from one of a number of action research projects that I have been involved in over the past decade with a number of different colleagues (see, for example, Rapoport and Bailyn, et al., 1996; Rapoport, et al., 1998; Bailyn, Fletcher, and Kolb, 1997). In these projects, based on what we have called the "dual agenda," we work with organizations to change work practices to meet the double goal of easing employees' lives and at the same time making the work more effective. The particular example I want to give deals with the portfolio analysis group of a large bank (Bailyn and Rayman, et al., 1998; Rayman, et al., 1999).

The work of this department consists in preparing financial reports for senior management and the board. The department is divided into groups, each of which has its own area of specialization but is sequentially involved with the work of the other groups. Thus there are both many independent areas of work and much need for coordination. Deadlines are often tight and top managers frequently ask for re-dos or for specific information that is not part of the standard reports, but *ad hoc*. Thus workload is heavy and hours are long.

Because of a recent reorganization the group, when we worked with them, consisted of a number of people who had very long commutes. To ease their personal problems they had requested permission to work from home one or two days a week. But this was not allowed by the bank. The manager was concerned about problems of coordination. She had tried hard to get the group to set up a plan for their work that would make it easier to ensure that all parts of these reports were ready at the appropriate time, but this had never happened.

As part of the action research project, the bank agreed to a three-month experiment where members of the group could work at home up to two days a week; others were allowed to have flexible hours, again something that had not previously been approved. The bank even contributed equipment to the telecommuters. And though these workers could not at home be attached to the office LAN, they could be linked through another city to the system that carried the data they needed.

The telecommuters were now working in a different temporal mode. They had shifted from control by objective clock time to a more personally responsive approach. People reported that for the first time they were able to participate in family events, and could do their work at those times of the day and night that fitted best into their personal productivity and their family temporal patterns. They also created more time by not commuting every day of the week. And when the office LAN went down for three days and they were the only ones able to get any work done, the advantage of a variety of responses to the tasks of the organization became obvious to everyone.

The results of the experiment were increased productivity and increased ability to respond to personal needs. And, perhaps most telling, in accomplishing these goals the unit found a different way of coordinating work. Now the plan that their manager had tried vainly to put into place became a reality, because it was deemed necessary to support this more responsive, expansive use of time. When eveyone was in the office, governed by the norms of clock time, there was no obvious need to shift to this more effective way of working. Also, morale was up in the unit, and people were less stressed. As one bank employee who interacted with this unit said, "they look much less frenzied."

This example shows that work designed around a less rigid, more encompassing sense of time can indeed meet the dual agenda. It can ease employees' lives and at the same time be more effective for accomplishing work goals. Both time and energy expand.

# Conclusion

One of the reasons it continues to be difficult to create gender equity in the workplace, even after years of affirmative action, equal opportunity legislation, and goodwill on the part of most employers, is the dominance that clock time has over our lives. It is critical, therefore, to consider what work practices would look like if they were designed in accordance with a more responsive and expansive sense of time. By relinquishing the time bounds on work, this approach would allow work activity to follow the ebb and flow of organizational tasks. By necessity it would create a more collaborative environment, and coordination would have to be more planned because it would no longer be possible to coordinate by immediate access. There would have to be more multiskilling, more human redundancy and slack. In many ways, this is already the direction organizations are trying to go. But they are often not successful because their efforts continue to be embedded in an objective, abstracted conception of time.

Most important, such a different approach to the design and practice of work will allow all employees, men and women alike, to integrate their work with their personal lives, and help to make gender equity in the workplace more of a reality. But creating such a situation will not be easy. It will require a different synchronization between the public and private spheres, where these are not seen as separate, or as differentially valued by society, or as differently committed to by employees. Clearly this is a distant ideal, but one that will never occur if we continue to construct time and its role in our lives as objective and external, and as based entirely on the clock and a fixed calendar.

## REFERENCES

Ancona, D. and Chong, C-L. (1996): Entrainment: Pace, cycle, and rhythm in organizational behavior. *Research in Organizational Behavior*, 18, 251–84.

Adam, B. (1990): *Time and social theory*. Philadelphia: Temple University Press.

Bailyn, L. (1988): Freeing work from the constraints of location and time. *New Technology, Work and Employment*, 3, 143–52.

Bailyn, L. (1993): *Breaking the mold: Women, men, and time in the new corporate world*. New York: Free Press.

Bailyn, L. (1994): Toward the perfect work place? The experience of home-based systems developers. In T. J. Allen and M. S. Scott Morton (eds), *Information technology and the corporation of the 1990s: Research studies*, New York: Oxford University Press.

Bailyn, L., Fletcher, J. K., and Kolb, D. (1997): Unexpected connections: Considering employees' personal lives can revitalize your business. *Sloan Management Review*, summer, 11–19.

Bailyn, L. and Rayman, P., et al. (1998): *Creating work and life integration solutions*. Cambridge, MA: Radcliffe Public Policy Institute.

Barnett, R. C. and Baruch, G. K. (1985): Women's involvement in multiple roles and psychological distress. *Journal of Personality and Social Psychology*, 49, 135–45.

Barnett, R. C., Marshall, N. L., and Pleck, J. H. (1992): Men's multiple roles and their relationship to men's psychological distress. *Journal of Marriage and the Family*, 54, 358–67.

Bluedorn, A. C. and Denhardt, R. B. (1988): Time and organization. *Journal of Management*, 14, 299–320.

Cohen, A. R. and Gadon, H. (1978): *Alternative work schedules: Integrating individual and organizational needs*. Reading, MA: Addison-Wesley.

Daly, K. J. (1996): *Families and time: Keeping pace in a hurried culture*. Thousand Oaks, CA: Sage.

Davies, K. (1990): *Women, time and the weaving of the strands of everyday life*. Aldershot, England: Gower.

Fabian, J. (1983): *Time and the other: How anthropology makes it object*. New York: Columbia University Press.

Fletcher, J. K. (1999): *Disappearing acts: Gender, power and relational practice at work*. Cambridge: MIT Press.

Giddens, A. (1987): *Social theory and modern sociology*. Stanford: Stanford University Press.

Glucksman, M. A. (1998): "What a difference a day makes": A theoretical and historical exploration of temporality and gender. *Sociology*, 32, 239–58.

Hall, E. T. (1983): *The dance of life: The other dimension of time*. Garden City, NY: Anchor Press/Doubleday.

Henry, J. (1965): *Pathways to madness*. New York: Random House.

Hewitt, P. (1993): *About time: The revolution in work and family life*. London: IPPR/Rivers Oram Press.

Judkins, P., West, D., and Drew, J. (1985): *Networking in organisations: The Rank Xerox experiment*. Aldershot, England: Gower.

Jurczyk, K. (1998): Time in women's everyday lives: Between self-determination and conflicting demands. *Time and Society*, 7, 283–308.

Kanter, R. M. (1977): *Work and family in the United States*. New York: Russell Sage Foundation.

Marks, S. R. (1977): Multiple roles and role strain: Some notes on human energy, time and commitment. *American Sociological Review*, 42, 932–6.

Melbin, M. (1978): The colonization of time. In T. Carlstein, D. Parkes, and N. Thrift (eds), *Human activity and time geography*, New York: Wiley.

Nowotny, H. (1975): Time structuring and time measurement: On the interrelation between time keepers and social time. In J. T. Fraser and N. Lawrence (eds), *The study of time II: Proceedings of the second conference of the International Society for the Study of Time*. Berlin: Springer-Verlag.

Olmsted, B. and Smith, S. (1994): *Creating a flexible workplace: How to select & manage alternative work options*. New York: AMACOM.

Orlikowski, W. J. and Yates, J. (1999): It's about time: An enacted view of time in organizations. MIT Sloan School of Management Working Paper, WP#4055, Cambridge, MA.

Perin, C. (1991): The moral fabric of the office: Panopticon discourse and schedule flexibilities. In P. S. Torbert and S. R. Barley (eds), *Research in the sociology of organizations: Organizations and professions*, Greenwich, CT: JAI Press.

Perlow, L. (1997): *Finding time: How corporations, individuals and families can benefit from new work practices*. Ithaca, NY: Cornell University Press.

Perlow, L. (1999): The time famine: Toward a sociology of work time. *Administrative Science Quarterly*, 44, 57–81.

Rapoport, R. and Bailyn, L., et al. (1996): *Relinking life and work: Toward a better future*. New York: Ford Foundation.

Rapoport, R., Bailyn, L., Kolb, D., and Fletcher, J. K., et al. (1998): *Relinking life and work: Toward a better future*. Innovations in Management Series. Waltham, MA: Pegasus Communications.

Rayman, P., Bailyn, L., Dickert, J., and Carré, F. (with the assistance of M. Harvey, R. Krim, and R. Read) (1999): Designing organizational solutions to integrate work and life. *Women in Management Review*, 14, 164–76.

Ronen, S. (1984): *Alternative work schedules: Selecting, implementing, and evaluating*. Homewood, IL: Dow Jones-Irwin.

Thompson, E. P. (1967): Time, work-discipline and industrial capitalism. *Past and Present*, 38, 56–97.

Whipp, R. (1994): A time to be concerned: A position paper on time and management. *Time and Society*, 3, 99–116.

# 16

# POSITIVE PSYCHOLOGY AT WORK: SAVORING CHALLENGE AND ENGAGEMENT

*Bret L. Simmons*

Through the lens of positive psychology, this chapter will present a new way to think about stress for women at work. Positive psychology at work emphasizes the attitudes and actions that lead to well-being, positive individuals, and thriving workplaces, in contrast to a familiar focus on pathology that results in a model of the human being lacking the positive features that make life worth living. Researchers have come to understand quite a bit about how people survive and cope when confronted with adversity, but we know comparatively little about how normal people thrive under normal conditions. Positive psychology advocates a preoccupation with building positive qualities in individuals and workplaces in addition to repairing the bad things about work and careers (Seligman and Csikszentmihalyi, 2000).

This chapter will discuss some of the new directions in the study of work and stress that are consistent with positive psychology. A comprehensive model of stress that incorporates positive as well as negative responses, shown in figure 16.1, will be introduced. This chapter will focus on the positive responses and their affect on well-being. Traditional treatments focus on the pathology of stress, and excellent recent reviews exist of stress for working women in general (Davidson and Fielden, 1999), for women executives (Nelson and Burke, 2000), and for work/family conflicts (Barnett, 1998). Gender differences for positive responses will be discussed where appropriate, but in most cases the research has not developed to the point where gender differences have been examined. Finally, implications of this model for women at work will focus on suggestions for women to savor the positive attitudes, emotions, and outcomes that result from the challenging and engaging work that they are increasingly gaining access to.

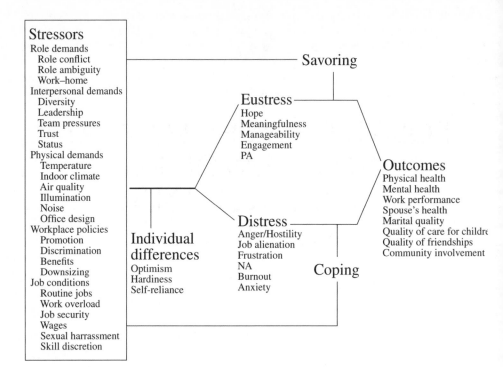

**Figure 16.1**  A model of eustress

## ■  Stressors and distress  ■

The physical or psychological stimuli to which the individual responds are commonly referred to as either "stressors" or "demands." Stressors at work take the form of role demands, interpersonal demands, physical demands, workplace policies, and job conditions (Quick et al., 1997; Barnett, 1998). There is some evidence for gender differences in stressors as a function of job characteristics. Many stressors reported more frequently by women (for example, inadequate salary, personal insults, periods of inactivity) are associated with low-level, low-control jobs. It is most likely that it is the characteristics of the jobs that are typically held by women, and not gender *per se*, that account for stress differences for women. As the number of women in the workforce continues to increase, equality in employment conditions (both good and bad) should lead to a reduction in variation between the sexes in experienced stressors (Jex, 1998). A study of male and female doctors in Scotland found that increased role complexity (home–work) was related to stress for both female and male doctors, which the researchers interpreted to suggest an increasing convergence in the occupational and domestic roles of male and female doctors (Swanson, Power, and Simpson, 1998).

When a person encounters a stressor, she or he evaluates the encounter with respect to its significance for well-being. This evaluative process is the essence of cognitive appraisal. The negative response to stressors that results from appraisals where stressors are perceived by the individual to be either threatening or harmful is commonly termed "distress." It is distress that is commonly studied for its relationship to adverse health outcomes, absenteeism, and turnover (Quick et al., 1997). Distress, as such, is negative and dysfunctional (that is, bad stress). Appropriate indicators of the distress response are negative work attitudes and psychological states (for example, anxiety, burnout, negative affect, frustration, job alienation, anger/hostility).

It has already been pointed out that there may be differences in the level of stressful job conditions reported by women; however, when appropriate controls are utilized, gender generally does not affect the relationship between job conditions and distress. Time pressures, conflicting demands, and dull, monotonous work are equally distressful for both men and women (Barnett and Brennan, 1997). A longitudinal study of male and female urban bus drivers confirmed that when men and women are exposed to stressors that are objectively identical, they tend to react in the same way (Rydstedt, Johansson, and Evans, 1998).

### ■ Eustress: the positive response to stress ■

Some have suggested that there is also good stress, which Selye (1976a, 1976b) termed "eustress." Quick et al. (1997) associate eustress with healthy, positive outcomes. Positive appraisals of stressors "occur if the outcome of an encounter is construed as positive, that is, if it preserves or enhances well-being or promises to do so," (Lazarus and Folkman, 1984, p. 32). As indicators of the positive response to stressors resulting from positive appraisals, they suggest looking for the presence of positive or pleasurable psychological states and attitudes. A major issue in the study of eustress is to simultaneously establish the presence of both positive and negative psychological states rather than merely inferring eustress by the absence of negative states. Instead of representing opposite ends of a single continuum, positive (eustress) and negative (distress) states may represent two distinct constructs, which would require separate multivariate indices for their measurement (Edwards and Cooper, 1988).

Consider the analogy of a bath-tub to illustrate the point of thinking of eustress and distress as two distinct constructs. As a minimum, we are concerned about two things when we settle in for a bath – the level of water in the tub and the temperature of water in the tub. Essentially two things determine the level of water in the bathtub – the flow of water into the bath-tub and the flow of water out of the bath-tub over time. Likewise, the simultaneous flow of both hot and cold water into the bath-tub determine the temperature of the water in the tub. If we liken the study of stress to the study of water in the bath-tub, our current approach is like studying a bath-tub with a single water faucet – cold water, representing distress. We know a lot about the sources of cold water, and we can tell individuals how to either decrease the flow of cold water into or increase the flow of cold water out of their bath-tub. We also know quite a bit about the physiological, behavioral, and psychological consequences of sitting in a tub of cold water for a prolonged period of time. Our knowledge of cold water (distress) is important, but does not present a complete understanding of the water (stress) in the bath-tub. A more complete model of stress would acknowledge that the bath-tub does indeed have two faucets – hot and cold – and both are necessary to get the level and temperature of the water just right for a comfortable bath.

The field of positive psychology is about valued subjective experiences. The approach to stress that incorporates subjective experiences is the cognitive appraisal approach most commonly associated with the work of Richard Lazarus (1966). The essence of this approach to understanding stress is that people can have different responses to stressors they encounter depending on whether they appraise a relevant stressor as positive or negative. Although Lazarus acknowledged the existence of positive responses, he, like the majority of stress researchers, focused almost exclusively on negative responses.

According to the cognitive appraisal approach, two individuals with significantly different perceptions of the same stressor (or a single individual with differing interpretations at different times) would respond differently. Likewise, two individuals with similar perceptions of the same (or different) stressors would experience similar responses (Roseman, 1984).

When a person encounters a stressor, she or he evaluates the encounter with respect to its significance for well-being. This evaluative process is the essence of cognitive appraisal. If a stressor is not appraised as irrelevant, Lazarus and Folkman (1984) assert, appraisals can be complex and mixed, depending on person factors and the situational context. They essentially describe two types of appraisals and associated response patterns: positive and stressful.

Positive appraisals "occur if the outcome of an encounter is construed as positive, that is, if it preserves or enhances well-being or promises to do so," (Lazarus and Folkman, 1984, p. 32). As indicators of positive appraisals, they suggest looking for the presence of positive or pleasurable psychological states (for example, exhilaration).

Stressful appraisals can also be thought of as negative appraisals. Negative appraisals include harm/loss, threat, and challenge. In harm/loss, some damage to the person has already occurred (for example, injury, illness, loss of a loved one, damage to self-esteem). Threat involves harms or losses that have not yet occurred but are anticipated. Challenge appraisals occur if the outcome of an encounter holds the potential for gain or growth. As indicators of challenge appraisals, Lazarus and Folkman (1984) suggest looking for some of the same positive or pleasurable psychological states they identify as indicators of the positive response (for example, exhilaration).

Lazarus and Folkman (1984) do not view challenge and threat as poles of a single continuum. They believe that challenge and threat responses can occur simultaneously, as the result of the same stressor, and should be considered as separate but related constructs. While threat is clearly a negative appraisal, challenge is better thought of as a positive appraisal (they share the same indicators).

As such, the reasoning they apply to the distinction between challenge and threat to the higher levels of positive and negative response can be extended. Accordingly, positive and negative responses can occur simultaneously, as a result of the same stressor, and should be considered as separate but related constructs. Thus, for any given stressor, an individual can have both a degree of positive and a degree of negative response. This is consistent with Lazarus and Folkman's (1984) view that any psychophysiological theory of stress or emotion, which views the response as unidimensional disequilibrium or arousal, is untenable or at least grossly incomplete. They support this with research of emotions and autonomic nervous system activity (Elkman, Levenson, and Friesen, 1983) as well as research of hormonal response to arousing conditions (Mason, 1974; Frankenhauser, et al., 1978). The evidence is accumulating that our brains may indeed be wired to simultaneously experience positive and negative emotions separately (Davidson, 2000; Tomarken et al., 1992; Wheeler, Davidson, and Tomarken, 1993).

Rose's (1987) longitudinal study of air traffic controllers (ATCs) provides physiological evidence of the positive stress response. Over a three-year period, the cortisol values of 201 men were measured every 20 minutes for five hours on three or more days and compared to both objective and subjective assessments of workload. Cortisol is a hormone secreted by the hypothalamic-pituitatary-adrenal system that has been found to be responsive to a variety of different environmental challenges. Cortisol acts on a variety of the body's organs, but its primary effect is to increase the supply of glucose and fatty acids in the bloodstream. Cortisol can also have harmful effects on the body's digestion, immune response, and muscular-skeletal system (Quick et al., 1997).

While the increases in cortisol for all levels of workload were slight, the men who showed the highest increase in cortisol to increased work reported themselves as more satisfied and were regarded by peers as more competent. These high cortisol responders also showed less frequent illness than those with lower cortisol levels, who for any given level of work tended to have more minor health problems. Rose concludes: "individuals who were busily engaged in work and who report a *challenge* but not a sense of being threatened or overwhelmed are better described as *engaged* rather than stressed and this appears to be a desirable state of affairs" (Rose, 1987, p. 145). Elsewhere, the happiness derived from engagement in mindful challenge has been termed "flow" (Csikszentmihalyi, 1990). In their review of Rose's study, Ganster and Schaubroek (1991) described the healthy state of physiological arousal experienced by the "engaged" workers as eustress.

While Rose's (1987) work provides physiological evidence for eustress, it does not provide specific insight for women at work. Frankenhauser (1979, 1983, 1986) provided additional support for the concept that different psychological processes affect the physiological response pattern in different ways, and these response patterns were found to have slight gender differences. Through a series of experiments, she and her colleagues consistently found that two components of psychological arousal determined cortisol and catecholamine responses. The psychological state characterized by positive emotions was labeled "effort", and the psychological state characterized by negative emotions was labeled "distress." Indicators of effort were variables labeled effort, tenseness, and concentration, while indicators of distress were variables labeled boredom, impatience, tiredness, and lack of interest (Lundberg and Frankenhauser, 1980). Frankenhauser (1979) notes the general resemblance of these two factors and the "cortisol factor" and "catecholamine factor" reported by Ursin, Baade, and Levine (1978) in their study of parachute trainees.

Frankenhauser (1983) asserted that these findings support the notion that psychologically different conditions produce a selective response. In general, cortisol secretions were associated with the negative feelings of distress, and catecholamine secretions were associated with the positive feeling of effort. The general patterns of hormonal secretions were the same for males and females; however, there was a distinct sex difference in the magnitude of the response, with women reporting less intense effort, and, accordingly, less of the catecholamines associated with positive emotions. Frankenhauser (1981) emphasized that "neurendocrine responses to the psychosocial environment are determined by the individual's cognitive appraisal of the situation and the emotional impact of the stimuli rather than by their objective characteristics" (p. 493).

This was confirmed in a study of positive and negative stress differences between male and female managers and clerical workers using several physiological indicators of stress (Frankenhaueser et al., 1989). Positive stress was operationalized with self-report measures of engagement and ability to concentrate, and negative stress was indicated with time pressures and pressure by demands. This study found that both men and women experienced more positive stress than negative stress, but the positive stress levels were lower for women. Although the women in the study experienced a high degree of engagement and enjoyed their work, they had a harder time unwinding after work than did the men in the study.

A recent study of high-level white-collar male and female managers again found that both women and men at these high levels experienced their jobs as challenging and stimulating, although the situation was less favorable for women. Women experienced more distress as a result of their higher unpaid workload and commitments to home and family (Lundberg and Frankenhaeuser, 1999).

In summary, an individual's cognitive appraisal of a situation produces positive and negative emotions, as well as a differential physiological response. The growing evidence of the positive physiological response to demands is critical to establishing a persuasive case for eustress. Managers, however, deal more with the attitudes and emotions of their workers than their hormonal responses.

## ■ Indicators of eustress ■

Engaged workers are enthusiastically involved in and pleasurably occupied by the demands of the work at hand. Workers can be engaged and perceive positive benefits even when confronted with extremely demanding stressors. A study of female and male soldiers participating in a US peacekeeping mission in Bosnia found that soldiers who were engaged in meaningful work during the deployment found it to be a positive experience (Britt, Adler, and Bartone, 2001). Interestingly, a factor such as witnessing the destruction caused by warring factions was associated with reporting greater positive benefits. In the context of the mission, the destruction was likely seen as justification for the mission, which added meaning to the soldier's work. Female soldiers in this study self-reported more positive benefits as a result of the deployment than men, although the effect size for gender was small.

Eustress reflects the extent to which cognitive appraisal of a situation or event is seen to either benefit an individual or enhance their well-being. When assessing eustress, the indicators of eustress should be positive psychological states, for example attitudes or emotions. Stable dispositional variables are not acceptable indicators of eustress, which must be subject to change according to changes in cognitive appraisal of stressors. Work attitudes are preferable indicators, and the measures should not overlap conceptually. The work attitudes positive affect (PA), meaningfulness, manageability, and hope may be good indicators of eustress (Simmons, 2000; Simmons and Nelson, 2001a; Simmons, Nelson, and Neal, 2001). While conceptually distinct, these constructs all represent an aspect of engagement, one of the primary indicators of the eustress response.

## Positive affect

Positive affect (PA) is a state of pleasurable engagement and reflects the extent to which a person feels enthusiastic, active and alert (Watson, Clark, and Tellegen, 1988). PA can be measured as a state or trait, with state PA capturing how one feels at given points in time, whereas the trait represents stable individual differences in the level of affect generally experienced (George and Brief, 1992; Watson and Pennbaker, 1989). State and trait PA are both conceptually and empirically distinct, and state PA is a separate factor from negative affect (George and Brief, 1992).

People in a positive state process information more heuristically or strategically, while people in a negative state process information more systematically. Positive affect is associated with seeing the opportunity in an issue as well as lower levels of risk taking (Mittal and Ross, 1998). Others have described those in a positive mood as "smarter" at processing information than those in a negative mood (Staw and Barsade, 1993). PA has been shown to be effective in medical contexts, improving decision making among medical students and creative problem solving and diagnostic reasoning processes among practicing physicians (Estrada, Isen, and Young, 1994; Isen, Rosenzweig, and Young, 1991; Estrada, Isen, and Young, 1997).

## Meaningfulness and manageability

These two constructs are part of a new scale developed by a nurse to measure situational sense of coherence (Artinian, 1997). Sense of coherence (SOC) was a term developed to denote factors that promote a healthy response to stressful situations (Antonovsky, 1987). It has traditionally been measured as a trait variable, but was adapted by Artinian (1997) as a situational or state measure. Two of three subscales are appropriate as indicators of eustress.

*Meaningfulness* is the extent to which one feels that work makes sense emotionally, that problems and demands are worth investing energy in, are worthy of commitment and engagement, and are challenges that are welcome. A representative of one of the scale's four items is, "At work, do you have the feeling that you don't really care about what goes on around you (very seldom/very often)?"

In their study of peacekeepers in Bosnia, Britt et al. (2001) operationalized meaningful work with indicators of job importance, soldier engagement, and the relevance of peacekeeping to the soldier's identity. The meaningfulness of work was a significant predictor of deriving benefit from the mission. The strongest zero-order correlation in the study was the significant positive relationship between soldier engagement and job importance.

*Manageability* is the extent to which one perceives that resources are at one's disposal that are adequate to meet the demands posed by the work situation. Representative items of this five-item scale are, "When you think of the challenges you are facing at work, do you feel that (there is no solution/you can find a solution)?" and, "People you count on at work often disappoint you (always happens/never happens)."

## Hope

Hope has been identified as a positive emotion reflecting a degree of expected benefit resulting from an evaluation of a particular situation (Lazarus, 1993; Smith, et al., 1993). Hope was defined as a cognitive set that is based on a sense of successful goal-directed determination and planning to meet goals (Snyder et al., 1996). As a belief that one has both the will and the way to accomplish one's goals, hope has also been suggested as an attribute of emotional intelligence (Huy, 1999). The state hope scale thus provides a snapshot of a person's goal-directed thinking and engagement.

Gender differences in state hope did not emerge in any of the studies conducted to develop and validate the scale. The lack of gender differences for hope is consistent with findings of the scale for dispositional hope, which has been administered to thousands of men and women of different backgrounds, education, and occupations (Snyder, 1994). The positive spin on this finding is that men and women are equally hopeful.

Conversely, it may be that the goals toward which hope is applied are different for women and men (Snyder, 1994). Like a glass ceiling effect, women may not really expect to have many of life's goals, especially those associated with work, open to them. If women perceive that many goals at work are beyond their reach, they may not even think of certain goals as being attainable. In effect, women may limit their goals to those left open to them. Thus, women may report high hope for the goals they believe they are allowed to have.

However, organizations now employ a significant number of women who have reached mid life and mid career (Gordon and Whelan, 1998). Women at mid career often have more positive models for thinking about success, career progression, and work and family responsibilities. Their desire for new challenges will likely find them directing their hope toward levels of career advancement that may have seemed unattainable when they first began their careers.

The positive psychological states meaningfulness, manageability, hope, and positive affect are examples of constructs that may be good indicators of eustress. In theory, any positive psychological state could be a potential of eustress. Much more research needs to be done to identify other effective indicators of eustress, as well as potential gender differences in these indicators.

## ■ Individual differences that promote the positive response ■

Several individual difference variables may be especially salient in their potential to influence the extent to which demands are seen as positive versus negative. The most important of these may be trait optimism (Seligman and Csikszentmihalyi, 2000). People high in optimism have consistently better moods, are more persevering and successful, and experience better health. Optimism is also consistently associated with finding benefit in difficult life situations (Tedeschi and Calhoun, 1996). Optimists may be expected to have a higher degree of eustress even when faced with traumatic events at work, such as downsizing, layoffs, or mid-life career changes. Optimistic people see the positive in difficult situations and understand that these situations are temporary, limited, or caused by something other than themselves (Quick et al., 1997).

Hardiness has been described as a stable tendency to find meaning in events, especially demanding events that challenge the individual (Kobasa, 1979). People with hardy personalities are more likely to view change as a challenge and opportunity for personal development, which leads them to be open to the positive aspects of change (Quick et al., 1997).

Attachment behavior may also moderate the relationship between demands and eustress. There are three patterns of attachment behavior that affect the ways individuals perceive and enact relationships at work (Quick, Nelson, and Quick, 1990; Nelson, Quick, and Joplin, 1991). Interdependence is a secure pattern of behavior that involves the formation of flexible, reciprocal relationships. Counter-dependence is an unhealthy pattern of behavior in which individuals, believing that no one will be available to turn to in stressful situations, isolate themselves and resist supportive overtures by others. Overdependence, another unhealthy pattern, is also based on the belief that others will not be there to help; however, overdependent individuals cling too tightly to others and may drain their support systems by failing to reciprocate support. Interdependent people have been described as self-reliant (Quick et al., 1997).

The relationship between attachment behavior, hope, and health was examined in a study of home health care nurses (Simmons and Nelson, 2001b). There was a positive relationship between interdependence and health that was fully mediated by state hope. The finding that hope mediates, rather than moderates, the relationship between attachment behavior and health suggests that it is not that hope has a greater effect on health in those that are interdependent, but that those who are interdependent are more likely to be hopeful, and therefore healthy.

■ **Eustress and health** ■

An extensive review of the subject of eustress suggested that eustress may improve health either directly through hormonal and biochemical changes or indirectly by facilitating effort and abilities directed toward coping with existing distress (Edwards and Cooper, 1988). Findings from a variety of sources, including anecdotal evidence, laboratory experiments, and studies of positive life events and job satisfaction were reviewed. This review of eustress provided suggestive, but not conclusive, evidence for the direct effect of eustress on health. Little research has focused on the effects of eustress on coping with existing distress, so evidence of the indirect benefits of eustress is scant. One study, however, did demonstrate that eustress is associated with an improvement in physiological functioning rather than merely a reduction in physiological damage (Sales, 1969).

A recent review of the literature stated that "positive emotional states *may* promote healthy perceptions, beliefs, and physical well-being itself" (Salovey, Rothman, Detweiler, and Steward, 2000, p. 110, emphasis added). Yet several recent empirical studies of hospital nurses operationalized eustress and distress as separate responses indicated by the presence of multivariate positive and negative psychological states (Simmons, 2000; Simmons and Nelson, 2001a). These cross-sectional studies hypothesized that in response to the demands of the job, hospital nurses would experience significant levels of both eustress and distress, and each stress response would have a separate effect on the nurses' perceptions of their health. They found that even in the presence of a demanding work environment, the hospital nurses were actively engaged in their work and reported significant levels of eustress, and eustress in turn had a significant positive relationship with their perception of their own health. Hope was the indicator of eustress with the strongest positive relationship with the nurses' perception (Simmons and Nelson, 2001a). In addition to being healthy and productive themselves, eustressed nurses may have a concrete impact on the health of patients by inspiring positive expectations and raising the patient's level of hope (Salovey, Rothman, Detweiler, and Steward, 2000).

Positive aspects of work for women is also a positive influence in the home environment (Barnett and Marshall, 1992; Barnett, Marshall, and Sayer, 1992). In a study of licensed practical nurses and social workers, there were no negative spillover effects from job to parenting or from parenting to job, but there were positive spillover effects from job to parenting (Barnett and Marshall, 1992). Women with rewarding jobs experienced less of the mental health effects of troubled relationships with their children. Challenge was the specific factor of a rewarding job that provided the positive-spillover effect (Barnett, Marshall, and Sayer, 1992). When employed mothers enjoyed high rewards from challenge at work, they reported low distress, regardless of their level of disaffection they experienced in their relationship with their children.

## ■ Savoring the challenge and engagement ■

The contrast between the view of positive psychology presented in this chapter and the more common view is captured in a very recent article by Folkman and Moskowitz (2000). As this chapter does, they accept the fact that positive and negative affect can cooccur during a stressful period of time. In contrast to the theory presented here, they suggest that positive and negative responses are produced by different events (stressors). In contrast to this chapter, the effects of the positive response are viewed as a coping strategy, a way to adapt to distress and its negative effects. While it is encouraging to see attention given to the effects of positive psychological states, this approach simply reinforces the prevailing primacy of distress and the associated psychology of pathology. A legitimate positive psychology will shift from an exclusive focus on pathology to the independent and direct effects of positive psychological states on important indicators of well-being as well as disease (Seligman and Csikszentmihalyi, 2000). The theory of eustress presented in this chapter thus makes a legitimate contribution to the advancement of a positive psychology.

The importance of eustress lies in its relationship to health and other positive outcomes. Engaging, challenging work can have positive health consequences for women.

Similar to stress, health has also been viewed as a unidimensional construct representing the absence of the negative, that being disease. Yet health should be defined not just as the absence of illness, but also as the presence of a sense of purpose, quality connections with others, positive self-regard, and mastery (Ryff and Singer, 1998). Work in general and careers with no imposed limits on upper goals stand to provide a significant source of these aspects of health for women.

One of the most important questions that research on future research on eustress must address relates to the potential to generate the positive stress response. This is analogous to the extremely valuable work that has been done on stress management, which is essentially focused on preventing the negative stress response (Quick et al., 1997). I hope that researchers will avoid the temptation to attempt to assign valence to stressors as a way to prescribe formulas for eustress. That would be totally inconsistent with the theory of eustress presented here. The cognitive appraisal approach to stress requires that any assignment of valence be reserved for the stress response.

Thus, any model of eustress generation must recognize the individualistic nature of the endeavor for which individuals must assume personal responsibility. The concept of coping, finding ways to reduce the negative stress response or distress, is familiar. I suggest a new concept I call "savoring," that does for the eustress what coping does for distress. Savoring is recognizing and appreciating the positive response to demands at work, and attempting to self-identify the sources that seem to most elicit the greatest sense of engagement and challenge.

Working women should be encouraged by the fact that despite the challenges, work can be a significant source of engagement, challenge, and health in their lives. Work, and for that matter life, will always be a mosaic of positive and negative experiences that are more than likely occurring simultaneously and interacting with each other in complex ways. In addition to valence, responses to work experiences differ with respect to their duration and intensity. Keep the bath-tub analogy in mind, and try to think of your career as an opportunity for a warm bath as opposed to a cold shower.

## REFERENCES

Antonovsky, A. (1987): *Unraveling the mystery of health: How people manage stress and stay well.* San Francisco: Jossey-Bass.

Artinian, B. M. (1997): Situational sense of coherence: Development and measurement of the construct. In B. M. Artinian and M. M. Conger (eds), *The intersystem model: Integrating theory and practice*, Thousand Oaks, CA: Sage.

Barnett, R. C. (1998): Toward a review and reconceptualization of the work/family literature. *Genetic, Social, and General Psychology Monographs*, 124, 125–82.

Barnett, R. C. and Brennan, R. T. (1997): Change in job conditions, change in psychological distress, and gender: a longitudinal study of dual-earner couples. *Journal of Organizational Behavior*, 18, 253–74.

Barnett, R. C. and Marshall, N. L. (1992): Worker and mother roles, spillover effects, and psychological distress. *Women & Health*, 18, 9–40.

Barnett, R. C., Marshall, N. L., and Sayer, A. (1992): Positive-spillover effects from job to home: a closer look. *Women & Health*, 19, 13–41.

Britt, T. W., Adler, A. B., and Bartone, P. T. (2001): Deriving benefits from stressful events: the role of engagement in meaningful work and hardiness. *Journal of Occupational Health Psychology*, 6, 53–63.

Csikszentmihalyi, M. (1990): *Flow: The psychology of optimal experience*. New York: Harper & Row.

Davidson, R. J. (2000): Affective style, psychopathology, and resilience: Brain mechanisms and plasticity. *American Psychologist*, 55, 1196–214.

Davidson, M. J. and Fielden, S. (1999): Stress and the working woman. In G. N. Powell (ed.), *Handbook of Gender & Work*, Thousand Oaks, CA: Sage.

Edwards, J. R. and Cooper, C. L. (1988): The impacts of positive psychological states on physical health: A review and theoretical framework. *Social Science Medicine*, 27, 12, 1147–59.

Elkman, P., Levenson, R. W., and Friesen, W. V. (1983): Autonomic nervous system activity distinguishes among emotions. *Science*, 221, 1208–10.

Estrada, C. A., Isen, A. M., and Young, M. J. (1994): Positive affect improves creative problem solving and influences reported source of practice satisfaction in physicians. *Motivation and Emotion*, 18, 285–99.

Estrada, C. A., Isen, A. M., and Young, M. J. (1997): Positive affect facilitates integration of information and decreases anchoring in reasoning among physicians. *Organizational Behavior and Human Decision Processes*, 72, 117–35.

Folkman, S. and Moskowitz, J. T. (2000): Positive affect and the other side of coping. *American Psychologist*, 55, 647–54.

Frankenhauser, M. (1979): Psychobiological aspects of life stress. In S. Levine and H. Ursin (eds), *Coping and Health*, New York: Plenum Press.

Frankenhauser, M. (1981): Coping with stress at work. *International Journal of Health Services*, 11, 491–510.

Frankenhauser, M. (1983): The sympathetic-adrenal and pituitary-adrenal response to challenge: Comparison between the sexes. In T. M. Dembroski, T. H. Schmidt, and G. Blumchen (eds), *Biobehavioral bases of coronary heart disease*, New York: Karger.

Frankenhauser, M. (1986): A psychobiological framework for research on human stress and coping. In M. H. Appley and R. Trumbull (eds), *Dynamics of stress: Physiological, psychological, and social perspectives*, New York: Plenum Press.

Frankenhaeuser, M., Lundberg, U., Fredrikson, M., Melin, B., Tuomisto, M., and Myrsten, A. (1989): Stress on and off the job as related to sex and occupational status in white collar workers. *Journal of Organizational Behavior*, 10, 321–46.

Frankenhauser, M., Von Wright, M. R., Collins, A., Von Wright, J., Sedvall, G., and Swahn, C. G. (1978): Sex differences in psychoendocrine reactions to examination stress. *Psychosomatic Medicine*, 40, 334–43.

Ganster, D. C. and Schaubroeck, J. (1991): Work stress and employee health. *Journal of Management*, 17, 235–71.

George, J. M. and Brief, A. P. (1992): Feeling good–doing good: A conceptual analysis of mood at work-organizational spontaneity relationship. *Psychological Bulletin*, 112, 310–29.

Gordon, J. R. and Whelan, K. S. (1998): Successful professional women in midlife: How organizations can more effectively understand and respond to the challenges. *Academy of Management Executive*, 12, 8–24.

Huy, Q. N. (1999): Emotional capability, emotional intelligence, and radical change. *Academy of Management Review*, 24, 325–45.

Isen, A. M., Rosenzweig, A. S., and Young, M. J. (1991): The influence of positive affect on clinical problem solving. *Medical Decision Making*, 11, 221–7.

Jex, S. M. (1998): *Stress and job performance*. Thousand Oaks, CA: Sage Publications.

Kobasa, S. C. (1979): Stressful life events, personality, and health: An inquiry into hardiness. *Journal of Personality and Social Psychology*, 37, 1–11.

Lazarus, R. S. (1966): *Psychological stress and the coping process*. New York: McGraw-Hill.

Lazarus, R. S. (1993): From psychological stress to the emotions: A history of changing outlooks.

In L. W. Porter and M. R. Rosenzweig (eds), *Annual Review of Psychology, Vol. 44*, Palo Alto, CA: Annual Reviews Inc.

Lazarus, R. S. and Folkman, S. (1984): *Stress, appraisal, and coping.* New York: Springer Publishing Company.

Lundberg, U. and Frankenhauser, M. (1980): Pituitary-adrenal and sympathetic-adrenal correlates of distress and effort. *Journal of Psychosomatic Research*, 24, 125–30.

Lundberg, U. and Frankenhauser, M. (1999): Stress and workload of men and women in high-ranking positions. *Journal of Occupational Health Psychology*, 4, 142–51.

Mason, J. W. (1974): Specificity in the organization response profiles. In P. Seeman and G. Brown (eds), *Frontiers in neurology and neuroscience research*, Toronto: University of Toronto.

Mittal, V. and Ross, W. T. Jr (1998): The impact of positive and negative affect and issue framing on issue interpretation and risk taking. *Organizational Behavior and Human Decision Processes*, 76, 298–324.

Nelson, D. L. and Burke, R. J. (2000): Women executives: Health, stress, and success. *Academy of Management Executive*, 14, 107–21.

Nelson, D. L., Quick, J. C., and Joplin, J. R. (1991). Psychological contracting and newcomer socialization: An attachment theory foundation. *Journal of Social Behavior and Personality*, 6, 55–72.

Quick, J. C., Nelson, D. L., and Quick, J. D. (1990): *Stress and challenge at the top: The paradox of the successful executive.* Chichester: John Wiley & Sons.

Quick, J. C., Quick, J. D., Nelson, D. L., and Hurrell, J. J. (1997): *Preventive stress management in organizations.* Washington, DC: American Psychological Association.

Rose, R. M. (1987): Neuroendocrine effects of work stress. In J. C. Quick, R. S. Bhagal, J. E. Dalton, and J. D. Quick (eds), *Work stress: Health care systems in the workplace.* New York: Praeger.

Roseman, I. J. (1984): Cognitive determinants of emotion: A structural theory. In P. Shaver (ed.), *Review of personality and social psychology: Emotions, relationships, and health*, Beverly Hills, CA: Sage.

Rydstedt, L. W., Johansson, G., and Evans, G. W. (1998): A longitudinal study of workload, health, and well-being among male and female urban bus drivers. *Journal of Occupational and Organizational Psychology*, 71, 35–45.

Ryff, C. D. and Singer, B. (1998): The contours of positive human health. *Psychological Inquiry*, 9, 1–28.

Sales, S. M. (1969): Organizational role as a risk factor in coronary disease. *Administrative Science Quarterly*, 14, 325–36.

Salovey, P., Rothman, A. J., Detweiler, J. B., and Steward, W. T. (2000): Emotional states and physical health. *American Psychologist*, 55, 110–21.

Seligman, M. E. P. and Csikszentmihalyi, M. (2000): Positive psychology. *American Psychologist*, 55, 5–14.

Selye, H. (1976a): *Stress in health and disease.* Boston: Butterworths.

Selye, H. (1976b): *The stress of life*: Revised edition, New York: McGraw-Hill.

Simmons, B. L. (2000): *Eustress at Work: Accentuating the Positive.* Unpublished doctoral dissertation, Oklahoma State University.

Simmons, B. L. and Nelson, D. L. (2001a): Eustress at work: the relationship between hope and health in hospital nurses. *Health Care Management Review* (in press).

Simmons, B. L. and Nelson, D. L. (2001b): Health for the hopeful: A study of attachment behavior in home healthcare nurses. Paper presented at the 2001 Annual Meeting of the American Psychological Assosication in San Francisco.

Simmons, B. L., Nelson, D. L., and Neal, L. J. (2001): A Comparison of the Positive and Negative Work Attitudes of Home Healthcare and Hospital Nurses. *Health Care Management Review* (in press).

Smith, C. A., Haynes, K. N., Lazarus, R. S., and Pope, L. K. (1993): In search of the "hot" cognitions: Attributions, appraisals, and their relation to emotion. *Journal of Personality and Social Psychology*, 65, 916–29.

Snyder, C. R. (1994): *The psychology of hope: You can get there from here.* New York: The Free Press.

Snyder, C. R., Sympson, S. C., Ybasco, F. C., Borders, T. F., Babyak, M. A., and Higgins, R. L. (1996): Development and validation of the state hope scale. *Journal of Personality and Social Psychology*, 70, 321–35.

Staw, B. M. and Barsade, S. G. (1993): Affect and managerial performance: A test of the sadder-but-wiser vs. happier-and-smarter hypothesis. *Administrative Science Quarterly*, 38, 304–31.

Swanson, V., Power, K. G., and Simpson, R. J. (1998): Occupational stress and family life: A comparison of male and female doctors. *Journal of Occupational and Organizational Psychology*, 71, 237–60.

Tedeschi, R. G. and Calhoun, L. G. (1996): The posttraumatic growth inventory: Measuring the positive legacy of trauma. *Journal of Traumatic Stress*, 9, 455–71.

Tomarken, A. J., Davidson, R. J., Wheeler, R. E., and Doss, R. C. (1992): Individual differences in anterior brain asymmetry and fundamental dimensions of emotion. *Journal of Personality and Social Psychology*, 62, 676–87.

Ursin, H., Baade, E., and Levine, S. (1978): *Psychobiology of Stress.* New York: Academic Press.

Watson, D., Clark, L. A., and Tellegen, A. (1988): Development and validation of brief measures of positive and negative affect: The PANAS scale. *Journal of Personality and Social Psychology*, 54, 1063–70.

Watson, D. and Pennebaker, J. W. (1989): Health complaints, stress and distress: Exploring the central role of negative affectivity. *Psychological Review*, 96, 234–54.

Wheeler, R. E., Davidson, R. J., and Tomarken, A. J. (1993): Frontal brain asymmetry and emotional reactivity: A biological substrate of affective style. *Psychophysiology*, 30, 82–9.

# 17

# ORGANIZATIONAL CULTURE: A KEY TO THE SUCCESS OF WORK AND FAMILY PROGRAMS

*Ronald J. Burke*

As an increasing number of women enter the workforce, concerns about balanced commitment to work and personal life have heightened (Schwartz, 1992; Davidson and Burke, 1994). These concerns are not only women's concerns; as societal values change, men have expressed interest in a more balanced work commitment as well (Burke and Nelson, 1998).

It has been suggested that it may be even more difficult now to manage a balanced commitment (Hochschild, 1997). Organizations today face heightened competition on a worldwide basis, employees are experiencing increasing performance pressures, and hours spent at the workplace – for managers and professionals particulary – may be increasing (Schor, 1991). High-performance organizations have raised their expectations regarding time, energy, and work commitment from employees.

These expectations may be particularly difficult for women, since women perform the bulk of household tasks (Hochschild, 1989, 1997), and men with families. This combination of factors likely contribute to the relatively slow influx of women into senior levels of corporate management (Burke and McKeen, 1992; Powell, 1999) and to the high levels of work–family conflict reported by both women and men (Greenhaus and Parasuraman, 1999; Perlow, 1997).

This research was supported in part by the School of Business, York University. Graeme Macdermid and Cobi Wolpin assisted with data collection and analysis; Sandra Osti prepared the manuscript.

The phrase "family friendly" was coined to describe those firms attempting to support work–personal life balance (Rodgers and Rodgers, 1989; Konrad, 1990). Many of these early efforts involved the creation of workplace policies more conducive to balanced investments in work and personal life. The efforts of these innovative organizations have been chronicled in lists of "best places to work" as well as described in the more mainstream professional and academic journals (see *Women in Management Review*, 1995; *Equal Opportunities International*, 1997; *Women in Management Review*, 1999). Unfortunately, some of these efforts have not made much difference or have not had staying power (Bailyn, 1994). More promising are attempts to fundamentally address workplace norms that reduce both work–personal life balance and organizational performance (Bailyn, Fletcher, and Kolb, 1997; Fletcher and Bailyn, 1996; Fletcher and Rapaport, 1996).

The term family friendly is an umbrella term describing a variety of policies and programs having the goal of facilitating the ability of employees to fulfill their family responsibilities (for example, on-site daycare, flexible working hours). However, Scheibl and Dex (1998) believe that the term family-friendly is vague, lacking a concise definition. An increasing number of organizations have developed such policies and programs over the past twenty years in response to both demographic changes in the workforce and competitive pressures to attract and retain quality staff.

Thompson, Thomas, and Maier (1992) note that the most popular family-responsive programs and policies fall into four major categories: (1) dependent care; (2) parental leave programs; (3) spouse relocation and job locator programs; and (4) alternative work schedules (for example, flexible work hours, job sharing, part-time work, and reduced workload arrangements).

It is believed that the provision of such programs will have benefits for both employees and employing firms. Unfortunately, relatively little research has examined this belief (Kossek and Ozeki, 1998). Most evaluations are anecdotal; the more substantial research studies present mixed findings (Gonyea and Googins, 1992; Lobel, 1999).

## ■  Do work–family programs and policies work?  ■

Rosin and Korabik (2001) found that it is satisfaction with family-friendly policies rather than mere access to or utilization of them that produces a reduction in work–family conflict and positive work and personal outcomes. It is critical that these policies and programs meet employee needs (that is, they must work), and are implemented in a supportive environment, if companies are to benefit from the development of such initiatives. Otherwise, family-friendly policies and programs will be underutilized and not achieve their objectives.

Thus the presence of these policies and programs does not guarantee that they will be used or will work effectively. Finkel, Oswang, and She (1994) found that 77 percent of women faculty thought that taking a maternity leave would have negative career consequences, and only 30 percent who gave birth took the full leave provided by their universities. Others (Hammonds, 1997; Perlow, 1995; Schwartz, 1995) have found that similar concerns exist among various groups of women employees. And these concerns are warranted. Judiesch and Lyness (2000) found that taking a family leave was negatively associated with subsequent promotions and salary increases.

Perlow (1997) has shown how the way work gets done in organizations (individual heroics) and the way work is rewarded perpetuate crises and continuous interruptions while discouraging cooperation. These policies reduce organizational productivity and the quality of people's lives outside of work. Working with a group of employees, she helped them develop times during the work week which would be quiet times (no interruptions) and times during the week which would be interaction times.

Thompson, Thomas, and Maier (1992) identify four barriers to the successful implementation of work–family programs. These were: (1) prevailing assumptions about gender roles and their relation to work and family, primarily the masculinization of work and the feminization of the family; (2) the lack of consensus and national leadership on national policy regarding work–family issues; (3) the difficulty of managing flexibility; and (4) the clash of work–family programs and company cultures.

Thompson and Beauvais (2000) noted six barriers to implementing work–life programs in organizations: (1) ingrained cultural assumptions and values regarding work and non-work domains; (2) structural difficulties in implementing programs; (3) lack of support from managers and supervisors; (4) the perception that family issues are women's issues; (5) maintaining equity among all employees; and (6) lack of evaluation data on work–life programs. Thompson and Beauvais (2000) believe that the values and assumptions in the culture about work and non-work domains are the most significant.

## ■ Clashes of corporate culture and corporate policies ■

Thompson and Beauvais (2000) report the results of an survey by RHI Managerial Resources of 1,400 chief financial officers on the importance of organizational support in helping employees balance work and other aspects of their lives. They found that 55 percent said this was "very important" and 39 percent said it was "somewhat important" (p. 172). The most frequently offered benefit was flexible hours (45 percent said they offered it), followed by part-time work (40 percent) job sharing (27 percent) and telecommuting (13 percent). But offering a variety of work–family programs does not guarantee that a company will be seen as family friendly by its employees. A key factor is whether the company's informal culture supports work–family balance (Smith, 1992).

A company may develop a wide range of innovative work–family programs only to have them resisted by line managers. Managers may continue to hold traditional views on what is important to business success (Bowen, 1998). The corporate culture can thwart the use of particular programs. Some corporate values work against the use of flexibility. Employees may not use particular programs because of the potential impact they believe using them will have on their careers.

Unfortunately, the most commonly used work–family programs do nothing to challenge the underlying structure of organizations or the culture that supports the masculinization of work. Instead, these programs blend into existing structures and organizational values.

What is needed? At a minimum, organizations need to look at their corporate culture, the norms that define commitment, success, and appropriate behaviors (Friedman and Johnson, 1996). Top-management support is critical in this regard.

Although there has been considerable writing on specific work–family policies and programs, and their effects, little attention has been devoted to the overall climate (for example, cultural values) of organizational work–family support. The phrase family friendly has been used to include the climate or culture notion. Jahn, Thompson, and Kopelman (2000) report the results of a study of perceived organizational family support (POFS) involving 310 employees from 96 organizations. They advocate a more subjective approach based on employee perceptions of organizational support for balancing work and family. They do so because policies and practices purported by a firm may not reflect reality. They distinguish between organization family support and perceived organizational family support. The former encompasses all the policies and programs offered by an organization; the latter is the employee's perception of the assistance available from the organization in terms of instrumental support, informational support, and emotional support. Jahn et al. (2000) colleagues found significant positive relationships between scores on the POFS and two more objective measures of organizational support (or family friendliness). (Interestingly, as predicted, POFS scores were independent of measures of lateness and absenteeism). They also found evidence of high interrater agreement (people working for the same firm tended to report similar POFS scores).

Thompson and Beauvais (2000) suggest that we can discover how barriers to successful implementation of work–life programs have been overcome by studying companies known for their successful work–life policies and programs. The offer three common themes of successful company efforts: (1) work–life integration is considered a strategic initiative of the business (a bottom line issue); (2) research is conducted on the behavioral and organizational effects of work–life policies and programs; and (3) cultural assumptions about the link between work and other life domains are examined and changed.

Lyness, Thompson, Francesco, and Judiesch (1999) examined individual and organizational factors associated with organizational commitment and planned timing of maternity leaves and return to work after childbirth in a sample of 86 pregnant women. Women who perceived supportive work–family cultures were more committed to their organizations and planned to return more quickly after childbirth than women who perceived less supportive cultures.

Thompson, Beauvais, and Lyness (1999) considered work–family culture as "the shared assumptions, beliefs and values regarding the extent to which an organization supports and values the integration of employee's work and family lives." They proposed three dimensions of work–family culture: (1) managerial support for work–family balance; (2) fewer negative career consequences associated with using work–family benefits; and (3) fewer organizational time demands that might interfere with family responsibilities. They found that employee's perceptions of a supportive organizational work–family culture were positively related to affective commitment and negatively related to intention to quit.

Thompson, Beauvais, and Lyness (1999) also observed that employees were more likely to use work–family programs when they perceived a more supportive work–family culture. In addition, experiencing a more supportive work–family culture was related to greater organizational commitment, lower intentions to quit, and less work–family conflict.

Galinsky, Bond, and Friedman (1996), in a national study of about 3,000 employees, found that individuals reported less conflict and stress, and developed better coping strategies, when their supervisors and workplace cultures were supportive. These employees also were more committed to their employers, had greater job satisfaction, and were more willing to work harder to help their firms succeed. The way the policies and programs were implemented and managed by line mangers and given credibility by the organization's culture seemed to be more important than the actual policies *per se*. They conclude that to get bottom-line business results from work–life policies and programs, both corporate cultural values and mangers' attitudes toward these policies and programs (and work–life integration more broadly) must be taken into account.

Kolb and Merrill-Sands (1999) describe collaborative action research projects with organizations having a dual aim – promoting gender equity and increasing organizational effectiveness. Running through these are the connections between work and family life. Policies and programs exist in many workplaces that keep people accommodated, but do not integrate their work and family lives. Family are accommodated (on-site child care) or individuals accommodated (part-time work). These policies and programs failed to question work policies and organizational cultures that made using these family-friendly policies and programs problematic. Kolb and Merrill-Sands believe that it is critical to focus on work practices and organizational cultures by challenging the assumptions (values) on which they are based and making efforts to change these if real progress is to be made.

They ask questions such as the following: "To what degree do informal work practices and cultural assumptions reinforce certain work processes and outputs and narrow definitions of what it means to be a committed and competent worker?", and "How do current work practices make it difficult for people to integrate their work and personal lives and what repercussions does this have for women and men in the workplace and in the family?" The goal of their approach is to have people identify and question these cultural assumptions and develop a collaborative strategy to deal with the dysfunctional aspects of these cultural assumptions. There really is a connection between how a firm deals with gender and work–personal life issues and how effective it is.

## NEW RESEARCH FINDINGS

Two recent research studies were conducted to examine the role of organizational culture on work and family issues, and the usefulness of work–family policies and programs.

### ■ Organizational values and work–personal life balance ■

This research project examined the relationship of managers' perceptions of organizational values supporting a balanced commitment to work and personal life, and their work experiences, work and life satisfactions, and levels of psychological well-being. The general hypothesis underlying the study would be that managers reporting organizational values conducive to a balanced commitment to work and personal life would be more satisfied and healthier. It is not clear, however, how values supporting work–personal life balance would influence other work experiences (for example, future career prospects, job involvement).

Questionnaires were mailed to about 1,000 male and 1,000 female MBA graduates of a single university in Canada in late 1996. Names were randomly selected from a listing of graduates from 1970 to 1994. Responses were received from 591 individuals, a response rate of about 35 percent when questionnaires that were returned because the respondent had moved were excluded. The sample became 530 when individuals who indicated they were no longer working full time were excluded.

A fairly wide range of response was present on most demographic items. Respondent ages ranged from under 35 to over 50, with about half falling between 36 and 45. Almost 80 percent of respondents were married and 70 percent had children. MBA degrees were obtained over a range of years, most (almost 60 percent) before 1985. Almost 40 percent had also achieved one or more professional designations (CA, CFA, etc.). Almost one-third worked 46 to 50 hours per week. About half had incomes between $50,000 and $100,000 (Canadian $). About 80 percent placed themselves into middle- or senior-management levels. Almost three-quarters had been with their present employers ten years or less and in their present jobs five years or less. Employing organizations ranged in size from 1 to 85,000 with about 33 percent in firms of less than 100 employees. The sample contained slightly more men ($N = 278$) than women ($N = 252$).

Organizational values encouraging work–personal life balance or imbalance were measured by scales proposed by Kofodimos (1995). Organizational values encouraging balance was measured by nine items ($\propto = 0.86$) (for example, Setting limits on hours spent at work). Organizational values supporting imbalance ($\propto = 0.83$) was measured by eight items (for example, Traveling to and from work destinations on weekends). Respondents indicated how positively valued each item was in their organization or represented desired qualities in managers (1 = very negatively valued, 3 = neither positively or negatively valued, 5 = very positively valued). A total balance score was obtained by combining both scales, reversing the imbalance scores.

## Work experiences

Four work experiences, measured by single items and multiple items, were included.

**Hours worked.** was assessed by a single item. Respondents indicated the number of hours they worked in a typical week.

**Extra hours worked.** ($\propto = 0.68$) was measured by six items. Respondents indicated how frequently they did each item (for example, go to work early).

**Job involvement.** ($\propto = 0.81$) was measured by an eight-item (for example, "I am deeply committed to my job") scale developed by Spence and Robbins (1992).

***Job stress.*** ($\propto$ = 0.89) was measured by nine items (for example, "Sometimes I feel like my work is going to overwhelm me") developed by Spence and Robbins (1992).

## Work satisfactions

Four aspects of work satisfaction were assessed.

***Job satisfaction.*** was measured by a seven-item scale ($\propto$ = 0.79) developed by Kofodimos (1995). An item was "I feel challenged by my work."

***Career satisfaction.*** was measured by a five-item scale ($\propto$ = 0.91) developed by Greenhaus, Parasuraman, and Wormley (1990). One item was "I am satisfied with the success I have achieved in my career."

***Career prospects.*** was measured by a three-item scale ($\propto$ = 0.66) developed by Greenhaus, Parasuraman, and Wormley (1990). An item was "I expect to advance in my career to senior levels of management."

***Intent to quit.*** ($\propto$ = 0.83) was measured by two items (for example, "Are you currently looking for a different job in a different organization?") This scale had been used previously by Burke (1991).

## Non-work satisfactions

Three measures of satisfaction in non-work domains were used.

***Family satisfaction.*** was measured by a seven-item scale ($\propto$ = 0.89) developed by Kofodimos (1995). One item was "I have a good relationship with my family members."

***Friends satisfaction.*** was measured by three items ($\propto$ = 0.85) developed by Kofodimos (1995). An item was "Friends and I do enjoyable things together."

***Community satisfaction.*** was measured by four items ($\propto$ = 0.80), also developed by Kofodimos (1995). A sample item was "I contribute and give back to my community."

## Psychological well-being

Three dimensions of health and well-being were measured.

***Psychosomatic symptoms.*** was measured by 19 items ($\propto$ = 0.84) developed by Quinn and Shepard (1974). Respondents indicated how often they experienced each physical condition (for example, headaches) in the past year.

**Physical well-being.** was measured by five items ($\propto$ = 0.72) developed by Kofodimos (1995). One item was "I participate in a regular exercise program."

**Emotional well-being.** was measured by six items ($\propto$ = 0.77) developed by Kofodinos (1995). An item was "I actively seek to understand and improve my emotional well-being."

Let us now consider some of the results.

## Organizational values

Respondents indicated a mean of 26.5, SD = 5.73 (N = 497) on the nine-item Balance scale, the mean item value of 2.9 falling at the "Neither agree nor disagree" point (3.0). The mean obtained on the eight-item Imbalance scale was 29.4, SD = 4.52 (N = 496), with an item mean of 3.7 which approached "Somewhat agree" (4.0). The mean on the Total Balance scale was 45.1, SD = 9.18 (N = 492) with an item mean of 2.6, falling between the "Somewhat disagree" (2) and "Neither agree or disagree" label (4). These data, in summary, showed that managers described their organizations as not particularly supportive of work–personal life balance. Scores on the Balance and Imbalance scales, as expected, were significantly and negatively correlated ($r = -0.61$, $p < 0.001$).

## Sex differences

As hypothesized, females score significantly lower on balance values and significantly higher on imbalance values. These differences were no longer statistically significant however when four demographic characteristics (age, marital status, number of children, and year of MBA) were controlled. These data showed that although women reported less organizational support for work–personal life balance than did men, when statistical controls of demographic characteristics likely to influence work–personal life balance were introduced, women and men indicated similar levels of support for work–personal life balance. Organizational support for both women and men was only moderate.

## Organizational values, work experiences and satisfactions

Table 17.1 presents the correlations between the measure of organizational values supporting work–family balance and measures of work experiences, work and life satisfactions, and psychological well-being for the samples of managerial and professional women and men. It should be noted that both samples were relatively large and many of the measures of work experiences, work and extra-work satisfactions and psychological well-being were themselves positively and significantly intercorrelated.

Women indicating organizational values more supportive of balance also reported less job stress; greater satisfaction with their jobs, careers, and family; less intent to quit;

**Table 17.1**  Organizational values, job experiences, and satisfactions

| Job experiences | Women Organizational values[a] | Men Organizational values[b] |
|---|---|---|
| Hours worked | 0.06 | −0.23*** |
| Extra-hours worked | −0.04 | −0.25*** |
| Job involvement | 0.04 | −0.02 |
| Job stress | −0.30*** | −0.38*** |
| Work satisfactions | | |
| Career satisfaction | 0.24*** | 0.16*** |
| Career prospects | 0.10 | 0.18** |
| Job satisfaction | 0.27*** | 0.32*** |
| Intent to quit | −0.20** | 0.28*** |
| Non-work satisfactions | | |
| Family satisfaction | 0.14* | 0.06 |
| Friends satisfaction | 0.05 | 0.18* |
| Community satisfaction | 0.02 | 0.13* |
| Psychological well-being | | |
| Psychosomatic symptoms | −0.28*** | −0.31*** |
| Emotional health | 0.14* | 0.20** |
| Physical health | 0.04 | 0.24*** |

[a]  *Ns range from 201 to 223.*
[b]  *Ns range from 257 to 265.*
*** $p < 0.001$.
** $p < 0.01$.
* $p < 0.05$.

fewer psychosomatic symptoms; and higher levels of emotional well-being. Among these women, organizational support and work–personal life balance values had no relationship with hours worked; extra-hours worked; job involvement; future career prospects; levels of satisfaction with friends and community involvement; and physical well-being (positive lifestyle behaviors).

Men indicating organizational values more supportive of work–personal life balance also reported working fewer hours per week and fewer extra hours; less job stress; greater satisfaction with their jobs, careers and career prospects; less intent to quit; greater satisfaction with friends and community; fewer psychosomatic symptoms; more positive lifestyle behaviors; and higher levels of emotional well-being. Among these men, organizational values supporting balance had no relationship with levels of job involvement and family satisfaction.

## Regression analyses

The data presented in Table 17.1 showed a greater number of statistically significant correlations between the measure of organizational values supporting work–personal life balance and the other measures used in the study for men than for women. It was

**Table 17.2**   Regression analyses

| Outcomes – Work and well-being | | | |
| --- | --- | --- | --- |
| Females (N = 187) | R | R² | Adj.R² |
| Psychosomatic symptoms (–0.25) | 0.29 | 0.08 | 0.08 |
| Intent to quit (0.18) | 0.34 | 0.12 | 0.11 |
| Males (N = 229) | | | |
| Job satisfaction (0.22) | 0.32 | 0.10 | 0.10 |
| Psychosomatic symptoms (–0.17) | 0.36 | 0.13 | 0.12 |
| Intent to quit (0.16) | 0.38 | 0.15 | 0.16 |

| Outcomes – Job experiences | | | |
| --- | --- | --- | --- |
| Females (N = 208) | | | |
| Job stress (0.32) | 0.32 | 0.10 | 0.10 |
| Males (N = 229) | | | |
| Job stress (0.18) | 0.40 | 0.16 | 0.16 |
| Joy in work (–0.28) | 0.44 | 0.20 | 0.19 |
| Hours worked (–0.20) | 0.49 | 0.24 | 0.23 |
| Feeling driven to work (0.20) | 0.51 | 0.26 | 0.25 |

unlikely that this pattern resulted from the larger sample size of the men's versus the women's groups. These findings suggested that men appeared to benefit more (that is, a greater number of statistically significant correlations) from organizational values supporting work–personal life balance.

Regression analyses were undertaken to examine this possibility further. Multiple regression analysis takes into account the modest intercorrelations among the predictors in identifying those that have significant and independent relationships with a given criterion measure.

Table 17.2 shows the results of these analyses. In the top half of this table, the ten indicators of work and extra-work satisfaction and psychological well-being were regressed on the organizational values measure separately for women and men. In the bottom half of the table, six measures of job experiences were regressed on the organizational values measure separately from women and men.

The regression findings showed a similar pattern for women and men when work and well-being outcomes were regressed on the organizational values measure (top half of table 17.2). Women reporting organizational values supportive of work–personal life balance also indicated lower levels of psychosomatic symptoms and less intention to quit. Men reporting organizational values supportive of work–personal life balance indicated greater job satisfaction in addition to lower levels of psychosomatic symptoms and less intention to quit. Similar levels of variance were accounted for in both analyses.

A somewhat different pattern of findings was observed for women and men when the job experiences measures were regressed on the organizational values measure (bottom half of table 17.2). Women reporting values more supportive of work–personal life balance also indicated less job stress. Men reporting values more supportive of work–personal life balance also indicated less job stress; men reporting values more supportive of work–personal life balance also indicated more joy in work, working fewer hours per week, and less feeling driven to work. The job experiences explained more variance on the organizational values measure for men than women (Adj. $R^2$s = 0.25 and 0.10, respectively).

The findings reported here support two conclusions, one expected and one unexpected. First, women and men indicate benefits in working in organizations having values supportive of work–personal life balance. This conclusion is consistent with other writing (Friedman and Greenhaus, 2000). Second, men appeared to benefit more from organizational values supportive of work–personal life balance than did women (tables 17.1 and 17.2). This finding was unexpected.

Why should men benefit more than women from organizational values supportive of work–personal life balance? Several speculations are possible. Men in the sample worked more hours per week and were more work involved than were women. More men than women were married or living with a partner, and more men had children. Men reported higher levels of organizational support for work–personal life balance than did women. Women still shoulder greater responsibility than men for "second shift" duties such that the combination of work and extra-work demands might be a greater burden for women than for men. Future research is needed to examine these, and other, possible explanations.

These results may also be consistent with findings from research examining models of career advancement for women and for men. Several of these studies (for example, Tharenou, Latimer, and Conroy, 1994; Stroh, Brett, and Reilly, 1992) have found that men more than women show greater career advancement benefits from identical characteristics (for example, education) and experiences (job tenure, mobility). Our findings may show that an organizational characteristic, believed to be very important for women (personal life friendliness), may in fact be of greater benefit to men than women.

## ■ Organizational values, performance and family friendliness ■

There has been considerable interest shown in the past decade in the influence of organizational culture, particularly cultural values, on work performance, productivity, learning and adaptability, and ultimately, organizational effectiveness (Deal and Kennedy, 1982; Peters, 1987; Schein, 1992). An increasing number of studies, both qualitative and quantitative, have examined the ways in which cultural values influence important work outcomes (Denison, 1990; Kotter and Heskett, 1992; Schneider, 1990). And although it has been suggested that cultural values have an influence on the work experiences of women in organizations (Bailyn, 1994; Schwartz, 1992; Konrad, 1990), little research has been devoted to this topic.

The absence of research findings here may be important since many firms believe that being family friendly conflicts with being productive (Fierman, 1994). This raises the question of whether cultural values that support productivity and quality of service are different from, and at odds with, cultural values that support a level playing field and family friendliness.

The present study examined the relationship between existing values in a professional services firm and a range of level playing field and family friendly measures. There has generally been very little effort to study management and organizational processes in professional service organizations. This has resulted, in part, from the priority attached to technical skills and professional expertise in explaining the success of such firms. It is only fairly recently that issues of leadership and management, teamwork, the utilization and development of talents of an increasingly diverse workforce (Schwartz, 1992), mission, and values have been considered.

The following general questions were considered. Are cultural values related to family friendliness, and in what way? Are cultural values related to level playing field measures, and in what way? Do the same cultural values predict both family friendliness and the presence of a level playing field?

This study represents a secondary analysis of attitude survey data collected within a single large professional services firm. The firm had about 2,150 employees at the time of the survey. About three-quarters were university graduates, many having also obtained professional designations in their areas of special expertise. The survey was distributed via internal organization mail. It was accompanied by a cover letter explaining the purposes of the survey and guaranteeing anonymity. Conducting the study within a single organization controls context variables such as industry structure, technology, policies, and procedures. The downside of such a strategy is that it limits the generalizability of the results to similar kinds of organizations in similar industries.

The sample ($N = 1,608$) represented a 70 percent response rate. There were slightly more women than men, but men were at significantly higher organizational levels than were women. About 60 percent of respondents were married and about 40 percent of respondents had children. About 65 percent of the respondents had been with the firm six years or less and about 40 percent were under 30 years of age. Four organizational levels were present: partners, managers, professional field staff, and clerical/support staff.

## Cultural values

Respondents indicated both the importance of and the current existence of ten values in the organization (1 = not at all, 5 = to a great extent). These items included: people in this organization are dedicated to outstanding service to clients; maintain the highest standards of professionalism; will not compromise integrity, objectivity or independence; have respect for each other; and are committed to making the firm a better place.

## Family friendliness measures

Three features of a family-friendly environment were assessed.

***Supportive work–family policies.*** was measured by a three-item scale ($\propto = 61$). Respondents indicated the extent (1 = not at all, 5 = to a great extent) that the firm's current work and family policies recognize the flexibility you need to balance work and personal life.

***Sacrifice career.*** was measured by a two-item scale ($\propto = 0.35$). Respondents indicated the extent ($1$ = not at all, $5$ = to a great extent) they believed that you needed to sacrifice career advancement to raise a family.

***Work–Family conflict.*** was measured by a single item. How often do you face a conflict between your work and your family/personal responsibilities? ($1$ = never, $3$ = about once a month, $5$ = almost every day).

## Level playing field measures

Five aspects of a level playing field were considered.

***Sexual harassment.*** was measured by the following question: Have you been subject to unwelcome behavior that you regard as sexual harassment a) by a partner, b) by a supervisor, c) by a co-worker, d) by a client? Responses were made on a three-point scale ($1$ = yes, more than once; $2$ = yes, once; $3$ = no).

***Biased decisions.*** was measured by a five-item scale ($\propto = 0.84$). Do you believe that decisions in the following matters in the firm are subject to bias? ($1$ = yes, $2$ = no). These were: job assignments, tours of duty, promotions, compensation and terminations.

***Experienced bias.*** Respondents were asked whether they had been subject to treatment at the firm that they believed demonstrated a bias against them. Three response alternatives were provided: (1) yes, more than once, (2) yes, once, and (3) no.

***Due process.*** Three questions ($\propto = 0.77$) enquired into the perception of due process and organizational action following harassment. If you were harassed at the organization is there someone within the firm you would feel comfortable reporting it to? If you were treated in a biased manner, is there someone within the firm you would feel comfortable reporting it to? If you were to report being harassed or treated in a biased manner, are you confident appropriate action would be taken? Respondents indicated yes (1) or no (2) to each question.

***Firm's commitment to fair treatment.*** was measured by a single item. To what extent do you consider that the firm is committed to the fair treatment of all staff, regardless of gender, race, disability, etc? ($1$ = not at all, $5$ = to a great extent).

## Importance, presence and gaps in cultural values

Table 17.3 shows, for each of the ten cultural values, their rated importance, the extent to which each was observed in the firm, and the difference between the two ratings.

**Table 17.3**   Importance versus actual values

| Values | Importance of Values | | | Actual Values | | | Difference | Rank |
|---|---|---|---|---|---|---|---|---|
| | Mean | SD | N | Mean | SD | N | | |
| Dedicated to outstanding service to clients | 4.7 | 0.53 | 1,598 | 4.0 | 0.79 | 1,564 | 0.7 | 8 |
| High value on staff development | 4.6 | 0.60 | 1,599 | 3.4 | 0.90 | 1,566 | 1.2 | 4 |
| Respect for each other | 4.8 | 0.52 | 1,595 | 3.4 | 0.91 | 1,569 | 1.4 | 2 |
| Not compromise integrity | 4.7 | 0.59 | 1,570 | 3.9 | 0.87 | 1,498 | 0.8 | 7 |
| Work as team for clients | 4.6 | 0.61 | 1,594 | 3.5 | 0.93 | 1,541 | 1.1 | 5 |
| Dedicated to continuous improvement | 4.5 | 0.60 | 1,590 | 3.5 | 0.84 | 1,540 | 1.0 | 6 |
| Balance responsibilities to selves, families | 4.6 | 0.67 | 1,587 | 3.0 | 1.00 | 1,516 | 1.6 | 1 |
| Support worldwide organization | 3.5 | 1.00 | 1,526 | 3.4 | 0.87 | 1,217 | 0.1 | 10 |
| High standards of professionalism | 4.6 | 0.56 | 1,588 | 4.0 | 0.78 | 1,552 | 0.6 | 1 |
| Committed to making firm better | 4.6 | 0.63 | 1,594 | 3.3 | 0.90 | 1,535 | 1.3 | 3 |

The most prevalent cultural values were: dedicated to outstanding service to clients; high standards of professionalism; and will not compromise integrity. The least prevalent cultural values were: balancing responsibilities to themselves, families, communities and the firm; committed to making the firm a better place; having respect for each other; supporting the worldwide organization; and placing a high value on staff development.

For each of the ten organizational values the presence in the firm was always lower than their rated importance, the average difference being 1.0, a full scale point on the five-point scale. The largest gaps existed on balance responsibilities toward families (1.6); respect for each other (1.4); committed to making firm better (1.3); high value for staff development (1.2); work as a team for clients (1.1); and dedicated to continuous improvement (1.0).

Three conclusions follow from these data. First, the organizational values in practice in this firm generally fell short when compared to their espoused importance. Second, the largest discrepancies were directly or indirectly related to work–family issues (for example, balance, respect). Third, discrepancies in these organizational values were likely to reduce organizational performance as well (for example, teamwork; continuous improvement; staff development).

## Regression analyses

Hierarchical regression analyses were undertaken in which measures of family friendliness and level playing field were regressed, one at a time, on the ten organizational values. The results of these regressions are shown in table 17.4. The table shows the amount of explained variance ($R^2$); increases in explained variance with the addition of other significant predictors ($\Delta R^2$); levels of significance of explained variance and increments in explained variance; and the significance of relationships between predictors and criterion variables ($\beta$).

**Table 17.4**  Organizational values, family friendliness, and a level playing field

|  | $R^2$ | $\Delta R^2$ | $P$ |
|---|---|---|---|
| Family Friendliness | | | |
| Supportive Work–Family policies ($N$ = 1,041) | | | |
|     Balanced responsibilities (0.47) | 0.26 | 0.26 | 0.001 |
|     Dedicated to outstanding service (0.09) | 0.27 | 0.01 | 0.001 |
|     Have respect for each other (0.06) | 0.27 | 0.00 | 0.01 |
| Sacrifice Career ($N$ = 1,009) | | | |
|     Balanced responsibilities (−0.26) | 0.09 | 0.09 | 0.001 |
|     Committed to making firm a better place (−0.13) | 0.10 | 0.01 | 0.001 |
|     Dedicated to continuous improvement (0.12) | 0.10 | 0.00 | 0.05 |
|     Work as a team for clients (−0.08) | 0.11 | 0.00 | 0.05 |
| Work–Family Conflict ($N$ = 1,160) | | | |
|     Balanced responsibilities (−0.37) | 0.15 | 0.15 | 0.001 |
|     Dedicated to continuous improvement (−0.10) | 0.15 | 0.00 | 0.01 |
|     Will not compromise integrity (0.08) | 0.16 | 0.00 | 0.01 |
| Level Playing Field | | | |
| Sexual Harassment ($N$ = 1,113) | | | |
|     Have respect for each other (0.14) | 0.03 | 0.03 | 0.001 |
|     Will not compromise integrity (0.10) | 0.04 | 0.01 | 0.01 |
| Biased Decisions ($N$ = 751) | | | |
|     Have respect for each other (0.18) | 0.07 | 0.07 | 0.001 |
|     Will not compromise integrity (0.11) | 0.08 | 0.01 | 0.01 |
|     Making the firm a better place (0.12) | 0.08 | 0.01 | 0.05 |
|     Dedicated to continuous improvement (−0.12) | 0.09 | 0.01 | 0.05 |
|     High value on staff development (0.11) | 0.10 | 0.01 | 0.05 |
|     Support the worldwide organizations (−0.08) | 0.10 | 0.00 | 0.05 |
| Due Process ($N$ = 769) | | | |
|     Have respect for each other (−0.22) | 0.12 | 0.12 | 0.001 |
|     Making the firm a better place (−0.15) | 0.15 | 0.03 | 0.001 |
|     High value on staff development (−0.11) | 0.16 | 0.01 | 0.01 |
|     Support worldwide organization (0.10) | 0.17 | 0.01 | 0.05 |
|     Balanced responsibilities (−0.10) | 0.17 | 0.01 | 0.05 |
| Personal Bias ($N$ = 1,106) | | | |
|     Have respect for each other (0.21) | 0.07 | 0.07 | 0.001 |
|     High value on staff development (0.12) | 0.08 | 0.01 | 0.01 |
|     Will not compromise integrity (0.08) | 0.08 | 0.00 | 0.05 |
|     Dedicated to continuous improvement (−0.08) | 0.09 | 0.00 | 0.05 |
| Firm Committed to Fair Treatment ($N$ = 1,148) | | | |
|     Making the firm a better place (0.18) | 0.11 | 0.11 | 0.001 |
|     Have respect for each other (0.17) | 0.15 | 0.04 | 0.001 |
|     Will not compromise integrity (0.11) | 0.16 | 0.01 | 0.001 |
|     High value on staff development (0.06) | 0.16 | 0.00 | 0.05 |

The following comments are offered in summary. First, a considerable number of organizational values, ranging from two to six, had significant and independent relationships with the criterion measures. On average, four organizational values showed such relationships. These ranged from two significant predictors for Sexual Harassment and six significant predictors for Biased Decisions.

Second, these predictors accounted for modest levels of explained variance ($R^2$) in the criterion measures, ranging from a low of 0.04 for Sexual Harassment to a high of 0.27 for Supportive Work–Family policies.

Third, three of the organizational values (dedicated to continuous improvement; support for the worldwide organization; and not willing to compromise integrity) had negative consequences for family friendliness and level playing field concerns. That is, women and men reporting higher levels of these organizational values also described their work setting as less family friendly and more biased.

Fourth, although nine of the ten organizational values had at least one significant and independent relationship with the criterion variables (maintaining the highest standards of professionalism did not), a few had a disproportionate number of significant relationships with the criterion measures. Thus, respect for each other had significant relationships with six of the eight criterion measures. This was followed by: not compromising integrity objectivity, or independence (five of eight); balanced responsibilities to themselves, their families, their communities as well as to the firm (four of eight); a high value on staff development (four of eight); making the firm a better place (four of eight); and dedication to continuous improvement (four of eight).

Fifth, four of the six most significant organizational values (respect; staff development; a better place; balance) emphasize human resources – personal balance, respect, development – rather than technical concerns. In addition, these particular organizational values were ones that were less commonly observed. That is, these four organizational values appeared in the bottom five rankings (see table 17.3).

The findings obtained in this single large professional services firm reveal an association between particular organizational values present in the firm and measures of both family friendliness and women friendliness (table 17.4). Not surprisingly, these particular values were human resource oriented as opposed to being technical or performance driven. In fact, particular organizational values were associated with less women and family friendliness. Fierman (1994) suggests that companies may be becoming less family friendly because they need greater contributions from their employees. Bailyn (1994) raises the same concerns: that is, values associated with high performance, high involvement workplaces, while exciting and associated with both personal and career development, may make it more difficult for employees to achieve (or even want) balance in their work lives. This raises the possibility that, for some firms, the values that are being espoused may be creating conflict for particular employees.

The most important organizational value related to level playing field measures was respect for each other. It is useful to begin to define what this value entails more specifically. The following come to mind. It includes supporting and encouraging all staff; acknowledging staff and their value; treating staff as equals; spending time with staff; listening to staff; getting to know staff; appreciating and valuing staff; and responding to the unique needs of staff.

The most important organizational value related to family friendliness was the endorsement of balance. This value, while significant to staff, was not being realized in the firm for reasons suggested by Bailyn (1994) and Fierman (1994): that is, this firm required increasing levels of performance in a more competitive marketplace, requirements that may be at odds with the realization of balance. The firm had created work–family policies to support greater balance, but these had been embraced half-heartedly and were not having the desired effect. Balance involves the provision of flexibility, the recognition and rewarding of performance not face-time (putting in long hours), and acknowledging legitimate needs of staff to nourish themselves, their families and their communities.

An interesting issue is whether organizational values related to family friendliness and the presence of a level playing field were different from, and perhaps opposed to, organizational values more supportive of a business or a bottom-line orientation.

We examined these relationships in this firm, using the same measure of organizational values but different outcomes indicators (Burke, 1997). For these analyses, measures of basic performance indicators and work outcomes were used. They included: employee perceptions of the firm's quality of services and products compared to its competitors; barriers to service observed in the firm; support for service excellence; job satisfaction; and intention to quit. The results showed that essentially the same organizational values predicted both work and organizational outcomes (for example, performance) *and* family-friendliness, and presence of a level playing field. It does not appear to be an either/or situation; that is, particular organizational values were antecedents of both firm effectiveness and family and women friendliness. It should be remembered, however, that some organizational values had a negative relationship with family friendliness and presence of a level playing field, as well as with one or more work outcomes. Thus a sensitive balancing act among organizational values may be necessary under the best of circumstances. Considerably more research must be undertaken to shed light on these conclusions and their implications.

Regression analysis were also undertaken in which the ten discrepancies in organizational values were regressed on both family-friendly measures and indicators of organizational performance. These results are presented in table 17.5. The following comments are offered in summary. First, balanced responsibilities had a significant and independent relationship with each of the four family-friendly policies and work–family conflict measures. In all cases, respondents indicating smaller discrepancies on this value also reported more favorable perceptions of the work–family policies (opportunities; not having to sacrifice one's career; less work–family conflict; less sexual harassment). Second, gap in balanced responsibilities also had significant and independent relationships with the three organizational performance measures (job satisfaction; office morale; intent to quit). Respondents indicating larger discrepancies in balance to self and family also reported less job satisfaction, greater intent to quit, and lower office morale.

## Conclusions

What can organizations do to develop such work–personal life balance values? The most common approach is to create workplace policies that promote them. Unfortunately, accumulating evidence suggests that the presence of such policies has produced at best inconsistent benefits (Bailyn, 1994). In some cases such policies have brought about value, attitude, and behavior changes; in other cases, such policies have existed only on paper. These latter organizations have only paid token lip service to the existence of such policies (Hochschild, 1997).

**Table 17.5**  Multiple regression – value differences

|  | $R^2$ | $\Delta R^2$ | $P$ |
|---|---|---|---|
| Family friendliness |  |  |  |
| Supportive Work–Family policies ($N$ = 1,028) |  |  |  |
|   Balanced responsibilities | 0.18 | 0.18 | 0.001 |
|   Have respect for each other | 0.20 | 0.02 | 0.001 |
| Sacrifice Career ($N$ = 995) |  |  |  |
|   Balanced responsibilities (0.22) | 0.07 | 0.07 | 0.001 |
|   Make firm a better place (0.11) | 0.07 | 0.01 | 0.01 |
|   Support worldwide organization (−0.10) | 0.08 | 0.01 | 0.01 |
| Work–Family Conflict ($N$ = 1,142) |  |  |  |
|   Balanced Responsibilities (0.35) | 0.12 | 0.12 | 0.001 |
| Sexual Harassment ($N$ = 1,096) |  |  |  |
|   Have respect for each other (−0.14) | 0.04 | 0.04 | 0.001 |
|   Maintain highest standards of professionalism (−0.07) | 0.05 | 0.01 | 0.01 |
|   Balanced responsibilities (−0.08) | 0.05 | 0.00 | 0.05 |
|   Support worldwide organization (−0.06) | 0.06 | 0.00 | 0.05 |
| Organizational Performance |  |  |  |
| Job Satisfaction ($N$ = 1,063) |  |  |  |
|   Respect for each other (−0.19) | 0.11 | 0.11 | 0.001 |
|   High value on staff development (−0.18) | 0.15 | 0.04 | 0.001 |
|   Balanced responsibilities (−0.03) | 0.16 | 0.02 | 0.001 |
|   Not compromise integrity (−0.09) | 0.17 | 0.01 | 0.001 |
|   Support worldwide organization (0.08) | 0.18 | 0.00 | 0.05 |
|   Highest standards of professionalism (−0.09) | 0.18 | 0.00 | 0.05 |
|   Work as a team for clients (0.07) | 0.19 | 0.00 | 0.05 |
| Office Morale ($N$ = 1,151) |  |  |  |
|   Respect for each other (−0.21) | 0.16 | 0.16 | 0.001 |
|   Balanced responsibility (−0.16) | 0.20 | 0.04 | 0.001 |
|   Making the world a better place (−0.15) | 0.23 | 0.03 | 0.001 |
|   High value on staff development (−0.12) | 0.24 | 0.01 | 0.001 |
|   Support the worldwide organization (0.09) | 0.24 | 0.00 | 0.01 |
|   Work as a team for clients (−0.07) | 0.25 | 0.00 | 0.05 |
| Intent to Quit ($N$ = 820) |  |  |  |
|   Balanced responsibilities (−0.19) | 0.08 | 0.08 | 0.001 |
|   High value on staff development (−0.14) | 0.11 | 0.02 | 0.001 |
|   Support the worldwide organization (0.18) | 0.13 | 0.02 | 0.001 |
|   High value on staff development (−0.15) | 0.15 | 0.02 | 0.001 |

These findings have interesting implications if borne out in other samples. It has been suggested that women who work in demanding jobs experience work–personal life concerns (Hochschild, 1989). Our data indicated that those concerns are also shared by their male colleagues. As a consequence, organizations may come under increasing pressure to be more family friendly.

The most common initiatives undertaken by organizations to address work–personal life concerns is to develop supportive policies and programs (Morrison, 1992). Unfortunately, such policies and programs often exist only on paper, and lack the support and commitment necessary to make them effective. Work and personal life concerns tend to be pitted against each other with the organization all too often, not surprisingly, giving priority to work. The more viable approach would be to link work and personal life in an integrative way. That is, satisfying work and personal life concerns simultaneously, while challenging and requiring the investment of some organizational resources may achieve work and personal life objectives (Rayman, Bailyn, Dickert, Carré, Harvey, Krim, and Read, 1999).

More recently, several researchers have begun to describe and evaluate more intensive collaborative projects with organizations interested in addressing work–personal life concerns. These projects make an explicit link between employee's personal needs (for example, family responsibilities) and business objectives with the intention of changing work practices so that both the organization and its employees benefit (Rapaport, Bailyn, Kolb, and Fletcher, 1998).

The work of Bailyn and her colleagues describes several collaborative action research projects in which researchers work jointly with companies to bring about change in the work culture and the organization of work that would facilitate work–personal life integration in a meaningful way (Bailyn, 1997; Bailyn, Fletcher, and Kolb, 1997; Fletcher and Bailyn, 1996; Fletcher and Rapaport, 1996). Other compelling evaluations of additional organizational initiatives (see Burke, 1999) show that changes in organization values and practice can be accomplished. These efforts require considerable commitment to be successful, however. The benefits to employees may be far reaching.

One of the major barriers standing in the way of meaningful workplace changes that address the work–personal life balance question is the tendency to see work and personal life (or family) as either/or concepts. That is, organizations can have a work-committed employee, a personal life or family committed employee, but not employees who are both work committed and family committed. Given this way of framing the problem it is no wonder that work–family programs are grudgingly implemented and usually fall short. Having a family continues to be a career liability for many women.

The real challenge for organizations is to identify ways that work is being undertaken that interferes with both performance and productivity goals and personal life needs. Only when personal life needs and job performance are linked, and both related to the bottom line, will lasting and significant progress be made. Examining organizational culture is a promising place to start.

## REFERENCES

Bailyn, L. (1997): The impact of corporate culture on work–family integration. In S. Parasuraman and J. H. Greenhaus (eds), *Integrating work and family: Challenges and choices for a changing world*. Westport, CT: Quorum Books.

Bailyn, L. (1994): *Breaking the mold*. New York: The Free Press.

Bailyn, L., Fletcher, J. K., and Kolb, D. (1997): Unexpected connections: Considering employee's personal lives can revitalize your business. *Sloan Management Review*, 38, 11–19.

Bowen, G. L. (1998): Efforts of leaders support in the work unit on the relationship between work spillover and family adaptation. *Journal of Family and Economics Issues*, 19, 25–52.

Burke, R. J. (1991): Early work and career experiences of female and male mangers: Reasons for optimisim? *Canadian Journal of Administrative Sciences*, 8, 220–4.

Burke, R. J. (1997): Organizational values, work–family issues and the "bottom line." *Equal Opportunities International*, 16, 34–40.

Burke, R. J. and McKeen, C. A. (1992): Women in management. In C. L. Cooper and I. T. Robertson (eds), *International Review of Industrial and Organizational Psychology*. New York: John Wiley.

Burke, R. J. and Nelson, D. L. (1998): Organizational men: masculinity and its discontents. In C. L. Cooper and I. T. Robertson (eds), *International Review of Industrial and Organizational Psychology*. New York: John Wiley.

Davidson, M. J. and Burke, R. J. (1994): *Women in management: Current research issues*. London: Paul Chapman Publishing.

Deal, T. E. and Kennedy, A. A. (1982): *Corporate cultures*. Reading, MA: Addison-Wesley.

Denison, D. (1990): *Corporate culture and organizational effectiveness*. New York: John Wiley & Sons.

*Equal Opportunties International* (1997): The sounds of shattering glass: Corporate initiatives for advancing managerial women. *Equal Opportunities International*, 16, 1–40.

Fierman, J. (1994): Are companies less family-friendly? *Fortune*, 130, 3, 64–7.

Finkel, S. K., Olswang, S., and She, N. (1994): Childbirth, tenure and promotion for women faculty. *Review of Higher Education*, 17, 259–70.

Fletcher, J. K. and Bailyn, L. (1996): Challenging the last boundary: Re-connecting work and family. In M. B. Arthur and D. M. Rousseau (eds), *Boundaryless Careers*, Oxford: Oxford University Press.

Fletcher, J. K. and Rapaport, R. (1996): Work-family linkages as a catalyst for change. In S. Lewis and J. Lewis (eds), *Rethinking employment: The Work Family Challenge*. London: Sage Publications.

Friedman, D. E. and Johnson, A. A. (1996): Moving from programs to culture change: The next stage for the corporate work/family agenda. In S. Parasuraman and J. H. Greenhaus (eds), *Integrating work and family: Challenges and choices for a changing world*, Westport, CT: Quorum Books.

Friedman, S. D. and Greenhaus, J. H. (2000): *Work and family-allies or enemies? What happens when business professionals confront life choices?* New York: Oxford University Press.

Galinsky, E., Bond, J. T., and Friedman, D. E. (1996): The role of employers in addressing the needs of employed parents. *Journal of Social Issues*, 52, 111–36.

Geiger, K. (1989): Long-held bias impedes efforts to support work/family needs. *Business Link*, 4, 4–5.

Gonyea, J. G. and Googins, B. K. (1992): Linking the worlds of work and family: Beyond the productivity trap. *Human Resource Management*, 31, 209–26.

Greenhaus, J. H. and Parasuraman, S. (1999): Research on work, family, and gender: Current studies and future directions. In G. N. Powell (ed.), *Handbook of gender and work*. Thousand Oaks, CA: Sage Publications.

Greenhaus, J. H., Parasuraman, S., and Wormley, W. (1990): Organizational experiences and career success of black and white managers. *Academy of Management Journal*, 33, 64–86.

Hammonds, K. H. (1997): Work and family. *Business Week's* second survey of family-friendly corporate policies, *Business Week*, September 15, 96–9, 102–4.

Hochschild, A. R. (1989): *The second shift*. New York: Avon.

Hochschild, A. R. (1997): *The time bind*. New York: Metropolitan Books.

Jahn, E. W., Thompson, C. A., and Kopelman, R. E. (2000): Rationale and construct validity evidence for a measure of perceived organizational family support (POFS): because purported practices may not reflect reality. *Community, Work and Family*, 3, 63–79.

Judiesch, M. K. and Lyness, K. S. (2000): Left behind? The impact of leaves of absence on managers' career success. *Academy of Management Journal*, 43, 142–57.

Kofodimos, J. (1995): *Balancing Act*. San Francisco: Jossey-Bass.

Kolb, D. M. and Merrill-Sands, D. (1999): Waiting for outcomes: Anchoring a dual agenda for change to cultural assumptions. *Women in Management Review*, 14, 194–202.

Konrad, W. (1990): Welcome to the women-friendly company. *Business Week*, August 6, 48–53.

Kossek, E. I. and Ozeki, C. (1998): Work–family conflict, policies and the job–life satisfaction relationship: A review and direction for organizational behavior-human resources research. *Journal of Applied Psychology*, 83, 139–49.

Kotter, J. P. and Heskett, J. L. (1992): *Corporate culture and performance*. New York: The Free Press.

Lobel, S. A. (1999): Impacts of diversity and work–life initiatives in organizations. In G. N. Powell (ed.), *Handbook of gender and work*, Thousand Oaks, CA: Sage Publications.

Lyness, K. S., Thompson, C. A., Francesco, A. M., and Judiesch, M. K. (1999): Work and pregnancy: Individual and organizational actors influencing organizational commitment, timing of maternity leave, and return to work. *Sex Roles*, 41, 485–508.

Morrison, A. M. (1992): *The new leaders*. San Francisco: Jossey-Bass.

Perlow, L. A. (1995): Putting the work back into work/family. *Group and Organization Management*, 20, 227–39.

Perlow, L. A. (1997): *Finding time: How corporations, individuals and families can benefit from new work practices*. Ithaca, New York: Cornell University Press.

Peters, T. (1987): *Thriving on Chaos*. New York: Alfred A. Knopf.

Powell, G. N. (1999): *Handbook of gender and work*. Thousand Oaks, CA: Sage Publications.

Quinn, R. P. and Shepard, L. J. (1974): *The 1972–73 Quality of Employment Survey*. Ann Arbor, MI: Institute for Social Research, University of Michigan.

Rapaport, R., Bailyn, L., Kolb, D., and Fletcher, J. K. (1998): *Relinking life and work: Toward a better future*. Waltham, MA: Pegasus Communications, Inc.

Rayman, P., Bailyn, L., Dickert, J., Carre, F., Harvey, M., Krim, R., and Read, R. (1999): Designing organizational solutions to integrate work and life. *Women in Management Review*, 14, 164–76.

Rodgers, F. S. and Rodgers, C. (1989): Business and the facts of family life. *Harvard Business Review*, 67, 121–9.

Rosin, H. M. and Korabik, K. (2001): Do family-friendly policies fulfill their promises?: An investigation of their impact on work–family conflict and work and personal outcomes. In D. L. Nelson and R. J. Burke (eds), *Gender, Work Stress and Health*, Washington, DC: American Psychological Association (in press).

Schein, E. H. (1992): *Organizational culture and leadership*. San Francisco: Jossey-Bass.

Scheibl, F. and Dex, S. (1998): Should we have more family-friendly policies? *European Management Journal*, 16, 585–99.

Schneider, B. (1990): *Organizational climate and culture*. San Francisco: Jossey-Bass.

Schor, J. (1991): *The overworked American: The unexpected decline of leisure*. New York: Basic Books.

Schwartz, D. B. (1995): The impact of work–family policies on women's career development: Boom or bust? *Women in Management Review*, 7, 31–45.

Schwartz, F. N. (1992): *Breaking with tradition: Women and work, the new facts of life*. New York: Warner Books.

Smith, D. (1992): Corporate benefits only a start for family friendliness. *Employee Benefit Plan Review*, 3, 46–52.

Spence, J. T. and Robbins, A. S. (1992): Workaholism: Definition, measurement, and preliminary results. *Journal of Personality Assessment*, 58, 160–78.

Stroh, L. K., Brett, J. M., and Reilly, A. H. (1992): All the right stuff: A comparison of male and female managers. *Journal of Applied Psychology*, 77, 251–60.

Tharenou, P., Latimer, S., and Conroy, D. (1994): How do you make it to the top? An examination of influences on women's and men's managerial advancement. *Academy of Management Journal*, 37, 899–931.

Thompson, C. A. and Beauvais, L. L. (2000): Balancing work/life. In D. Smith (ed.), *Women at work: Leadership for the next century*. Upper Saddle River, NJ: Prentice-Hall.

Thompson, C. A., Beauvais, L. L., and Lyness, K. S. (1999): When work/family benefits are not enough. . . . The influence of work/family culture on benefit utilization, organizational attachment, and work/family conflict. *Journal of Vocational Behavior*, 54, 392–415.

Thompson, C. A., Thomas, C. C., and Maier, M. (1992): Work–family conflict: Reassessing corporate policies and intitiatives. In U. Sekaran and F. Leong (eds), *Woman power: managing in times of demographic turbulence*. Newbury Park, CA: Sage Publications.

*Women in Management Review* (1995): The sounds of shattering glass; Corporate initiatives for advancing managerial women. *Women in Management Review*, 10, 3–53.

*Women in Management Review* (1999): Work–family initiatives: From policies to practices. *Women in Management Review*, 14, 157–202.

# 18

# BEST PRACTICES FOR RETAINING AND ADVANCING WOMEN PROFESSIONALS AND MANAGERS

*Mary C. Mattis*

The growing recognition in the business community that competitive advantage for organizations derives from continuous improvement of processes for managing *both* material and human resources has resulted in an increased interest in methods for benchmarking HR best practices. This chapter focuses on effective methods for benchmarking best practices for recruiting, retaining, and advancing women professionals and managers in business organizations – the business case for benchmarking gender diversity "best practices;" the benefits of internal versus external benchmarking; pros and cons of the "best practice" model; continuing challenges relating to knowledge transfer and implementation of gender diversity best practices; and descriptions of outstanding initiatives that have produced measurable results.

## ■ The business case for benchmarking gender diversity best practices ■

### Women are a large part of the available talent pool and a growing economic force

In the US, changing demographics have created a business imperative for companies to attract and retain female talent. In 1999, women made up 46.5 percent of the total US labor force, and held 49.5 percent of managerial and professional specialty positions (US Bureau of Labor Statistics, 1999). Women now earn more than half the bachelor's and master's degrees awarded every year and one-third of MBAs. Today, half of the undergraduate degrees in business and management, accounting, and mathematics go to women (Digest of Education Statistics, 1996–97).

Outside of the walls of major corporations, women-owned businesses have also become a force to be reckoned with. As of 1997, there were 8.5 million women-owned businesses in the US, employing over 23.7 million people and generating close to $3.1 trillion in sales (National Foundation of Women Business Owners, 1999).

Aside from their role as business owners, women make more than 85 percent of total household purchasing decisions, including such major items as homes, cars, and, vacations (Barstow, 2000). Improving customer focus demands that businesses hire and retain people who reflect the demographics of the consumer base, especially at senior levels to provide leadership.

## A glass ceiling continues to block women's advancement to senior levels

To date, US companies have been more successful at attracting women to their workforce than at advancing them to meaningful leadership roles. Catalyst's annual censuses of women's representation in corporate management and governance, along with other studies, support the contention that a glass ceiling continues to operate to the detriment of women's advancement in US companies/firms (Catalyst, 1999, 2000b). In 2000, women held just 11.7 percent of corporate board seats and just 12.5 percent of corporate officer positions in *Fortune* 500 companies. Women corporate officers make up only 4.1 percent of top earners in *Fortune* 1000 companies and represent just 6.2 percent of individuals holding the most powerful and prestigious titles of chairman, CEO, vice-chairman, president, COO, SEVP, and EVP. Even when they achieve the rank of corporate officer, few women hold line jobs – those positions with profit-and-loss or direct client responsibility: among corporate officers men hold 92.7 percent of line jobs. The fact that, for whatever reason, women's experience continues to be largely on the staff side of business organizations limits their potential to obtain powerful and prestigious titles and commensurate salaries.

Catalyst and other researchers have identified the following as the most powerful barriers to women's career advancement (Catalyst, 1998):

- negative assumptions and stereotypes about women, their abilities, and their commitment to careers
- perceptions that women's style of leadership does not fit with generally accepted norms
- lack of career planning that leaves women with a limited breadth of exposure to their organizations, in particular, lack of general management and line experience
- lack of mentoring and exclusion from informal networks, where men have typically learned the unwritten rules of success
- failure to make managers accountable for advancing women
- absence of or inadequate succession planning processes
- "negative mentoring" and self-selection that channels women into staff roles
- appraisal and compensation systems that are not uniform for men and women

- other forms of "cultural discouragement," such as a work environment that values long hours over actual performance or that offers limited support for work–family initiatives and limited commitment to diversity programs in general
- discrimination and sexual harassment.

## Retention of women professionals and managers is surpassing recruitment as a key concern of companies/firms

Historically, the business case for retaining and advancing women has been most compelling for professional firms and service organizations where people are the primary business asset. Service organizations and, somewhat later, professional firms were the first business organizations to attract and eventually attain a critical mass of women professionals. The entry of women into careers in the service sector occurred before there was widespread recognition of the so-called "glass ceiling" – organizational and attitudinal barriers to women's full participation and advancement in companies and firms. So it is not surprising that professional firms and service organizations were among the first to experience high turnover of women professionals, with the attendant high costs of losing seasoned talent. J. Michael Cook, the former CEO of Deloitte and Touche LLP, used to refer to the phenomenon of firms like his own which were hiring increasing numbers of women and losing them at an equally high rate as the "stupid curve."

Today, with close to half of professional and managerial positions occupied by women across industries, the business case for stemming the turnover of women in business organizations is compelling. Studies have shown that the cost of replacing exempt employees, especially senior managers and highly marketable personnel such as high-tech professionals and engineers, is substantial. Other "invisible" costs of turnover include the impact on the morale and productivity of work units, discontinuity of customer/client service with resultant negative impact on customer/client satisfaction, and lost of intellectual capital with the associated possibility that a former employee may become a future competitor.

### ■ Benchmarking gender diversity performance and outcomes ■

Simply put, benchmarking is the process of identifying, understanding, and adapting outstanding practices both inside and outside of an organization. The goals of benchmarking gender diversity are: to improve a company's competitive advantage in recruiting, retaining, and developing diverse talent so as to enhance business results, and to provide a corporate culture and work environment where everyone has equal access to opportunities and equal encouragement to contribute and succeed.

Specific objectives of benchmarking gender diversity best practices include:

- developing the business case for gender diversity
- tying diversity strategies to short- and long-term business imperatives and strategic business plans

312    MARY C. MATTIS

- identifying and recruiting the best and brightest talent
- eliminating barriers to success
- enhancing access to opportunities.

Although the concept of measuring business activities/outcomes internally and against peers and competitors is not new, use of the term "best practice" to describe state-of-the-art initiatives and approaches in business and other disciplines does not appear in the literature until the 1970s. Early references to "best practices" include Blackwood's (1976) analysis of the development of a standard statement of auditing and Glaser's (1980) description of an iterative review paradigm for synthesizing the knowledge base of a given subject in the behavioral sciences. Also in 1980, Higgins and Ramano presented the findings from a survey investigating corporate practice in the areas of monitoring and forecasting social trends, noting that the sample frame was divided into three areas: industrial and financial concerns; nationalized industries and public corporations; and best practice companies. In 1982, Sutton discussed the need for a database that would allow the accounting profession to analyze to what extent best practice has been implemented and to shed light on why organizations adopt and then change internal accounting. Other early uses are found in articles on the subject of productivity in service organizations in the US (Clutterbuck, 1984) and among small businesses in the UK (Sherman, 1984).

In what may be the first use of the term "best practice" in reference to human resources management, Wolfe (1978) proposes a model for computerization of personnel records based on an analysis of best practices from a survey of corporate personnel systems.

In the mid 1980s Catalyst – a non-profit organization that works with business to advance women – introduced a competitive award for best practices to recruit, retain, and advance women in US business organizations. The purpose of the Catalyst Award nomination and evaluation process was twofold: to increase awareness among business leaders that, by expanding the pool of senior management talent to include women, companies/firms would enhance the quality of their senior management teams and, hence, their overall business results; and to enhance management's understanding that, in order to attract and retain a segment of the most talented female professionals, corporations/firms must establish policies and programs that would enable women to pursue both career and family goals and that would address attitudinal barriers that inhibit women's career growth.

The genius of the Catalyst Award was in recognizing that corporations routinely benchmark their business processes and outcomes against their competitors. The award increased awareness in the business community that effective management of all the available talent, both male and female, was a competitive advantage and stimulated companies' interest in being recognized by business peers for best practices in this area.

## ■ Internal versus external benchmarking ■

Benchmarking women's advancement involves two major areas of research activity: internal and external research benchmarking. However, most discussions of benchmarking focus on external benchmarking – the process of gathering information on practices and outcomes of industry peers, competitors, or companies with recognized best practices. In this regard, Jac Fitz-enz (1997), founder of the Saratoga Institute – noted for its national benchmarking studies – observed that the search for best practices frequently embodies an organization's wish for a "magic wand." It follows that companies searching for a magic wand to solve a problem or enhance a business process/outcome are not likely to stop to consider that it may exist within their own organization.

Catalyst finds that internal benchmarking is equally important as – if not more important than – external benchmarking in preparing a company or firm for the transformation process that follows benchmarking research.

Internal research provides meaningful metrics that enable companies to:

- establish the current status of women at the organization, reviewing such information as recruitment, retention and advancement statistics
- develop short- and long-term goals for improvement after the process of internal and external benchmarking is concluded
- evaluate the effectiveness of initiatives that result from benchmarking by measuring and reporting progress toward specified goals.

Thus, before it even begins to look at external data, the organization gains a concrete sense of where and what it is doing well and not so well in the area of gender diversity. Without this information, it is impossible to carry out successful external benchmarking.

## Internal benchmarking – quantitative measures

While it is fairly easy to develop quantitative meaures for a variety of gender diversity areas, many companies either do not maintain such or have not designed their human resources management information systems in a way that enables them to look at the different components of women's advancement in relation to each other. For example, compensation, benefits, leave, and promotion data may be separately maintained and reported. It is also fairly common for companies to have a general sense of the representation of women by levels within the organization, but not to know how they are represented across functions or business areas, or to know the attrition rate of employees in these groups. In the US, companies that receive federal contracts are more likely to maintain at least some of these data for purposes of reporting to the US Office of Federal Contract Compliance Programs.

Research by Catalyst (1996) shows that cross-functional development opportunities are essential for advancement in most corporations and firms and the lack thereof prevents women from competing for the highest-level positions in their organization. However, many companies do not know the extent to which women are represented in line or staff positions in their business units. Research also shows that while entry-level male and female managers and professionals generally receive comparable compensation packages, a wage gap between men and women frequently develops as they advance within their organization, one that cannot always be explained by differences in tenure or performance (Catalyst, 1997). Compensation studies can uncover differences in the way women and men are rewarded for their contributions.

Another important performance area that should be examined in assessing gender diversity performance is the whole complex of activities around performance appraisal, career pathing, and access to opportunities. A simple measure of the effectiveness of career development systems is a comparison of the representation of gender diversity in the top three tiers of management and in the management pipeline. Internal benchmarking activities in this area, such as those conducted at the Bank of Montreal, demonstrate that time alone will not remedy women's lack of representation in senior management.

Organizations should also examine their succession planning processes to determine whether men or women are making it on to slates of candidates, and, more important, whether their names reappear on slates year after year without explanation for their lack of mobility. Time in grade is another quantitative measure of managers' effectiveness in developing diverse talent.

These measures and others that may be identified as important, in combination, move a company in the direction of understanding how women are positioned in the organization and whether they are likely to be able to compete for top-level jobs without deliberate intervention to improve the opportunity structure of the organization.

## Internal benchmarking – qualitative measures

Internal benchmarking also involves understanding how different employee groups, in this case women, perceive the corporate culture and work environment. Organizations sometimes neglect this aspect of gender diversity performance. In their efforts to develop a data-based approach, they fail to understand the importance of employee perceptions. Qualitative research involves collecting data about employees' subjective experience and evaluations of the work environment. This feeling side of the work experience affects morale, productivity, organizational commitment, loyalty, and, ultimately, retention.

Qualitative gender diversity performance measures focus on employee satisfaction with:

- the work environment in general, that is, how it feels to come to work every day
- content of specific jobs
- access to key networks, mentors and key developmental opportunities
- support from supervisor
- quality of feedback from supervisors
- recognition and rewards systems
- optimism about future opportunities for career growth and advancement.

Many of the opportunities associated with advancement to senior ranks in companies are accessed through informal networks and channels of communications. Historically, women have lacked access to the informal opportunity structure. To assess various employee groups' perceptions of access to informal opportunities, companies and firms use surveys, focus groups and individual interviews. An analysis of performance appraisal forms can identify disparities in the feedback, evaluation, and career coaching that supervisors provide to men and women in the organization.

Research shows that the extent to which a manager is willing to provide information about organizational politics or to explain career path options is critical to both the retention and advancement of women. For example, Catalyst's (1999) research on women of color shows that women who reported supportive manager behaviors were also more likely to say that they intended to remain with their organization. In another unpublished, proprietary Catalyst study, male and female professionals received substantively different feedback in written performance evaluations: male managers' reviews of female reports focused almost exclusively on their current performance whereas their reviews of male reports discussed both their current performance and how to position them for future developmental assignments and promotions.

Several other benchmarking activities include:

- *Cohort analysis.* This provides an examination of the career paths of "classes" of men and women recruited to entry-level positions in the organization at year three, year five, and year ten, or at other specified career checkpoints in order to understand how women have progressed compared to men who entered the organization at the same time. Other questions that cohort analyses address are: To what extent have men and women had equal opportunities to work on both line and staff sides of the organization? Who is most likely to have been given critical assignments on task forces or in high-visibility teams? Is there a higher rate of attrition for women?
- *Officer career path assessment.* This type of analysis diagrams the career paths of individuals who have reached the highest levels of leadership in their organization to determine what credentials are valued, what critical assignments position managers for advancement, and whether there are positions that most managers occupy en route to the top. This type of research enables companies to confirm or dispel beliefs about historical leadership profiles (for example, all top management were engineers, or had significant sales leadership experience) and to begin to identify the competencies that will be critical to future corporate leadership needs. Too frequently, the "do as I did" model of career development operates to exclude women from consideration for developmental assignments and promotions.

At the conclusion of internal benchmarking, a company or firm should be able to answer the following questions:

- What are we doing well in gender diversity performance areas critical to our business?
- Where do we need to improve?

Equally important, internal benchmarking also provides data from which the organization can shape its specific business case for implementing new initiatives. As an example, internal benchmarking at Deloitte & Touche documented the high level and cost of turnover of female professionals in the firm and became a central component of the business care for change articulated by the former CEO J. Michael Cook.

There is no one right way of internal benchmarking, just as there is no "magic bullet" external practice that can be adopted by every company. Each company must find its own way through the process guided by both employee needs and business imperatives as well as other contextual factors. When an organization has reached the point when it knows what it is doing well and what needs improvement, then it is time to consider external benchmarking.

## Barriers to internal benchmarking

O'Dell and Grayson (1998), discussing the challenges and benefits of internal benchmarking, cited Jerry Junkins, the late chairman, president and CEO of Texas Instruments as saying, "If TI only knew what TI knows." In a similar vein, the authors also cite Lew Platt, the late chairman of Hewlett Packard as saying, "I wish we knew what we know at HP." These remarks from the leaders of two of America's greatest corporations acknowledge the challenge of internal benchmarking – the process of identifying, sharing, and using the knowledge and practices inside one's own organization. In the same article, O'Dell and Grayson identify some of the reasons why companies don't benchmark internal best practices:

- ignorance – neither the "source" nor the "recipient" knew someone else had knowledge they required or would be interested in the knowledge they had
- lack of absorptive capacity – even if a manager knew about the better practice, he or she may have had neither the resources (time or money) nor enough practical detail to implement it
- lack of a relationship between the source and the recipient of knowledge.

Even when an organization is able to overcome these barriers, the lag in time for a knowledge transfer to occur, that is, for a best practice to be identified internally before it is implemented, is substantial: Szulanski (1994) found that even in the best of firms, in-house best practices took an average of 27 months to wind their way from one part of the organization to another. As a representative from a Baldridge winner company observed: "We can have two plants right across the street from one another, and it's the damnedest thing to get them to transfer best practices."

Other factors preventing internal benchmarking and transfer that are identified by O'Dell and Grayson (1998) include:

- a culture that values personal technical expertise and knowledge creation over knowledge sharing
- the lack of contact, relationships, and common perspectives among people who don't work side by side
- an overreliance on transmitting "explicit" rather than "tacit" information. Polanyi (1967) and Nonaka (1991) also identified the importance and value of recognizing and trying to capture tacit knowledge – the know-how, judgment, intuition, and little tricks that constitute the non-codifiable knowledge that may make the difference between failure and success in knowledge transfer

- not allowing to take the time to learn and share and help each other outside of their own small corporate village, or not rewarding them for doing so
- organizational structures that promote "silo behavior" or what Catalyst has referred to as "glass walls." As an example, in Catalyst's research on women in sales (1995), managers and sales representatives in field sites frequently were unaware of or failed to implement best practice flexible work arrangement and leave policies that were available to head-quarters' staff.

Brown and Duquid (2000) and Wenger and Snyder (2000) suggest that "communities of practice" – a group of people informally bound by shared expertise and passion for a joint enterprise – is a way that some companies are attempting to improve performance and expedite the knowledge transfer required for the organization-wide roll-out of an isolated best practice.

## External benchmarking

Companies do not operate in a vacuum. They are competing with industry peers and, in many instances, organizations in other industry sectors for talent and for markets. The "war for talent" is a reality that companies cannot ignore. Therefore, it is critical that they understand how the opportunities and rewards they offer to their employees compare with those of other companies.

External benchmarking, however, is costly in terms of both financial and people resources, requiring interviewing and visiting companies against which an organization is benchmarking which is costly to both the company doing the research and to best practice organizations. Many world-class companies are weary of requests for benchmarking. Therefore, the goal should be to identify only a few external benchmarking partners and to make the best choices.

Getting to the heart of another company's initiatives is another challenge of external benchmarking since many best practices are not embodied in discrete visible programs. The challenge for benchmarking teams is to identify the underpinning values and contextual factors that contribute to the initiatives effectiveness and to discern whether the initiative could be tailored to their own organization.

Catalyst's experience benchmarking gender diversity initiatives in a wide range of business and professional organizations shows conclusively that isolated programs transplanted to new environments usually don't work. For example, there is a limited value in implementing generous dependent care leave policies without flexibility of work scheduling and work sites; training is useful as part of a comprehensive career development system, but produces only limited, short-term change as a stand-alone approach. No turnkey gender diversity initiatives exist, although it is true that isolated programs can be copied or purchased "off the shelf." An organization should resist the temptation to seize what appears to be a magic bullet before top-level support and communication systems are in place and gender diversity goals have been integrated into broad business strategies.

In considering internal and external benchmarking one might conclude that each, as a singular approach, has drawbacks: External benchmarking alone overlooks the vast amount of untapped knowledge and best practices already residing inside organizations. Internal benchmarking alone leaves a company without a comparative perspective with regard to how competitors and peers are faring. Together, both approaches provide the most comprehensive picture of what tools are available inside and outside the organization to improve an organization's performance in recruiting, retaining and advancing women.

## Fundamental underpinnings of successful gender diversity initiatives

No matter how original and compelling an initiative may be, it will not succeed without a supportive infrastructure. Catalyst's (2000a) research demonstrates that successful gender diversity best practices are supported and sustained by:

- motivation and rationale linked to business strategy
- commitment and support from the highest levels of the organization
- built-in communication and training plans clearly stating how the initiative is linked to business issues/strategies
- built-in accountability mechanisms with specific metrics to measure results
- early-win and long-term goals
- assumptions and approaches that challenge the status quo.

In a decade and a half of evaluating gender diversity initiatives, Catalyst has observed the following trends. Today, companies are much more likely to undertake internal and external benchmarking against other organizations before they begin to design their own initiatives. Companies used *ad hoc*, informal approaches to barriers to women's advancement in many of the earliest initiatives that were evaluated. Today, companies are much more likely to use formal policies to make change, which offers the advantages of uniformity of communication and implementation, integration into manager training, and equal access.

Many early initiatives to address the glass ceiling were characterized primarily by successful programs to address specific problems and populations. More recently, winning initiatives are multifaceted and have as their goal systemic change. Today, companies are more aware of the business case for effective use of all of their talent. Today's initiatives are more likely to involve HR/line management partnerships and, on occasion, collaboration with other companies.

Fitz-enz (1997) identified eight factors that Saratoga Institute studies have found to be antecedents of "best" human asset management practices, many of which overlap with those identified by Catalyst:

1   *Values.* A constant focus on adding value in everything rather than simply doing something. In addition, there is a conscious ongoing and largely successful attempt to balance human and financial values.

2   *Commitment.* Dedication to a long-term core strategy. Avoidance of the temptation to change management fads.
3   *Culture.* Proactive application of the corporate culture. Management is aware of how culture and systems can be linked together for consistency and efficiency
4   *Communication.* An extraordinary concern for communicating with all stakeholders. Constant and extensive two-way communication using all media and sharing all types of vital information is the rule.
5   *Partnering.* New markets demand new forms of operation. They involve people within and outside the company in many decisions. This includes the design and implementation of new programs/practices.
6   *Collaboration.* A high level of cooperation and involvment of all sections within functions. They study, redesign, launch, and follow-up new programs in a collective manner enhancing efficiency and cohesiveness.
7   *Innovation and risk.* Innovation is recognized as a necessity. There is a willingness to risk shutting down present systems and structure and restarting in a totally different manner while learning from failure.
8   *Competitive passion.* A constant search for improvement. Systems and processes are designed to actively seek feedback and incorporate ideas from all sources.

Opportunity Now, an advocacy organization based in the United Kingdom that works to realise the economic potential and business benefits that women contribute to the workforce, also names a number of the aforementioned factors as critical to the development of effective gender diversity initiatives including (Cherry and Mattis, 2000):

- *Demonstrate commitment.* It is important to make a clear and unequivocal commitment to gender equality, starting at the very top of the organization.
- *Investment counts.* The extent of an organization's investment, whether financial, time and/or human resources will have a significant impact on success with gender issues. This investment is necessary to enhance access to opportunities and provide developmental support.
- *Change behavior.* Progress toward goals for gender issues will be measured by changes in organizational culture to allow more flexible and inclusive working practices.
- *Communicate ownership.* The extent to which goals for gender activities are communicated is an essential factor in achievement. It is important to build executive and employee awareness of gender issues and foster a more inclusive work environment.
- *Share ownership.* Listening to employee views helps to ensure that the organization will achieve its gender issue goals by keeping track of what really makes a difference. Gender policies and practices should be dynamic, and constantly monitored and re-evaluated. Benchmarking the retention and advancement of women professionals provides essential data for the evaluation of gender diversity initiatives.

## ■ Pros and cons of the best practice model ■

The best practice model is not without its critics. Brown and Duguid (2000) discuss the dilemma of "how to capture knowledge without killing it." Purcell (1999) raises questions about the applicability of the best practice model with regard to the universality of high commitment management. Fitz-enz (1997) observed that: "many believe that a publicized process is an example of a best practice. In actuality, it is only the visible result of something much more fundamental within the organization, which is itself the true best practice." In the same article, he observes that best practice is subjective and transitory, and describes a Saratoga Institute study of 200 companies "best practices," for which only 54 of the companies could provide verifiable, hard data that the practice had led to improvements. Furthermore, there were several instances where two companies reported diametrically opposed practices and yet both came out with excellent performance.

Catalyst (2000a) outlined the following dangers inherent in benchmarking gender diversity best practices.

- Best practices are transitory and time bound, that is, a number of gender diversity initiatives that were once considered outstanding are now mainstream. In order for initiatives to remain relevant, they must continue to evolve as the context within which they were constructed evolves.
- Best practices don't exist in isolation or out of context. It follows that while one organization's practice can be useful as a guide to addressing another organization's issues, it will need to be tailored to the second organization's specific context. Also, since policies, programs, and practices are context-specific, there can be more than one "best" practice for addressing barriers to the retention and advancement of women; for example, disproportionate turnover of female employees requires different solutions in corporations than in professional firms.
- Best practices are shaped by several factors: industry, organization size and market reach, structural considerations, etc. What works in one company or industry may not work in another.
- Benchmarking is not an end in itself but a means to an end: to create a more inclusive corporate culture where women, among others, have equal access to resources and opportunities to enable them to succeed.

With these caveats in mind, we would argue that the best practice model is a useful one for several reasons. First, it provides a starting point for organizational transformation when and where there is the will and the resources to improve gender diversity. Second, use of benchmarking research and identification of best practices for gender diversity is consistent with the way corporations/firms do business. Thus, use of this model for human resources management brings credibility to the endeavor and optimizes the chances that resulting initiatives will be integrated into existing business strategies. Finally, companies are by nature competitive. In the US, Catalyst, and in the UK Opportunity Now, have found that benchmarking and recognizing gender diversity best practices of prominent companies is *an effective means of raising awareness of women as a business resources and of motivating companies to compete for female talent*.

The best practices outlined below were selected from a range of initiatives that have been identified and recognized by Catalyst and other organizations as exceptional approaches to retaining and advancing women. Each example focuses on an initiative that was designed to address one of the specific barriers to women's retention and advancement discussed above.

# BEST PRACTICES FOR RETAINING AND ADVANCING WOMEN PROFESSIONALS AND MANAGERS[1]

## ■ Corporate initiative – benchmarking ■

### Bank of Montreal's Advancement of Women Initiative

Early in 1991, F. Anthony Comper, the bank's president and chief operating officer, commissioned the Employee Task Force on the Advancement of Women to identify barriers to female advancement and to devise strategies to break them down. The mandate of the task force was to "identify the constraints to the advancement of women" and to "recommend goals and measures."

The bank's investigative phase broke new ground as part of a gender diversity initiative. The task force reviewed the bank's human resource database, interviewed 270 people, conducted 11 focus groups, and surveyed 500 former managers. But the most important thing it did was a survey of 15,000 women and men employees, asking such questions as "What is the No. 1 thing that's holding women back?" and "What would you like the bank to do to help you advance?". The key finding from the task force was: "Women were not advancing because of stereotypical attitudes, myths of conventional wisdom."

The task force set out on a "myth-busting" venture, countering each of the stereotypes with facts gleaned from the human resources files. The most common erroneous assumptions about women's failure to advance in the bank's executive ranks, as revealed by the survey, were:

- Women at the bank were either too young or too old to compete equitably with men.
- Because of child-rearing responsibilities, women are less committed to their careers.
- Women do not have the educational credentials to compete with men.
- Women don't have 'the right stuff' to compete for senior jobs.
- Women haven't been in the pipeline long enough to advance to senior levels.
- Time will take care of the problem.

The task force learned that these myths were false and required refutation. As a result of its rigorous research, the bank was able to demonstrate that women are equally as qualified, equally as educated, and equally as committed to their careers as men. The survey also uncovered similarities in the approaches men and women felt the bank should take to help them advance. Both talked about needing flexibility in scheduling work hours, both wanted more control over their careers, more information about management vacancies, and more access to mentoring.

To build a foundation for eliminating barriers to women's advancement, the task force issued a report detailing the information about women employees at the bank that they had compiled. Based on the survey research and the analysis of demographic data on male and female employees, the report used a myths-and-realities approach and was distributed to all staff. It included this information:

- On average, women and men are the same age.
- Although women have babies and more responsibility for childrearing, they have longer service records at the bank, except at senior levels.
- An analysis of performance appraisals revealed that a higher percentage of women than men were ranked in the top two tiers of each level.
- The percentage of women in senior positions had grown so slowly – 1 percent a year – that it was not practical to wait for time to take care of the problem.

The initiative that resulted from the bank's research and communication efforts has several components that fall into the categories of training, career planning and performance review, and flexible work arrangements.

- *Training.* The bank has incorporated "Managing Diversity" and "Men and Women as Colleagues" into its management training curriculum and added a leadership curriculum to help managers develop a leadership style that emphasizes coaching and teamwork. It has also instituted several accreditation programs to help men and women gain credentials that will help them advance. The program addresses historical inequities in employment, in which women were concentrated in personal banking, with limited authority on how much they could lend. The bank's goal is for half the trainees in each program to be female.
- *Career planning.* Among programs that were implemented are: 1) computer-assisted self-learning courses for branch staff to increase their knowledge and skill base and become eligible for more senior positions; 2) a career information network that provides listings of job vacancies for mid-to-senior management positions; 3) a job posting system for regional positions in lower-level jobs. Managers and supervisors, starting at the executive level, establish annual hiring, retention, and advancement targets, and they determine how flexibility will fit into that plan. They review and update business plans quarterly.
- *Performance reviews.* Annual performance reviews include each manager's progress in reaching individual goals, as well as his or her contribution to workplace equality. Employees rate their managers on their management of flexibility.
- *Flexible work arrangements.* Employees are able to work out flexible arrangements with supervisors. "Flexing Your Options," a 100-page handbook distributed to all employees and managers, offers detailed advice on how to implement a flexible work arrangement, including common questions asked by managers, how to develop a proposal for a flexible schedule, and a description of varying types of arrangements. The bank assesses the impact of flexible arrangements on work. For example, the impact of a work-at-home program on translators was measured, with a finding that the amount translated by those working at home was either the same or exceeded the amount translated by persons working at an office site.

**Results.** In six years, from late 1991 to late 1997, the representation of women in executive ranks increased from 9 percent to 24 percent. Among senior vice presidents, women have increased from 3 percent to 27 percent, and their representation among senior management has increased from 13 percent to 26 percent.

# ■ Corporate initiatives – moving women into line positions ■

## Consolidated Edison – Management Intern Program

Consolidated Edison – Con Ed, as it is referred to by residents of New York City and Westchester County, NY – is one of the largest publicly owned gas and electric utilities in the United States. Motivated by changing workforce demographics and a bottom-line concern to develop and diversify management talent, Con Edison created a comprehensive strategy called "Commitment to Women With Technical Talent." The strategy was designed to recruit, develop, and promote qualified women. The centerpiece of this strategy is the Management Intern Program, which was launched in 1981 to intensify efforts to recruit women and to develop future female managers of the company. The initiative has continued to evolve. In 1993, Con Edison divided the program into several organization-based programs – the:

- Field Supervisory Program for Engineers
- Assistant Engineer Program
- Gas Operation Management Development Program
- Information Resources Assistant Computer Analyst Program
- Business Intern Program (organizationwide).

Another recent change is in the administration of the program. The Management Intern Program was once run solely by the College Programs Department. Now, the Recruitment and Staffing Department hires and places the interns, and Con Ed's Learning Center is responsible for the administration of the program. Mentors assist the director of the Learning Center by providing feedback to evaluate the effectiveness of the program.

The programs generally recruit between 10 and 20 students annually. Managers conduct campus interviews with potential candidates, who are assessed according to skills identified by the Competitive Skills Team. The managers in the recruiting and staffing department select candidates for the program. They are looking for technical competence, leadership potential, and communication skills. The Gas Operations Management and the Business Intern Programs both run for two years, while the Assistant Engineer and Field Supervisory Intern Programs take three years. Each program involves several short-term, rotational assignments where the interns receive on-the-job supervision and mentoring from an assigned advisor.

After the first year, engineers go into a three-year position as first-line supervisors followed by three years in central operations. For interns who are not engineers, a one-year administrative training job follows the Management Intern Program. That year is spent in a field assignment in operations. These programs provide participants with a wide range of experience and expose them to the field environment.

Each intern is assigned a mentor from mid or upper-level management who is responsible for tracking the intern's progress. Managers meet regularly with interns to provide guidance and assistance. The assignments are evaluated by a Functional Review Committee made up of senior-level managers and chaired by general managers. The program administrator is part of every review committee.

**Results.**  While women make up only 17 percent of engineering students nationally, they are more than 30 percent of the participants of the Management Intern Program. There has been a great demand for program graduates from departments. And graduates are placed into departments upon completion of the program.

## Corning Incorporated – Women in Manufacturing Initiative

Corning's Women in Manufacturing Initiative (WIM) is specifically designed to increase and advance the pool of women in manufacturing leadership positions at the company. It provides women employees with critical career pathing information and development opportunities.

In 1992, Norman Garrity, then EVP of Corning's Specialty Materials Division and currently president of the Corning Technologies and co-chief operating officer, recognized a lack of women in key manufacturing positions. He formed the WIM team, comprising ten men and women in manufacturing leadership. Their mission was to identify potential issues or barriers that were keeping women from progressing into key manufacturing positions, and then to implement initiatives to break these barriers and monitor progress.

The team discovered there were issues in the advancement, retention, and recruitment of women in manufacturing. They set out to shape a clearer understanding of the women's perception of the manufacturing environment. From these data, the team constructed a powerful initiative to develop and advance women into manufacturing roles.

Corning realized its work environment in manufacturing was not working for women because the environment was decreasing productivity and causing unacceptable levels of attrition (in 1992, twice as many women as men left jobs in the manufacturing sector). Corning intends that every employee have the opportunity to fully participate, to grow professionally, and to develop to her or his highest potential. The WIM initiative helps ensure Corning uses its available pool of talent by developing women to their fullest potential, thus providing the company with a competitive advantage.

The WIM initiative includes communication and data gathering, coaching, mentoring, a process for recruiting women into manufacturing career planning, work–life balance integration, and networking. A key element of the program is strong commitment from senior leadership.

Specifically, the initiative:

- works to recruit women into manufacturing positions
- encourages managers to provide women with key developmental and networking experiences
- analyzes career paths to senior-level positions, thereby identifying and communicating feeder positions and key developmental experiences

- ensures that women who are interested in manufacturing are included in succession planning
- develops a manufacturing ladder to encourage movement between manufacturing and engineering
- emphasizes zero tolerance for any form of sexual harassment
- places importance on achieving a balance between work and personal life
- encourages increased use of both formal and informal flexible work arrangements.

To support the initiative's objectives, a career path brochure, which clarifies career planning for the manufacturing sector of the company, was developed. In addition, coaching and mentoring programs ensure that women are mentored on career development issues.

*Results.*  The positive impact of the initiative is clear, through an increase in women employees in key positions, as well as improved employee satisfaction on diversity-related issues. From 1992 to 1996, women manufacturing employees increased from 22.4 percent to 28.5 percent, while women in "A-payroll" positions (the highest layer of management in the company) increased from 15 percent to 26 percent. There were no women plant managers when the initiative was founded. Today, five of Corning's 20 plant managers are women; an additional two women plant managers have been promoted into higher-level management positions. At the same time, the attrition rate of women employees has dropped from 8 percent to 3.5 percent.

Employee surveys reveal an improved work environment within the plants that is marked by an increased comfort level on the part of women. Employees also report an improvement in their ability to balance their work and personal lives.

## ■  Corporate initiative – mentoring programs  ■

### Knight-Ridder – Bench Strength Program

Knight-Ridder, the newspaper and information company, is competing in a fast-changing, volatile industry. Understanding that it does business in a diverse world in which economic power is increasingly wielded by women as well as men, the company recognized that newspapers and other forms of media need to reflect the communities they cover; both to maintain a standard of excellence and to be prepared to recognize business and product opportunities that might arise. In light of women's growing economic influence, Knight-Ridder wanted particularly to strengthen its position with women readers.

In 1989, Knight-Ridder's diversity task force created a mandate to advance women. And business units were required to develop numeric targets based on regional populations and to design programs to advance women in senior positions.

Knight-Ridder's "Bench Strength" program is a formal mentoring system targeted at high-level employees who are identified by senior managers at newspapers as being within two to three years of taking on significantly broader leadership roles. More than 40 percent of the participants are women. Corporate officers take responsibility for a

group of six to eight mentees. Officers serving as mentors have a number of responsibilities – to

- talk with each mentee's editor or publisher to get an assessment of his or her strengths,
  weaknesses, and career aspirations
- have a similar in-depth talk with the individual
- have the mentees and their editors devise a career development plan, looking forward two
  to three years and including a timetable, a cost projection, and a clearly understood
  outcome
- review the plan and fine-tune it with the editor and the individual
- support and assist in implementing the plan and make sure the timetable is met.

Officers meet annually to discuss the individuals in the program. This creates a
familiarity with these individuals for the time when job openings arise.

Knight-Ridder holds vice-presidents and supervisors accountable for results for the
Bench Strength program and all other diversity initiatives. At the corporate officer
and local company executive levels, bonuses are tied to performance on advancing
diversity, including women. Performance reviews also contain requirements relating
to diversity hiring and development. From 1990 to 1995, Knight-Ridder significantly
moved the needle on women and minorities in the workforce and management representation through a five-year plan. Today, each company's strategic plan specifies steps
toward its clearly defined goals for advancing diversity, including women, at management and non-management levels. The elements of the plan include:

- any specific recruiting and hiring
- a program for accelerating the training and experience of women and minorities,
  identifying individuals, and projecting assignments and opportunities
- a specific program for enlarging the pool of qualified women and minorities for jobs
- plans for aiding organizations in the community that promote opportunities for women
  and minorities
- plans for conducting diversity training (including gender, sexual harassment, and
  work–life issues) in the workplace
- steps to be taken to assure both the reality and perception of fairness to all employees.

**Results.** Women represent about 40.1 percent of Knight-Ridders's workforce and
they are equally reflected among its executive ranks, at 39.6 percent, up 17 percent
from 1991. A survey of the paper's readers showed a significant increase in female
readership from 1991 to 1994.

■  **Firm initiative – retention**  ■

## Ernst & Young – use of technology

Professional services firms are known for their long hours, intense work environments,
and demanding travel regimens. For many firms in the early 1990s, this translated into
a struggle to retain women professionals. One such firm, Ernst & Young, annually lost

22 percent of its women professionals and spent $150,000 per job to hire and train replacements. According to a 1996 unpublished Catalyst study of the firm, 60 percent of women employees and 57 percent of men in senior management were dissatisfied with working long hours. In response to those dramatic statistics and client demands for consistency in service, in 1996 Ernst and Young created the Office of Retention to address issues of work–life balance and women's particular needs in this area.

Ernst & Young's Office of Retention has leveraged technology to generate innovative ways to "convince employees it is safe to use flexible work arrangements (FWA)." Employees now use the electronic *FWA Roadmap* and *FWA Database* to research and apply for flexible work arrangements.

- The FWA Roadmap is an interactive tool that guides individuals through the flexible work arrangement application process by providing detailed information about the available programs.
- The FWA Database provides the personal stories of more than 500 individuals who work on flexible work arrangements. For those who worry about the potential impact of a flexible work arrangement on their career, the database provides some reassuring statistics:
  (a)  99 percent are satisfied with their arrangement
  (b)  98 percent say their colleagues are supportive of their arrangement
  (c)  97 percent say their supervisor is supportive of their arrangement
  (d)  25 percent of people profiled have had a least one promotion since the database was established, five of them to partner.

By sharing these internal success stories, Ernst & Young is communicating to partners and employees alike that a flexible work arrangement does not hinder career advancement or jeopardize client relationships. Now 1,700 of 23,000 staff members – 7 percent – work a flexible work schedule, up from 1,000 in 1988. Of those who benefit from flexible work arrangements, 12 percent are men.

## ■  Firm initiative – culture change  ■

## Charles Schwab & Co. – Building a culture: no ceilings, no barriers, no limits

Over twenty-five years ago, Charles Schwab recognized that it could gain a market advantage by building a brokerage firm dedicated to customer needs and the recruitment and development of traditionally underrepresented segments of the financial services sector. His firm was founded with the notion that an open, respectful, and inclusive culture was the key to achieving this advantage. Today, founder Charles Schwab and co-CEO David Pottruck continue to implement the original vision by demonstrating support for diversity in all business decisions and employees programs.

The Vision Quest program is a key component of Schwab's approach. Vision Quest featured a nationwide event that simultaneously brought together 5,000 Schwab employees from ten geographic locations. Its purpose was to achieve coherent thinking about Schwab's culture, vision, values, business, and marketplace. The event included speeches from the co-CEOs, videos, and an interactive business-related game. Schwab continues to conduct Vision Quest events with smaller groups of new hires as an official part of the Schwab orientation and enculturation process in order to communicate and maintain a shared vision, culture, and work approach.

Schwab focuses on recruiting diverse talent through the following programs:

- Wings is a recruitment program for college seniors that focues on hiring ethnically and gender-diverse candidates. Upon graduation, candidates are placed in a month-long training program, followed by interim assignments in various Schwab departments.
- The Management Associate Program is a seven-month training program that focuses on developing leadership skills for high-potential business school students and Schwab employees. Participants have the opportunity to work with long-standing Schwab employees, leaders, and senior management in one field with two headquarter-based rotations.
- Schools to Careers is an internship program for high school students interested in intellectually and technically demanding careers. The program – which includes mentoring programs, job shadowing, work-site visits, part-time work, and paid summer internships – is an additional way of promoting the company's goal of developing a talented and diverse future workforce.

Schwab also features a host of work–life programs, including:

- informal and formal flexible work arrangements
- a hoteling program that offers 50 off-site workstations to San Francisco employees with the goal of easing their daily commute
- the Balancing Work–Life training program offered by Schwab University, and led by senior women in the organization
- Les Concierge Service which acts as a "personal assistant" and is available on an unlimited basis, at no charge, to all Schwab employees. Services provided include running personal errands, doing household chores, and helping busy employees plan family vacations.

The company also offers development programs.

- Schwab has a formal mentoring program, and is a founder of Mentium 100 in the San Francisco Bay area. Mentium 100 is a cross-company mentoring program placing senior managers with mid-level executives.
- The Women's Interactive Network is an active employee resources group that sponsors training, speakers, and seminars on women's issues.

Schwab encourages employees to become active in their communities.

- Volunteerism is encouraged, and business units frequently participate in programs such as Habitat for Humanity during business hours.
- An employee "sick bank" allows employees to donate extra, unused sick days to colleagues with life-threatening illnesses.

**Results.** Women currently comprise 39 percent of Schwab's workforce and 36 percent of its corporate officers. Two of the company's five vice-chairs are women and two women sit on the 12-member board of directors. Due to the strong presence of women in senior management, 77 percent of Schwab's employees ultimately report to a woman.

## ■ Corporate initiative – succession planning ■

### Motorola – succession planning with clout

Motivated by changing workforce demographics, Motorola broadened its longstanding succession planning practice in 1989 to accelerate the advancement of women to the vice-president level. Yet, by 1995, the company realized that most of the women who reached the VP level were white women. As a result, then-chairman and CEO Gary Tooker challenged his direct reports to closely monitor and develop women of color so that they would be more fully represented among vice-presidents. Motorola made sure that each mechanism supporting its succession planning process is actually targeted to women of color.

Motorola established Officer Parity Goals requiring that by year-end 2000, the percent representation of women and people of color at every management level mirror the representation of these groups in specific areas of import to the company. Human resources also monitors and provides analyses of the company's progress toward its officer parity goals and the representation of women and people of color in each of the key areas and in staff versus line positions.

Motorola's succession planning process – the Organization and Management Development Review – identifies and tracks employees who have the potential to be promoted two levels in five years. This process is unique in that it embraces the entry and middle levels of management as well as the upper levels, which are more commonly the focus of succession planning. By developing a high-potential list that reaches lower into the organization the company ensures that there is enough representation of women and people of color, and specifically, women of color, in the pool which feeds the senior management levels. In addition, for each high potential, managers must include individual career development plans. In situations where a woman or person of color has left the company, their manager is responsible for ascertaining the reason for the departure.

An annual succession planning chart – the Management Resources and Replacement Chart – is completed to identify three successors who could fill each key position. On the chart, managers first provide their "immediate successor" should their positions suddenly open. Managers also designate their planned successor or a person who is being trained and developed for the job. This "planned successor" may be the same person as the immediate successor. Finally, managers must specify the most qualified woman or person of color candidate at the time, in addition to any woman or person of color already designated as the immediate or planned successor.

Senior managers must complete development planning forms for women and people of color who are identified as having the potential to become vice-presidents within a specified time period. The development plan specifies timelines for promotions and lateral moves as well as a mentor for the high potential so that both the high potential's supervisor and mentor become responsible for helping the individual carry out her or his development plan.

Motorola's current chairman and CEO Chris Galvin drives the initiative with strategic assistance from the HR department. Chris Galvin's direct reports, who lead Motorola's six major business operations, are each responsible for developing plans to meet the parity goals for their organizations. Progress toward these goals is reviewed on a quarterly basis. Motorola believes it is essential to have top leadership commitment and an understanding that diversity of talent is necessary to the company's success. The company uses similar processes for diversity as it does for any business initiatives: establish clear goals, timetables, and milestones to be reviewed.

Key elements for women of color include:

- strong leadership commitment to advance women of color to the vice-president level
- integration of diversity and business objectives
- representation goals for women and people of color at every management level
- succession planning that includes the widest talent pool and strategic planning to develop high potentials
- managerial accountability for success.

**Results.** In 1991, there was only one woman of color among nine female vice-presidents compared with today when there are 11 women of color vice-presidents out of 54 women vice-presidents.

## ■ Corporate initiative – work–life ■

### Baxter International Inc. – Work and Life Strategic Initiative

Baxter Healthcare's Work and Life Strategic Initiative began with an 18-month study to investigate work–life issues. The initial goals of the initiative were to evaluate current work–life programs, understand employees' work and life needs, and uncover management attitudes toward employees' work–life conflicts. Subsequent goals included using the fact-finding process to motivate senior managers to address work–life as a critical business issue and to dispel fears and stereotypes surrounding work–life issues. During the course of the study, the scope of work–life issues was found to be broader than anticipated, and new findings significant to human resources and the work–life field were discovered. The reach of work–life expanded to encompass more categories of employees who experience conflicts, as well as more approaches to alleviate them.

The initiative provided the impetus to incorporate work–life support mechanisms into operational aspects of Baxter. The initiative has helped to identify the extensive breadth and depth of work–life conflicts and reveal the impact the results made and continued to make on the entire organization.

The Work and Life Strategic Initiative was developed under the direction of Alice Campbell, Baxter's Director of Work and Life Initiatives. Initial input for the project was received from the Work–Life Forum, a group of HR managers that represented Baxter business units. The business unit HR staff identified how many locations would participate in the study, the findings of which would represent that particular business unit. Managers at most locations were interviewed, as well as managers at the headquarters office for that division. The CEO champions the initiative, providing ongoing role modeling and communication of his commitment.

Baxter communicates its commitment to work–life issues through a variety of methods.

- Each business unit communicated specifics about its participation in the survey to the management team, following up with a detailed report.
- The Operating Management Team used voicemail to distribute standards to all employees.
- A Work–Life homepage on Baxter's intranet site supports and provides information to employees about Baxter's work–life initiatives.
- CEO Harry Kraemer writes a monthly update to all staff that includes information about his own family and efforts to achieve balance. On the "Ask Harry" intranet site, Kraemer responds to employee questions about the company and the initiative.
- Baxter shared results of the Work and Life Initiative, internally as well as with the business community, in a full report, *The Work and Life Pyramid of Needs*.

Baxter allows for review of work–life issues for individuals and managers using the variety of mechanisms available. Supervisors at the highest level monitor results for each employee and take them into account when establishing objectives for any given year. The all-employee survey monitors results on employee issues that take into account the overall corporation.

Figures are monitored quarterly for activity relating to alternate work arrangements and the "Inside Advantage" job posting system. A sharp increase in the number of jobs that could be considered for alternate work arrangements occurred as a direct result of these enhancements.

***Results.*** Between 1996 and 1998, there has been an 8 percent increase of women at the managerial level, a 17.7 percent increase at the director level, and a 29.6 percent increase at the vice-president level. The percentage increase of employees of color who are officials and managers increased by 8.8 percent – women of color increased by 20.4 percent.

## NOTE

1   The best practices presented here were collected by Catalyst and approved by the companies for reprinting. Many result from the Catalyst Award evaluation process, undertaken annually, and currently headed by Marcia Kropf, VP, Research and Information Services and Paulette Gerkovich, Director, Research. Prior to their tenure, the author of this chapter headed the Awards evaluation process at Catalyst for eight years. Meredith Moore, Senior Associate, Research, compiled these practices into a database for internal use at Catalyst and developed a format for presenting them in a uniform fashion. Best practices used here are excerpted from *Cracking the Glass Ceiling: Catalyst's Research on Women in Corporate Management 1995–2000*.

## REFERENCES

Barstow, A. (2000): Women as Targets: The gender-based implications of online consumer profiling. *Online Profiling Project*. Comment, P994809/Docket No. 990811219-9219-01, November 1, Washington, DC.

Blackwood, M. (1976): Bank Reports for Audit Purposes, *Accountancy*, 87, 99, London: UK.

Brown, J. S. and Duguid, P. (2000): Balancing Act: How to Capture Knowledge Without Killing It. *Harvard Business Review*, Boston, MA.

Catalyst (1995): *Knowing the Territory: Women in Sales*. New York, NY.

Catalyst (1996): *Women in Corporate Leadership: Progress and Prospects*. New York, NY.

Catalyst (1997): *Women of Color in Corporate Management: A Statistical Picture*. New York, NY.

Catalyst (1998): *Advancing Women in Business – The Catalyst Guide*. San Francisco, CA: Jossey-Bass.

Catalyst (1999): *Women of Color in Corporate Management: Opportunities and Barriers*. New York, NY.

Catalyst (2000a): *Cracking the Glass Ceiling: Catalyst's Research on Women in Corporate Management, 1995–2000*. New York, NY.

Catalyst (2000b): *2000 Catalyst Census of Women Corporate Officers and Top Earners*. New York, NY.

Cherry, J. and Mattis, M. C. (2000): *Women in Senior Management in the United Kingdom*. London: Opportunity Now.

Clutterbuck, D. (1984): How to Plant the Seeds of Productivity. *Management Today*, July.

Digest of Education Statistics (1999): Postsecondary Education, Chapter 3. Table 258, Bachelor's, master's, and doctor's degrees conferred by institutions of higher education, by sex of student and field of study: 1996–1997.

Fitz-enz, J. (1997): The Truth About "Best Practice," *Human Resource Planning*, 16, 3, Tempe, AZ.

Garvin, D. A. (1993): Building a learning organization. *Harvard Business Review*, July/August.

Glaser, E. M. (1980): Using Behavioral Science Strategies for Defining the State-of-the-Art. *The Journal of Applied Behavioral Science*, Jan/Feb/Mar.

Higgins, J. C. and Ramano, D. (1980): Social Forecasting: An Integral Part of Corporate Planning? *Long Range Planning*, April.

Hiltrop, J.-M. (1996): The impact of human resource management on organisational performance: Theory and research. *European Management Journal*, December.

Hiltrop, J.-M. (1996): The impact of human resource management on organisational performance: Theory and research. *European Management Journal*, December.

National Foundation of Women Business Owners (1999): *Key Facts*. Silver Spring, Maryland.

Nonaka, I. (1991): The Knowledge-Creating Company, *Harvard Business Review*, 69, 6, November/December.

O'Dell, C. and Grayson, C. J. (1998): If Only We Knew What We Know: Identification and Transfer of Internal Best Practices. *California Management Review*, 40, 3.

Polyani, M. (1967): *The Tacit Dimension*. New York: Doubleday.

Purcell, J. (1999): Best practice and best fit: Chimera or cul-de-sac? *Human Resource Management Review*, 9, 3.

Sherman, H. D. (1984): Improving the productivity of service businesses, *Sloan Management Review*, 25, 3.

Sutton, T. G. (1982): Management Accounting Needs a Data Base. *Management Accounting*, 63, 9.

Szulanski, G. (1994): *Intra-Firm Transfer of Best Practices Project*. Houston: TX. American Productivity and Quality Center.

US Bureau of Labor Statistics (1999): Household Data Annual Averages. Washington, DC.

VWenger, E. C. and Snyder, W. M. (2000): Communities of Practice: The Organizational Frontier. *Harvard Business Review*, January.

Wolfe, M. N. (1978): Computerization – It Can Bring Sophistication Into Personnel. *Personnel Journal*, 57, 6.

# 19

# ADVANCING WOMEN'S EXECUTIVE LEADERSHIP

*Val Hammond*

In global corporations, whether large manufacturers or fleet-of-foot service providers, and in public bodies, those working at the highest levels can and do wield power that affects the day-to-day lives of countless individuals. Yet across the world, and despite their predominance in the working population, women form only a tiny minority of those at the top.

Wanted: more uppity women (*Financial Times* headline)

Having more women in top level executive posts impacts on our society in various ways.

Boards, therefore corporations and their shareholders, or public bodies and their users, benefit when there are different perspectives with which to view problems and opportunities. Few, given the upheaval in numerous organizations, would argue with the opinion of Denise Kingsmill, herself an experienced director: "Most boards could use a healthy dose of diversity in their make-up. This would make them more dynamic and energetic" (Kingsmill, 2000).

The wider business community, as well as public life, benefits. As the number of women with experience in top management increases, so they become eligible for non-executive posts or for bigger roles on public bodies. This, in turn, brings a broader range of perspectives into the fabric of business and society. To quote Dame Rennie Fritchie, The UK Commissioner for Public Appointments, we need "a broader range of people available in the pool . . . to choose from – more women, more from ethnic minorities but, above all, more good people" (Nowak, 2000).

Employees, men as well as women, benefit by having a greater variety of role models with whom to identify and a wider range of people who can offer mentoring and coaching skills. This can help unstick the organization from outdated ways of managing, introduce new models and styles, and thereby assist in retaining quality performers and in attracting high grade recruits.

Customers for goods and services benefit especially when, as is often the case, women are the decision makers or are themselves the end consumers. The growth in the number of talented women who become successful entrepreneurs indicates that women are adept at being in touch with the market and at spotting new opportunities.

## ■ Tracking top executive women ■

At the beginning of the twenty-first century most developed countries have a track record of sustained action over a period of thirty years or more to improve the situation for women in the workplace and in the wider community. Among advanced nations, there has been a major thrust aimed to increase the numbers of women entering management and professional careers, then to promote serious attention to development and promotion so that they reach senior levels in line with their ability. This work has seldom been out of the headlines during the last quarter century and it reflects a continuation of effort that was evident through the whole of the twentieth century. There were just some temporary setbacks in the immediate aftermath of each of the two World Wars. Now the focus is on the situation for women at the very top.

In the USA, the annual Catalyst Census of Women Board Directors (Catalyst, 1999) tracks the changes in representation in the Top 500 *Fortune* Companies. In 1999 the census was extended to the Top 1,000 *Fortune* companies and found that America's 500 largest companies were significantly more likely than the second group of 500 companies to have at least one woman on their board. The top 500 returned 11.2 percent women directors while those ranked 501 to 1,000 returned only 8.5 percent. In a country where so much emphasis has been placed on achieving diversity it is disappointing to note that the same census recorded only 1.9 percent "women of colour" directors from the 777 companies which provided data.

The situation is no better elsewhere. The Catalyst Census for Canada for 1998 (Catalyst, 1998) recorded 7.5 percent women board directors. Pajo et al.'s 1997 study (McGregor and Cleland, 1997) reported that among New Zealand's top 200 companies only 4.4 percent of the directors were women. By 1999, Devlin (1999) suggested that in the broader span of New Zealand companies women hold 7.4 percent of directorships which seems to gain support from the fact that women form 8 percent of the membership of the Institute of Directors.

Across the European Union as a whole the Commission says that women fill only 3 to 6 percent of senior executive posts although women hold up to 30 percent of middle management appointments. Illustrating the extremes, in Sweden (EU, 2000) women hold 29 percent of senior management roles on public bodies but only 9 percent in the private sector, whereas in the Republic of Ireland (EEA, 2000) only 3 percent of women in employment hold the position of managing director. In the European Commission itself, although 50 percent of the officers are women, only 11.9 percent of the director generals/directors are women (Women in Europe, 2000). The Commission is, though, making progress toward its target of 20 percent by 2005.

In the UK a new FTSE Female Index (Industrial Society and Fawcett Society, 2000) was launched. This showed that women's representation on the boards of the FTSE 100 companies was only 5.2 percent. However, if only the employed, executive, directors were considered, the proportion fell to 1.8 percent. In a well-publicized launch of the Index one of Britain's top women Denise Kingsmill said, "It is becoming a corporate governance issue." Kingsmill, a high-profile lawyer with a history of working with boardroom disputes, is now Deputy Head of the UK Competition Commission, the body that regulates major mergers and acquisitions, and so is well acquainted with the workings of Britain's corporate top teams. The Index reveals differences between the companies. A handful have two women board members while the majority of companies, including those which in other respects are equally prestigious, have none. The slow pace of change is demonstrated through a study that followed up on the appointment of women directors in ten large companies in 1989 and again in 1999 (Pye, 2000). In 1989 not one of the 78 executive directors in the ten companies was a woman. There were two non-executive directors and this made women's representation just 2 percent. A decade later, with 2 out of 53 executives and 6 out of 61 non-executive directors, women's representation on the boards of these companies had reached 7 percent.

It's incredibly important to choose the right career (Nicola Horlick, Managing Director, SG Asset Management)

In the early 1980s Rosalie Silverstone and Audrey Ward charted the progress of UK women in different professions (Silverstone and Ward, 1980). They showed the long time-lag between early, isolated women pathfinders and the breakthrough that occurs when large numbers of women find similar employment. The first women accountant qualified in the late nineteenth century but was not accepted into the Chartered Institute of Accountants until 1910. It then took until the 1970s for numbers to swell to the stage where they could be referred to as a gender revolution in accountancy. By the 1990s, although few women had achieved leading positions in the major accountancy firms, accountancy became a fast-track route into senior management for women in business. Similar progress is apparent in other professions. The first women lawyer was called to the British Bar in 1922. In the following year, the first woman solicitor took out a practising certificate. It was another 26 years before a women was appointed King's Counsel and a further 16 years to 1965 before the first women was made a High Court Judge. Today, while more than 50 percent of law students are women, there are relatively few at barrister or partner level and fewer still in the judiciary. Despite high-profile women, including Cherie Booth, the British Prime Minister's wife, the profession continues to be strongly masculine in person and style. Perhaps because of this, more women with law degrees are attracted to business.

The two professions, accountancy (including finance more generally) and law, are particularly relevant to executive leadership since women directors in today's corporations have very often grown through them into top positions or into general management. They are well-defined specialisms with skill sets and knowledge that are highly valued in a regulated and legalistic business world. Women who have role-model status by achieving leading roles often have these skills. Nicola Horlick, a brilliant young fund manager, built an outstanding reputation with one finance house, left, fought a dramatic and public boardroom dispute and eventually established herself as joint managing director with another finance company – SG Asset Management. Yve Newbold, now Chair of The Ethical Trading Initiative, previously a partner at Heindrick

& Struggles Executive Search firm and for many years company secretary at the hard-nosed international conglomerate Hanson Industries, built her career on law.

While it would be a wrong to suggest that disciplines like finance and law are the only avenues to senior business leadership for women, the principle that study – education and qualifications – provides a route into senior roles is well taken. Women are flowing into universities, attaining good degrees, and winning success in the recruitment stakes. Many employers say that it means that they have taken virtually equal numbers of men and women graduates for ten years or more. Of equal significance is that recruiters from major consultancies, multinationals, and similarly large corporations often comment on the high quality of women entrants to graduate management schemes. Usually such schemes include placements, training, mentoring, and often fast-track promotions. Women are also continuing with their studies and achieving MBAs, the "gold standard" for business qualifications.

### ■  Women set to run the world?  ■

The result of this earlier progress is played out in the evident changes in the distribution of women in management roles. UK employers record significant proportions of women in management roles, sometimes 30 percent or more. Closer examination shows, though, that the women are predominantly in junior and middle-management roles. In US, where the pace has been somewhat faster than in the UK, a recent survey by Catalyst found that women held 49 percent of the middle management posts (Catalyst, 2000).

The concentration at middle-management level does not appear to relate to qualifications. Even highly qualified scientists and specialists find it hard to rise through the ranks. However, it may relate to women's expectations. Research by Ackah, Heaton, and McWhinney (1999) shows that women who have gained their MBA value it as much for its standing as for the knowledge they have acquired. They say that women are significantly more likely than men to be promoted on achieving their MBA (although from and to lower levels than men) but that they still perceive their future promotion prospects as poor. This view is somewhat justified as women's pay remains at a significantly lower rate than that of men even in comparable roles.

After a decade of recruiting high-calibre women, and despite the evidence that the pace of progress has slowed, many employers do not appear to think that more action from them is necessary. However, their optimistic view that change at the top is simply a matter of the time it takes to move up the hierarchy is challenged by closer analysis. This suggests that the glass ceiling is still in place and, moreover, that the response of women to corporate life is not necessarily as anticipated by employers.

> The salary was quite exciting, and the car . . . but there was no job satisfaction (Pauline Portas, Charterhouse Management)

A UK study by Catherine Hakim, a researcher with long experience of the employment situation, identifies different work–life choices now available to women (Hakim, 2000). She identifies the changes that have taken place over the last thirty years: access to contraception; the equality revolution and legislation; growth in white-collar occupations; creation of jobs for secondary earners; and the increasing importance of attitudes, values, and personal preferences in lifestyle choices. Hakim's three choices for women today, together with her estimates of the distribution, are:

- home centred – gives priority to children and family life; no preference for work (the option of 20 percent of women)
- adaptive – preference for combining jobs and family life (option favoured by 60 percent of women)
- work centred – gives priority to employment or other competitive activities in the public arena (option taken by 20 percent of women).

Of course, such choices are not necessarily available to all women, particularly those whose circumstances mean that they have to support themselves and their families. However, these choices are available to highly qualified women who are big earners and more likely to be candidates for developing senior management and executive leadership roles. Understanding the basis for choice is therefore important, particularly for those who have responsibility for attracting and retaining talent.

Family issues are not the whole picture. For some, maybe many, women it seems that the culture of senior management is not sufficiently attractive to keep them moving along the career track. While employers experience growing concern about scarce resources, women's own reaction falls into one of four categories.

Some women take a break for family or other reasons and find their employer insufficiently flexible to accommodate their return to the workplace. A study (WRN, 2000) involving more than 1,200 highly qualified women in UK, with smaller complementary studies in Spain and Italy, found that most looked to their professional association rather than to their employer for assistance in returning to work. This reflected the lack of help offered voluntarily by their organizations and their greater affinity to their profession than to any one employer. Unfortunately, the study identified that the professional bodies – associations of accountants, solicitors, clinicians, engineers, etc. – were even less organized to provide keep-in-touch and re-entry assistance than the employers. This resulted in many of these women either not returning to paid work or going to a different kind of job, usually at a much lower level where they could not make good use of their earlier training.

Some women are attracted by the opportunities and perceived greater flexibility offered by competitors. For example, the finance sector works hard to attract the best recruits, yet a UK government study revealed that only 10 percent of employers in banking and insurance allowed flexitime working. With increased emphasis on work–life balance highly qualified people, particularly women, will move to organizations that offer flexible work and benefit packages. Job sharing is becoming an attractive option at management level for both individual women and for employers. The industries at the forefront include banking and finance, IT and public services. Nicki Thomson shares the post of senior corporate manager at Barclays Corporate Banking in London with Maria Cussell (Sandler, 2000). To check they would work well together the bank carried out personality testing in the recruitment stage. After 18 months they describe their role as "like a marriage." They work closely and are assessed on shared objectives as well as on individually focused ones. In other organizations, such as UBS Warburg, and PriceWaterhouseCooper, a flexible benefits package includes funds to purchase benefits from a menu with choices ranging from company car, health care, additional holidays, gym membership, childcare vouchers, share options, and so on. Organizations as diverse as Cadbury, the food manufacturer, the BBC, and Alcatel Telecom offer similar benefit programs.

Some women who are seriously put off by a climate of hierarchy turn instead to entrepreneurship. This often takes employers by surprise. A study by the London Society of Chartered Accountants (2000) involved 350 London-based start-ups selected at random. They discovered that women set up 67 percent. Significantly, 71 percent of the women owners said that negative job experiences had driven them into entrepreneurship. Reasons varied from being regularly overlooked for promotion, being asked to work longer hours than men are, and being subjected to sexual harassment or suggestive remarks. Fiona Price, who set up her own financial advisory company in 1988, described how, at the time, her male colleagues "thought it hysterical" (Sullivan, 1999). Twelve years later, at the head of her own successful city-based business, she says that she could not imagine herself being happy in a large bureaucratic office with inflexible work practices. Sue Birley, Professor of Entrepreneurship at Imperial College Management School, endorses this view. She says, "More women are starting their own business as a way of developing their careers. Factors driving this growth include high divorce rate and an increase in female role models as well as a sense of not 'fitting'" (Birley, 2000).

Other women enjoy their work but dislike the culture at senior level, which they describe as overly political and pressured. They decide to stay with their employer but to "park" their career. These are the women who possibly cause most alarm in the corporate world. Employers often do not notice their strategy and even take comfort from the rising number of women at just below the senior levels. However, the action of these women can have profound consequences far beyond their own futures. If the company is not prompted into action, younger women may assume that a ceiling is in place and adjust their expectations or behaviour. This sends messages, perhaps unintended, to all employees.

Each of these strategies offers different benefits to the women concerned but all have severe implications for employers. The effects come into play just as the employers are expecting that they will start to see the results of their investment in selection and development. These women were often recruited as part of cohorts to provide for long-term succession. If, having formed 50 percent of the intake, women do not stay the course, for whatever reason, then the choice for top-level succession has to be made from a much-reduced pool to the detriment of the future of the company.

Even women who rise to the very top sometimes find it impossible to balance the pressures of their job with their desire to take a strongly hands-on role in the family. This is not necessarily a simple gender issue. It affects men as well as women, and is a reflection of an increasing desire for parents to spend time with their children. Nevertheless, the action of a high-profile woman makes the point. Penny Hughes enjoyed spectacular acclaim as the 33-year-old Chief Executive of Coca-Cola UK. She surprised everyone when, after three years, she suddenly resigned to spend more time with her son. This sent a message to other women about the potential challenges of combining a family with a high-flying career. It may also have influenced board members who were contemplating the appointment or promotion of women to top roles. Just a few years later Penny Hughes, although not in a full-time role, has several non-executive directorships with prestigious companies including Vodafone, Mirror Group, and Bodyshop. She is also featured as a "woman to watch", indicating that she is tipped for big new roles in the future. This is good news for women who want to challenge the necessity for an unbroken career route. Corporations also should take note that a career pause does not mean that the investment in the individual is lost. However, it is noticeable that Hughes's comeback is less reported in the press than her leaving.

In the USA, commenting on "back home support", Meyerson and Moen (2000) note that those executive posts are still based on having someone behind them. Meyerson notes that executive posts are two-person jobs and says that "senior level jobs are still based on the notion that people have someone behind them, that there is a division of labour." Moen, quoting from her 1999 survey of dual-income couples, adds that "in 40 percent of marriages, one person had a 'career' and the other had a 'job'." In a twenty-first century take on the theme, the careerist is now sometimes the woman and her partner the stay-at-home or job-holding partner. A prominent example is Carly Fiorina, Chief Executive of Hewlett Packard, whose husband Frank says that he chose to retire early because he recognized her career potential.

The realization that these issues exist is prompting some employers to look more deeply at their organizational cultures, at their policies and practices, and at their strategies for developing staff, specifically women employees. This attention is not new. Leading employers have been working consistently for many years on these issues but the focus on executive leadership is fresh. Earlier work has generally concentrated on opening recruitment channels, on getting women into management or other types of work regarded as non-traditional for women. Assessment centres, with a clear focus on competence, have proved useful, allowing women to demonstrate their individual abilities and, at the same time, causing assessors to question any stereotypes they may hold about women. However, the assumption as outlined above was that once women were in the career streams, promotion through to the highest levels would follow naturally.

## ■ Winning the war for talent ■

In a tone now markedly more aggressive, corporate recruiters talk about there being "a war for talent." Today's virtually full employment and the burgeoning e-sector means that the competition for high-calibre people has never been stronger. It exists at graduate recruitment level where firms as diverse as Andersen Consulting, Merrill Lynch, and UBS Warburg are vying with each other to offer the greatest "golden hello", usually described as a sum payable on entry to pay off education costs. However, it is even more striking that further along the career path, the pressure is on to hold on to talented people. The company rationale is financial – to reap the benefit of several or even many years of investment in development – but, more than, that it is to ensure the competitive advantage that comes from the deployment of the best brains and skills.

The shortage of highly trained people is causing some firms to rethink their employment strategies and their terms and conditions. In Germany, Professor Sissi Closs, who started her own company, Comet Computer GmbH, says that "Many of our employees come to us from other companies where, for various reasons such as pregnancy or child related part-time working, they could not find appropriate work that used their professional abilities." This is a point of view reflected in a report from a survey carried out by Hay Management Consultants (Falconer, 2000) which worried that "companies too late to adapt to family friendly working can expect to receive a battering from their more enlightened rivals." Then again, many companies seem to overlook the obvious fact that people are likely to leave for the very reasons that attracted them. If money is the carrot but financial rewards do not keep pace with expectations, then people will leave. If flexibility is the carrot but it is not available further up the ladder, then people will look elsewhere. If travel is the attraction but postings are restricted, then experience will walk.

## ■ Award-winning organizational strategies to keep women moving upwards ■

The powerful place of the "war for talent" driver is demonstrated through entries for the Year 2000 UK Opportunity Now Best Practice Awards for UK employers acting to improve the situation for their women employees. Of the 20 finalists, 15 employers cited the need to attract or retain talent in their rationale for introducing new polices. They identified a range of different strategies but the goal was the same: to attract and then keep high-calibre women. The companies weighed their success by measuring the numbers of women moving up through the ranks to senior management.

In the UK financial sector, Halifax plc's Fair's Fair program oversees a series of linked projects to enhance the possibilities of women who form 75 percent of employees. Programme leadership is with an executive steering group and high-level champions formally encourage flexibility. They introduced a glass ceiling forum, awareness-raising workshops for all, and monitored achievement through business plans, staff appraisals, and surveys. Among measurable results, 75 percent of women now return from maternity leave (50 percent taking the part-time option). The proportion of women appointed to senior management moved from 21 to 26 percent. The number of women executives increased from 7 to 19 with one appointment taking effect while the individual concerned was on maternity leave. Ethnic minorities generated more business from within the ethnic minorities. And, home-based women managers increased their productivity by 20 percent.

Again in the UK, in the public sector, specifically the Inland Revenue, a program "Challenging Preconceptions" aimed to change the picture of the stereotypical "taxman." To get to the top it is essential that credible candidates have completed their Inspector of Taxes training. The Inland Revenue adapted their approach as to how such training is delivered, offering home study modules, distance learning, and help with child care costs to permit study. They also paid attention to the subliminal messages conveyed through recruitment literature for the training, ensuring, for example, that one featured candidate was an obviously pregnant woman. The result is that now 58 percent of trainee tax inspectors are women and that the first part-time tax inspector has been appointed.

In Biotechnology and Biological Sciences Research Council that employs women scientists the issue was that women seemed to cluster at the bottom of the pay scales. The result was a tendency for them to drop out of employment before reaching the higher end of the pay bands. A study identified the cause as a structure based on length of service. An equal pay audit involving management and trade unions studied the grading system and made measures against the private sector and revised the standard pay point system (SPP). When the initiative started, the pay of some 60 percent of staff was below SPP. After the changes this fell to 32 percent and is subject to regular review. Just as significant, the attitude to part-time work has improved and women scientists are taking this option. The notion that promotion is viable only for full-timers is fast disappearing.

In Cummins Engine Company, a firm with 4,500 employees at six major plants, an anti-harassment policy was introduced in 1997 as part of a drive to attract talented women and other underrepresented groups and to create a harassment-free workplace. The policy was backed with rigorous training for all staff with a code of conduct that held every employee responsible for its enforcement. The company's serious intent is demonstrated by the fact that the way individuals conduct themselves in relation to the code could affect performance reviews and job status. Progress is monitored through surveys, and all complaints about harassment are logged and shared with counsellors. As a result, the number of women managers has increased by 34 percent since the policy began and 2 percent more women are employed overall.

At Procter and Gamble UK they offer workshops entitled, somewhat provocatively, "Sex@work" to look at behavioural differences and as a means of raising awareness. The result, they say, is that women feel more able to use their own style. At the same time the company has included in its balanced scorecard measures of diversity alongside other performance indicators. These ways of raising awareness in the UK, where quotas are unlawful and even targets are viewed with suspicion, have brought change. Apart from women's growing self-confidence they increased their representation at assistant director (senior manager) level from 13 to 19 percent in three years.

A similar approach by GlaxoWellcome also brought fast progress. With women comprising 42 percent of their workforce, this pharmaceutical giant set aside a budget for diversity projects and ensures that every manager has diversity training. Promotion criteria are firmly based on competence and merit. This creates open competition for jobs and ensures that no one with talent is debarred just because they are in the "wrong" place. For example, it has allowed progression from secretarial into managerial work. At the same time, the company has attended to the needs of working carers through its flexible work program so that they now see 93 percent of women returning from maternity leave. This is a major achievement in an industry where the loss of skilled, experienced people is particularly telling. Research projects typically take years and the investment in training and development of scientists and other specialists is huge. The program, Diversity in Business, is credited with raising the number of women in senior management from 13 to 16 percent in one year and – with an eye to the future – to increasing women at middle management from 27 to 32 percent over the same period. The company's serious intent is also evident at the very top where they now have three women on the board – the only FTSE 100 company where this is the case.

## ■ Expatriates lead the way ■

In many instances the prompt for action comes from the chairman or chief executive who has become, perhaps uncomfortably, aware of the lack of women at the top table. Often, such realization arises as a result of questions from the parent organization, usually in these cases, American. In others, women who have achieved senior-level posts take or are given responsibility for encouraging other women. This is a recent trend perhaps reflecting the greater confidence of women today. Again, where the senior woman is American, the challenge tends to be sharper, perhaps reflecting the experience of her home country. In this respect the study carried out by Catalyst in the USA has worrying implications for American women and those in other countries (Catalyst, 2000). This showed that although 49 percent of middle managers are women only 13 percent achieve expatriate roles. This is due as much to misconceptions about women's willingness to move as to the challenges that arise when the move affects a dual-career couple. Clearly American, and indeed other nationalities who arrive as expatriates at senior levels, are able to influence and engender a more inclusive culture which benefits the host site and the individual managers.

There is a noticeable "outsider" effect that seems to make it more possible for people to move forward once they are removed from the own culture – a phenomenon that Nancy Adler identified and labelled the "Gaijin Syndrome" (Adler, 1994). Her research showed that in some countries foreign women were more likely to be accepted than indigenous women. It seemed that once the outsider was admitted, local "rules" and customs were overridden making it possible for women to be accorded positions of responsibility and eminence. This is most evident in public life. For example, Madeline Albright, the US Secretary of State, found acceptance even in those environments where it is unusual for women to take a high-profile public role.

A similar outsider role exists in business, and it is striking that in the UK many women who have achieved outstanding success are not British. When *Management Today* produced its list of "the women who move Britain" half of those in the top ten are not British, have an immigrant background, or have substantial out-of-UK experience (Hamilton, 1999). Marjorie Scardino (Chief Executive of Pearson) and Deanne Julius (Bank of England Monetary Policy Committee, formally with Shell and BA) are both American. Elisabeth Murdoch (formerly Programme Director of BSkyB, now setting up her own production company) is Australian. Anita Roddick (Founder of Bodyshop) is the child of Italian immigrants. Rosie Boycott (journalist and newspaper editor) has lived in India and Kuwait. Among other examples are the American Barbara Cassani who as Chief Executive Officer of Go was the first CEO of an airline; the Norwegian Wenche Marshall-Foster,UK Head of Perrier, South African Prue Leith renowned businesswoman, restauranteur and cookery writer who was famously identified as every chairman's favourite for non-executive appointments, New Zealander Denise Kingsmill (mentioned previously), Steve Shirley, Founder and President of FI Group (daughter of immigrants), and Christine Wuillamie, the French-Vietnamese Chairman and Chief Executive of CWB Systems Services. Incidentally, thus far BA seems to have managed to keep pace with Cassani's rising expectations as she has been with them for 12 years in a string of interesting jobs. But, they should note her itchy feet and her belief that she will have five or six careers (Davidson, 1999). She has a practical down-to-earth approach that allows her to recognize what she shares in common with other working women (dual career, family, mortgage, and so on) while also acknowledging that she can afford paid help. Her determination, proven achievements, and accessibility make her a great role model.

While it can be argued that people with outstanding skills and experience rise to the top in any environment, in the case of women it lends support to Nancy Adler's view that Gaijin or foreigners are allowed to operate outside the norms. They have the scope to challenge and break stereotypes and so to create the possibility for new pathways for local women. The effect of this is seen in the *Management Today* list with clear streams of change. For example, Helen Alexander, Chief Executive of The Economist Group, is identified as following the Scardino route, and Pippa Wicks, who left Courtaulds Textiles to join Pearson, is also marked out as "one to watch".

## ■ Views differing ■

The results claimed for corporate initiatives seem to indicate that improvements are taking place. However, a survey recently carried out in the UK and involving 1,188 senior women and 117 chief executives/chairmen found that the two groups offered different perspectives on the situation (Catalyst and Opportunity Now, 2000). According to the report, "chief executives are more than twice as likely as senior women to believe that opportunities for women to advance to senior leadership in their organizations compared to five years ago have greatly improved." While 58 percent of the chief executives quoted the beneficial effects of their equality policies, only 40 percent of the women expressed similar views. They tended instead to explain that there were both positive and negative effects. Only 29 percent of the senior women felt that the equality policies and practices had had an effect on their own careers, although whether this is because the current measures were not in place at critical stages in their life is not clear. This study suggests, though, that people at the very top might be placing too much weight on top-down change and overlooking the subtle challenges that typically face all who are involved in cultural and behavioural change.

There is agreement on key impediments to advancing women: family responsibilities, stereotyping and preconceptions about women's roles and abilities, shortage of accessible role models of successful women, and lack of line and general management experience. However, chief executives seem unaware of women's continuing felt or actual state of exclusion from informal networks, as well as barriers arising from differences in style and women's awareness or response to organizational politics. This report concludes that chief executives fail to recognize specific manifestations of a hostile organization culture. If this is the case, then it seems inevitable that many of the well-intentioned initiatives are doomed unless they are sustained for the many years it takes to embed a new culture. In this scenario, ambitious women seek highly personal and individualized routes to the top jobs, based on performing beyond expectations, adapting their style, and on developing and sticking to their own career goals.

Such a strategy undoubtedly works for the determined but the cost in personal terms is high. There is also the risk that the company will lose their rising star to another employer or to self-employment.

This risk is underlined by another study involving 2,000 senior managers and professionals, 25 percent of whom women (Rice, 2000). The findings showed that nearly 43 percent expressed loyalty to themselves and to their own career rather than to their employers, whom they expected to leave within two years. These respondents were disenchanted by people-friendly initiatives (regarded as "just vocabulary") and 46 percent would switch jobs for a better quality of life. The researchers suggest the causes are the working through of the social changes that began in the 1980s, the rise of two-career couples, working mothers, and the equal presence of women in the workforce, and say that this has changed the dialogue between employer and employee.

> Know who you are, and be that person, good or bad. (Marjorie Scardino, Chief Executive, Pearson Group)

Some companies and organizations have harnessed women's determination by making explicit the need to equip women to take charge of their own possibilities. This aspect of change was mentioned by nearly one-third of the entrants for the UK's Opportunity Now 2000 Best Practice Awards. It exists at Halifax plc in the "Change rests with me" program that aims to raise awareness of what is possible. Women executives in the company set about helping other women to make progress through discussion groups and informal mentoring, thus ensuring that up-coming women are able to learn from those who have gone before. This mirrors the experience of women studied in Australia where it was found that the majority of high achievers acknowledge the barriers and are actively helping others to overcome them (Rindfleish, 2000).

Several UK universities have outreach or specially designed programs to enable women to either restart or to update their studies, thus ensuring the possibility of a continuing stake in the new economy. In HSBC plc a program to raise awareness of the role of professional qualifications in accelerating progress to the top has resulted in the proportion of women studying rising from 30 to 52 percent in three years.

Networking is a strong feature of women's development processes. The benefit of shared experience is offered formally as well as informally. In Europe, an innovative "Crossing the Boundaries" program brings together women for five four-day modules over a nine-month period. The stimulus, contacts, and confidence that come from moving around the Continent as well as learning how to leverage Europe's public and private institutions provides a powerful and sustainable network for these women. Similar programs are offered through the European Women's Foundation for senior women in the Eastern and Central European countries, building links between them and with EU countries. Less formally, local, national, and international networks provide forums for women to share experience.

## Conclusion

The question now is not whether women are capable or desirous of achieving executive leadership. There are already examples of highly successful women in many different areas of leadership. More women, suitably qualified and experienced, are in the frame. The challenge is whether organizations are prepared to adapt to accommodate the different life requirements and styles of talented women and men who want broader and more enriched lives. If they are, then these organizations, as well as the individuals, will benefit from the greater diversity of talent that is available. Some companies are already innovating with new ways of working, a process that can only accelerate in line with technological change. Competition will ensure that women will increase their presence and influence in executive leadership.

## REFERENCES

Ackah, C., Heaton, N., and McWhinney, G. (1999): Women in management: the case of MBA graduates. *Women in Management Review*, 14, 4, 136–45.

Adler, N. (1994): Competitive Frontiers: Women Managing Across Boarders. In N. J. Adler and D. N. Izraeli (eds), *Competitive Frontiers – Women managers in a global economy* Cambridge, MA, Blackwell Business Books.

Birley, S. (2000): quoted in *the Financial Times*, October 19, 20.

Catalyst (1998): *Women Board Directors of Canada*. New York.

Catalyst (1999): *Census of Women Board Directors*. New York.

Catalyst (2000): Passport to Opportunity: US Women in Global Business. New York.

Catalyst and Opportunity Now (2000): Breaking the barriers, women in senior management in the UK. London: Opportunity Now.

Davidson, A. (1999): Barbara Cassani. *Management Today*, August, 66–71.

Devlin, P. (1999): Top corporate jobs elude women especially in bigger companies. *National Business Review*, May 10, quoted in R. Fawcett and J. K. Pringle Women CEOs in New Zealand: where are you? *Women in Management Review*, 15, 5/6, 253–60.

EEA, *Women in the Labour Force*. Quoted by National Women's Council of Ireland Women in Europe Newsletter (2000): 93.

EU (European Union) (2000): Bridging the gender gap: reducing segregation in the labour market. Employment and Social Affairs, European Union.

Falconer, H. (2000): HR holds the key to firms' survival in flexible future. *Personnel Today*, July 4, 7.

Hakim, C. (2000): Work–Life Style Choices in the 21st Century. Oxford: Oxford University Press.

Hamilton, K. (1999): The women who move Britain. *Management Today*, March, 39–45.

Industrial Society and Fawcett Society (2000): FTSE Female Index, an initiative of Harriet Harman, MP, The Industrial Society and The Fawcett Society.

Kingsmill, D. (2000): quoted in The Financial Times, November 7, 22.

London Society of Chartered Accountants Survey (2000): quoted in *Financial Times*, October 19, 20.

Pajo, K., McGregor, J., and Cleland, J. (1997): Profiling the pioneers: women directors on New Zealand Corporate Boards. *Women in Management Review*, 12, 5, 174–81.

Meyerson, D. and Moen, P., (2000) quoted in The return of the stay-at-home-spouse. *Financial Times*, October 6, 13.

Nowak, S. (2000): Quango Queen. *Professional Manager*, November, 24–7.

Pye, A. (2000): *People Management*, October 12, 13.

Rice, M. (2000): Age of the Flex Exec, MT-Ceridian Work/Life survey. *Management Today*, August, 46–52.

Rindfleish, J. (2000): Senior Management Women in Australia, diverse perspectives. *Women in Management Review*, 15, 4, 172–83.

Sandler, D. (2000): Job shares can work for everyone. The *Financial Times*, November 8, 22.

Silverstone, R. and Ward, A. (eds) (1980): *Careers of Professional Women*. London: Croom Helm.

Sullivan, R. (1999): Skirting the issue? *The Director*, June, 42–6.

WRN (Women Returners to Work) (2000): The role of professional associations in facilitating the re-entry of highly qualified women into employment. London: WRN.

# INDEX